MIRACLES
—of the—
BOOK OF
MORMON

MIRACLES
— of the —
BOOK OF
MORMON

A GUIDE TO THE SYMBOLIC MESSAGES

ALONZO L. GASKILL

CFI
An imprint of Cedar Fort, Inc.
Springville, Utah

ISBN 13: 978-1-4621-1685-0

Published by CFI, an imprint of Cedar Fort, Inc.
2373 W. 700 S., Springville, UT 84663
Distributed by Cedar Fort, Inc., www.cedarfort.com

LIBRARY OF CONGRESS CATALOGING-IN-PUBLICATION DATA

Gaskill, Alonzo L., author.
Miracles of The Book of Mormon : a guide to the symbolic messages / Alonzo L. Gaskill.
    pages cm
Includes bibliographical references and index.
ISBN 978-1-4621-1685-0 (hardback w/dustjacket : alk. paper)
1. Symbolism in the Book of Mormon. 2. Book of Mormon--Criticism, interpretation, etc.
3. Church of Jesus Christ of Latter-day Saints--Doctrines. 4. Mormon Church--Doctrines. I.
Title.
BX8627.G37 2015
289.3'22--dc23
                                2015025377

Cover design by Shawnda T. Craig
Cover design © 2015 Lyle Mortimer
Edited and typeset by Jessica B. Ellingson

Printed in the United States of America

10 9 8 7 6 5 4 3 2 1

Printed on acid-free paper

In memory of Dr. Hugh Nibley (1910–2005), whose love for the Book of Mormon and whose approach to that sacred text have forever influenced the way I read it.

Other Books by Alonzo L. Gaskill

Miracles of the New Testament:
A Guide to the Symbolic Messages

Love at Home:
Insights from the Lives of Latter-day Prophets

The Truth about Eden:
Understanding the Fall and our Temple
Experience

Sacred Symbols:
Finding Meaning in Rites, Rituals &
Ordinances

The Lost Language of Symbolism—An Essential
Guide for Recognizing and Interpreting
Symbols of the Gospel

Odds Are You're Going to Be Exalted—
Evidence that the Plan of Salvation Works!

Know Your Religions, Volume 1—A
Comparative Look at Mormonism and
Catholicism

CONTENTS

Contents

CONTENTS

Acknowledgments

I wish to express my sincere appreciation to the numerous individuals who helped me in the process of writing this manuscript; chief among them are Jan Nyholm, Debbie Parker, Andy Skelton, and Drs. Todd Parker, Charles Swift, and Stanley Johnson. I have earnestly sought to incorporate each of their suggestions or, at the very least, to clarify what I have written based on their comments and recommendations. I sincerely appreciate the sacrifices of each of those who were kind enough to offer their time and expertise to help me with this project. Their suggestions and insights have greatly improved the manuscript.

INTRODUCTION

As I noted in my book *Miracles of the New Testament*, a good universal definition of what constitutes a "miracle" is difficult to come by.[1] By that I mean, most will acknowledge that miracles are those events that are largely unexplainable by *known* natural laws; yet what falls into the category of "miraculous" is not always agreed upon. Should one, for example, include visions in a list of scriptural miracles? For surely they are miraculous events. Or what about the manifestation of any of the gifts of the Spirit, such as speaking in tongues or prophecy? Those are also quite miraculous. If one speaks technically, must one not acknowledge that events largely taken for granted—such as the birth of a human being—are miracles also? Thus, the definition of what constitutes a miracle is not always cut and dried, and the ability to create a complete list of Book of Mormon miracles is therefore difficult.[2]

That being the case, the list of miracles we will examine here largely ignores traditional life events, such as giving birth or using the human brain to think and reason—even though most readers will feel a measure of awe at God's handiwork manifest through such events. Instead, our focus will be on that which most would acknowledge as extraordinary, on those events in the Book of Mormon that confront us with a sense that God's power is absolutely incomprehensible and unexplainable to finite humans. We will look at stories where prophets and holy men on the Western Hemisphere employ the powers of heaven to change lives, heal the hopeless, and cast out demons. We will examine miracles that evidence that God is in charge and that what He wills certainly comes to pass. Each of these—and many others—is prevalent in the Book of Mormon. Indeed, miracles appear in every book of that sacred text; and miracles are central to the message of the Book of Mormon.[3] It constantly testifies of the miraculous, and its coming forth is no less than miraculous.

One of the difficulties in a study like this has to do with deciding the approach one should take. Is there a place for a systematic look at the miracles in the Book of Mormon? Surely there is. But which *approach* or *system* should one employ? Is it best, for example, to categorize the miracles by their type (healings vs. signs in the heavens)? Or would it be better to look at the miracles based on who performed them (the miracles of Nephi vs. the miracles of Alma)? Should the focus be on the details of the miracle or instead on the meaning of the miracle for the reader today? Not all will agree on what constitutes the right approach. Yet, because our interest here is on application, it seems best to examine each of the miracles individually, and aside from any overarching structure that one scholar or another might propose. (It should be noted, while much has been written on miracles of the Old and New Testaments, very little has been written on the miracles of the Book of Mormon. Thus, we are venturing into unfurrowed territory.) While we acknowledge the value of a structured approach to this subject, for what we are seeking to do here, it will be best to look at the smaller picture rather than the bigger one.

The reader should be aware that we are taking the position that the miracles described in the Book of Mormon actually happened—that they are historical events. And we acknowledge with those who believe that each miracle in some way testifies of Christ and His divine power. Certainly those performed by the Master Himself (during His post-Resurrection visit to the Nephites) evidence that He possessed the power of God. But those miracles brought to pass by the various prophets of the Book of Mormon also testify of Christ's power, in that they remind us that He endows those whom He calls to preside with authority and gifts akin to His own. This was the case with those who succeeded Him in His ministry in the Eastern Hemisphere, and it was also the case with those whom He called to preside over the Church in the Western Hemisphere. Though we will examine each of the miracles of the Book of Mormon for their symbolic value—for their application—we take the position of Augustine (AD 354–430), who said (of the miracles of the New Testament): "We do not, because we allegorize facts . . . lose our belief in them as facts."[4]

While all scriptural miracles *are* testaments to Jesus as the Son of God, the plethora of miracles in the standard works seems to suggest that something is intended by them (in addition to witnessing that Jesus is divine or that His prophets hold the priesthood). In other words, they certainly testify of Jesus's divinity, but to what else might they be a testament? What else might they communicate to the reader? As one studies the various miracles of the Book of Mormon, it becomes evident that they serve well as great teaching devices that can help us understand gospel truths buried within the miraculous events. One commentator penned this explanation: "Miracles were designed to symbolize the spiritual blessings that God is able and willing to bestow upon our needy hearts. The majority of miracles were acts of mercy and are conspicuous as emblems of redemption. . . . The miracles Christ performed, for example, were parabolical illustrations of the great salvation which He preached."[5] In other words, Jesus (and others) preformed many mighty miracles in the lives of the *ancients*, but each of those can symbolize blessings He has in store for you and me *today*! One of my BYU colleagues put it this way: "It is interesting that while people are concerned about the historicity of symbols, rarely do they concern themselves with the symbolism of history. Just as symbols can correspond to actual events, actual events can be symbolic. I am not just referring to ritual and ceremony, such as the sacrament or temple worship, which are by definition symbolic actions. I am referring to events in everyday life that . . . actually point to meaning outside of themselves."[6] The trick is seeing symbolically so that we might draw out of the historic miracle application to our lives today.

It is well known that in antiquity there were a variety of approaches to reading and applying scripture. For example, the exegetical[7] school of Antioch tended to look for the "literal" or "historic" sense of scripture, whereas the Alexandrian school very much fostered an allegorical approach to the sacred text.[8] Which approach was right? I suppose that largely depends on your school of thought and what it is you feel you need from scripture. As one scholar pointed out:

> Every text is capable of different levels of apprehension. At the most elementary level, early Rabbis made a distinction between what was "written" (*kitab*) and what was "read" (*qere*) in the text of Torah; more elaborate distinctions between *peshat* ("literal meaning"), *darash* ("applied or extended meaning"), and *sod* ("mystical meaning") were to

follow. Christianity would develop similar distinctions between literal, moral, and allegorical readings of its texts.[9]

Such variety in approach is as applicable to the study of the Book of Mormon as it is to the Bible. Contingent upon what one is using scripture for, or what one needs personally from the text, there are a variety of ways to approach the reading and applying of scripture. So, for example, a study of chiasmus in the text attempts to do something entirely different than drawing a homily from one of the Book of Mormon narratives. Neither is necessarily wrong, but each has a different purpose and different "rules of engagement," *per se*. Elder Dallin H. Oaks made this point:

> For us, the scriptures are not the ultimate source of knowledge, but what precedes the ultimate source. The ultimate knowledge comes by revelation. . . .
>
> The word of the Lord in the scriptures is like a lamp to guide our feet (see Psalm 119:105), and revelation is like a mighty force that increases the lamp's illumination many-fold. We encourage everyone to make careful study of the scriptures and . . . to prayerfully seek personal revelation to know their meaning for themselves. . . .
>
> Such revelations are necessary because, as Elder Bruce R. McConkie of the Quorum of the Twelve observed, "Each pronouncement in the holy scriptures . . . is so written as to reveal little or much, depending on the spiritual capacity of the student."
>
> Elder Bruce R. McConkie [also] said, "I sometimes think that one of the best-kept secrets of the kingdom is that the scriptures open the door to the receipt of revelation." This happens because scripture reading puts us in tune with the Spirit of the Lord. . . .
>
> Many of the prophecies and doctrinal passages in the scriptures have multiple meanings. The Savior affirmed that fact when he told his disciples that the reason he taught the multitude in parables was that this permitted him to teach them "the mysteries of the kingdom of heaven" (Matthew 13:11) while not revealing those mysteries to the multitude. His parables had multiple meanings or applications according to the spiritual maturity of the listener. They had a message for both children and gospel scholars. . . .
>
> Those who believe the scriptural canon is closed typically approach the reading of scriptures by focusing on what was meant at the time the scriptural words were spoken or written. In this approach, a passage of

scripture may appear to have a single meaning and the reader typically relies on scholarship and historical methods to determine it.

The Latter-day Saint approach is different.

"In the wise words of St. Hilary, . . . 'Scripture consists not in what one reads, but in what one understands.'"

One trouble with commentaries is that their authors sometimes focus on only one meaning, to the exclusion of others. As a result, commentaries, if not used with great care, may illuminate the author's chosen and correct meaning but close our eyes and restrict our horizons to other possible meanings. Sometimes those other, less obvious meanings can be the ones most valuable and useful to us as we seek to understand our own dispensation and to obtain answers to our own questions. This is why the teaching of the Holy Ghost is a better guide to scriptural interpretation than even the best commentary.[10]

Elder Oaks added that "scripture is not limited to what it meant when it was written but may also include what that scripture means to a reader today."[11] I could not agree more with Elder Oaks's point. While there is value in scholarly commentaries (and we shall draw upon many in this text), there is also great value in openness to applications beyond "what was meant at the time the scriptural words were spoken or written."[12] Thus, our purpose here will be to find meaning and personal application in the stories of the miracles preserved for us on the pages of the Book of Mormon. I will *not* seek a singular dogmatic interpretation or application. *Nor* will it be my intention to suggest to the reader what the ancients necessarily saw in or meant by a given miracle. Rather, we will look at various potential applications of the miracles and their surrounding story line to the lives of those of us living in "the dispensation of the fulness of times" (D&C 124:41). My target audience is the laity of the Church—not the scholars. And instead of a scholarly or academic treatment of these miracle narratives, what I offer here is a series of homilies—ways to apply the passages to the life of the reader—fodder for the teacher and preacher. I acknowledge this is but one approach to these miraculous events; but it is one that many have personally found meaning and benefit from. I remind the reader of the prophet Nephi's familiar declaration: "I did liken all scriptures unto us, that [they] might be for our profit and learning" (1 Nephi 19:23). This is the task in which we seek to engage. Thus, the following should be understood and kept in mind as the reader digests the concepts presented on the pages of this book:

- What is offered herein is a modern application of an ancient story. In other words, while the original author may not have intended us to see symbolism in a given miracle story, nevertheless, there are some interesting and thought-provoking analogies that can be drawn from these miracles. Thus, what this book seeks to present is not necessarily what the ancients saw in these stories but, instead, what you and I can draw from them by way of modern applications. This is important for the readers to understand, both as they read this book, but also as they look for personal applications.[13]

- In addition, as Elder Oaks suggested, the commentary from various authors I have offered herein should not be seen as the *only* way to apply these miracles, nor necessarily as the best or most correct way. But what others have said about these miracles and their application serve the purpose of getting you and me to think about these stories and what they might potentially offer by way of application to the lives of those of us living many hundreds of years after these stories were initially penned.

- As to sources, I've relied on various types. I have drawn freely from scholarly commentaries on the Book of Mormon for insights into the historical, cultural, and linguistic portions of the miracles. I've relied on doctrinal commentaries for their insight into doctrines taught by the miracles. And I've relied on homiletic[14] commentators for their applications of these events to our day.[15]

- A distinction should be made between the historical meaning of an event, what that event symbolizes, and analogies or allegories that might be drawn from the event under consideration. The historical meaning is what the event meant for those who actually witnessed the miracle. (This is not so much our focus herein.) The symbolic meaning would be what the author who penned the story was trying to teach his audience. (We have occasionally pointed these out, particularly as other commentators have highlighted such meanings.) Analogies and allegories are those things you and I may draw from these stories as personal applications. (These are the primary focus of this text.) Our modern analogies and allegories may be such that they would be completely foreign to those living in the era when the Book of Mormon was compiled. To say that they are what was meant by the original author would in *some* circumstances be inaccurate at best and dishonest (or misrepresentative) at worst. Thus, I emphasize here that the analogies and allegories presented in this book are simply modern applications. This book is largely *not* about how the ancients saw these events *nor* about what they meant for those living in their day. I am simply asking the questions, "How can a given miracle apply to my life today?" or "How can it teach me principles for the twenty-first century?" But the reader should be careful to distinguish between the historical event, the ancient symbolic connotation, and the modern application and allegorization offered herein.

• The commentary I will be offering on each of the miracles follows a consistent pattern. In order, I will offer a discussion of the following things for each of the narratives under examination:

SCRIPTURAL CITATIONS: I have provided the scriptural references wherein the miracle is recorded in the Book of Mormon. Some of the miracles are recorded in (or referenced in) multiple places, and by more than one author. Thus, each of these is listed at the beginning of each section.

SUMMARY OF THE MIRACLE: Rather than citing the actual scriptural text, I have summarized each miracle. This seemed preferable for two reasons. First, some of the miracles are discussed in more than one location in the Book of Mormon—and not all recitations give all of the details of a given miracle. Thus, it seemed important to offer a harmony or summary of each, which included the insights of all of those who recorded it. Second, as the summary approach had been used in the first volume of this set (*Miracles of the New Testament*), it seemed best to be consistent in my approach by summarizing the miracles here also.

BACKGROUND ON THE MIRACLE: This section deals less with the symbolism and more with historic, geographic, cultural, or linguistic insights into the miracle. This is offered by way of clarification and less with the intent of seeking application.

STANDARD SYMBOLS: In this section we list various common symbols employed in the miracle under examination, symbols that appear in the story but have familiar or well-known meanings aside from the miracle being discussed.

APPLICATION AND ALLEGORIZATION: This portion of the commentary offers insights into what various commentators have written by way of personal application in these miracles. These are offered non-dogmatically. They are intended only as springboards to encourage the readers to think about ways they might apply these miracles to their personal life or to the lives of those whom they teach.

Now, before you and I begin our foray into a study of the symbolic meaning of the miracles, I think it worth highlighting for the reader the uniqueness of the miracles found in the Book of Mormon. Whereas the New Testament's miracles lean heavily toward healings, the Book of Mormon contains a greater variety of miracles—many, many different types of encounters with the divine. In addition, the miraculous in the Book of Mormon is often more evident than in the New Testament. Highlighting the differences between miracles in the New Testament and those recorded in the Book of Mormon, BYU's Dr. Charles Swift notes:

In a number of accounts in the Gospels, the Lord performs miracles. . . . In many ways, however, the miracles he performs with the Nephites . . . go beyond those recorded in the Gospels. . . . Even the

Lord teaches about the differences [between His New Testament and Book of Mormon miracles]: "So great faith have I never seen among all the Jews; wherefore I could not show unto them so great miracles, because of their unbelief" (3 Nephi 19:35). . . .

In the New Testament, the Lord feeds thousands of people from only five loaves of bread and two fish; in 3 Nephi, he provides the sacrament to the multitude without even one loaf of bread or cup of wine, miraculously producing the bread and wine from nothing [3 Nephi 20:6–7]. . . . In the Gospels, the Lord heals a number of people, but the general pattern is that individuals seek him to be healed. In [the] Book of Mormon account of the Lord's ministry, he invites everyone present who is afflicted to come forth and be healed [3 Nephi 17:7]. . . . Matthew gives the account of people bringing little children to Jesus so that he could "put his hands on them, and pray," and "he laid his hands on them" (Matthew 19:13, 15). In 3 Nephi, however, the Lord prays for the people, then tells them to look at their children. "And as they looked to behold they cast their eyes towards heaven, and they saw the heavens open, and they saw angels descending out of heaven as it were in the midst of fire; and they came down and encircled those little ones about, and they were encircled about with fire; and the angels did minister unto them" (3 Nephi 17:24). . . .

We can find one of the Lord's prayers in John 17, when he offers what is often called the Intercessory Prayer. The Savior offers a similar prayer on behalf of the Nephites. This 3 Nephi prayer, though, is accompanied with miraculous events that we do not find with the prayer recorded in John [3 Nephi 19:14–15]. . . .

The Gospels provide us with brief glimpses of the resurrected Savior [see Matthew 28, Luke 24, John 20–21]. . . . While there is no doubt that the four Gospels are testimonies that Jesus was resurrected, the 3 Nephi account is an even stronger witness of his resurrection. We read of his descending from heaven and of his ministry as a resurrected being to the Nephites for several days. After reading this gospel, there can be no doubt that the Lord was resurrected with a physical body and that he could continue to minister to his people even after his death. It could not be more poignantly stated than in 3 Nephi [11:14–17]. . . . The resurrected Savior in the Book of Mormon is no metaphor, but a living, breathing God who walks among the people, preaching to them and allowing thousands to touch his wounds and bear witness of his reality.[16]

Professor Swift goes on to offer example after example of miracles in the New Testament that have parallels in the Book of Mormon—and that seem much more miraculous in the latter of these than in the former.[17] Just as the Book of Mormon has its own unique and powerful spirit that accompanies its pages, so also its list of divinely inspired miracles are unique and stand out for their details, in addition to their application to the lives of those living in the latter days.

I suppose I should also impress upon the reader my personal witness that the greatest of all miracles is the Atonement of the Lord Jesus Christ. Unfathomable as God's love is, and as incomprehensible as Christ's passion was, they encompass all other miracles and supersede them all. The Book of Mormon has much to say about Christ's ransom sacrifice for us, and in many ways I will discuss the Atonement on the pages of this book—and in the context of the miracles I will examine. But unlike so many of the miracle stories of the Book of Mormon, the application of Jesus's Atonement—wrought on our behalf—is not metaphorical. It is real, necessary, and salvific; and because of its sacred nature, we will make no attempt to allegorize or spiritualize it here. But it is our hope that our discussion of the many miracles Jesus and His Western Hemisphere prophets brought to pass will bring a greater sense of appreciation for that *ultimate miracle* in the lives of all who read this work.

NOTES

1. See Alonzo L. Gaskill, *Miracles of the New Testament: A Guide to the Symbolic Messages* (Springville, UT: Cedar Fort, 2014), xii. Nibley offered this insight into the definition of the word *miracle*: "What is a miracle? It's a *miraculum*. It means 'a little thing that makes you wonder.' Notice, it's a diminutive. *Mirara* is to wonder, to admire with open mouth in admired amazement" [Hugh Nibley, *Teachings of the Book of Mormon: Transcripts of Lectures Presented to an Honors Book of Mormon Class at Brigham Young University, 1989–1990*, four volumes (Provo, UT: Foundation for Ancient Research and Mormon Studies, 2004), 4:199].

2. The Book of Mormon is saturated in the miraculous: 1 Nephi 1:14, 18; 14:7; 17:51; 19:13; 22:7; 2 Nephi 1:10; 3:24; 4:17; 10:4; 18:18; 25:17; 26:13, 20; 27:26; 28:6; 29:1; Jacob 4:8; Mosiah 3:5, 15; 8:18, 20; 15:6; 23:24; Alma 9:5–6; 19:4; 23:6; 26:12, 15; 37:27, 40–41; Helaman 5:12, 26; 10:13; 14:6–7, 28; 15:3, 15–17; 16:4, 13, 16, 20, 23–24; 3 Nephi 1:4, 22; 2:1–3; 5:8; 7:20, 22; 8:1; 14:22; 17:16–17; 19:35; 21:9; 26:16; 28:31–33; 29:7; 4 Nephi 1:5, 13, 29–31; Mormon 1:13; 7:9; 8:26, 34; 9:10–20; Ether 12:12–18; Moroni 7:27, 29, 35, 37; 10:12.

3. Note some of what the Book of Mormon says about miracles: "Jesus is the Christ, the Eternal God; And . . . he manifesteth himself unto all those who believe in him, by the power of the Holy Ghost; yea, unto every nation, kindred, tongue, and people,

working mighty miracles, signs, and wonders, among the children of men according to their faith" (2 Nephi 26:12–13). "I am a God of miracles" (2 Nephi 27:23). "If ye have imagined up unto yourselves a god who doth vary . . . then ye have imagined . . . a god who is not a God of miracles. But behold, I will show unto you a God of miracles. . . . God has not ceased to be a God of miracles. . . . And if there were miracles wrought [in the days of Christ], why has God ceased to be a God of miracles and yet be an unchangeable Being? And behold, I say unto you he changeth not; if so he would cease to be God; and he ceaseth not to be God, and is a God of miracles. And the reason why he ceaseth to do miracles among the children of men is because that they dwindle in unbelief" (Mormon 9:10–11, 15, 17, 19–20). "For if there be no faith among the children of men God can do no miracles among them; wherefore . . . all they who wrought miracles wrought them by faith. . . . And neither at any time hath any wrought miracles until after their faith; wherefore they first believed in the Son of God" (Ether 12:12, 16, 18). "Have miracles ceased because Christ hath ascended into heaven, and hath sat down on the right hand of God, to claim of the Father his rights of mercy which he hath upon the children of men? . . . And because he hath done this, my beloved brethren, have miracles ceased? Behold I say unto you, Nay; . . . Has the day of miracles ceased? Behold, I say unto you Nay; for it is by faith that miracles are wrought. . . . If these things have ceased wo be unto the children of men, for it is because of unbelief, and all is vain" (Moroni 7:27, 29, 35, 37). "For behold, to one is given by the Spirit of God . . . that he may work mighty miracles" (Moroni 10:9, 12).

4. Augustine, "On Eighty-Three Varied Questions," 65, in Joel C. Elowsky, editor, *Ancient Christian Commentary on Scripture: John 11–21* (Downers Grove, IL: InterVarsity Press, 2007), 25.

5. Herbert Lockyer, *All the Miracles of the Bible: The Supernatural in Scripture—Its Scope and Significance* (Grand Rapids, MI: Zondervan, 1965), 15. Lockyer also noted that the miracles were visible emblems of what Jesus is and what He came to do for each of us [see Lockyer (1965), 15].

6. Charles L. Swift, Doctoral Dissertation, *"I Have Dreamed a Dream": Typological Images of Teaching and Learning in the Vision of the Tree of Life* (Provo, Utah: Brigham Young University, 2003), 115n33.

7. *Exegesis* means to "draw out" of a text its meaning. An "exegetical" approach, therefore, is one that seeks to "draw out" of a text the meaning or application intended by the original author who penned the text.

8. See Frank Lloyd Cross and Elizabeth A. Livingstone, editors, *The Oxford Dictionary of the Christian Church*, second edition (New York: Oxford University Press, 1990), 490, s.v., "Exegesis"; John Bowden, editor, *Encyclopedia of Christianity* (New York: Oxford, 2005), 552; Joseph W. Trigg, "Allegory," in Everett Ferguson, editor, *Encyclopedia of Early Christianity* (New York: Garland Publishing, 1990), 23–26; Fredrick W. Norris, "Antioch," in Ferguson (1990), 54.

9. Luke Timothy Johnson, *Sacra Pagina: The Acts of the Apostles* (Collegeville, Minnesota: The Liturgical Press, 1992), 155. While I acknowledge that a fifth- or sixth-century source does not tell us how the first-century Church read scripture, it

does seem quite clear that the New Testament Church read the Old Testament—which was their "scripture"—in very symbolic and Christocentric ways, thus giving us some sense of their tendency to see scripture as symbolic and typological. That being said, I am not here arguing for an ancient interpretation. What I am saying is that, just as many ancients read the scriptures symbolically—as the New Testament often does of the Old, the Rabbis did of the Hebrew Bible, and the early post-New Testament Christians did of the Bible generally—herein I too will look for messages of application that can be drawn from the texts generally, and from their symbols specifically.

10. Dallin H. Oaks, "Scripture Reading and Revelation," *Ensign*, January 1995, 7–9. See also Charles L. Swift, "Three Stories," in *My Redeemer Lives*, Richard Neitzel Holzapfel and Kent P. Jackson, editors (Provo, UT: Brigham Young University Religious Studies Center and Deseret Book, 2011), 125–46.

11. Oaks (1995), 8.

12. Regarding sources, I have largely drawn upon two types of commentaries for the writing of this text: homiletic and scholarly. While academicians sometimes don't like—or don't see as legitimate—homiletic commentaries, because of my stated purpose in this book, those really *are* the most appropriate for engaging in a discussion about modern applications. I have also employed a handful of scholarly commentaries, in part because of their historical, cultural, or linguistic insights into the text, but also because they too sometimes offer symbolic insights into the text. Hence my mixture of sources, which to some, no doubt, will seem like rather strange bedfellows.

13. While I will offer occasional points of clarification as they relate to language, culture, or history surrounding these miracles, this work is *not* intended as a historical analysis of the facts, *nor* as a scholarly examination of the miracles. To read what I've done here as such would be to entirely miss the point of this work. I acknowledge that for some academics such an approach will be frustrating. Nevertheless, I personally see value in asking, "How does this speak to me personally, owing to the circumstances in my life today?" And so, rather than asking, "What did this mean for the first-century Church?" our question will be, "What *can* I see in this for my life today?"

14. The word *homiletic* simply means that which resembles or relates to a homily. Of course, *homilies* are short messages or talks that typically have a religious or moral message.

15. As already noted, a number of the scholarly commentaries I used also interpreted these miracle stories in symbolic ways—occasionally finding modern application in the ancient accounts and with an intent of promoting application among readers of the scriptural texts.

16. Charles Swift, " 'So Great and Marvelous Things': The Literary Portrait of Jesus as Divine Lord in 3 Nephi," in Andrew C. Skinner and Gaye Strathearn, *Third Nephi: An Incomparable Scripture* (Provo, UT: Maxwell Institute for Religious Scholarship, 2012), 244–45, 248–49.

17. See Swift, in Skinner and Strathearn (2012), 244–50.

NEPHI *Imitates* LABAN

1 NEPHI 4:20–26

THE MIRACLE

In one of several attempts by Lehi's sons to obtain the plates of brass, Nephi entered the city and headed toward the house of Laban. Unexpectedly, he discovered his nemesis inebriated and unconscious, lying upon the ground.

While Nephi looked upon Laban, the Spirit surprised this future prophet by commanding him to do what, to Nephi, was the unthinkable. He was commanded to slay Laban. For, said the Spirit: "It is better that one man should perish than that a nation should dwindle and perish in unbelief" (verse 13). Accordingly, Nephi—no doubt hesitantly—slew Laban "that he might obtain the records according to God's commandments" (verse 17).

Once Laban was no longer a threat, Nephi employed his ingenuity, coupled with the dictates of the Spirit, in order to accomplish what his father and the Lord had sent him to do.

Nephi removed Laban's clothing—apparently consisting of a uniform coupled with armor—and quickly dressed himself in the decedent's clothing. Then Nephi went forth to the home of Laban.

Upon arriving at Laban's domicile, Nephi encountered Zoram, Laban's servant who was responsible for the treasury and its contents. Zoram held the keys, and, thus, Nephi was forced to interact with him in order to obtain the plates.

Nephi, imitating the voice of Laban, ordered Zoram to follow him to the treasury. Zoram showed no evidence of suspecting that Nephi was not actually Laban. Indeed, the servant carried on a rather casual conversation with Nephi regarding the meeting Laban had attended that evening. Nibley pointed out, "No one dares challenge 'big brass' too closely (least of all a grim and hot-tempered Laban)."[1] In an attempt to continue the charade, Nephi answered Zoram's questions as best he could. He noted in his account of the exchange that Zoram, "supposing that I . . . was truly that Laban whom I had slain, . . . did follow me" (verse 26).

BACKGROUND

The miracle in this episode is found in the Lord's ability to disguise Nephi's voice—not just his appearance—so that he could obtain the plates without being discovered.[2] While an attempt at impersonating Laban would be possible, the successful imitation of his voice—particularly to one of his closest associates—seems incredibly difficult at best. The Lord's intervention would be needed. Of course, how this miracle was accomplished is a matter of conjecture. However, one commentary on the Book of Mormon suggested,

> In the dark, wearing the armor of Laban, he might be mistaken for Laban. But how could he disguise his voice, especially when speaking to a servant who would surely know Laban's voice? Nephi recognizes Zoram, the servant, as the one who had the keys to the treasury. He must certainly have learned that information on an earlier visit. When seeing the very person he needed, Nephi probably felt renewed confirmation that he was being guided by the Spirit. Thus, he found that he spoke with Laban's voice. That discovery would have further affirmed his sense that Yahweh was behind his actions. . . .
>
> Nephi's appearance was so completely that of Laban that the servant accepted the illusion without hesitation. Even if the voice were somewhat different, the servant's expectation of hearing Laban would have encouraged him to hear what he expected to hear and [to act] accordingly. . . .
>
> Nephi's experience was more than a simple generic deception, however, as Nephi had to appear as Laban in Laban's house and before a servant who knew him well. Doubtless Yahweh provided assistance to the illusion.[3]

Another similarly stated,

Nephi was so convincing in speaking in the voice of Laban that the servant obediently followed him (vv. 20–25). He also conversed freely with Nephi as he carried the plates of brass outside the walls of Jerusalem (v. 27). The time involved and the distance covered could have been quite extensive. Therefore, this was no temporary misidentification. . . . It is logical that Zoram knew Laban's voice well. . . . What was the secret to Nephi's voice change? Was it not a gift of the Spirit, a form of the gift of tongues, a power poured out on him because of his faith? It was God's will that Nephi obtain the plates of brass, therefore he could bless Nephi, because of his faith, with the ability to sound like Laban.[4]

These explanations both highlight the miraculous nature of Nephi's imitation of Laban and the source. It seems Nephi may have experienced something akin to what Brigham Young is said to have experienced when (according to tradition) he was "transfigured" after the death of Joseph Smith. Brigham—who is said to have appeared and sounded like Joseph to those in the audience—was not seeking to imitate the prophet.[5] The Lord simply made him look and sound like Joseph to many of those in attendance. It may well be that the Lord performed a similar miracle for Nephi, inspiring him to don Laban's clothing (so that he would *look* like Zoram's master), but then miraculously *causing* his voice to sound like Laban's (so that Zoram would not detect him).

While Western culture naturally causes us to recoil at the idea that Nephi was commanded to cut off Laban's head, in the culture of the East in Nephi's day, this may have not seemed quite as unthinkable. Hugh Nibley shared an experience he had that highlights the difference in how Eastern cultures might see this story in comparison to the way Westerners perceive it:

For seven or eight years, my classes consisted entirely of Arab Moslems. From all the Arab countries they came to BYU to study because President Harris had started the 4-H program over there. They had to take religion, and the consul didn't want them to take Christian religion. They took Book of Mormon and loved it; it was their book. They ate it up, except for little Fayek. . . . There were two sitting in the front row [one day when I shared the story of Nephi slaying Laban], Salim and Fayek Salen. . . . [Fayek] was only seventeen years old when he came here, and he lived at our house. He was a very bright little guy. . . . Well, I told the story of cutting off the head of Laban there, which has always shocked everybody as being immoral. Well, it is. It shocked Nephi too. He had to argue with himself for an hour. He wouldn't do it. . . . But anyway, these boys were worried. I could hear murmurs all over the class. They didn't like this story of cutting off Laban's head like that. Fayek Salim raised his hand and said, "Mr. Nibley, there is something very wrong about this story; this is not a good story. When he found Laban lying in the street like that, why did he wait so long to cut off his head? That doesn't ring true—any Arab would have done it like that, of course." In other words, the story *does* ring true.[6]

As Nibley's story highlights, what would be appalling to one culture is not necessarily inexcusable in another. Nibley also reminds the Western reader that "the slaying of Laban is no more reprehensible than was the beheading of the unconscious Goliath."[7] In the Arab culture in which he was reared, Nephi's hesitancy to kill Laban may simply reveal the goodness of his heart, and the innate spirituality of this approximately fifteen-year-old boy who would one day preside over the Church in the promised land.[8]

The fact that both Lehi and Laban were descendants of Joseph suggests that the two men were related—though how closely is unclear.[9]

The statement that Laban's death would prevent a "nation" from "perishing in unbelief" (verse 13) seems to imply that if Lehi's family did not take the plates with them, they would not have what was necessary to preserve their faith in the new land (see 1 Nephi 4:15–16). As one commentator put it, "Nephi needs a powerful reason to overcome his reluctance to shed blood; that reason is his people's future ability to know the commandments. Because those commandments are contained on the brass plates, they are therefore necessary to Lehi's posterity."[10]

One commentary on the Book of Mormon suggested that the name Zoram might come from the Hebrew *Zur*, meaning "rock"—implying the trustworthy and reliable character of Zoram.[11] Whether or not this is the meaning of Zoram's name, he certainly turned out to be exactly that, siding with Nephi over the prophet's older and highly rebellious brothers, Laman and Lemuel.

We speak of Zoram as Laban's "servant," but he may have been much more than that. It has been suggested that he was an "important official, and no mere slave." The title "servant," by which Nephi refers to Zoram, has been said (at that time) to mean "official representative"—and implied an honorary position rather than one of servitude (as we might think of it today).[12]

SYMBOLIC ELEMENTS

While clothing, contingent upon the article and its usage, can have myriad meanings, in this narrative Laban's clothing does not appear to be intended as a symbol. It is practical—just clothing. That being said, what he wore the night he lost his life overtly stands as a symbol of the state of things in Jerusalem at the time. One commentator pointed out: "Laban . . . was wearing his full dress armor. What a world of inference this is! We sense the gravity of the situation in Jerusalem which 'the elders' are still trying to conceal; we hear the suppressed excitement of Zoram's urgent talk as he and Nephi hasten through the streets to the city gates (1 Nephi 4:27), and from Zoram's willingness to change sides and leave the city we can be sure that he, as Laban's secretary, knew how badly things were going."[13] Thus, the open mention of armor covertly informs us that things are not good in and about Jerusalem—a fact of which Lehi and his family were already well aware.

Nephi also employs Laban's clothing as a symbol, simply by donning it. When the future prophet dresses himself in Laban's garb, he is attempting to symbolize Laban—and thereby to access that which only Laban had a right to. Thus, in that sense, the clothing of Laban functioned as a symbol of authorization and authority—hence Zoram's choice to willingly follow.

In scripture, the voice of God is often a symbol of His power and His person.[14] Curiously, the voice of Laban (through Nephi) actually is used similarly in this narrative. When Zoram hears Laban's voice (or supposes he does), he associates it with both the power and person of his employer. Coincidental as it may be, Laban certainly acted as though he were God, and thus, the parallel in the symbolism seems fitting.

In this miracle, the brass plates contain the word of God and also represent the desperate need we each have to have access to God's word. Nephi's commitment to do anything within his power to obtain the plates—even if it required the laying down of his own life (see 1 Nephi 3:15)—is reminiscent of the Protestant Reformers (like Wycliffe and Tyndale) who gave their lives for access to the word of God. The plates symbolize God's word. But Nephi's devotion to obtaining them can metaphorically represent a demeanor that God desires all of His children manifest toward His words. Each of us may be benefited by personal introspection regarding whether our personal use of the standard works sends a message to the Father that we love and cherish His word as Nephi loved it.

APPLICATION AND ALLEGORIZATION

Nephi famously declared, "I know that the Lord giveth no commandments unto the children of men, save he shall prepare a way for them that they may accomplish the thing which he commandeth them" (1 Nephi 3:7). This miracle is but one example of how God can do that. We know Nephi entered the city being "led by the Spirit" and "not knowing beforehand" what he was going to do (1 Nephi 4:6). He was proactive and filled with faith, but beyond that, he had no idea how God would secure for him the plates. And as the text testifies, it didn't happen at all in a way Nephi would have predicted. So it is in our own lives. God will fulfill His promises to us (as we faithfully seek to do His will). However, few of us experience a life that has gone the way we predicted it would. This miracle seems to testify of the need to be willing to be used in the way God wants to use us. It also testifies of the need to do whatever difficult things He asks us to do—even when those seem contrary to our plan or will.

The miracle of Nephi being enabled to speak in Laban's voice reminds us of the truth that God can make us into something different than we are by nature. That means that He can certainly squeeze out of us the "natural man" or woman (Mosiah 3:19) who persuades us to sin on a daily basis. But it also implies that God can make us what He needs us to be in a challenging calling, a hard career, or in a difficult marriage. We don't always know how He will accomplish that, but if we move forward with the same level of faith manifested by Nephi, God will equip us with the gifts and attributes necessary—even if those are not ones innate to us.[15]

On a related note, Nephi's miracle of speaking with Laban's voice brings to mind the gift of tongues (Articles of Faith 1:7; Omni 1:25; Alma 9:21; D&C 109:36). While we typically associate this gift with speaking a language we do not know—particularly so that we can share the gospel with others[16]—this particular gift of the Spirit goes well beyond that singular purpose. The gift of tongues can certainly be manifest through speaking a foreign language, but it can also be manifest though God's inspiring a man or woman with wisdom and words beyond their own. We can be given utterance to accomplish God's work and will in our callings; in counseling others; in interacting with a spouse, boss, or child; or in many other circumstances where we do not have the ability or the words necessary to communicate what needs to be communicated in the way it needs to be said. But God knows what needs to be said and how it must be spoken, and He can give us the gift of tongues so that we have utterance. "Open your mouths and they shall be filled, and you shall become even as Nephi of old" (D&C 33:8).

Finally, while Nephi sought to imitate Laban, as we seek to imitate God and Christ, we will find the attributes of God manifest in our nature—in our character. As we imitate our Father and our Savior, we will begin to speak with Their voice and develop Their countenance. With Alma, we should each ask, is "the image of God engraven upon your countenance?" (Alma 5:19). If not, perhaps we should work harder on our imitation of Him.

NOTES

1. Hugh Nibley, *An Approach to the Book of Mormon*, third edition (Provo, UT: Foundation for Ancient Research and Mormon Studies, 1988), 117.

2. We cannot help but ask, What does it mean to speak with Laban's voice? Was it his accent? His tone? His inflection? Or was Zoram's perception simply obscured by the Spirit? While such questions naturally arise, the text is silent on the answers. All we know is that in some miraculous manner, God caused Zoram to perceive Nephi as Laban—in both appearance and voice.

3. Brant A. Gardner, *Second Witness: Analytical and Contextual Commentary on the Book of Mormon*, six volumes (Salt Lake City, UT: Greg Kofford Books, 2007), 1:122.

4. Monte S. Nyman, *Book of Mormon Commentary*, six volumes (Orem, UT: Granite Publishing, 2003–2004), 1:70. It seems appropriate here to offer a general definition of faith. In *Lectures on Faith* we are informed that faith "is the principle of power in the Deity as well as in man. Hebrews 11:3: 'Through faith we understand that the worlds were framed by the word of God, so that things which are seen were not made of things which do appear'" [*Lectures on Faith* (Salt Lake City, UT: Deseret Book, 1985), 7]. This first of seven lectures goes on to say, "Secondly, [faith] is the principle of power in man also. . . . The mountain Zerin, by the faith of the brother of Jared, is removed. How do you convey to the understanding more clearly [than through such

an example] that faith is the first great governing principle which has power, dominion, and authority over all things? By it they exist, by it they are upheld, by it they are changed; . . . and without it there is no power" [*Lectures on Faith* (1985), 7, 8–9].

5. Many Latter-day Saints in attendance at the succession meeting spoke of how Brigham was transfigured so that he appeared much like Joseph. But one of the strongest testimonies, repeated time and again, was that Brigham sounded exactly like Joseph: "When he spoke, it was in Brother Joseph's voice"; "His voice was like that of the Prophet"; "Brigham Young came to the stand and commenced to speak with the voice of Joseph the Prophet"; "Joseph's voice was clear and distinct as I ever heard Joseph speak"; "I heard the voice of the Prophet Joseph"; "Brigham, speaking with an angel's voice"; "It was the voice of Joseph Smith—not that of Brigham Young"; "I know that it is Joseph Smith's voice! Yet I knew that he had gone" [*The Eyewitness History of the Church, Volume Three, Journey to Zion's Hill, 1845–1869*, Jennifer Johnson, Claire Koltko, Brittany McEwen, and Natalie Ross, compilers (Springville, UT: Cedar Fort, 2006), 17–22]. The author acknowledges that many Latter-day Saint historians today see the "transfiguration" of Brigham as a "collective memory" that developed over time and years after the event. My reference to the said "transfiguration" here is not intended to embrace late recollections nor to challenge the "collective memory." I only reference the tradition to suggest that its traditional telling may color how we read the event Nephi experienced.

6. Nibley (2004), 1:94, 80; see also 1:126.

7. Hugh Nibley, *Lehi in the Desert/The World of the Jaredites/There Were Jaredites* (Provo, UT: Foundation for Ancient Research and Mormon Studies, 1988), 100. See also D. Kelly Ogden and Andrew C. Skinner, *Verse by Verse: The Book of Mormon*, two volumes (Salt Lake City, UT: Deseret Book, 2011), 1:32.

8. Reynolds and Sjodahl conjecture that Nephi was born in 617 BCE and married in 600 BCE. If that was the case, Nephi would be somewhere between fifteen and seventeen when he slays Laban. [See George Reynolds and Janne M. Sjodahl, *Commentary on the Book of Mormon*, seven volumes (Salt Lake City, UT: Deseret Book, 1955–1961), 1:16].

9. Nibley (2004), 1:71, 75, 107.

10. Gardner (2007), 1:119.

11. See Reynolds and Sjodahl (1955–1961), 1:22. See also 1:42. Nibley, on the other hand, claimed the name was not Hebrew but Canaanite or Aramaic and that it likely meant "a strong, refreshing rain" [Nibley (2004), 1:127].

12. See Nibley, *An Approach* (1988), 128.

13. Nibley, *An Approach* (1988), 112. See also Ogden and Skinner (2011), 1:31.

14. See Leland Ryken, James C. Wilhoit, and Tremper Longman III, editors, *Dictionary of Biblical Imagery* (Downers Grove, IL: InterVarsity Press, 1998), 918.

15. One wonders to what extent Nephi was strengthened *because of* the constant opposition of his brothers. There was no middle ground for him, nor should there be for us either.

16. The prophet Joseph spoke of the primary purpose of the gift of tongues as preaching the gospel to individuals in their own language [see Willard Richard's

report in Joseph Smith's Journal, 26 December, 1841, cited in *The Joseph Smith Papers—Journals, Volume 2: December 1841—April 1843*, Andrew H. Hedges, Alex D. Smith, and Richard Lloyd Anderson, editors (Salt Lake City, UT: The Church Historian's Press, 2011), 18. See also *History of the Church*, seven volumes (Salt Lake City, UT: Deseret Book, 1978), 2:162, 3:379, 5:31–32. See also Larry E. Dahl and Donald Q. Cannon, *The Teachings of Joseph Smith* (Salt Lake City, UT: Bookcraft, 1998), 670–71].

NEPHI'S BANDS *Are* LOOSED

1 NEPHI 7:16–18

THE MIRACLE

As they traveled through the wilderness, Nephi's brothers Laman and Lemuel (along with four of Ishmael's children and their families) began to murmur about the difficulty of the trip and the sacrifices that had been required of them. It was their desire to return home to Jerusalem, and they made that known in typical obnoxious Laman and Lemuel fashion.

Nephi, filled with faith, was "grieved for the hardness of their hearts" (verse 8). So he spoke to them, hoping they would soften their hearts. He emphasized the importance of keeping the commandments. He reminded them that they had seen an angel. He recounted for them the "great things the Lord had done" in delivering them from Laban's wrath and in conveying to them the plates of brass, which they had been seeking (verse 11). Nephi testified to them that those who exercise faith in God receive of His blessings and aid. And, finally, he warned them that returning to Jerusalem would result in their captivity or, even worse, their deaths.

Nephi's words so infuriated his brothers and their cohorts that they took him and bound him with strong cords with the intention of leaving him in the wilderness to be eaten by wild beasts.

Trusting in God, Nephi prayed, saying, "O Lord, according to my faith which is in thee, wilt thou deliver me from the hands of my brethren; yea, even give me strength that I may burst these bands with which I am bound" (verse 17). Upon the conclusion of his prayer,

Nephi received the strength necessary, the bands were loosed from his hands and feet, and he stood before them a free man.

BACKGROUND

The reader will recall that the point of this trip to Jerusalem was the retrieval of Ishmael's family, so that Lehi's sons and daughters would have companions to marry, and so that they could raise up a posterity in the wilderness and in the new promised land (1 Nephi 7:1–2).[1] Nibley conjectures that Lehi and Ishmael were brothers—and that would explain why Lehi sent his sons back for that specific family.[2]

The return trips to Jerusalem (after their initial departure) required the sons of Lehi to travel 800–1,000 miles through an inhospitable desert region.[3] The difficulty of the task was made worse by the fact that they were never committed to it in the first place. While this is no excuse for their murderous behavior, we can certainly see how it added to it.

When, at the conclusion of his prayer, Nephi's bands break in a seemingly miraculous manner, his brothers are not humbled. Rather, they only become angrier with their younger brother (7:19). It is only the pleading from members of Ishmael's family that *temporarily* softens the hearts of Laman and Lemuel. One commentator explained, "From our perspective, the event seems miraculous. However, in context of the moment, it was not considered particularly remarkable. Nephi has described himself as physically large and strong. Laman and Lemuel may have seen his release as nothing more than a demonstration of Nephi's strength or their own ineptitude in tying knots. They are certainly not awed into cooperation by it."[4] The dismissing of miracles comes easily to those who lack faith. The Prophet Joseph indicated that at the Second Coming of Christ there will be those who will see the sign of His advent—a light coming from the east, growing brighter and brighter as it nears the earth—and yet they will still deny its reality all the way up until they are destroyed by the descending fire. Said Joseph, "But what will [they] do? They will say it is a planet, a comet, etc."[5]

Angry as they were, Laman and Lemuel stopped their abuse of Nephi, likely in response to the pleadings of Ishmael's wife and one of his daughters (verse 19).[6] What remains to be understood, however, is what softened the heart of Ishmael's family. Monte Nyman suggested this:

> There were five single daughters of Ishmael, and four sons of Lehi, plus Zoram, the servant of Laban who had joined them. Their purpose in returning to Jerusalem to get Ishmael's family was to get wives to raise up seed unto the Lord. Had one of Ishmael's daughters and her mother counted the eligible bachelors, and realized there would be one short if Nephi's life was taken? This seems to be more a probability than a possibility.[7]

The reason for Laman and Lemuel's sudden "change of heart," and also the reason for the shift in feeling of Ishmael's family, may be found in factors other than sincere repentance. The continued bad behavior of that group suggests godly sorrow is not what we are seeing manifest here.

SYMBOLIC ELEMENTS

While the text does not explicitly emphasize the parallels, there seems to be a symbolic connection between Nephi's experience with his brothers and Joseph (who was sold into Egypt) and his brothers. One commentator noted:

> Whether by coincidence, divine irony, or Nephi's literary recasting, Nephi's story continues to parallel that of his ancestor Joseph. Like Joseph he is younger than his brothers over whom, like Joseph, he is predicted to rule. Also, like Joseph, he arouses his brothers' anger. Nephi's brothers appear to have the same designs upon him as Joseph's brothers did before they sold him to the Midianites. In this case, however, the outcome of the brotherly conflict is different, though Nephi (again like Joseph) will end up ruling in a foreign country.[8]

The parallels are numerous enough and significant enough for us to believe that the connection between the two prophets is more than mere coincidence.

Cords can symbolically represent "imprisonment and limitation."[9] Thus, the act of binding someone often carries the connotation that he or she has lost agency or power, that the bound person is in a state of oppression or in a state of being controlled.[10] Thus, we read of Abraham binding Isaac (Genesis 22:9) or those carried into exile being bound (2 Chronicles 25:7; 33:11). We're also told Satan will be bound during the Millennium (Revelation 20:1–3); and we think of ourselves as bound by sin or addiction.

To be loosed, on the other hand, represents being "empowered" and being given "freedom." It is an image of "liberation from bondage" and highlights one's ability to be an agent unto himself.[11] Thus, the psalmist praises God for "loosening his bonds" (Psalm 116:16). That from which one is "loosed" can be an enemy, an addiction, temptation, debt, and so on. God is often depicted as the liberator of the one previously bound.

APPLICATION AND ALLEGORIZATION

Laman and Lemuel get angry with Nephi *because* he has the Spirit with him and because he speaks the truth by that same Spirit. So it is with Satan. The adversary of all unrighteousness does not like it when you and I follow the Spirit. He seeks to thwart us—and to accost us—anytime we get close to God. He hates it when converts seek baptism, he despises it when you and I repent, and he is frustrated when individuals pursue a path that leads to the holy temple. Anytime you or I seek to do good, to change our lives, to stand for truth and righteousness, his only desire is to thwart us. He wants to bind us—to prevent us from acting in holy and faithful ways—and he'll do all that he can to bind us in order to prevent us from becoming as God is, or from drawing nearer to our Creator and our Savior. When he does so—and sometimes he'll have success—we need to follow the example of Nephi and cry out, "O Lord, according to my faith which is in thee, wilt thou deliver me from the hands of my adversary; yea, even give me strength that I may burst these bands with which I am bound" (see 1 Nephi 7:17).[12]

This same principle is true of any addiction with which we are bound: drugs, alcohol, pornography, anger, same-sex attraction, dishonesty, greed, avarice. Whatever binds us, as we cry out to the Lord, He has the power to loose us. He has the power to restore the agency we lose when we succumb to temptation and addiction. If we spiritually allow Him to place His hands upon our heads, He can free us—regardless of how strong the temptation is or how badly we are addicted.[13]

This miracle also reminds us of the dangers of pride. Laman and Lemuel have been taught at the feet of a prophet, their father, Lehi. Their younger brother, though annoying to them, also has great spiritual endowments. Yet, because of pride, they frequently chafe at what is right, good, and true. We each will have encounters in our lives wherein we will be confronted with the wrongness of our own acts, words, or decisions. We can respond as did Laman and Lemuel, with a spirit of anger, which is self-destructive. Or we can choose a path of humility, where we simply acknowledge our mistakes and embrace the Spirit of the Lord. As we see in the Book of Mormon, the former choice leads to death, and the latter to life. Are we humble enough to choose that which leads to life and happiness?

Each of us will at times in our lives be wronged by others. Sometimes those wrongs will be so grave and egregious that we will have difficulty letting go of what has been done to us or said about us. We may feel justified in our anger—or perhaps even in feelings of hatred toward the one who has harmed or offended us. However, such feelings force the Spirit of God out of our lives and allow the person who originally victimized us to have even more power in our lives (by controlling our emotions and by robbing us of the companionship of the Holy Spirit). In such circumstances, which are bound to come to each and every one of us, we must choose to be like Nephi, who after abuse at the hands of his brothers—and after an encounter that was designed to take away his life—prayed to the Lord, softened his own heart, and then "did frankly forgive them of all that they had done" (1 Nephi 7:21). One source wisely noted, "There are only two choices: obedience is the pathway to vitality; murmuring is the pathway to death."[14] Nephi's choice to be obedient to the pathway that leads to the Spirit brought him vitality. Laman and Lemuel's choice to follow the path of murmuring—which we might be tempted to do when we're wronged—brought them spiritual death. May God bless us to have the mortal fortitude of Nephi and the courage and strength to take that higher road when our enemies take the lower one.

Noting the breaking of the bands with which Nephi was bound, David A. Bednar offered this interpretation and application of this miracle, stating,

I personally do not believe the bands with which Nephi was bound just magically fell from his hands and wrists. Rather, I suspect that he was blessed with both persistence and personal strength beyond his natural capacity, that he then "in the strength of the Lord" (Mosiah 9:17) worked and twisted and tugged on the cords and ultimately and literally was enabled to break the bands.

Brothers and sisters, the implication of this episode for each of us is quite straightforward. As you and I come to understand and employ the enabling power of the Atonement in our personal lives, we will pray and seek for strength to change our circumstances rather than praying for our circumstances to be changed. We will become agents who "act" rather than objects that are "acted upon" (2 Nephi 2:14).[15]

Surely God does miraculous things in our lives. But Elder Bednar is correct that often those miracles happen because you and I request God's help and strength, and then we do all that we personally can to make the miracle happen.

One last application seems worth making. Ishmael's wife's act of pleading with Laman and Lemuel may offer a potential message for us today. In 1834 Joseph and Hyrum had been on the Zion's Camp march. During that excursion, many of the men murmured because of their sufferings. Joseph warned them to cease murmuring, lest they provoke God's wrath. But the counsel was ignored, and sure to his word, the men in the camp come down with cholera. This sickness was devastating to those who acquired it. Joseph and Hyrum were called upon to administer to those who were sick, but in doing so, the Prophet and his brother became ill also. So bad was the disease that they thought they would die there in the Missouri wilderness, never having a chance to say good-bye to their wives or children. As Joseph and Hyrum pled with the Lord for deliverance, Hyrum had an "open vision" in which he saw his mother, Lucy Mack Smith, kneeling under an apple tree (in tears) praying that the Lord would spare their lives. Joseph and Hyrum were healed, and upon their return, the Prophet said to his mother: "Oh, my mother! How often have your prayers been the means of assisting us when the shadows of death encompassed us."[16] As the pleading of Ishmael's wife spared Nephi, the pleading of Lucy saved her sons. And while we do not know the intent or motivation of those in Ishmael's family who pled for Nephi's welfare, what we do know is that a righteous wife or mother who petitions the Lord on behalf of her posterity surely will be heard. (Of course, prayers are answered in the Lord's way and in His time. But they *are* answered. We must have the patience to trust in Him when it feels as though *our* pleadings have gone unheard or unmet.)

NOTES

1. See Erastus Snow, *Journal of Discourses*, 23:184.

2. Nibley (2004), 1:131. Nibley points out that it was culturally the practice (during that time) for the children of brothers to marry. Thus, Ishmael daughters are the natural choice for Lehi's sons' wives. [See also Nibley (2004), 1:29.]

3. Ogden and Skinner (2011), 37. One text points out, "The distance from Jerusalem to the Red Sea (the Gulf of Aqaba) is about 180 miles through hot, barren country infested anciently by many marauders. And they had gone three days' journey beyond that. (See 1 Nephi 2:6.)" "They were *over* two hundred miles from Jerusalem" before they were sent back to get the plates, and then sent back again to get Ishmael's family. [See *Book of Mormon (Religion 121–122) Student Manual*, second edition, revised (Salt Lake City: The Church of Jesus Christ of Latter-day Saints, 1981), 16, emphasis added.]

4. Gardner (2007), 1:149.

5. Joseph Smith, in Dahl and Cannon (1998), 624.

6. See Nibley (2004), 1:133.

7. Nyman (2003–2004), 1:96n5.

8. Gardner (2007), 1:148–49.

9. David Fontana, *The Secret Language of Symbols* (San Francisco, CA: Chronicle Books, 1994), 75. See also J. C. Cooper, *An Illustrated Encyclopaedia of Traditional Symbols* (London: Thames and Hudson, 1982), 42.

10. See Ryken, Wilhoit and Longman (1998), 92. Of course, Satan has no power over us—only that which we give him. [Joseph Smith, *Teachings of the Prophet Joseph Smith*, Joseph Fielding Smith, compiler (Salt Lake City, UT: Deseret Book, 1976), 181.] Thus, if we find ourselves bound—if we find our agency has been lost—we can blame no one but ourselves. While Satan seeks to "destroy the agency of man" (Moses 5:4), he cannot do so except we willingly comply.

11. See Ryken, Wilhoit and Longman (1998), 516–17.

12. This theme of deliverance from bondage appears repeatedly throughout the Book of Mormon. It is central to the Book of Mormon's primary message.

13. See Howard W. Hunter, "Reading the Scriptures," *Ensign*, November 1979, 65.

14. Ed. J. Pinegar and Richard J. Allen, *Teachings and Commentaries on the Book of Mormon* (American Fork, UT: Covenant Communications, 2003), 34.

15. David A. Bednar, "In the Strength of the Lord," Brigham Young University Devotional, October 23, 2001, in *Brigham Young University 2001–2002 Speeches*, 4.

16. See Lavina Fielding Anderson, editor, *Lucy's Book: A Critical Edition of Lucy Mack Smith's Family Memoir* (Salt Lake City, UT: Signature Books, 2001), 575–78.

NEPHI *Is* TRANSPORTED *To a* HIGH MOUNTAIN

1 NEPHI 11:1
2 NEPHI 4:24–25

THE MIRACLE

Nephi, desiring to know the things his father had seen (in his dream of the tree of life), sat pondering what Lehi had told him. He firmly believed that God could reveal to him knowledge of that which his father had been shown and taught during his prophetic dream.

In the midst of his pondering, Nephi "was caught away in the Spirit of the Lord, yea, into an exceedingly high mountain" (1 Nephi 11:1). The location was entirely unfamiliar to him, because he had never been there before.

The transporting of Nephi to this alternate location facilitated his receiving an answer to his prayer.

BACKGROUND

Hugh Nibley conjectured that the mountain to which Nephi was transported was in "another dimension."[1] In other words, just as the spirit world is in a separate dimension from our earthly (or mortal) dimension, Nibley surmises that Nephi was transported to a real location but one outside the dimension in which he lived.

SYMBOLIC ELEMENTS

Mountains were often used by the ancients as temples.[2] Mount Sinai certainly functioned in this capacity for Moses—and he, like Nephi, was "caught up into an exceedingly high mountain" (Moses 1:1).[3] One commentary on the Book of Mormon pointed out, "Mountains are frequently the meeting places between God and man; they are nature's temples, the point of intersection between the finite and the infinite."[4] Elsewhere we read, "Symbolically, Nephi has entered sacred space, a fit place for the presence [of] the Spirit of the Lord."[5] Thus, in this particular miracle narrative, the mountain to which Nephi is taken is a good symbol for the temple—not solely the location where sacred ordinances are performed, but more particularly, the place set apart from the world, the place of solace and quietude that each of us should seek out (or create) in order to draw closer to God.

APPLICATION AND ALLEGORIZATION

Meditation and ponderous thought are among the most effective tools we have in our attempts to draw closer to God and to rend the veil that separates us from the Divine. Millet and McConkie highlighted the commonality of this practice as a precursor to the major revelations of this dispensation:

> Who can assess the value of pondering, the impact of a righteous soul meditating upon the eternal word? Who can measure the worth of careful and deep reflection upon the things of God? "The things of God are of deep import," Joseph Smith wrote from the Liberty Jail, "and time, and experience, and careful and ponderous and solemn thoughts can only find them out" (*Teachings*, p. 137). Some of the greatest revelations of all time have come as a direct result of pondering. The boy prophet pondered upon the passage in James 1:5–6. . . . As a result of that pondering and prayer, the heavens were rent, the great Gods of heaven came to earth again, and thus was commenced a marvelous dispensation of grace. Joseph Smith and Sidney Rigdon . . . had a singular experience. "While we meditated upon [the resurrection], the Lord touched the eyes of our understandings and they were opened, and the glory of the Lord shone round about" (D&C 76:19). The Vision of the Glories—one of the grandest panoramic oracles of all time . . . —was vouchsafed to mortal man [through pondering]. Likewise, while President Joseph F. Smith pondered upon the first epistle of Peter and our Lord's postmortal ministry to the world of spirits, there was granted to him a "vision of the redemption of the dead," a vision that offered saving insights into the manner in which the Master organized

his righteous servants for the presentation of the message of the gospel to those who sit in darkness (see D&C 138).[6]

Prayer is important; but meditation must also not be neglected. Quiet, ponderous thought—aside from all the requests so common in our personal prayers—allows us to simply listen to the voice of the Spirit and to be guided to what He needs us to think about and know. We tend to govern the direction of our prayers. Meditation, on the other hand, is a means of allowing God to govern the conversation. Both have their place; but (as President Hinckley suggested) one is commonly neglected by the Saints.[7] Nephi's experience reminds us of the power and importance of pondering.

This miracle reminds us of God's ability to direct us to places we would not go were we not governed by the Spirit: something particularly important when one serves as Relief Society president, bishop, or in any calling within the Church. Just as the Holy Ghost took Nephi to a mountain he had never been to, so also (when we are in tune with the Lord) will the Spirit guide us down paths we have not traversed and to locations we had not intended to go. President Monson is famous for his stories about being guided by the Spirit to this home or that. The Lord seeks to do the same with each of us. I recall having a similar experience as a young missionary.

> My companion and I had awakened that morning and gotten ourselves ready for the day. The previous evening we had planned out what we would do the next day; but when morning arrived, somehow those plans just didn't seem right. We prayed and determined to change our plans—but for no apparent reason other than the Spirit seemed to be urging us. We got in our car and begin to drive with no specific destination in mind. In a few minutes we came upon a housing complex—several stories high with numerous units. We knocked every door in the complex and found but one family home—or, at least, one family willing to answer the door. They invited us in, we taught them the gospel, and they were baptized a short time later. The most significant aspect of this story, however, is that this family was moving to another country in only three weeks. Had we not been directed that morning to proselyte in a different location from the one in which we had been working, by the time we actually knocked the doors in that building this family would have been long gone. Thankfully, like Nephi, we wanted to know God's will, we prayed and pondered the feelings that

came, and ultimately we were "caught away in the Spirit of the Lord, yea, into an" apartment complex "which we never had before seen, and upon which we never had before set foot."

Nephi's miracle reminds us that the Lord can lead us to where He needs us. Indeed, He actually *wants* to lead us so that we can be His instruments in accomplishing His work. His Spirit will inspire us to go to the temple (as it transported Nephi to the sacred mountain). It will guide missionaries to where they are needed and to where their message will be accepted. It will guide bishops, home and visiting teachers, ward missionaries—transporting them to (or inspiring them to visit) the homes of those who need them. A woman in my stake shared an experience that also illustrates this principle:

> She had witnessed a young boy getting off a school bus, wearing a birthday hat. The Spirit spoke to her, saying, "You need to get that young boy a birthday present." She thought to herself, "That's just weird. I don't even know that little boy or his family." The Spirit continued to urge her until she finally decided to comply. Embarrassed by the strangeness of what she was doing, she approached the home that she saw the young birthday boy enter. She rang the doorbell and then nervously waited. When the boy's mother answered the door, my friend simply said, "I know this sounds weird, but I felt like I needed to bring your son a birthday present, so here it is." She handed the gift to the mom, turned around, and quickly walked down the street, embarrassed—and thinking, "That could not have been a prompting of the Spirit. I think I just made that up myself, and now I've embarrassed myself something terrible." The next thing she knew, the mother of the birthday boy was following her, crying as she called out. She caught up with my friend and explained, "My husband lost his job recently, and my son's birthday is today. We haven't had the money to buy him a present. My husband is supposed to get some severance pay tomorrow—so we were going to celebrate his birthday later, when we got a little money. Your gift is an answer to prayer! He will have a present on his birthday."

There are so many whom God has placed around us, individuals who have needs that you and I can meet. God is willing to guide us. Are we willing and prepared to be guided?

As a final application, it will be recalled that Nephi wanted to know the things of God. He had faith in God's ability to reveal, and thus he prayerfully pursued that which he desired. Amid all of the other applications we might draw from this miracle, a simple one is this: "We too can know and understand the things of God as we pay the price to pray and ponder over these precious truths—not just a cursory request, but rather a deep yearning of our very soul that requires the exercise of faith to the point of mental exertion."[8] As the LDS Bible Dictionary states, "Blessings require some work or effort on our part before we can obtain them. Prayer"—and we might add pondering—"is a form of work, and is an appointed means for obtaining the highest of all blessings."[9] The Saints must be willing to pay the price, and set the tone (in their personal lives), to receive the blessings the Lord offers.

NOTES

1. See Nibley (2004), 1:146.

2. Nibley (2004), 1:145–46.

3. Nephi and Moses are certainly not alone in this experience of utilizing a mountain as a temple. Enoch (Moses 7:2–3), Jesus, Peter, James, and John (Matthew 17:1–9) each used mountains for this purpose. "There were probably many more similar occasions throughout the history of the world" [Nyman (2003–2004), 1:137].

4. Joseph Fielding McConkie and Robert L. Millet, *Doctrinal Commentary on the Book of Mormon*, three volumes (Salt Lake City: Bookcraft, 1987–1991), 1:75.

5. Gardner (2007), 1:199.

6. McConkie and Millet (1987–1991), 1:74–75. See also Ogden and Skinner (2011), 1:48–50.

7. See Gordon B. Hinckley, *Teachings of Gordon B. Hinckley* (Salt Lake City: Deseret Book, 1997), 334–35.

8. Pinegar and Allen (2003), 44.

9. "Prayer," in LDS Bible Dictionary (Salt Lake City: The Church of Jesus Christ of Latter-day Saints, 1979), 753.

Lehi Discovers *the* Liahona

1 Nephi 16:10
Mosiah 1:16–17
Alma 37:38–47

The Miracle

During their travels southward through the wilderness, God guided Lehi and his entourage. He did so via the revelations this prophetic man had, and also through equally miraculous means.

God had commanded Lehi in a night vision to take his journey (on the morrow) into the wilderness. The next morning Lehi awoke and stepped out of his tent, and saw on the ground the Liahona—a "round ball of curious workmanship" with "two spindles," which "pointed the way whither they should go" (1 Nephi 16:10). This miraculous ball—with its no less miraculous appearance—led them on their journey to the promised land. In the process, it led them to the fertile parts of the wilderness, it kept them safe from enemies, and it steered them toward their ultimate destination—so long as they were worthy and followed it in faith (Mosiah 1:16–17).

Background

The word *Liahona* has been interpreted by Latter-day Saint commentators to be a Hebrew word (possibly with a Nephite or Egyptian termination) that means "Jehovah is light."[1] The implication of this name, then, is that Jehovah is the source of light—a suggestion substantiated by Doctrine and Covenants 88, which informs us that all light comes from God and Christ (verses 6–13). One text on the Book of Mormon explains the name in this way:

> Lehi had just received the divine command to begin his perilous journey. The question uppermost in his mind, after having received that call, must have been how to find the way. That must have been quite a problem. But he arose early in the morning, determined to carry out the command given. Undoubtedly he had prayed all night for light and guidance. And now, standing in the opening of the tent, perhaps as the first rays of the sun broke through the morning mists, his attention is attracted by a metal ball "of curious workmanship." He picks it up and examines it. And then, as he realizes that it is the guide for which he had been praying, he exclaims in ecstasy, *L-iah-on-a!* Which is as much as to say, This is God's delight; it has come from him! And that became the name of the curious instrument. . . . Lehi gave the metal ball a name commemorative of one of the great experiences of his life, just as these Old Testament worthies had done. [Genesis 16:13–14 or 27:7–8.] And, furthermore, he gave it a name that no one but a devout Hebrew influenced by Egyptian culture would have thought of. Is that not the strongest possible evidence of the truth of the historic part of the Book of Mormon?[2]

Presumably Lehi had been praying for light. The Liahona—a gift to him from God—was the source or means of the prophet having that light. Thus, perhaps this influenced Lehi's decision to call the ball Liahona ("Jehovah is the source of light!").

The Liahona is said to be of "curious" workmanship. The word *curious* in this verse has traditionally been understood to mean "skillful" or "impressive."[3] Rather than implying that it was "unusual," the word here seems to suggest (in 1828 English) that it was "wrought with care and art; elegant; neat; finished; as a curious . . . work."[4] This was no ordinary ball—in its functionality and also in the impressiveness of its craftsmanship or design.

In Alma 37, the Liahona is thrice referred to as a "compass" (verses 38, 43, 44). However, commentators have frequently pointed out, this is not a compass in the sense that you and I think of today. In other words, it was not a version of the instrument used by mariners to identify magnetic north. The word *compass* frequently appears in the Bible in reference to "a circle or a globe in general, a round, [or] a circuit"

(Exodus 27:5; 38:4; Numbers 34:5; Joshua 15:13; 2 Samuel 5:23; 2 Kings 3:9; Proverbs 8:23; Isaiah 44:13; Acts 28:13).[5]

How did the Liahona work? No one knows for certain. One text suggests a plausible explanation of how (from the perspective of an engineer) this two-spindled device directed Lehi and his family:

> As mentioned in Nephi's description above, one pointer necessarily provided directional information. But to appreciate the elegance of the Liahona's design, from an engineer's viewpoint, is to understand the function of the second pointer. Since a single pointer is always point-ing a direction, it was likely the role of the second pointer to provide the necessary additional information about whether the Liahona was "operational," meaning that the pointing information from the first pointer was reliable.
>
> There is but one engineering approach that provides the necessary functionality and meets all of the above requirements both efficiently and simply. This is how it would have worked: if an observer viewed the pointers and saw only a single pointer, . . . then they were both aligned in the same direction, one on top of the other, and the director was providing correct information. Lehi's party could then follow the indi-cated direction with confidence that it was the Lord's instruction. If, on the other hand, the two pointers were cross-ways to each other—form-ing an "x" . . .—then the device was not functioning, and the pointing information was not reliable. No other information was required of the Liahona, so no more than two pointers were needed. But the require-ments demand a minimum of two.[6]

This is certainly plausible—though, again, nothing more than conjecture. But it does offer a feasible explanation as to the purpose of the "second pointer" or "spindle" of the Liahona. Another possible explanation is that, while the one pointed the direction they should travel, the other pointed to instructions written around the rim of the ball—things like "Go slow," "Speed up," "Stay where you are," and so on.[7] After Nephi broke his bow, members of the family murmured because of the sufferings they had to endure. Nephi approached Lehi, asking that he inquire of the Lord regarding what they should do. Lehi did so, and the Lord commanded him to look upon the Liahona "and behold the things which are written" thereon (1 Nephi 16:26). Nephi informs us, "And it came to pass that when my father beheld the things which were written upon the ball, he did fear and tremble exceedingly, and also my brethren and the sons of Ishmael and our wives" (verse 27). What appeared is unclear, but we might assume it was some sort of dramatic warning about the consequences of the murmuring and their lack of faith in God. When Nephi declares that upon the Liahona there was written "new writing, which was plain to be read, which did give us understanding concerning the ways of the Lord; and it was written and changed from time to time," it may be that the engravings around the rim of the ball miraculously disappeared and were replaced by other writings (from time to time). But it may also simply imply that "pointer" or "spindle" number two changed "from time to time"—pointing to new directions.[8] And, in the case of this incident, pointing to a warning that had theretofore not been highlighted since they had first obtained the "curious" ball. In the first of these two theories, the writing on the Liahona was a bit like the writing on the plates of the Book of Mormon—when Joseph looked at the characters through the Urim and Thummim. Edward L. Stevenson explained that "sentences would appear and were read by the Prophet and written by Martin, and when finished he would say, 'Written,' and if correctly written, that sentence would disappear and another appear in its place."[9] In this third theory, writing would phenomenally appear around the outside of the face of the Liahona and then, from time to time, disappear—being replaced by other writings.[10] In this third theory, there is no explanation as to the place or purpose of the second "spindle" or "pointer." Again, we cannot say with any degree of certainty how all of this worked, but what commentators have offered is thought provoking, to say the least.

SYMBOLIC ELEMENTS

The Liahona has been defined as a symbol for the words of Christ, as found in the scriptures and the teachings of the living prophets (see Alma 37:38–47). Because it worked when they were faithful and did not work when they were disobedient to the Lord (and His prophets), it served as "a visible evidence of their standing before God."[11]

APPLICATION AND ALLEGORIZATION

The Liahona is the most obvious type in this miracle, and its meaning is elucidated in the Book of Mormon itself. Of it, Alma the

Younger explained that it was prepared by God, but it only functioned according to the user's faith in the Father and diligent heed to the Liahona itself. If those who used it doubted its instructions or neglected to follow them, then it would cease to function—and those who possessed it would be "afflicted" (see Alma 37:42). Of course, because the miracles of the Liahona were brought to pass by "small means," the Nephites "were slothful and forgot to exercise their faith and diligence and then those marvelous works ceased and they did not progress" (Alma 37:41). We read,

> I would that ye should understand that these things are not without a shadow; for as our fathers were slothful to give heed to this compass (now these things were temporal) they did not prosper; even so it is with things which are spiritual. For behold, it is as easy to give heed to the word of Christ, which will point to you a straight course to eternal bliss, as it was for our fathers to give heed to this compass, which would point unto them a straight course to the promised land. And now I say, is there not a type in this thing? For just as surely as this director did bring our fathers, by following its course, to the promised land, shall the words of Christ, if we follow their course, carry us beyond this vale of sorrow into a far better land of promise. O my son, do not let us be slothful because of the easiness of the way; for so was it with our fathers; for so was it prepared for them, that if they would look they might live; even so it is with us. The way is prepared, and if we will look we may live forever. And now, my son, see that ye take care of these sacred things, yea, see that ye look to God and live. (Alma 37:43–47)

Alma the Younger makes it clear that the Liahona is a type—a symbol—for the words of Christ, as found in scripture and in the teachings of the living prophets and apostles. As we follow them diligently, they will lead us in the way of eternal life. Indeed, they will lead us to the promised land—the celestial kingdom of our God. However, slothfulness to these sacred things will surely leave us in darkness and confusion, just as the Nephites' slothfulness to the Liahona left them similarly situated. Faithfulness to the words of Christ, as given through His authorized messengers, is the only safe way to live our lives. We are promised rich blessings of the Spirit as we have faith in them. We are promised consequences as we neglect them.

The following table describes some of the most obvious symbolism present in this miracle of the Liahona.

ELEMENT IN NARRATIVE	SYMBOLIC INTERPRETATION
The Liahona (16:10)	Christ and His words—as found in the scriptures, in teachings of the living prophets, via the Spirit, in priesthood blessings—as our guide and compass through life.
Lehi's "astonishment" and the curious nature of the Liahona (16:10).	God uses simple means to bring to pass His miraculous work. Even Jesus, according to the prophet Isaiah (53:2), had an ordinary look to His appearance that left some inattentive to who He was and what He had come to offer.
The Liahona's spindles (16:10)	The directions, counsel, and promptings that come to us through the various divinely appointed sources.
The Liahona led the Nephites along the Red Sea (16:14, 16).	That which is of God—that which serves to inspire and direct us—will always lead us to the "living waters" (John 7:38–39).
The Liahona led the Nephites to the "more fertile parts" (16:14).	Christ and His Spirit will always make our lives fertile, rich, and blessed.
Asking the ball for directions (16:24).	Calling upon the Lord in prayer and studying His words—through scriptures, conference talks, and so on.
The Liahona worked according to the faith, diligence, and heed given it (16:28).	We must have faith in Christ and His words and be diligent in keeping His commands if we wish for His direction in our lives.
The Liahona would get new writing from time to time (16:29).	The Church receives modern revelation as needed to guide and direct it.
The Liahona sent Nephi to the mountain to get nourishment (16:30).	The Lord's word will always point us toward the temple.
On the mountain, Nephi obtained nourishment for himself and his entire family (16:31).	As we attend the temple, we too will be spiritually nourished and will receive the Lord's will for our own families.

As a related point, because the Nephites thought *some* of the "counsel" of the Liahona seemed insignificant ("small"), they neglected to obey it and thus suffered. Hugh Nibley pointed out,

Moreover, while both [Lehi and Nephi] marvel at the wonderful work-manship of the brass ball in which the pointers were mounted, they refer to the operation of those pointers as "a very small thing," so famil-iar to Lehi's people that they hardly gave it a second glance. So con-temptuous were they of the "small means" by which "those miracles were worked" for their guidance and preservation that they constantly "forgot to exercise their faith," so that the compass would work. This suggests that aside from the workmanship of the mounting, there was nothing particularly strange or mystifying about the apparatus, which Alma specifies as a "temporal" thing.[12]

Some Latter-day Saints also downplay the significance of some of the "small" counsel given by the presiding Brethren—or some of the "small miracles" that take place in their lives. We sometimes assume that things the prophets and apostles advise us are really just "sugges-tions." President Boyd K. Packer once noted, "You can put it down in your little black book that if you will not be loyal in the small things, you will not be loyal in the large things. If you will not respond to the so-called insignificant or menial tasks which need to be performed in the Church and kingdom, there will be no opportunity for service in the so-called greater challenges."[13] Selective obedience is never wise and never safe. Like the Nephites with the Liahona, such an attitude toward the words of prophets and apostles is incredibly harmful and can keep us from "progressing in our journey" (Alma 37:42). Over the years I've had students ask, "How do we know when they are giving us their opinion as opposed to the word and will of the Lord?" I have traditionally responded, "What does it matter? The Brethren are extremely cautious. They have sixty, seventy, eighty years of experience. Even their personal advice is based on maturity and wisdom. To want to quibble about whether they are speaking by revelation or from a life of faithfulness and experience with counseling those who have sinned, I think we're pretty safe heeding their counsel and warning regardless of which is its source." The Liahona worked, not because the Nephites possessed it, but because they followed its directions. So also having living prophets is of no value to us if we only believe in their prophetic mantle. We must do more than just believe—we must faithfully follow their "smallest" of directions. Thus, President Harold B. Lee stated,

We must learn to give heed to the words and commandments that the Lord shall give through his prophet, "as he receiveth them, walking in all holiness before me; . . . as if from mine own mouth, in all patience and faith" (D&C 21:4–5). There will be some things that take patience and faith. You may not like what comes from the authority of the Church. It may contradict your political views. . . . It may interfere with some of your social life. But if you listen to these things, as if from the mouth of the Lord Himself, with patience and faith, the promise is that "the gates of hell shall not prevail against you" (D&C 21:6).[14]

An additional application can be found in Alma's declaration "that by small and simple things are great things brought to pass; and small means in many instances doth confound the wise" (Alma 37:6). One of the personal meanings we can draw from this miracle is the reality that, if we are seeking and are spiritually preparing ourselves, God sends us revelatory experiences. However, they sometimes come in surprising ways and through unexpected people, events, or things. In other words, "small and simple things" can be the source of revelation—just as it was for the Nephites, who found a weird little compass on the ground outside of their tent one day. As a singular example, I was recently participating in some sealings at the temple and noticed that one of the participants had brought a family file name in to be sealed—just one name. However, I couldn't help but notice that the blue card was wrinkled and heavily soiled. It looked as though it had been eaten off of, stepped on, and quite possibly pulled out of a kitchen trash can. Though I didn't say anything about it, the sealer noticed its condition too and made reference to it. The brother who brought the card explained that he came out of his house one morning and it was sitting there in the yard. He tried to contact the folks who had originally printed the name, but to no avail. The card weighed on his mind for some time, so he determined that he should probably take the name to the temple and get the ordinances done for this person whom he had never known and to whom he was not related. Curiously, the brother had suggested that this miraculously found card had been the source of motivation for him to return to the temple—something he had not done for quite some time. "By small and simple means are great things brought to pass." This brother found a Liahona at his doorstep in the form of a family file card. The *Book of Mormon Reference Companion* points out, "The counsel of the modern prophets, inspiration of the Holy Ghost, and teachings of the scriptures can all be viewed as modern-day Liahonas."[15] President Thomas S. Monson spoke of our patriarchal blessings as Liahonas.[16] Elder Lowell M. Snow (of the Seventy) spoke of general conference as a "modern Liahona."[17] In addition to these obvious examples, what Liahonas has the Lord sent you in your life? They are there. Look for them. And heed the promptings they bring.

One additional application comes to mind. Shortly after discovering the Liahona, Nephi had his father inquire of the Lord to find out where he should hunt for food. In 1 Nephi 16:30 we read, "I, Nephi, did go forth up into the top of the mountain, according to the directions which were given upon the ball." Anciently, mountains were common symbols for the temple.[18] The Lord sent Nephi to the mountain. Likewise, as we sup from the Liahonas that the Lord gives us—as we read our scriptures, study the words of the living prophets, and say earnest and meaningful prayers—we will find ourselves, like Nephi, drawn to the mountain, even the holy temple. A natural consequence of faithfulness to the "small and simple things" is a desire to be in the Lord's house, and to be there frequently. Similarly, a natural consequence of not engaging our modern Liahonas is a lack of desire to be close to the Lord—to be in His presence and about His work. Like Nephi, Lehi, and the rest of their family, we can neglect the compasses God has given us, and we will find ourselves spiritually stranded— destitute for the nourishment our spirits and our testimonies need to survive.

NOTES

1. See McConkie and Millet (1987–1991), 3:282; Hyrum M. Smith and Janne M. Sjodahl, *Doctrine and Covenants Commentary,* revised edition (Salt Lake City: Deseret Book, 1978), 78; Reynolds and Sjodahl (1955–1961), 4:178. Whether these commentators are right or not on the meaning of this name is conjectural. However, their explanation makes some sense and fits into the larger picture of the place and purpose of the Liahona.

2. Reynolds and Sjodahl (1955–1961), 4:178–79.

3. McConkie and Millet (1987–1991), 1:124.

4. See Gardner (2011), 1:272; Ogden and Skinner (2011), 1:70.

5. See Reynolds and Sjodahl (1955–1961), 4:182. See also McConkie and Millet (1987–1991), 1:124.

6. Robert L. Bunker, "The Design of the Liahona and the Purpose of the Second Spindle," in *Journal of Book of Mormon Studies,* Volume 3, Number 2 (Fall 1994), 6.

7. See Nibley (2004), 1:170–71.

8. Because of this episode with the broken bow, one commentator suggested, "One of the spindles pointed the direction the family should travel in the wilderness. The other pointed the direction they should go for food" (Richard L. Ricks, *Partly Cloudy: 76 Miracles from the Book of Mormon* (Standard Copyright License: 2006), 11.

9. See Edward L. Stevenson, cited in Paul R. Cheesman, *The Keystone of Mormonism: Early Visions of the Prophet Joseph Smith* (Provo, UT: Eagle Systems International, 1988), 69. See also Michael H. MacKay, et al, *The Joseph Smith Papers—Documents Volume 1: July 1828–June 1831* (Salt Lake City: The Church Historians Press, 2013), xxix–xxxii.

10. See Nyman (2003–2004), 1:234.

11. See McConkie and Millet (1987–1991), 3:282. The fact that the Liahona only worked when the possessor was obedient reminds us of the experience of the Prophet Joseph when he was translating the Book of Mormon. Joseph had been preparing to translate one morning when something happened between him and Emma, and the Prophet was quite put out by it. Joseph tried to work on the Book of Mormon but could not translate a single syllable. He left the house, spent about an hour in the orchard supplicating the Lord, came home and asked Emma's forgiveness, and then resumed his work of translation. He found that when he was disobedient, or even when he "dwelt too much on earthly things," he would be "incapable of proceeding with the translation" [See David Whitmer, *An Address to All Believers in Christ* (Richmond, Missouri: David Whitmer, 1887), 30]. Any revelation—whether through the Liahona, the Urim and Thummim, or personal prayer—requires that we be obedient to the principles and promptings of the Holy Spirit. That Spirit is fragile, and it is easy for our natural proclivities to disrupt it.

12. Hugh Nibley, *Since Cumorah* (Provo, UT: Foundation for Ancient Research and Mormon Studies, 1988), 259.

13. Boyd K. Packer, "Follow the Brethren," *BYU Speeches of the Year*, 23 March 1965, 4, cited in Ogden and Skinner (2011), 2:29.

14. Harold B. Lee, *The Teachings of Harold B. Lee*, Clyde J. Williams, editor (Salt Lake City: Bookcraft, 1998), 525–26.

15. Neil E. Lambert, "Liahona," in Dennis L. Largey, *Book of Mormon Reference Companion* (Salt Lake City: Deseret Book, 2003), 520.

16. Thomas S. Monson, cited in K. Douglas Bassett, *Doctrinal Insights to the Book of Mormon*, three volumes (Springville, UT: Cedar Fort, 2007), 1:68.

17. Lowell M. Snow, cited in Bassett (2007–2008), 1:70.

18. See Nibley (2004), 1:145.

GOD *Makes* RAW MEAT SWEET

1 NEPHI 17:2–3, 12–13

THE MIRACLE

As Lehi's party traveled through the wilderness in an eastward direction, they were commanded by God to not "make much fire" (verse 12). Thus, they largely subsisted on raw meat and whatever food-stuffs they could find along the way that did not require cooking.

Nephi testified, however, that God blessed them so that, in spite of the unusual diet, the raw meat was palatable—even "sweet" (verse 12)—and their nursing wives were able to provide for their newborns. Indeed, Nephi indicated that the women were granted abnormal strength so that they had the power and stamina of men, and there was no murmuring.

BACKGROUND

Technically, the eating of raw meat (and the consumption of blood) would have been against the law of Moses. Thus, one commentary reasoned, "There must have been some pressing reason for not making fires regularly."[1] As a possible explanation for God's willingness to make an exception to His own law, Hugh Nibley explained,

> The Book of Mormon makes no mention of Lehi's people meeting any other party in their eight years of wandering. Casual meetings with stray families of Bedouins then as now would merit no special

attention, but how were they able to avoid any important contacts for eight years and some 2500 miles of wandering?

One illuminating "aside" by Nephi explains everything. It was only after they reached the seashore, he says, that his people were able to make fires without danger, "for the Lord had not hitherto suffered that we should make much fire, as we journeyed in the wilderness; for he said: I will make thy food become sweet, that ye cook it not; and I will also be your light in the wilderness" (1 Nephi 17:12–13).[2]

Nibley's point is that the Lord likely commanded Nephi and those traveling with him to not make fire as it would attract others. Any who were seeking them—because of Laban's death—might more readily find them, but so might marauders looking for unsuspecting travelers to rob. Thus, in an effort to protect this divinely guided group, God gave them the command to not build fires to cook their food. Perhaps there were also other reasons for not making fire: time, fuel, the trail it would leave. We can only conjecture as to the Lord's ultimate intent.

One commentator offered another perspective on this miracle. He suggested that we need not "visualize them gnawing at a freshly cut bloody haunch. The Arabs today still eat a spicy, raw, partially dried meat called 'bastern' (lit., 'raw meat'). Probably Lehi's band consumed something similar on their journey."[3] So, while raw, perhaps this new diet was not as disgusting as the imagination leads us to assume.

SYMBOLIC ELEMENTS

East is the direction that symbolically represents God, His abode, and His influence.[4] Thus, if something came from the east, it was representative of the idea that it was of God, sent by God, or godly in nature.[5] Both blessings and punishments were believed to have been sent from the east (from God).[6] People from the east were often respected for their wisdom and perceived as being messengers of God.[7] If someone moved toward the east, symbolically the implication was that they were moving toward God. Thus, the fact that the Nephites are traveling in an easterly direction implies that they were moving toward God, or following God's will and directives.

Meat has multiple symbolic connotations in scripture.[8] However, in our application of these verses, it seems best interpreted as a representation of that which God calls us to do—our "work" in the kingdom and in the world. That work can pertain to a calling, to a professional occupation, to our burdens or trials, to efforts at gaining a testimony. Any challenging task can well be represented by the "meat" described herein.

Like meat, fire has many symbolic meanings in scripture.[9] It can represent the presence of God, His glory, His heavenly abode, His power to destroy the wicked, His sanctifying influence upon the righteous, the purging or removing of sin, the dangers of temptation and sin, and so on.

APPLICATION AND ALLEGORIZATION

The ultimate lesson of this miracle is shared by Nephi himself, who recorded, "And thus we see that the commandments of God must be fulfilled. And if it so be that the children of men keep the commandments of God he doth nourish them, and strengthen them, and provide means whereby they can accomplish the thing which he has commanded them; wherefore, he did provide means for us while we did sojourn in the wilderness" (1 Nephi 17:3).[10] Simply put, when we keep the commandments of God, He "nourishes us" and "strengthens us" (physically and spiritually) and "provides the means whereby" we "can accomplish the thing which he has commanded" us (1 Nephi 3:7). In other words, He makes us more than we would be in and of ourselves.

As noted, fire has many symbolic meanings. But the meaning that seems most germane to this passage has to do with "the outward sign of God's guiding presence."[11] In other words, among other things, fire was often a symbol for God's presence, protection, and providence. Thus, the absence of fire in this episode can well represent the notion that sometimes we are called by God to trust in Him as He invites us to take a step or two into the dark. The first verse of the autobiographical hymn "Lead, Kindly Light" speaks of this very thing. In a prayer to God, the lyricist, John Henry Newman, writes,

> Lead, kindly Light, amidst th'encircling gloom;
> Lead thou me on!
> The night is dark, and I am far from home;
> Lead thou me on!
> Keep thou my feet; I do not ask to see
> The distant scene—one step enough for me.[12]

Newman, stranded for days at sea in a fog that would not let up, began to doubt what the future held for him. He was trapped in darkness and pled for God's intervention. Willing to do what he could to have faith and move forward, he prayed that God would allow him to see "one step" in front of him, and in turn he would then walk in faith into that darkness that encircled him.[13] So long as we are faithful to Him, God will never leave us alone; nonetheless, He will occasionally require of us that we trust Him when we cannot see Him—or what lies ahead. The command of God that the Nephites travel without "much fire" (toward the east) reminds us that we, too, are asked at times to move forward without the evident presence or guidance of God. Like the Nephites, God promises that "inasmuch as ye shall keep my commandments ye shall be led . . . and ye shall know that it is by me ['east'] that ye are led" (17:13); nevertheless, also like the Nephites, such action might require a measure of faith on our part as we move forward without being allowed to rely upon the things in which we are comfortable placing our trust.

An additional but related insight is to be found in Nephi's declaration that the people were able to do a difficult—*even disgusting and painful*—task without murmuring. In Mosiah 24:14–15, we read,

> And I will also ease the burdens which are put upon your shoulders, that even you cannot feel them upon your backs, even while you are in bondage; and this will I do that ye may stand as witnesses for me hereafter, and that ye may know of a surety that I, the Lord God, do visit my people in their afflictions.
>
> And now it came to pass that the burdens which were laid upon Alma and his brethren were made light; yea, the Lord did strengthen them that they could bear up their burdens with ease, and they did submit cheerfully and with patience to all the will of the Lord.

God does not promise to *always* take our burdens away, but He does promise to ease the pain of that which we are called to bear. If we turn to Him in life, and particularly in our trials, the Lord has the power to make it possible for us to carry our crosses without feeling the full measure of the pain associated with those crosses. He can make our burdens light. We may still be called to feel some of the pain, but we will be comforted by Him. Nephi and his entourage experienced the fulfillment of this divine promise. The Lord offers you and me the opportunity to experience it too. As one text notes, "Nephi does not suggest that Yahweh made [their] life easy, but rather that he made the Lehites equal to its demands."[14] As we sincerely turn to Him, God will make hard things doable and burdens endurable.[15]

Nephi is promised by God that He will make their raw meat "sweet" to them, so that they can travel without fire. Symbolically speaking, we are reminded of the reality that the Father can also make bitter (or hard) things "sweet" to us. Each of us will be required to do some difficult things in life. God does not simply expect us to endure those trials and tests. He actually has the power to make them both endurable and "sweet" to us. You and I can truly find joy in the process of being sanctified and developed by God—not in some narcissistic manner, but in feeling love *for* God as we sense God's love *for us*, manifest through His efforts to make us as He is.

The raw meat God commanded the Nephites to eat ultimately provided strength to those who ate of it, even though the thought of eating raw meat may have been disgusting to them. Likewise, the hard things—the naturally distasteful things—God requires of us can make us strong. As they say, our trials are blessings in disguise; or, at least, they can be, if we embrace them rather than fight against them. If we seek to be developed by them instead of being angered by them, God can use them to our benefit and blessing. Rather than rejecting those things God calls us to do or bear, simply because they are not naturally palatable, we would do well to remember this miracle and expect that strength will come to us as we accept what God sends to us.

The language of the Lord to Nephi is instructive: "I will . . . be your light in the wilderness" (17:13). The emphasis appears to be on the word *I*. There may be other things you are tempted to rely upon—including man-made sources or those things you know well and with which you feel comfortable. However, God reminds the prophet-to-be that *He* must be their source of "light." No one, nor anything else, will suffice. And so He must be for each of us.

NOTES

1. Reynolds and Sjodahl (1955–1961), 1:173.
2. Nibley, *Lehi in the Desert* (1988), 63. See also Nibley, *An Approach* (1988), 237–38; Reynolds and Sjodahl (1955–1961), 1:173; Daniel H. Ludlow, Ed J. Pinegar,

Richard J. Allen, Leaun G. Otten, and C. Max Caldwell, *Unlocking the Book of Mormon* (American Fork, UT: Covenant Communications, 2007), 37.

3. Gardner (2007), 1:293. See also Lynn M. Hilton and Hope Hilton, *In Search of Lehi's Trail* (Salt Lake City: Deseret Book, 1976), 102, cited in Bassett (2007–2008), 1:75–76.

4. J. E. Cirlot, *A Dictionary of Symbols*, second edition (New York: Philosophical Library, 1971), 245.

5. Cooper (1995), 59; Joel F. Drinkard Jr., "East" in David Noel Freedman, editor, *The Anchor Bible Dictionary* (New York: Doubleday, 1992), 2:248; Joseph Fielding McConkie and Donald W. Parry, *A Guide to Scriptural Symbols* (Salt Lake City: Bookcraft, 1990), 44; Allen C. Myers, editor, *The Eerdmans Bible Dictionary* (Grand Rapids, MI: Eerdmans, 1987), 300; Ryken, Wilhoit, and Longman (1998), 225.

6. Drinkard, "East" (1992), 2:248; Ryken, Wilhoit, and Longman (1998), 225.

7. Drinkard, "East" (1992), 2:248; Drinkard, "Direction and Orientation," in Freedman (1992), 2:204; Myers (1987), 299.

8. See Walter L. Wilson, *A Dictionary of Bible Types* (Peabody, MA: Hendrickson, 1999), 275–76.

9. See Ryken, Wilhoit, and Longman (1998), 286–89.

10. Brant Gardner pointed out, "This passage is a homily, embedded in the narrative so that the spiritual lesson will become apparent" [Gardner (2007), 1:300].

11. Ryken, Wilhoit, and Longman (1998), 288.

12. "Lead, Kindly Light" *Hymns*, no. 97.

13. President Boyd K. Packer shared the following related experience: "Shortly after I was called as a General Authority, I went to Elder Harold B. Lee for counsel. He listened very carefully to my problem and suggested that I see President David O. McKay. President McKay counseled me as to the direction I should go. I was very willing to be obedient but saw no way possible for me to do as he counseled me to do. I returned to Elder Lee and told him that I saw no way to move in the direction I was counseled to go. He said, 'The trouble with you is you want to see the end from the beginning.' I replied that I would like to see at least a step or two ahead. Then came the lesson of a lifetime: 'You must learn to walk to the edge of the light, and then a few steps into the darkness; then the light will appear and show the way before you.' Then he quoted these 18 words from the Book of Mormon: 'Dispute not because ye see not, for ye receive no witness until after the trial of your faith' (Ether 12:6). Those 18 words from Moroni have been like a beacon light to me" [Boyd K. Packer, "The Edge of the Light," *BYU Magazine*, March 1991, 22–23].

14. Gardner (2007), 1:293.

15. See Ogden and Skinner (2011), 1:72–73.

GOD FREES *the* ISRAELITES *from* EGYPTIAN BONDAGE, PARTING *the* RED SEA *for* THEIR ESCAPE

1 NEPHI 17:23–27
MOSIAH 7:19
ALMA 36:28
HELAMAN 8:11–12

THE MIRACLE

Once they arrived at the coastline, God commanded Nephi to build a ship in which he and his family could travel across the ocean to the promised land. However, when Nephi's brothers saw that he was attempting to build a vessel, they began to murmur and say, "Our brother is a fool, for he thinketh that he can build a ship; yea, and he also thinketh that he can cross these great waters" (1 Nephi 17:17).

Nephi indicated that Laman and Lemuel did not simply doubt his ability to build the ship the Lord had commanded him to construct, but they emphatically denied that any such command had come to him from God (1 Nephi 17:18).

When the brothers saw that their mocking caused Nephi to sorrow, "they were glad in their hearts" and "did rejoice," saying, "We knew that ye were lacking in judgment; wherefore, thou canst not accomplish so great a work. And thou art like unto our father, lead away by the foolish imaginations of his heart" (1 Nephi 17:19–20).

Nephi, perhaps fed up with the faithlessness of his brethren, rebuked them and reminded them of the many miracles God had performed in the lives of the covenant people. Among other things, he reminded them of how the Lord brought the children of Israel across the Red Sea—and freed them from the hands of their captors—because of their faith in Him (Exodus 14). For Nephi, this miracle of the past testified of God's ability and willingness to do miracles in the prophet's day.

Regarding the miracle Nephi described, it will be recalled that after Jehovah had poured out a series of debilitating and even fatal plagues upon Egypt, Pharaoh told Moses that the Israelites were no longer his slaves and that they could leave Egypt if they so desired. However, once they began their exodus, Pharaoh had a change of heart, as he had so many times before. He began to think of the economic loss his nation would incur by not having the slave labor of the Israelites, and so Pharaoh called together his armies and pursued the Israelites.

In the process of their escape, Israel found themselves with their backs up against the Red Sea and with Pharaoh's army speedily approaching them. Their deaths seemed assured. However, when they thought themselves about to be destroyed, Jehovah commanded Moses to stretch forth his hand and staff and part the Red Sea so that the Israelites could pass through on dry ground—and so the Egyptians would seek to follow them into a watery grave. The east wind came, the sea was parted, and the pillar of fire that had been leading the Israelites moved to their rear, dividing them from the Egyptians and giving them a head start across the Red Sea.

Eventually the Egyptians were able to pursue the Israelites, but as they did so, they encountered difficulties. The Lord "troubled" them or threw them into confusion (Exodus 14:24). The book of Psalms suggests that God sent a rather sudden thunderstorm or rainstorm upon the Egyptians (see Psalm 77:16–20). Also, we are told that He caused the wheels of their chariots to get stuck in the mud and then jam or fall off.[1] According to extra-canonical Jewish tradition, Pharaoh's armies were even made physically ill by God.[2] All of this scared the Egyptians, who felt that God was fighting for the Israelites, and so they turned around and headed out of the sea, toward Egypt.[3]

The Lord commanded Moses to close up the Red Sea, which he did, and Pharaoh's entire army drowned in the midst of it.[4] "And Israel saw that great work which the Lord did upon the Egyptians: and the people feared the Lord, and believed the Lord, and his servant Moses" (Exodus 14:31).

During their rebuke, Nephi reminded his brothers of all of this miraculous history so as to say, in so many words, *If God could do such a great and mighty miracle for our fathers, He certainly could show me how to build a little boat!*[5]

BACKGROUND

It has been estimated that at the time of the exodus the Israelites numbered around two million souls.[6] While some have suggested that Israel's lack of military training would have made it easy for Pharaoh to have rounded them up with only a few soldiers,[7] it seems very unlikely that two million Jews would simply surrender to an estimated 500,000 troops. Thus, the situation would have required a measure of organizing on the part of Pharaoh's armies—and perhaps a bit of time to so organize. Thus, the children of Israel had a head start.

In its deepest parts, the Red Sea is some six thousand feet in depth and several miles across (in its narrowest portion).[8] Thus, the profound and divine nature of this miracle is highlighted by the magnitude of the body of water Moses parted and Israel crossed.

It has been suggested that a sort of "tit-for-tat" is at play here in the taking of Egyptian lives by water. Some eighty years earlier, Pharaoh had taken the lives of the male Israelite children by drowning them in the Nile. Now Israel's God would drown Pharaoh and his armies in the Red Sea. Ironically, the very man God used to bring to pass the watery destruction of the Egyptians was Moses, who himself was rescued by God from the Nile slaughter when he was but an infant.[9]

One commentary on the Book of Mormon suggests that Nephi's use of this story actually fulfills a scriptural dictate to teach the story of the Passover:

> Nephi's use of the Exodus story to teach and inspire (17:23–43) . . . is much like the practice of Jews today in recounting the Exodus story on the eve of Passover. Lehi and Nephi were following the Mosaic injunction to teach the children of the family the Passover miracles and God's goodness to the house of Israel (Exodus 12:26–27; 13:8, 14). Nephi used the phrase "ye know" eight times in five verses. Laman and

Lemuel "knew" the Exodus story and its lessons because they had been taught [it many times] before.[10]

SYMBOLIC ELEMENTS

Symbolically speaking, the sea has a number of different, but related, meanings that seem applicable here. One typologist wrote, "It may be used to represent extremely difficult problems and situations which arise in the Christian's path and [which] are impossible to conquer unless the Lord performs a miracle."[11] This certainly applies to the Israelites' situation in Exodus 14. Another referred to the sea as a symbol of the "restless masses of humanity, [and of] the wicked nations" of the earth.[12] Because the sea is commonly linked to chaos, death, disorder, and the abode of Satan, such an interpretation would make sense.[13] Thus, one text states, "It is only at the sea that the forces of chaos are decisively overcome and the world is reestablished on firm moorings. . . . The Egyptians . . . drown in the midst of a chaos of their own making. . . . Chaos, in all of its creational-historical manifestations, has been overcome."[14] Therefore, in this miracle the sea well serves as a symbol of that which Satan uses to thwart God's plans and our righteousness. But, as the miracle suggests, God will always conquer, and whatever Satan seeks to use to move forward his wickedness, God can use to accomplish His good. Indeed, the very traps Satan sets for the Saints are the exact devices Deity uses to destroy the devil.

In this miracle, as in others, Pharaoh is a standard symbol of Satan and his influences in the world. He represents evil and those who oppose the true and living God.[15] The land of Egypt, of course, can represent this fallen world, spiritual death, and the bondage they provide to those who love them more than God.[16]

In this miracle, a pillar of fire or a cloud protected God's covenant people from their enemies (Exodus 14:19–20), just as Jesus can protect us from ours.[17] Thus, in Exodus 14:20 we are told that the pillar of fire, which represented Jehovah's presence, "was a cloud and darkness" to the Egyptians, though "it gave light by night" to the Israelites. Of this one commentator wrote, "What was light for Israel became darkness for the Egyptians (verse 20). Thus the double nature of the glory of God in salvation and judgment . . . could not have been more graphically depicted."[18] The day of Christ's return is known as "the great and dreadful day of the Lord" (Malachi 4:5; 3 Nephi 25:5; D&C 110:16) because it will be great for the righteous and dreadful for the wicked. This truth is well represented by the presence of God in this miracle, which brought darkness to the Egyptians and light to the Israelites.[19]

The staff or rod of Moses is a common symbol of strength, authority, priesthood power, judgment, and divine guidance.[20] Moses used it on Israel's behalf to exercise each of these elements against Pharaoh, just as Christ uses—on our behalf, and against the adversary—His strength, authority, priesthood, revelation, and judgment.

As noted above, anciently the east wind was a common representation of God's influence or power. Things that came from the east were believed to have been sent by God, or to be representative of God.[21] As one commentator noted, "Winds . . . are often described poetically in the Bible as almost personified messengers of the God who controls them."[22] Thus, symbolically speaking, we are being told that it was God who divided the Red Sea, not some random or fortuitous wind.

While not an obvious standard symbol, the parting of the waters actually has a well-established meaning. Throughout the Hebrew Bible, the phrase translated in English as "make a covenant" would be rendered more literally to "cut a covenant." Anciently one did not "make" covenants, one "cut" them. Thus, when making a covenant in biblical times, it was common to take an animal and slay it in a ritualistic manner and then to say (often while gripping the hand of the party with whom one is making the oath or covenant), "If I break my covenant with you may this same thing (which we've done to this animal) happen to me." The concept behind the "cutting of a covenant" was that the persons making promises would be reminded as they entered into a covenant that there are blessings for keeping an oath, but there are also penalties for breaking one. Thus, at Schechem Moses divided Israel into two groups—half on Mt. Ebal and the other half on Mt. Gerizim—and he passed between them as he had them recite the blessings and curses for covenants kept or broken (Deuteronomy 27–29:1).[23] Symbolically speaking, for breaking the covenant, one would be rent in two, just as the animal used to make the covenant was rent. In a more literal sense, the person making the covenant knew it would be forfeiting the promised blessings associated with the covenant if that person did not keep his or her part of the covenant. Numerous times throughout the Bible this concept of "cutting a covenant" appears in situations and settings that do not seem innately covenantal. Of course, in this miracle Moses divided the Red Sea and the people passed between the parts (Exodus 14). Later, Joshua would part the Jordan River and have Israel pass through the parts (Joshua 4:1–24). We learn that Israel was rent in two kingdoms because of their disobedience (1 Kings 11:29–40; 12:1–24). Mark informs us that at the death of Jesus the veil of the Jewish temple was rent in two, enabling individuals other than just the Jewish high priest to pass between the veil's parts (Mark 15:38). When Christ returns, He will split the Mount of Olives in two, and the Jews will run between the parts—where they will see their Messiah (Zechariah 14:1–5; D&C 45:48–59). The episode at the Red Sea appears to have covenant-making elements as part of it. In every case of "cutting a covenant," the idea was that if one kept covenants, that person would be protected, blessed, and exalted. If one broke covenants, that person would be "cut" (or penalized) by the covenant. In passing through the Red Sea, the Israelites passed through safely and were blessed to make it to the "land on the other side," but the Egyptians were drowned in the depths (so that they didn't get to inherit the "land on the other side"). The former group is a symbolic depiction of the faithful, and the latter of the unfaithful. The dividing of the Red Sea, therefore, can remind us of the idea that there are blessings and penalties associated with the covenant-making process.[24]

APPLICATION AND ALLEGORIZATION

As with many of the miracles we have been examining in this book, the parting of the Red Sea, as recounted by Nephi, has a number of potential symbolic applications. One of the most obvious would be the reality that there are consequences if we do not keep our covenants, and blessings if we do. If we are unfaithful to the true and living God, as the Egyptians were, we should expect to drown in the chaos we will create through our disobedience to prophetic light. If, on the other hand, we seek to obey God and trust in His counsel, we will successfully make the long journey to the promised land—representative of the celestial kingdom. Nephi shared this miracle because "this was an obvious lesson of history applied upon their own case, and also a solemn warning of what the consequences of their own disobedience might be."[25] For Laman and Lemuel the lesson made no difference. Will it make a difference in the lives of you and me?

Pharaoh's anxious pursuit of departing Israel reminds us of an important principle in life: "Pharaoh . . . did not want to lose his slaves, and with a great army he began to pursue. Satan never willingly gives up any of his servants."[26] As the time for Christ's return nears, Lucifer is more anxious than ever to place us in bondage and to enslave us to desires, passions, and addictions. Like Pharaoh (who worried about Israel following Moses), the devil worries about us following Christ and, consequently, finding a means by which we can escape Satan's power. Now more than ever, we need to trust in and follow the Lord and His appointed prophets so as to escape the bondage the evil one has in store for us.

In spite of all of the miracles they had seen, as soon as things *seemed* to be going wrong, Israel doubted God and chastised Moses for ruining their lives (Exodus 14:10–20). Laman and Lemuel were no different. At the drop of a hat, they would turn on their prophet father and brother, and on the Lord, who had revealed Himself to them in so many miraculous events. Of this wishy-washy behavior, one commentator wrote, "We recognize ourselves again and again in Israel"—and, perhaps, in Laman and Lemuel too.[27] How often, when things seem to be going differently than we wish, do we forget the many miracles and blessings God has performed in our lives? As humans, we are so quick to doubt, so apt to turn from the Lord. He still loved Israel, even in her disobedience, and He'll still love us. But we must ever be conscious of such faithless attitudes and fight to suppress them. One commentary summarizes the episode in this way:

> In his inspired response to his brothers, Nephi compared their situation with that of their forefathers during the period of their Egyptian bondage and subsequent wilderness wanderings. Surely faith was required to accept Moses as a prophet and follow him into the wilderness. Certainly there were those in Egypt who asked how they were to cross the Red Sea. Others asked how they would find food. And what of water? and clothes? And what army would protect them, should Pharaoh come after them? And what of their other enemies in the desert, so anxious to attack and plunder? Could not countless questions be asked by the doubters?
>
> Yet Israel followed their prophet, and miracle followed miracle. The Lord parted the Red Sea so that they might pass through on dry ground. He destroyed the pursuing army of Egypt, fed the Israelites

manna or food from heaven, and brought forth water from a rock. He scattered their enemies before them, leading them in a cloud by day and a pillar of fire by night. Notwithstanding it all, still there were those who murmured and reviled against Moses and against God.

Is it easier in one day to follow a living prophet than in another? Would those who murmured against Moses and his God not also murmur against Nephi and his God? And what of our day? Should there not be unanswered questions? Should it not require faith to accomplish that which the Lord has asked of us? And would we not expect modern Israel to have among its numbers those who would murmur against our prophets and our God?[28]

As an additional application, we note that the Israelites found themselves in a rather hopeless situation. Their backs were up against the Red Sea so that they had nowhere to which they could escape. Their archenemy was about to attack them, and they doubted their deliverance was possible. Nevertheless, God *did* save them, and in the most miraculous of ways. This miracle is a testament to the fact that God promises those who follow the prophets a means of escape from trials, temptations, and enemies. As one commentator put it: "We see . . . deliverance from *our* enemies in the crossing of the Red Sea."[29] As with the ancient Israelites—and even the faithful Nephites—so also with us: God provides the way by which we can escape whatever threatens us.

Moses had commanded his people to stand firm and watch God fight for them, and they had seen Him do just that as the waters enveloped their pursuers. God has not stopped fighting for His people. He still protects them from their enemies and watches their backs. If the Israelites could trust Him when their backs were to the sea [leaving them seemingly nowhere to go], can we do any less? No matter what we face today, if we've trusted in Him, we are His children. He will never fail us. What enemy need we fear?[30]

God's deliverance of Israel out of Egyptian bondage and slavery typified Christ's deliverance of His Church out of this fallen, corrupt, and enslaving world.[31] "Moses in the baptism of the Red Sea shook off the powers and principalities of Egypt, and Christ, in the baptism of Calvary, made possible a perfect deliverance for a sin-bound race."[32]

It is a curious fact that there were other ways into the promised land in addition to passing through the Red Sea. Indeed, a number of commentators have pointed out that traversing the Red Sea was likely the most difficult way to the promised land—but it was the one the Lord chose for Israel.

> The attainment of moral ends is more important than physical convenience. The Israelites could have entered Canaan by a much nearer way than through the Red Sea, but that way was chosen for them to teach them many important truths in connection with God. The shortest way to attain an end is not always the best way. A short way to a fortune may not be so conducive to the formation of a character, as one which it takes much longer to travel. This truth is taught in the temptations of our Savior. Satan proposed a short way to that universal dominion which our Lord knew could only be safely and truly attained through Gethsemane and Calvary.[33]

So it is in our lives: the easiest and quickest way is not necessarily the best or most beneficial way.[34] Often we simply need to accept the Lord's path and be willing to set aside the one we prefer. Just as the children of Israel needed this specific miracle in their lives to convince them that God was there for them, watching over them, and providing for them, you and I need to remember that He knows exactly what we need, but He may want to show us from time to time just how involved He is in the details of our lives. We must to be willing to let Him perform the miracles He wants to in our lives, even if that means taking a different or even harder road.

One of the most commonly mentioned symbolic applications of this miracle is that which the Apostle Paul highlighted. In 1 Corinthians 10:1–2 he wrote, "Moreover, brethren, I would not that ye should be ignorant, how that all our fathers were under the cloud, and all passed through the sea; and were all baptized unto Moses in the cloud and in the sea." Paul saw the crossing of the Red Sea as ancient Israel's baptism—or more particularly as a representation of the need for covenant Israel to accept baptism and thereby come unto Christ. Paul was not alone in seeing this symbol in the crossing of the Red Sea. One early Christian source stated, "The very name of the Red Sea is not superfluous. Just as it is known as Red, so the baptismal water can be labeled red, for it came forth mixed with blood from the Lord Savior's side."[35] Elsewhere we read:

According to the view of the inspired Paul, the people, . . . by passing through the Red Sea, proclaimed the good tidings of salvation by water. . . . For even now, whensoever the people [are] in the water of regeneration, fleeing from Egypt, from the burden of sin, it is set free and saved. But the devil with his own servants . . . is choked with grief and perishes, deeming the salvation of men to be his own misfortune.[36]

In other words, just as the Red Sea made an end of Israel's enemies, so also baptism can make an end of ours, if we are but true to the covenant associated with it.[37]

Finally, in the sixth century one church father noted how Moses used a rod—a piece of wood—to perform many of his miracles, including the parting of the Red Sea. In this story he was commanded to "lift up" the staff or rod of wood (Exodus 14:16) that Israel's deliverance might be provided via the water. This was a typological reminder of how Christ would need to be "lifted up" upon a cross of wood (1 Nephi 11:33) that covenant Israel might be delivered from the bondage of sin, again, via the waters of baptism.[38]

Finally, Nephi did liken this miracle of olden times to his day, saying, just as God did this for our fathers, He can do as great of things for us. We must take a page from Nephi's playbook. We too must recognize that God's act of saving the Israelites—and His act of doing the same (in a different way) for the Nephites—is a testament that He will intervene and save us today. In what ways has He intervened in your life when the "way out" was hedged up and your enemies were staring you down?

NOTES

1. The Hebrew, Syrian, and Septuagint are inconsistent and can, therefore, have the meaning that the wheels were "bound," "jammed," "bogged down," or "came off" [Walter C. Kaiser, Jr., "Exodus," in Frank E. Gaebelein, editor, *The Expositor's Bible Commentary*, twelve volumes (Grand Rapids, MI: Zondervan, 1976–1992), 2:390–91].

2. See Avivah Gottlieb Zornberg, *The Particulars of Rapture: Reflections on Exodus* (New York: Doubleday, 2001), 213–14.

3. See Kaiser, in Gaebelein (1976–1992), 2:391.

4. The text never states that Pharaoh drowned, only that his entire army did. However, Psalm 136:15 states that God "overthrew Pharaoh and his host in the Red sea," implying that Pharaoh also drowned. See also Paulus Orosius, "Seven Books of History Against the Pagans," 1:10, in Joseph T. Lienhard, editor, *Ancient Christian*

Commentary on Scripture: Exodus, Leviticus, Numbers, Deuteronomy (Downers Grove, IL: InterVarsity Press, 2001), 76; Clement of Rome, "Letter to the Corinthians," 51, in Lienhard (2001), 77; Zornberg (2001), 89; Lockyer (1965), 63. Josephus claimed that the wind blew the bodies of Pharaoh's army toward the eastern shore, where Moses and Israel were assembled, thereby enabling them to obtain their weapons and armor [see Josephus, "Antiquities of the Jews" Book II, Chapter 16:6, in William S. La Sor, translator, *The Complete Works of Josephus* (Grand Rapids, MI: Kregel Publications, 1981), 65. See also Kaiser, in Gaebelein (1976–1992), 2:390].

5. Nephi previously used this same analogy with his brothers (in 1 Nephi 4:1–2) when they doubted it was possible to get the plates. King Limhi retold this miracle (in Mosiah 7:18–19), as did Alma the Younger (in Alma 36:28), and also Nephi, the son of Helaman (Helaman 8:11), each to make basically the same point: God can and will intervene in our lives if we will but believe in Him and be faithful to His commands.

6. See Kaiser, in Gaebelein (1976–1992), 2:387; Lockyer (1965), 61.

7. See, for example, Lockyer (1965), 61.

8. See Lockyer (1965), 62.

9. See Lockyer (1965), 62.

10. Ogden and Skinner (2011), 1:77–78.

11. Wilson (1999), 361.

12. Kevin J. Conner, *Interpreting the Symbols and Types*, revised and expanded edition (Portland, OR: City Bible Publishing, 1992), 166.

13. John S. Kselman and Michael L. Barré, "Psalms," in Raymond E. Brown, Joseph A. Fitzmyer, and Roland E. Murphy, editors, *The New Jerome Biblical Commentary* (Englewood Cliffs, NJ: Prentice Hall, 1990), 541; Joseph A. Fitzmyer, *The Anchor Bible: Luke I–IX* (New York: Doubleday, 1970), 739n31; C. S. Mann, *The Anchor Bible: Mark* (New York: Doubleday, 1986), 278–79; Edwin Firmage, "Zoology," in David Noel Freedman, editor, *The Anchor Bible Dictionary*, six volumes (New York: Doubleday, 1992), 6:1132; Lamar Williamson, Jr., *Interpretation: A Bible Commentary For Teaching and Preaching: Mark* (Atlanta, GA: John Knox Press, 1983), 104; Adam Clarke, *Clarke's Commentary*, six volumes (New York: The Methodist Book Concern, 1846), 5:420; Sean Freyne, "The Sea of Galilee" in Freedman (1992), 2:900; Leon Morris, *Tyndale New Testament Commentaries: Revelation*, revised edition (Grand Rapids, MI: Eerdmans, 1999), 171; Walter L. Liefeld, "Luke," in Gaebelein (1976–1992), 8:913; Cooper (1995), 121.

14. Fretheim (1991), 153, 160.

15. See Ryken, Wilhoit, and Longman (1998), 639; Conner (1992), 140; Trench (1974), 33.

16. See Conner (1992), 140; R. C. Trench, *Miracles and Parables of the Old Testament* (Grand Rapids, MI: Baker Book House, 1974), 33; Ryken, Wilhoit, and Longman (1998), 639.

17. See Kenneth E. Trent, *Types of Christ in the Old Testament* (New York: Exposition Press, 1960), 46.

18. Kaiser, in Gaebelein (1976–1992), 2:389.

19. Ginzberg records, "To prevent the enemy from inflicting harm upon the Israelites, He enveloped the Egyptians in profound darkness, so impenetrable it could be felt. . . . Nevertheless, the Egyptians could see that the Israelites were surrounded by bright light . . . and when they tried to speed darts and arrows against them, the missiles were caught up by the cloud . . . hovering between the two camps, and no harm came to Israel" [Louis Ginzberg, *The Legends of the Jews*, seven volumes (Philadelphia, PA: The Jewish Publication Society of America, 1967–1969), 3:21].

20. Conner (1992), 164, 170; Ryken, Wilhoit, and Longman (1998), 733, 734; Cooper (1995), 140; Jack Tresidder, *Symbols and their Meanings* (London: Duncan Baird Publishers, 2000), 139.

21. Cirlot (1971), 245; Cooper (1978), 59; Drinkard (1992), 2:248; McConkie and Perry (1990), 44; Myers (1987), 300; Ryken, Wilhoit, and Longman (1998), 225. Pharaoh's heart was not softened by this plague (Exodus 10:20), so Moses was instructed to send another.

22. R. Alan Cole, *Tyndale Old Testament Commentaries: Exodus* (Downers Grove, IL: InterVarsity Press, 1973), 121.

23. Other symbolic references to this concept are found in the story of Abraham cutting a covenant with God (Genesis 15:5–18); in the narrative of Moroni and the title of liberty (Alma 46:21–22); in Joshua's ritual act of dividing the priests into two groups (Joshua 8:32–35; Deuteronomy 27); and so on.

24. The LDS Bible Dictionary states, "The traveling of Israel out of Egypt, through the wilderness, crossing over the Jordan River into the promised land, is similar to a man forsaking the worldly things, going through the wilderness of temptation, and finally passing through the veil of death into the celestial kingdom (cf. Alma 37:38–45; D&C 84:21–24)" [LDS Bible Dictionary (Salt Lake City: Intellectual Reserve, 1979), 747]. I express appreciation to Dr. Todd Parker for bringing this quotation to my attention.

25. See Reynolds and Sjodahl (1955–1961), 1:180.

26. Ada R. Habershon, *Hidden Pictures in the Old Testament* (Grand Rapids, MI: Kregel Publications, 1982), 71.

27. Cole (1973), 120.

28. McConkie and Millet (1987–1991), 1:133.

29. Ada R. Habershon, *Study of the Types* (Grand Rapids, MI: Kregel Publications, 1974), 45; emphasis added. We see this same principle represented in the angelic armies with Joshua at Jericho, and even with Joseph Smith when a miraculous storm beat down upon the mobs threatening Zion's Camp.

30. Pamela McQuade, *The Top 100 Miracles of the Bible* (Uhrichsville, OH: Barbour Publishing, 2008), 52.

31. See Lockyer (1965), 63.

32. Lockyer (1965), 63.

33. Trench (1974), 35–36.

34. See Jeffrey R. Holland, "The Inconvenient Messiah," *Ensign*, February 1984, 68–73.

35. Cassiodorus, "Exposition of the Psalms," 80:6, in Lienhard (2001), 71.

36. Gregory of Nyssa, "On the Baptism of Christ," in Lienhard (2001), 76. The Israelites were saved by water and fire. They were saved by water in that it drowned their enemies. They were saved by fire in that it held back the Egyptians so that Israel could get a head start in passing through the Red Sea. We too are saved by water and by fire (John 3:5; 2 Nephi 31:17) in that we are baptized by both water and fire as a means of entering into the Church through covenants are ordinances.

37. See Augustine, "Explanation of the Psalms," 107:3, in Lienhard (2001), 76. "Just as the Jews were saved and extricated through the waters of the Red Sea, so we are delivered from the land of Egypt, that is, from the sins of the flesh, and reborn through regeneration by the sacred water" which is baptism [Cassiodorus, "Exposition of the Psalms," 80:6, in Lienhard (2001), 71].

38. See Caesarius of Arles, "Sermon," 112:4, in Lienhard (2001), 74.

GOD FED ISRAEL MANNA
in the WILDERNESS

1 NEPHI 17:28
MOSIAH 7:19

THE MIRACLE

In continuing his discourse of rebuke (highlighted in the preceding miracle), Nephi moves from his discussion of the miracle of Israel crossing the Red Sea to God feeding them manna in the wilderness.

Again, Nephi's purpose in sharing these miracles was to say to Laman and Lemuel, 'You know these things happened. To deny that they did is to deny your historical identity as Israelites.' So, knowing that you believe these things happened in the past, how can you deny God's ability to do a miracle today? If He could feed Israel in a miraculous manner in the desert, He can surely enable us to build a ship to carry us across the ocean to the promised land.'

When Nephi reminded his brothers of this miracle, the following historical events (surrounding this miracle) surely came to mind:

Israel had been hungry as they traveled in the wilderness. Many of the Jews feared for their temporal well-being if they did not soon find some source of nourishment. Moses promised them God's blessing, and the next day it arrived in the form of manna from heaven.

Each morning it appeared like frost or dew on the ground, and when the Israelites initially saw it they said to each other, "What is it?" so unfamiliar were they with the strange heaven-sent food.[2] The substance had the appearance of a "fine flake-like thing" or like "frost" (*NASB* Exodus 16:14), which would literally dissolve or melt in the sun.

The color of the manna was white, like coriander seed (*KJV* Exodus 16:31), and its taste was honey-like (Exodus 16:31). It apparently could be used like flour to bake something akin to bread—indeed, bread from heaven. Though later supplemented by quail, the manna met Israel's dietary needs for some four decades.

They were commanded by Moses to gather the manna each day— and only take as much as they needed for that day, as it would not keep overnight. On the Sabbath there would be none to gather, so they were instructed to collect twice as much the day before the Sabbath and were promised that only on that day would the manna not spoil if kept overnight.

BACKGROUND

Manna means literally "what is it?" and, since the Israelites could not figure out what the unknown edible substance was, for want of a better name, they called it manna.

Numerous commentators—whether correct or incorrect—have suggested that manna may have literally been the seeds or by-product of some tree or plant that (though Israel was unfamiliar with it) was used by God to meet their needs in what appeared to be a miraculous occurrence. In the opinion of said commentators, the miracle took place via God using the natural resources of the earth, which He had previously prepared to meet the needs of His children. (God often works through natural means to bring to pass the miraculous.) For example, on the Sinai Peninsula there is said to be, even to this day, a type of "plant lice" that bore into the fruit of the tamarisk tree so common in the region. Utilizing the fruit juices, the lice excrete a "yellowish-white flake or ball," which is said to disintegrate in the heat of the daytime sun, but is also known to congeal in the cooler hours of the day. This lice excrement, known to be filled with sugary carbs, is even today gathered by the natives of the region, who utilize it to make a type of bread that they call "manna." Like the manna of Moses's miracle, this plant manna is said to decay quickly and also to readily attract ants and flies.[3] Thus, in a number of ways, this "plant lice" sounds like a possible cause of the miracle.[4] I personally take no position on whether this is the means by which God produced the manna. All that seems to matter is that God *did* produce it. How He did so is irrelevant.

SYMBOLIC ELEMENTS

While physical hunger was the problem the manna was sent to resolve, scripture often uses hunger as a symbol for a lack of spirituality, or a weak relationship with God (see Deuteronomy 8:3; Isaiah 49:9–10; Matthew 5:6; John 6:35). As one expert in symbolism suggested, hunger "represents a deep desire for God."[5] Thus the message of this miracle, as it relates to Israel's hunger, was not that they might die but rather that they were spiritually in need. They needed fed souls as much as they needed fed stomachs. You and I, if we have that "deep desire for God," should also expect to be fed from heaven with that which no man can provide—the "bread of life." Manna imagery is present in numerous places in the scriptures, and it is traditionally used to symbolically show God's ability and desire to provide for His children, even for those who complain from time to time. In the Gospel of John, Jesus makes reference to the symbol and states that it is a typological foreshadowing of His divine mission to sustain life—specifically eternal life.[6] The following chart shows some of the major parallels that exist between manna and Christ.

MANNA	JESUS
Manna is a form of bread.	Jesus was the Bread of Life (John 6:35), who came from Bethlehem (which means the "house of bread").
Manna appeared miraculously from heaven as a gift from God (Exodus 16; Deuteronomy 8:3).	Jesus was born into mortality in a most miraculous manner, having been sent by God as a gift to mankind. His second advent will be no less miraculous.
Manna sustained the life of ancient Israel for some forty years—forty being the standard symbolic number for trials or tests.[7]	Jesus sustains us both physically and spiritually throughout this life and into the life to come. Only He can enable us to endure life's trials.
Manna is a Hebrew word meaning, "What is this?"	Matthew records that of Christ the question was asked, "Who is this?" (Matthew 21:10).

MANNA	JESUS
Manna was said to taste sweet like honey (Exodus 16:31).	Not only are the words of Christ sweet to those who love God, but so also are the life, teachings, and ministry of the *Logos*, the actual word of God (John 1:1).[8]
Manna had a white color, which is a standard symbol for purity.	Christ's purity is known to be one of the elements that qualified Him to function as the Messiah.
Manna was sent to satisfy the physical hunger of the people.	Jesus was sent to satisfy the spiritual hunger of the people (John 6:35).
The sending of the manna glorified God and established His "loving mercy toward His people and His provision for their needs."[9]	Jesus glorified God and stood as a testament of His mercy and love for His people, and of His commitment to provide for their spiritual needs.
While the manna may have arrived in a miraculous way, it was quite normal in its appearance.	While Christ may have come to earth in a rather miraculous way, Isaiah suggests that there was nothing spectacular about His appearance (Isaiah 53:2).
Some read the text as saying that the manna needed to be individually appropriated.[10]	Certainly we must each individually develop a personal relationship to, and dependence upon, Christ.
One commentator suggested that the manna "was not to be . . . eaten in the form they gathered it; instead, it was to be prepared by milling and baking."[11]	Similarly, it is not enough to have heard of Jesus or to believe in Him. Rather, it is what we do with Him that determines whether or not we are true Christians.
The manna was freely available to everyone, regardless of position, rank, wealth, or race.	Christ and His gifts are freely available to everyone, regardless of position, rank, wealth, or race.
The manna was entirely undeserved by Israel, who had been murmuring even though they were the recipients of numerous miracles.	The gifts of Christ to us are entirely undeserved, and most of us are far guiltier than we realize of ingratitude for all God has done for us.

MANNA	JESUS
If Israel did not gather their manna before the Sabbath, it would be too late to do so once the Sabbath came (Exodus 16:22–30).[12]	When Christ returns for the Sabbath of the earth's temporal existence (the Millennium), those who have not gathered of His heaven-sent nourishment prior to His arrival will ever remain unfilled (Alma 34:33–34; Matthew 25:1–13).[13]

As a summary of this symbol, one dictionary states that the manna "invites all to taste and touch and smell and see that the Lord is good, his gifts delicious, nutritious, abundant and free, unearned and undeserved."[14]

One commentator on the Book of Mormon recounting of this miracle stated, "The manna and the Liahona, both directly related to the divine provision of food, is a parallel that Nephi would easily make. The Liahona was a gift from Yahweh that provided food just as the manna was a gift from Yahweh that provided food. . . . Obviously, he expects Laman and Lemuel to fill in the parallel of the Liahona as he articulates the miracle of manna."[15]

APPLICATION AND ALLEGORIZATION

The manna was a symbol—a sacred reminder—of Christ, and you and I must daily seek a relationship with Him, something Laman and Lemuel had neglected to do, even in spite of being reared in the home of a prophetic father. As did Israel of old with their manna, we must daily take Christ into our lives. We must ensure that it is He, and He alone, who fills our lives if we are to be sustained spiritually here and gain eternal life in the celestial kingdom of our God.

Israel was commanded to take some of the manna, place it in a pot, and put that in the ark of the covenant so that future generations would know that the miracle of the manna actually *did* happen and that God *did* take care of His own (see Exodus 16:32–34). This has been seen by commentators as a message about the importance of recording the mercies and miracles of God in our own lives, whether in a journal or otherwise, so future generations might know of how blessed we have been and how many miracles God has performed in our lives.[16] One of the great acts of ingratitude is to not record the sacred experiences that have been ours.

One text reminds us that the divinely supplied manna was given to Israel for the entire forty years that they traveled through the wilderness. However, the very day they entered the promised land and ate of the fruits of Canaan, the miracle of the manna ceased. God no longer gave, as it was no longer needed. "God never wastes His power," nor should we.[17] While we seek God's blessings, and even His intervention, we must be careful that we do not expect Him to do what we can do for ourselves.

We spoke above of the theory of a number of modern commentators, namely that manna might have come from the tamarisk tree or from "plant lice" associated with that tree. Again, it is unclear to me if this is an accurate view of how God accomplished the miracle. However, the following related insight seems valuable:

> It is important to stress the naturalness of the manna and the quail [miracles]. . . . It is precisely the "natural" that is seen as a gift from God. God's gifts to Israel are to be found not only in the unusual but also in the everyday. If the provisions of God in the wilderness are all subsumed under the extraordinary or miraculous, then the people of God will tend to look for God's providential care only in that which falls outside the ordinary. The all too common effect of this is to absent God from the ordinary and everyday and to go searching for God only in the deep-sea and mountaintop experiences. Consequently, the people of God will not be able to see in the very ordinariness of things that God is the one who bestows blessings again and again. The result will often be that, when the miraculous can no longer be discerned in one's life, there will be a profound experience of the absence of God altogether.[18]

This commentator is correct: Most of the miracles God performs in our lives—and He does them daily—come in such a way that they don't seem that miraculous. But if we only receive His intervention in the strange or out of the ordinary, we will be prone to look for, and possibly only accept, a God who is manifest in the miraculous but never in the mundane. God blesses us in the everyday experience just as much, if not more, than He does through the seemingly miraculous. Indeed, as we count our many blessings, that is when we realize how absolutely miraculous God is, providing for every little detail of our lives, day in and day out.

Ambrose compared the manna given to Israel in the wilderness to the "word of God," which is detailed in the "words of God." He said that the scriptures, which teach us of Christ, "nourish the soul of the wise." They "illuminate" and "sweeten" our lives with "truths," which are "soothing" and "sweeter than honeycomb." The scriptures have, in Ambrose's opinion, the power to delight and enlighten those who have the faith to believe in them.[19] As one commentator put it, "The scriptures are the manna given as from heaven to feed us in the desert of this world."[20] Another wrote, "The thoughts of God, revealed in His word, are the soul's manna."[21] Only those who have made it a practice to daily sup from God's words can truly understand and testify to the truth behind this description of scripture. When we read them so much that we love them, they become one of the richest and sweetest things God has given us to enjoy. They bring power, insight, direction, the Spirit, and numerous other blessings that only those versed can imagine.

One commentator suggested that Exodus 16:18, where Israel is commanded to gather enough manna that each family member has his or her needs met, "was used by the apostle Paul as an illustration for Christians to share with one another just as Israel had pooled the manna everyone had collected (2 Corinthians 8:15)."[22] Similarly, another wrote that Paul used the miracle of the manna "to enforce on the rich a charitable distribution of their means to the needy, so that there might be provided for all a sufficiency of these temporal goods."[23] The fact that those of a household each went out and gathered but then placed the gleanings in a common pot to be shared by all is a strong message to us of our need to consecrate all that we have to the building up of the kingdom and to the blessing of the lives of God's children.

In a simple application of this miracle, one author noted that the manna disintegrated or evaporated once the sun came out, and thus Israel had to act early if they were to secure the blessing available to them. So it is with you and me; this miracle reminds us that we must be diligent in fulfilling our duties if we are to lay hold upon the blessings God has in store.[24] A mission postponed may turn into a mission never served. A prompting postponed may be disaster developing. A calling neglected may be a blessing bypassed. God has many gifts and blessings for us, but if we are not diligent in our part, there may be a number of gifts we never get. Like the manna, they may fade before we gather them.

Finally, the manna's propensity to rot or decay and to produce worms—if more was gathered than was needed, or if it was hoarded and stored (against God's commands)—has been seen by many commentators as a symbol of the dangers of greed and covetousness. For example, John Chrysostom wrote, "Those who gathered in their houses more than the lawful quantity gathered not manna but . . . worms and rottenness. Just so both in luxury and in covetousness, the gluttonous and drunken gather not more delicacies but more corruption."[25] Elsewhere we read that the corruption that came upon the hoarded manna reminds us of the importance of being content with "that portion God has assigned for us."[26] Curiously, since Laman and Lemuel were so fixated on the wealth and comforts they were required to leave behind, perhaps Nephi had this very application in mind as he reminded his wayward brothers of the miracle of the manna.

NOTES

1. See Gardner (2007), 1:302.
2. One commentator has pointed out that, while Israel is clearly curious about the new food (Exodus 16:15), "the people give no sign of amazement" and "the report of these developments is matter-of-fact," almost "down playing" the miracle [Fretheim (1991), 182].
3. See Fretheim (1991), 182; Fairbairn (1989), 2:56–57; Cole (1973), 133; Lockyer (1965), 66; Trench (1974), 43–44; Katharine Doob Sakenfeld, *International Theological Commentary: Numbers—Journeying with God* (Grand Rapids, MI: Eerdmans, 1995), 69; Nyman (2003–2004), 1:256–57.
4. I am by no means denying the miraculous nature of the manna God sent Israel. I am only pointing out a common theory as to how God may have accomplished that miracle.
5. Wilson (1999), 234.
6. See Ryken, Wilhoit, and Longman (1998), 534.
7. One source states, "The manna was supplied throughout the entire sojourn of the Israelites and did not cease until they reached Canaan. [See Exodus 16:35] . . . As the children of Israel were blessed with the presence of the heaven-sent manna, so Christ, the heavenly bread, shall satisfy our hunger until, when we shall be like Him, we shall hunger no more (1 John 3:2)" [Trent (1960), 50].
8. "There is a legend among the Jews that the flavour of the Manna was just what each person liked best" [Habershon (1982), 81; Lockyer (1965), 66]. It is interesting to note, even within the Church, how varied peoples' approaches to and needs from Christ are. Just as the Apostle Paul said that he sought to be "all things to all

men, that [he] might by all means save some" (1 Corinthians 9:22), so also Jesus's approach to His disciples is to meet their every need—and to meet them in the ways that are best for them individually. The gospel and the Atonement are very much tailored to meet individual needs. There is nothing "one size fits all" about Christ's work on behalf of His brothers and sisters. He knows us individually, and He addresses our needs individually.

9. Trent (1960), 49.

10. See, for example, Trench (1960), 49–50.

11. Kaiser, in Gaebelein (1976–1992), 2:402. Another commentator wrote, "The manna needed to be ground in mills or beaten in a mortar. [This symbolizes] the sufferings of our Lord throughout His lifetime. . . . His whole life was one of suffering; and as we have this again and again brought before us in these types, we learn something of the meaning of the words, 'it pleased the Lord to bruise Him'" [Habershon (1974), 30].

12. One commentator put it this way: "Christ, the Bread of Life, is available to all who call upon Him, yet He must be accepted while we are in life's 'work week.' When the spiritual Sabbath (ceasing from earthly toil and labor) comes, then Christ cannot be found by those who have previously rejected Him (Prov. 1:28 and Isa. 55:6). Hence, the scripture sayeth [sic]: 'Now is the accepted time . . . [today] is the day of salvation'" [Trent (1960), 50].

13. Lenet Hadley Read, *Unveiling Biblical Prophecy* (San Francisco, CA: Latter-day Light Publications, 1990), 44.

14. Ryken, Wilhoit, and Longman (1998), 534.

15. Gardner (2007), 1:303.

16. See Trench (1974), 46.

17. Lockyer (1965), 66.

18. Fretheim (1991), 181–82.

19. See Ambrose, "Letter" 54 (64):2, in Lienhard (2001), 87.

20. Lockyer (1965), 66.

21. Trench (1974), 44.

22. Kaiser, in Gaebelein (1976–1992), 2:403.

23. Fairbairn (1998), 2:58.

24. See Trench (1974), 46.

25. Chrysostom, "Homilies on 1 Corinthians," 40:5, in Lienhard (2001), 88.

26. Trench (1974), 45.

God Gave Israel Water
in the Wilderness

1 Nephi 17:29; 20:21
2 Nephi 25:20

The Miracle

Nephi's chastisement of Laman and Lemuel continues here, as he cites one final miracle that God performed on behalf of ancient Israel—namely the quenching of their thirst by giving them water from a rock.

Again, Nephi's purpose in sharing this miracle—along with the miracles of the Red Sea and the manna—was to say to Laman and Lemuel, 'You are believers in these miracles of the past. You "know" that they happened (1 Nephi 17:29). So, if you profess a belief in such ancient miracles, how can you not believe in modern ones? If God could get water from a rock or part the Red Sea, surely He could safely carry you and me across the ocean in a boat He instructed us to make.'

When Nephi reminds his brothers Laman and Lemuel of the miracle of God giving Israel water from a rock, many things may have passed through the minds of these struggling sons of Lehi, not the least of which should have been the following:

In the first water-from-a-rock miracle (see Exodus 17) the children of Israel had been traveling in the Desert of Sin when they came to a place called Rephidim. They were tired and thirsty, and yet the wadi or gully there had dried up, and so there was no water for them to drink.

In the preceding six months, they had seen Moses bring the ten plagues upon Egypt, a pillar of fire by night and a cloud by day had led them on their way, God had parted the Red Sea for them and closed it on their enemies, the waters of Marah were miraculously made drinkable, and bread and meat had been sent from heaven to sustain them on their trek. With all of that happening in such a short window, Moses records that they still murmured and asked, have you "brought us up out of Egypt, to kill us and our children and our cattle with thirst?" (Exodus 17:3). They demanded that Moses provided them with water. There is almost a spirit of entitlement about their statement, as though they were taking for granted that Moses had the power to perform these miracles and was somehow withholding such from them.

Moses turned to the Lord with his problem, asking Him what he should do. God's solution was what it had always been: He will provide. He commanded Moses to take some of the elders of Israel with him, go to the rock at Horeb, and with his staff smite the rock so that water would flow out for the people to drink.

Moses did as commanded, and the water came as God had promised. However, because of the incident, Moses named the place *Massah* ("temptation") and *Meribah* ("contention" or "strife"), because the people there tested the Lord and quarreled with Moses.

In the second water-from-a-rock miracle (see Numbers 20) the Israelites were camped in Kadesh, very near Canaan (the promised land). Moses's sister, Miriam, had died and was buried there. Again, there was no water, so the people began to murmur, saying, "Why did you bring us into the desert? So that we and our livestock could die here?" (see Numbers 20:4–5).

Moses and his brother, Aaron, entered the Tabernacle and prostrated themselves before the Lord. His glory appeared to them (Numbers 20:6), as it had to the elders of Israel in the first miracle of water-from-a-rock (Exodus 17:5–6), and He commanded Moses to assemble the people and in their presence command the water to flow from the rock.

Not exactly following the Lord's instructions, Moses assembled the people and chastised them, saying, "Hear now, ye rebels; must [Aaron and I] fetch you water out of this rock?" (Numbers 20:10). At that point Moses smote the rock twice with his staff rather than just commanding the water to flow, as the Lord had instructed him to. The water flowed, but the Lord informed Moses and Aaron that they would not be entering the promised land because they "did not trust in [Him] enough to honor [Him] as holy in the sight of the Israelites" (*NIV* Numbers 20:12).[1]

Nephi's use of this story not only demonstrated God's intervention in the past but highlighted many parallels between rebellious and unfaithful Israel and Laman and Lemuel, who murmured, doubted, complained, and criticized, much as their ancient counterparts had. No doubt, Nephi noticed these similarities. Whether Laman and Lemuel had "ears to hear" (Deuteronomy 29:4; Mark 4:9) is another story.

BACKGROUND

This is actually a double miracle in that it is performed twice, though which one Nephi had in mind when he cited the miracle is anyone's guess. The first account of causing water to flow from a rock is recorded in Exodus 17:1–7, and the second in Numbers 20:1–13. The Exodus miracle takes place at the beginning of their forty-year sojourn, whereas the Numbers miracle takes place near the end of it. In the Exodus story the Lord goes before Moses (implying that His glory was present and seen), but in the Numbers account Moses and Aaron see God's glory in the Tabernacle, but then He does not visibly appear before them when the miracle is actually performed. In the Exodus narrative Moses is commanded to smite the rock with his rod, but in the Numbers miracle Moses is simply instructed by the Lord to command water to flow from the rock. Exodus mentions only Moses during the miracle, whereas Numbers mentions Moses and Aaron. Thus, these are not two separate accounts of the same miracle, though they are remarkably similar.[2] Nephi may have seen both as equally instructive for his purpose in teaching his brothers.

The location of the first miracle was *Rephidim*, which means "resting place." God had led them there, and it would be the location where He would have them camp, or rest, for a time. But the incidents and attitudes there turned this time for resting into a time of strife and their place for a miracle into a place of anger. (Oh, how Laman and Lemuel should be able to relate to this detail.) Thus, after the miracle had taken place, Moses renamed the site from *Rephidim* ("resting place") to *Massah* ("test") and *Meribah* ("contention," "strife," or "quarreling"), because there they tested the Lord and contended with Moses.

The location of the second miracle is Kadesh, just outside of

Canaan. As in the first miracle, the place is renamed *Meribah* because of Israel's "quarreling" and "contentious" attitude. One can almost envision Father Lehi—who had a propensity for naming places—dubbing their coastal camp *Meribah* (as every place seemed to be when Laman and Lemuel were at your side).

SYMBOLIC ELEMENTS

Jesus is the rock depicted in both of these water-producing miracles. He is the source of the "living waters" that saved Israel's life when it flowed forth from the stone. Regarding the rock in these two wonders, one text records,

> In some way the holiness of the Lord was assaulted by Moses' rash action (v.12; see also [Numbers] 27:14) [in the Numbers narrative], for he had not treated with sufficient deference the rock of God's presence. In some manner the rock speaks of God. This was a . . . symbol of his person, a gracious provision of his presence. In the [New Testament] we learn that the rock actually speaks of the person of the Lord Jesus Christ; it is called "Christ" by Paul in 1 Corinthians 10:4. Hence, unwittingly, Moses in his wrath had lashed out against the physical embodiment of God's grace [in the Numbers 20 miracle].[3]

In the mind of some commentators, Jesus was the intended symbol behind the rock that saved Israel's life, and thus, God's rebuke of Moses *may* have been, *in part*, because of his treatment of the rock.[4] In his book *Types of Christ in the Old Testament*, Kenneth Trent notes numerous ways in which the rock of Exodus 17 and Numbers 20 typifies Christ. The following chart is a summary of Trent's explanation of the parallels.[5]

THE ROCK	CHRIST
The ancient Israelites' lives were in danger because of want of physical water.	The lives of all of God's children are in danger because of their need for spiritual water.
The rock in Horeb was revealed to the people by God in answer to their great need.	Christ, the "Rock of Ages," was revealed to the people by God in answer to their great need as a fallen and sin-cursed people.

THE ROCK	CHRIST
In delivering its life-sustaining treasure, the rock served as a means of glorifying God.	Christ sought to glorify His Father in all that He said and did.
The rock in Horeb was filled with unrealized and hidden blessings that to the causal passerby were not evident.	Christ, our Rock, was filled with unrealized and hidden blessings that to the causal passerby were not evident (see Isaiah 53:2).
The rock at Horeb had to be smitten before its treasures of life could be unleashed for the people.	It was not until Christ's blood flowed that the treasures of His redemption for us could be unleashed on our behalf.
The rock at Horeb was smitten but once.	"Christ was *once* offered to bear the sins of many" (Hebrews 9:28).
Paul tells us that the rock "followed" Israel until they reached the land flowing with "milk and honey" (1 Corinthians 10:4).	Jesus has promised us that He will be with us "even until the end of the world" (Matthew 28:20).

Many aspects of these two water-producing miracles testify of Christ, our Rock and our Redeemer.

As noted earlier, the staff or rod of Moses is a common symbol of strength, authority, priesthood power, judgment, and divine guidance.[6] "The rod was in the hand of Moses, the power in the hand of God."[7] Even though Moses did not use his staff or rod in both of these miracles, he is commanded by God in each of the miracles to bring it with him (Exodus 17:5; Numbers 20:8), likely as a symbol that he was acting under God's delegated authority, rather than under his own power.

Also noted previously, water traditionally carries two symbolic meanings—chaos and death,[8] or life and the Holy Spirit.[9] In the case of this miracle, the water is clearly a symbol of the Spirit, which saves and then sustains the lives of covenant Israel.

APPLICATION AND ALLEGORIZATION

Ada Habershon, one of the nineteenth century's most prolific typologists, saw what so many of the Church Fathers saw in these two miracles—namely a foreshadowing of Jesus on the cross, where His smitten side produced water. She wrote,

> *The smitten rock* was the source of the rivers of water; just as the death of Christ must precede the descent of the Holy Spirit. In promising the outflowing rivers of water in John vii., the Lord evidently referred to this type. We read, "This spake He of the Spirit, which they that believe on Him should receive: for the Holy Ghost was not yet given; because that Jesus was not yet glorified." The Apostle Paul tells us that "that rock was Christ."[10]

As Habershon notes, millennia after the miracle, the Apostle Paul referred to this event with Christological application. He was quite clear that he understood the rock to have been a symbol of Christ (1 Corinthians 10:1, 4). Following Paul's lead, the Fathers of the Church took the symbolism one step further and offered a twist that may be surprising to many readers. For example, Augustine wrote, "The rock was Christ in sign. . . . The rock was smitten twice with a rod; the double smiting signified the two wooden beams of the cross."[11] Elsewhere Augustine penned this about the miracle recorded in Numbers 20:11:

> "Blessed are they that hunger and thirst after righteousness, for they shall be filled." And our thirst is quenched from the rock in the wilderness: for "the Rock was Christ," and it was smitten with a rod that the water might flow. But that it might flow, the rock was smitten twice: because there are two beams of the cross. All these things, then, which were done in a figure, are made manifest to us.[12]

Like Augustine, Caesarius of Arles (circa 470–542 AD) also saw a foreshadowing of Jesus's crucifixion in Moses's double smiting of the rock. He wrote, " 'Therefore Moses struck the rock twice with his staff.' What does this mean, brethren? . . . The rock was struck a second time because two trees were lifted up for the gibbet of the cross; the one stretched out Christ's sacred hands, the other spread out his sinless body from head to foot."[13] Though less specific, John of Damascus (circa 650–750 AD) clearly saw the same symbolic message in the Mosaic miracle. He wrote that "the rock [rent] and pouring forth streams of water" symbolized the "precious Cross" of Christ.[14] Around the same time Augustine began serving as Bishop of Hippo,

John Chrysostom (circa 347–407 AD) wrote, "Instead of water from a rock, [we have received the] blood from His side; instead of Moses' or Aaron's rod, the Cross."[15] Thus, for early Christians this second water-producing miracle of Moses serves to remind the believing reader of the staff that pierced Christ's side and the blood and water that flowed therefrom (John 19:34). To the Fathers of the Church, the rock was more than just Christ, as Paul explained it. Rather, it was "Jesus Christ, *and him crucified*" (1 Corinthians 2:2; emphasis added).[16] Though the water that came forth from the rock quenched Israel's physical thirst, in the mind of patristic exegetes it foreshadowed the reality that Jesus's atoning sacrifice would quench covenant Israel's spiritual thirst. As Habershon noted, "The smitten rock was the source of the rivers of water; just as the death of Christ must precede the descent of the Holy Spirit."[17] Surely Nephi, who had seen the Lord (2 Nephi 11:3), understood this. Oh, how he must have hoped his brothers could feel what he felt about Christ and understand what he understood.

Because of its durability, unchangeableness, solidity, and strength, a rock is a perfect symbol of Christ, the "Rock of Ages."[18] In the context of these two miracles, it not only highlights Christ's character but also the nature of God's dependability. We need never doubt nor fear that He will neglect to provide. If we are but striving for worthiness, He will tend to our every need. Clearly, both of these water-from-a-rock miracles depict Israel in less-than-perfect terms. So it is with you and me—we need not be perfect, but we must seek to be faithful and believing.

One commentator, drawing on the Church Fathers (who saw Atonement imagery in the smiting of the rock); acknowledged that the rock represents the crucified Christ of Calvary, whose blood flowed just as the water flowed[19] but then noted,

> In the first instance [or miracle] God told Moses to strike the rock. That represents the stroke of God on Christ Jesus at Calvary (Exodus 17:6). In [the second miracle] God told him to speak to the rock. That rock is Christ (1 Cor. 10:4). Christ is not to be smitten again, once was sufficient. . . . The rock was to be spoken to the second time, which indicates that we are only to come to Him in prayer and praise with our petitions and receive again the abundance of forgiveness and the outpouring of the Holy Spirit.[20]

Thus, according to this aforementioned source, in the first miracle we see Christ's sacrifice on our behalf. In the second we see His post-martyrdom intercessions.[21]

The fact that God answered Israel's prayers through a rock has been seen as significant, not simply because the rock was a symbol of Christ but also because of the unlikely source it was for water. In other words, if God had caused a desert spring to suddenly be discovered, such a resolution to their problem of thirst would be expected. But to use that which does not have water to produce water is a surprise. Hence, one text notes,

> God can bring good to His people from the most unlikely sources. Nothing seemed more unlikely to yield water than the barren rock of Horeb. So God often brings refreshing streams of comfort to His people out of hard circumstances. Paul and Silas could sing in the dungeon, and their imprisonment was made the means of adding to their converts in Philippi. The lot of John in Patmos seemed hard and dreary indeed, but at the bidding of Christ, streams of living water gushed forth there, which refreshed the soul of the apostle at the time, and have followed the church until the present. . . . Above all, out of the hard circumstances of the crucified Lord of glory, God has brought forth waters of everlasting life.[22]

How many times in your life has God brought answers or comfort from what appeared to be a trial or an unlikely source of relief? As the Lord reminded us through the prophet Isaiah, "My thoughts are not your thoughts, neither are your ways my ways, saith the Lord. For as the heavens are higher than the earth, so are my ways higher than your ways, and my thoughts than your thoughts" (Isaiah 55:8–9). We need not worry about *how* the Lord will answer our prayers or meet our needs. All we need do is trust that He *will*, in His own way and in His own time.

In his two-volume work *Typology of Scripture*, Patrick Fairbairn suggested that since the rock was Christ (1 Corinthians 10:4), and the passing through the Red Sea was baptism (1 Corinthians 10:1–2), and the manna was the body of Christ (John 6:31–33, 41), then the water that flowed from the rock might be seen as a symbol of Jesus's blood.[23] Thus, you have baptism and the sacrament (the bread and water) symbolized.

In the sixth century, Caesarius of Arles suggested a possible application of the symbolism behind Israel's thirst. He stated that most of us are "thirsty"—the righteous for God and the sinners for the fulfillment of their lusts.[24] The thirst of the righteous will always be quenched by God, but the wicked, no matter how much they "drink," will never quench their thirst. Indeed, the more they drink of their sins, the more thirsty they will become. Are you and I thirsting after the things that can be quenched, after living waters? Or are we craving that which cannot satisfy?

Moses indicated that the children of Israel continually "tempted" or tested God (Exodus 17:2). In his estimation, their request for water showed a lack of faith and implied their tendency to try the Lord. Of this, one commentator noted,

> Testing has to do with "putting God to the proof," that is, seeking a way in which God can be coerced to act or show himself. It is to . . . try to force God's hand in order thereby to determine concretely whether God is really present or not. Israel's testing of God consisted in this: if we are to believe that God is really present [they reasoned], then God must show us in a concrete way by making water materialize. ["Testing" God] is to make one's belief in God contingent upon a demonstration. It is, in essence, an attempt to turn faith into sight. . . . This approach to God is often characteristic of believers. [Or of those who *claim* to be "believers" but who struggle with conversion and faithfulness.] I will not take special precautions in the use of automobiles or guns or on dangerous ventures. God will take care of me. I will not take out insurance, God is my insurance policy. Such attitudes set God up for a test, holding God hostage, determining just how God is to show the divine power. It places God in the role of servant, at the beck and call of one in any difficulty.[25]

Does our approach to God suggest that we have faith in Him, or that we seek to test and tempt Him? While the line between these two may be subtle, it is, nevertheless, real.

We read that the Israelites, because of their thirst, "murmured against Moses," their prophet (Exodus 17:3; see also Numbers 20:2). So many miracles of preservation had already been performed, but they still doubted and complained. One text offers the following application of these two manifestations of God's power in giving water from a rock:

If we seek to criticize one of God's faithful leaders, we'd best beware. For God does not take such actions lightly. When we follow a leader who walks closely with God, it's better to appreciate him than grumble. Was God planning on letting His people die of thirst in the desert on their way to the Promised Land? That's unthinkable—except to those complaining Israelites. Had they trusted, they would have both received water and failed to malign Moses. Are we grumbling Israelites?[26]

Such a germane question: Are you and I, as modern-day Israel, prone to grumble and complain about our leaders—general or local? Do we speak critically of those whom the Lord has called to lead? If we do, we are as faithless as ancient Israel was on the occasions of these miracles. It must be remembered that by murmuring against Moses they were really murmuring against God, as He had called Moses. Thus, while you and I may believe that we can with propriety criticize an earthly leader of the Church (or a leader of one of its congregations), to do so is to criticize the God who called him to that position. Oh, how Laman and Lemuel struggled with this vice. One commentator on the Book of Mormon account of this miracle wrote,

> Verse 30 [of 1 Nephi 17] closes the logical trap on Laman and Lemuel. Just as the children of Israel murmured against their prophet and leader, so Laman and Lemuel have complained and resisted their leader on whom Yahweh's mantle rests. They cannot deny their national history nor the allusion to their own situation. Yet this condemnation contains hope along with accusation. The children of Israel murmured, but they also repented. Nephi holds out the same hope to Laman and Lemuel that all will be well if they repent. Nephi is not condemning his brothers outright, but calling them to repentance.[27]

Finally, one commentator pointed out that one of the most praiseworthy traits of Moses was his consistent practice of taking his trials and difficulties to the Lord—which is evidenced by this miracle and others (see, for example, Exodus 15:25; 16:4; 32:30; 33:8; Numbers 11:2, 11; 12:13; 14:13–19).[28] Laman and Lemuel, on the other hand, struggled to follow Moses's example, indicating that they did not pray simply because they were sure the Lord would not answer (1 Nephi 15:8–9).

NOTES

1. One of my peer reviewers suggested the following: "We know Moses was translated. Does God translate disobedient servants? The Old Testament says Moses died. We know that was not true. Could this Old Testament claim about why Moses was not allowed to enter the promised land also be wrong?" [Todd Parker, Review of *Miracles of the Book of Mormon*].

2. See Kaiser, in Gaebelein (1976–1992), 2:406.

3. See Kaiser, in Gaebelein (1976–1992), 2:406.

4. See Gordon J. Wenham, *Tyndale Old Testament Commentaries: Numbers* (Downers Grove, IL: Inter-Varsity Press, 1981), 149. It is worth noting that the book of Psalms highlights Moses's harsh words during the episode as playing some role in the penalty God doled out. "Rash words came from Moses' lips" (*NIV* Psalm 106:33). Moses's rebuke of Israel—asking rhetorically, "Must we fetch you water?"—could imply he was taking credit for the miracle, rather than giving God the credit [see Olson (1996), 126–27; Ginzberg (1967–1969), 6:91n490. See also Sakenfeld (1995), 114]. Unfortunately, the passage is simply unclear on what exactly Moses and Aaron did wrong. One text offers the following explanation: "Some commentators find it difficult to see how Moses' action could be construed as unbelief. The key to the problem is to be found in a comparison of God's instructions to Moses with their execution. . . . There is a marked divergence between what was commanded and what was done. Moses was instructed to *take the rod, assemble the congregation* and speak to *the rock* ([verse] 8), but in the event he *took the rod, gathered the assembly*, spoke to them instead of to the rock, and then *struck the rock* ([verses] 9–11). Though this brought forth water, it was not produced in the divinely intended way, and counted as rebelling against God's command ([verse] 24) and unbelief. . . . Thus, Moses' failure to carry out the Lord's instructions precisely was . . . an act of unbelief. . . . Moses' unbelief was compounded by his anger, expressed in his remarks to the people ([verse] 10), 'he spoke words that were rash' (Ps. 106:33), and by striking the rock twice ([verse] 11). DeVaulx suggests that there was an element of sacrilege in striking the rock, for it symbolized God. . . . Elsewhere God is often likened to a rock (e.g. Pss. 18:2; 31:3; 42:9). This understanding of the rock closely corresponds to that of the targums, and of Paul, who says 'they drank from the supernatural Rock which followed them, and the Rock was Christ' (1 Cor. 10:4). In disobeying instructions and showing no respect for the symbol of God's presence, Moses failed to *sanctify* God" [Wenham (1981), 150–51]. One Latter-day Saint commentator explained: "To meet the need, Moses was commanded to speak to a rock. He disobeyed, apparently not believing sufficiently (Num. 20:8–12, 24), and struck the rock with his symbol of power, the rod, as he had done once before—when he had been told he should do so (Ex. 17:6–7). He also took honor to himself, saying, 'Must we fetch you water out of this rock?' (Num. 20:10; 27:14; Deut. 32:51). Moses' punishment teaches us that great leaders must especially be exemplary in every way (Deut. 3:23–27; 4:21–23; 34:120)" [Ellis T. Rasmussen, *A Latter-day Saint Commentary on the Old Testament* (Salt Lake City: Deseret Book, 1993), 158].

5. See Trent (1960), 50–52.

6. Conner (1992), 164, 170; Ryken, Wilhoit, and Longman (1998), 733, 734; Cooper (1995), 140; Tresidder (2000), 139; Lockyer (1965), 76; Trench (1974), 64; McConkie, in Millet (1987), 203.

7. Trench (1974), 47.

8. For example, Kselman and Barré, in Brown, Fitzmyer, and Murphy (1990), 541; Fitzmyer (1970), 739n31; Mann (1986), 278–79; Firmage, in Freedman (1992), 6:1132; Williamson (1983), 104; Clarke (1846), 5:420; Freyne, in Freedman (1992), 2:900; Morris (1999), 171; Liefeld, in Gaebelein (1976–1992), 8:913; Cooper (1995), 121. See also Wilson (1999), 361; Conner (1992), 166.

9. For example, see John 7:37–39; Numbers 8:7; Wilson (1999), 452; Ryken, Wilhoit, and Longman (1998), 931; Cooper (1995), 189; Wilson (1999), 347, 452; Conner (1992), 163, 179; Habershon (1982), 237, 238; Hall (1974), 128; Habershon (1974), 40, 143, 152; Lockyer (1965), 68.

10. Habershon (1974), 43. See also 49.

11. Augustine, "On the Gospel of St. John," Tractate 26:12, in Philip Schaff, editor, *Nicene and Post-Nicene Fathers: First Series*, fourteen volumes (Peabody, MA: Hendrickson Publishers, 2004), 7:172.

12. Augustine, "On The Gospel of St. John," Tractate 28:9, in Schaff (2004), 7:182.

13. Caesarius of Arles, "Sermon" 103:3, in Lienhard (2001), 239. Caesarius also wrote, "Behold, . . . unless this rock is struck, it does not have any water at all. But when it has been struck, it produces fountains and rivers, as we read in the Gospel: 'He who believes in me, from within him there shall flow rivers of living water.' When Christ was struck on the cross, he brought forth the fountains of the New Testament. Therefore it was necessary for him to be pierced. If he had not been struck, so that water and blood flowed from his side, the whole world would have perished through suffering thirst for the word of God" [Caesarius of Arles, "Sermon" 103:3, in Lienhard (2001), 90].

14. See John of Damascus, "Exposition of the Orthodox Faith," Book IV, Chapter XI, in Philip Schaff and Henry Wace, editors, *Nicene and Post-Nicene Fathers: Second Series*, fourteen volumes (Peabody, MA: Hendrickson, 2004), 9:80–81.

15. John Chrysostom, "Homilies on Second Corinthians," Homily 11:18, in Schaff (2004), 12:333.

16. This is not to say that Paul missed the point of the type or its relationship to the cross. The only point I wish to make here is that Paul did not highlight the cross or Atonement symbolism, whereas the Church Fathers traditionally did.

17. Habershon (1974), 43.

18. See Joseph Smith, in *The Joseph Smith Papers—Journals Volume 1:1832–1839*, Dean C. Jessee, Mark Ashurst-McGee, and Richard L. Jensen, editors (Salt Lake City: The Church Historian's Press, 2008), 24. See also Smith, in Smith (1976), 41; "Rock of Ages," Augustus M. Toplady, lyricist, and Thomas Hastings, composer, in *Hymns of the Church of Jesus Christ of Latter-day Saints*, second revised edition (Salt Lake City: Intellectual Reserve, 2002), hymn number 111.

19. See Wilson (1999), 346–47.

20. See Wilson (1999), 347.

21. Commentators have called the second miracle a "spoilt type," and have suggested the reason God was angry with Moses is because he ruined the typology of the miracle [see Habershon (1975), 60, 143–44; Trent (1960), 52].

22. Trench (1974), 47–48. Christ as the source of living waters, as suggested by this miracle, brings to mind two passages from the Gospel of John—4:4–26; 7:37–39.

23. Patrick Fairbairn, *Typology of Scripture*, two volumes in one (Grand Rapids, MI: Kregel Publications, 1989), 2:65.

24. See Caesarius of Arles, "Sermon," 103:2, in Lienhard (2001), 90. "When we come to the Lord as thirsty sinners, and are satisfied by Him, He gives us His Holy Spirit to dwell in our heart" [Habershon (1982), 238].

25. Fretheim (1991), 189.

26. McQuade (2008), 54.

27. Gardner (2007), 1:303.

28. See Kaiser, in Gaebelein (1976–1992), 2:406.

THE SPIRIT *Makes* NEPHI UNTOUCHABLE

1 NEPHI 17:47–48, 52–55

THE MIRACLE

After chastising his brothers at length for their faithlessness and for their sinful lives, Nephi found that he had pushed them to the point of anger. So furious were they because of his rebuke that they reached forth their hands to grab Nephi and throw him into the depths of the sea.

In the name of Christ, Nephi commanded them, "Touch me not, for I am filled with the power of God, even unto the consuming of my flesh; and whoso shall lay his hands upon me shall wither even as a dried reed; and he shall be as naught before the power of God, for God shall smite him" (verse 48). Nephi then again rebuked them and reminded and encouraged them to believe that God has power to do all things.

The brothers, humbled by the Spirit they felt as Nephi reproved them, found that they could not contend verbally with him. They simply could not respond with any meaningful retort. Indeed, for many days they were afraid to touch Nephi because they feared what they had felt when he had spoken to them. They sensed not simply the power of Nephi's words, but the power of his person also.[1]

Several days after the experience, the Lord commanded Nephi, "Stretch forth thine hand again unto thy brethren, and they shall not wither before thee, but I will shock them, . . . and this will I do, that they may know that I am the Lord their God" (verse 53). Nephi did so, and "the Lord did shake them" (verse 55). In response to this additional undeniable manifestation of God's power, Laman and Lemuel testified: "We know of a surety that the Lord is with thee, for we know that it is the power of the Lord that has shaken us" (verse 55). Nephi's older brothers fell down at his feet—and began to worship him because of the power he manifested. But Nephi stopped them, encouraging them instead to worship God and honor their parents, that their lives might be lengthened.

BACKGROUND

When the Lord commanded Nephi to touch his brothers, He informed him that he need not worry, for the Lord would *not* cause them to wither when touched (verse 53). The fact that the Lord had to settle Nephi's concerns is evidence that Nephi did not wish harm on his brothers. Indeed, the fact that he didn't want to hurt them—even after all they had done to him and against him—shows the goodness of Nephi's heart and the sincerity of his words: "Behold, my soul is rent with anguish because of you, and my heart is pained" (verse 47). This episode is proof of Nephi's love for his siblings and his earnest desire that they be blessed rather than punished. As one commentator put it, "Nephi is speaking in sorrow, not in anger. His words communicate powerful compassion and deep spiritual pain over his brothers."[2]

The space of time between Nephi's rebuke of his brothers and his act of "shaking" or "shocking" them appears to be several days.[3] One commentary on the Book of Mormon explained why the span of time between the two dramatic encounters: "The fear of the rebellious brothers gradually gave way to a sensation of freedom from all danger. In all probability they were about to carry out their murderous plan— or, rather, make another attempt—when the Lord commanded Nephi to stretch forth his hand against them a second time, because He—the Lord—was about to give them a manifestation of his power."[4]

Nephi's exhaustion (verse 47) after testifying with force to his brothers is understandable. As one commentator noted, "An unusual outpouring of the Spirit of the Lord is typically followed by physical exhaustion (see 1 Nephi 1:7; Moses 1:10; Joseph Smith—History 1:20; Daniel 8:27; *Teachings*, pp. 280–81)."[5] Many men who have faithfully exercised the priesthood have had the experience of being physically drained after a powerful priesthood blessing. Even Jesus indicated that, after being touched by the woman with an issue of blood, "virtue" ("power" or "strength" according to the Greek) "had gone out of him" (Mark 5:30). The Prophet Joseph testified that "a man who exercises great faith in administering to the sick, blessing little children, or confirming, is liable to become weakened."[6]

The inability of Nephi's brothers to interfere with his testimony has been taken by some as evidence that he, like Abinadi (Mosiah 13:2–3, 5) or Stephen (Acts 6:15), was transfigured during this episode.[7]

Nephi's comment to Laman and Lemuel—"Ye are murderers in your hearts" (verse 44)—has been taken to mean that Nephi prophetically knew what his brothers were up to, even though they had yet to try to "take him" and "throw him into the depths of the sea" (verse 48). The Spirit of God was resting upon him, and he was enabled to know things that had yet to take place.[8]

Nephi testified to his brothers, "If God had commanded me to do all things I could do them. If he should command me that I should say unto this water, be thou earth, it should be earth; and if I should say it, it would be done" (verse 50). Of this, Millet and McConkie wrote, "The power of the priesthood which Nephi held enabled him to do more than ask for blessings—by that power the righteous man can command the very elements and they will obey (see JST, Genesis 14:30–32)."[9] This principle seems echoed in the words of Doctrine and Covenants 132: "Verily, if a man be called of my Father, as was Aaron, by mine own voice, and by the voice of him that sent me, and I have endowed him with the keys of the power of this priesthood, if he do anything in my name, and according to my law and by my word, he will not commit sin, and I will justify him" (verse 59; see also Moses 6:34; Helaman 10:5). That which a man does or promises by priesthood authority—if done in righteousness and under the influence of the Holy Spirit—will be honored by the Lord.[10]

In 1 Nephi 17:53 the Lord tells Nephi He will "shock" Laman and Lemuel. However, in verse 54 it says the Lord "shook" them. One text explained this seeming difference by suggesting that the word *shock* in Joseph Smith's day likely would not have brought to mind the idea of an electric shock—as it does for us today. Rather, the word would most likely have meant to Joseph and his contemporaries "to shake" or to "tremble," as that was the primary meaning of the verb in Webster's 1828 dictionary. Thus, Nephi may not have "shocked" his brothers in the electric sense, but may have caused them to convulse when he touched them.[11]

After their "shaking," Laman and Lemuel fell to the ground, prostrating themselves before Nephi. Nibley pointed out,

> This is called *proskynēsis*. It means "falling right down and kissing the ground." The *proskynēsis* is a very common way of demonstrating in the ancient world. When the emperor came, there was a *proskynēsi*. When the pope passed, everybody fell down flat. You're supposed to be overpowered; this is the idea. With the Romans you were supposed to blind yourself like this. The dazzling light of the king is so great that you put your hand in front of your face to protect your eyes. That's the *proskynēsis* and the salute.[12]

Laman and Lemuel respond just as one in their day would have been expected to. In our day, however, *proskynēsis* is something we reserve (in our mind's eye) for God or Christ. Thus, the act of Laman and Lemuel here seems all the more inappropriate.

SYMBOLIC ELEMENTS

While the hand is often a symbol for one's work or what one pursues, it also functions as a symbol of power, whether good or evil.[13] Thus, Nephi's extended hand represented God conveying a rebuking power (verse 54), and Laman and Lemuel's hands being retracted or withheld (verse 52) represented an acknowledged lack of power and a lack of support from the divine.

The "shock" or "shaking" (as Nephi describes it) of Laman and Lemuel is itself a symbol of divine wrath and power. Those described as shaking or trembling are symbols of fear and an acknowledgement of guilt along with feelings of pending destruction.[14]

APPLICATION AND ALLEGORIZATION

One obvious application of this story has to do with Laman and Lemuel's spiritual state. Prior to this dramatic episode, Nephi tells us that they were both "past feeling" (verse 45). "The Spirit's calm, quiet, peaceful voice was trying to reach them, but the noise of their sinful lifestyle and mind-set was obstructing the voice."[15] We cannot help but wonder if there are things that are keeping the Spirit from fully communicating with us. Are we less receptive than we should be? Are there things we should be changing—influences we should be removing—so that the Spirit of the Lord may be unrestrained? Like Laman and Lemuel, we need to remember: if we can't hear the "still, small voice" (1 Nephi 17:45; D&C 85:6), the Lord may send something louder (D&C 43:21–25). As one commentator put it, "Sometimes if a person cannot be reached by that quiet, gentle voice of the spirit, the Lord will employ other methods such as thunder, lightning, tempests, and earthquakes."[16] The best way to invite the Lord to humble you is to ignore the whisperings of the Spirit. Laman and Lemuel did this and, in so doing, bade the Lord to speak with them a bit more boldly. And, boy, did He "shake" them! It is best to learn this lesson through *their* lives rather than in *our own*.

Because Nephi manifested power and evident gifts of the Spirit, at the end of this encounter his brothers treated him in a worshipful manner. This same thing happened to Peter (Acts 10:26) and to Paul (Acts 14:14–15). One commentary on these verses wisely noted, "It is appropriate that we have a great respect for those the Lord has chosen as his leaders, and more especially that we honor the office they hold. It is wholly inappropriate, however, for one man to worship another."[17] We should be grateful for and treat with respect not only the fifteen men whom God has called as prophets, seers, and revelators but also all leaders of the Church—on a general and local level. But our reverence for them and their callings should never develop to the point of worship, nor should it cause us to expect perfection of them. Holy men and women serve and lead in the Church. However, they are, in the end, men and women—with a sacred calling and accompanying mantel. But they do not profess perfection or seek worship. We should not place them in the uncomfortable position of having to be perfect, nor should they have to endure excessive adulation from members of the Church who see their leaders more as "rock stars" than as humble, holy servants of the Lord.

On a related note, one commentary reminds us that "it is a common mistake to worship the man with the power instead of the *source* of the power."[18] We must never forget that all miracles—including priesthood miracles—are not wrought by the holder of the priesthood, but by God. In those sacred experiences where the Father allows us to be healed or to witness a priesthood miracle, we should turn first and foremost to the Father with our expression of gratitude. While it is appropriate to thank the man who administered to us, he was merely a conduit. The Lord is the sole source of such blessings.

By way of application, Monte Nyman suggested the following: "There is a great lesson to be learned from Nephi's declaration that he could do whatever God commanded him to do. Nephi believed he could do what the Lord commanded because Moses had been able to do what the Lord commanded him. In turn, we should believe that if Moses and Nephi were both able to do as the Lord commanded, we can also do as the Lord commands of us. This is a major precept of this chapter."[19]

One simple application of this miracle is the eternal truth that power comes into our lives when we have His Spirit with us. Nephi experienced it. You and I too can have the power of His Spirit as we live faithful to covenants and commandments.

Nephi's experience reminds us that the Lord has the power to protect us—and even to shake our enemies—when necessary. Like with Nephi, one of the ways this can be accomplished is through the bearing of our personal testimonies. Laman and Lemuel were humbled, not so much by their rebuke but by the strength of Nephi's witness (days before they were "shaken" by him). Because Nephi spoke by the Spirit, he spoke with power. As you and I testify via that same Spirit, our adversaries will feel of the force of our words, and like Laman and Lemuel, in some cases they will be humbled by the experience.

NOTES

1. One commentary suggests, "Perhaps they remembered Miriam, the sister of Moses, who was stricken with leprosy, when she engaged in a conspiracy against the prophet of the Lord. (Num. 12:1–5) Or, Korah, Dathan and Abiram who, for their rebellion, were swallowed up by the earth (Nub. 16:31–33)" [Reynolds and Sjodahl (1955–1961), 1:181].

2. Gardner (2007), 1:308.

3. See Nyman (2003–2004), 1:271; Ogden and Skinner (2011), 1:81.

4. Reynolds and Sjodahl (1955–1961), 1:182.

5. McConkie and Millet (1987–1991), 1:139. See also Gardner (2007), 1:308.

6. Smith, in Smith (1976), 281.

7. See McConkie and Millet (1987–1991), 1:139; Ogden and Skinner (2011), 1:335; Richard Dilworth Rust, "Recurrence in Book of Mormon Narratives," in *Journal of Book of Mormon Studies*, Volume 3, Number 1 (1994), 42.

8. See Gardner (2007), 1:309. Royal Skousen has suggested that 1 Nephi 17:53 may have originally been intended to read "shake" rather than "shock" (agreeing with verse 54); but Oliver (as scribe) may have misunderstood Joseph and inadvertently written the wrong word [see Gardner (2007), 1:311, quoting Skousen].

9. McConkie and Millet (1987–1991), 1:139.

10. See Joseph Fielding McConkie and Craig J. Ostler, *Revelations of the Restoration* (Salt Lake City: Deseret Book, 2000), 1076.

11. See Gardner (2007), 1:310; Ludlow, Pinegar, Allen, Otten and Caldwell (2007), 41.

12. Nibley (2004), 1:325.

13. See Maurice H. Farbridge, *Studies in Biblical and Semitic Symbolism* (London: Kegan Paul, Trench, Trubner and Co., 1923), 274–75; Conner (1992), 147; Joseph Fielding McConkie, *Gospel Symbolism* (Salt Lake City: Bookcraft, 1985), 261; Cirlot (1971), 137.

14. See Ryken, Wilhoit, and Longman (1998), 892.

15. Ogden and Skinner (2011), 1:79–80.

16. Ogden and Skinner (2011), 1:80.

17. McConkie and Millet (1987–1991), 1:139.

18. Ludlow, Pinegar, Allen, Otten, and Caldwell (2007), 41.

19. Nyman (2003–2004), 1:271.

Liahona Quits Working *When* Nephi's Brothers Bind Him *with* Cords

1 Nephi 18:9–22
Alma 37:38–47

The Miracle

Once their ship was built (according to the specifications of the Lord), Lehi and his family set sail for the promised land. Quite some time into the journey, the old, familiar, unrepentant Laman and Lemuel began to surface. As usual, others were adversely affected by their behavior.

Nephi noted that his two older brothers, along with the sons of Ishmael and their families, began to behave in unseemly ways: dancing and singing in apparently inappropriate way and speaking with "exceeding rudeness" to those around them (1 Nephi 18:9).

Nephi, fearing that the Lord's Spirit would be grieved and leave them to themselves on this dangerous journey, spoke to those in their party who were acting inappropriately. In soberness, he reminded them of the power that had brought them to that point in their journey and encouraged that they exhibit a measure of decorum.

As would be expected, this angered Laman and Lemuel, so they took Nephi and bound him (hand and foot) so that he could not move. No sooner than they had done so, the Liahona ceased to work and a terrible storm arose, threatening to sink their ship.

Lehi reprimanded his elder sons for their behavior, but this seemed only to agitate them all the more. They threatened their father and anyone else who spoke up for Nephi. Lehi and Sariah were so distraught because of the incident that they became physically ill and were brought near to death.

On the fourth day, with Nephi still bound and the storm raging, the brothers began to fear "the judgments of God were upon them," and so they loosed Nephi (verse 15). He immediately praised God for His goodness and His mercy—and did not murmur because of his afflictions. When Nephi picked up the Liahona, it began to work again, the storm did cease, and a great calm came upon the waters and their boat. Once again, they made progress toward the promised land.

Significantly, all the pleading of their parents, siblings, and Nephi's wife and children made no difference to Laman and Lemuel. As Nephi noted, "There was nothing save it were the power of God, which threatened them with destruction, [that] could soften their hearts; wherefore, when they saw that *they* were about to be swallowed up in the depths of the sea they repented of the thing which they had done" (verse 20; emphasis added).

BACKGROUND

As to what provoked the "rude" and raucous behavior of Laman, Lemuel, the sons of Ishmael, and their wives is unclear. To see Nephi's elder brothers act inappropriately is not unusual. Others had also caused problems from time to time. However, the collective misbehaving is less common in the story. Reynolds and Sjodahl suggested the following explanation:

> "Rude" (from the Latin, "rudis") means "rough," and it is synonymous with "barbarous"; "vulgar," and "impudent." I can account for their behavior, only on the supposition that they were intoxicated. In their stock of provisions they undoubtedly had preserved grapes and grape juice, as well as honey and certain spices. They could easily make an alcoholic mixture, the wine ("mesech"), of which we read in Prov. 23:29–34: "At the last it biteth like a serpent, and stingeth like an adder. Thine eyes shall behold strange women and thine heart shall utter perverse things." That, it seems to me, is what happened.[1]

This may well be the cause of their behavior—but it is certainly no excuse for it. These boys were "rude" well before this event. This seems to be a character trait they had nurtured for many years. Somehow they apparently felt they were above others, and the natural result of such a belief is pride and condescension. Laman and Lemuel were the poster children for this arrogant attitude.

SYMBOLIC ELEMENTS

As noted previously, the Liahona is a symbol of Christ and His words as given in scripture and through modern prophets. It also well represents the dictates of the Holy Spirit and the guidance that the Father sends to us through that third member of the Godhead.

While "cords" can carry various symbolic meanings (contingent upon how they are employed), in this particular narrative the cords that Nephi was bound with are a good representation of the limitations we place upon our leaders when we reject their counsel and warnings. The binding of Nephi also reminds us of the sinful and rebellious choices we make in life, which ultimately bring to us, and those around us, negative consequences.

The storms described in this miracle story well symbolize the tests and trials incident to the mortal experience. Each of us encounters them. Some come up quite naturally. Some are the result of our own doing. Some may even be sent by God as a means of developing us or testing us.

APPLICATION AND ALLEGORIZATION

"Reverence"—not rudeness (1 Nephi 18:9)—"invites revelation."[2] "Coarse behavior is never attractive to the Spirit, and when the Spirit withdraws it is natural to expect the protective blessings of heaven to withdraw also."[3] Laman and Lemuel were their own worst enemies. For all of their struggles to become converted, if they would have lived in a way that would have allowed them to have the Spirit operative in their lives, they would not have struggled so much with testimony and temptation. You and I can learn from their example. When one acts in a raucous and irreverent manner, one is not receptive to the Spirit of the Lord—and the corrective counsel of those in authority seems judgmental and harsh. As we live in such a way as to invite the Spirit, even correction is not offensive, because our desire is to become like God and to feel of His Spirit.

Commenting on the rudeness of Nephi's older brothers, Hugh Nibley said, "Now, Joseph Smith says that rudeness is a sin. *Reverentia* (reverence) is reverence for anything—there is no reason for being rude. We must hold nobody or nothing in contempt. We must never do that because we don't know the values of things; we don't know how to evaluate at all. . . . Rudeness is a sinful sort of thing. It is treating the world disrespectfully."[4] We live in a society that is so very rude. Much of our humor is rude. So many of the sitcoms and reality shows we consume are filled with rudeness. Because rudeness is a sin, we cannot act in rude ways and expect at the same time to have the guidance or direction of the Spirit of the Lord.

President Boyd K. Packer once noted that "irreverence suits the purposes of the adversary by obstructing the delicate channels of revelation in both mind and spirit."[5] Just as Laman and Lemuel's offensive acts caused the Liahona to cease to function and, thus, caused them to "know not whither they should steer the ship" (verse 13), so also when you and I live in a way that is not conducive to the Spirit, we are left to ourselves to grope in the dark, looking for our way without the aid of the Lord. Can we afford to sail the turbulent seas of life and endure their storms without the companionship and guidance of the Spirit of God? Any who have suffered a significant trial in life know the lack of wisdom in that choice.

Nephi suggests that the storms that arose—tossing their ship from one side to the other—were a direct consequence of the actions and attitudes of his elder brethren (verse 13). Like Laman and Lemuel, many of the challenges we incur in life are the direct result of our choices. Not all, but many! Unrighteousness almost always brings progress-halting "storms." Just as the Lehite ship was driven backward because of the storm that came upon them, you and I lose both our direction and progress we have made when we fail to follow the Lord's Spirit. Sin always puts us behind. It never helps us to progress. If we stew in our sins long enough, that act of stewing can sink our "ship."

In this miracle it is only the overwhelming trials that come to Laman and Lemuel that ultimately change their behavior (verses 15, 20). Tribulations sent from God are designed to inspire humility and repentance. Some of us need larger trials than others, simply because we are either too prideful to repent or too steeped in our wickedness to do so. Unfortunately, in the case of Laman and Lemuel, their repentance was not sincere, neither was it permanent. However, for us repentance can and should be. When God allows us to struggle with large and burdensome challenges, He does so because He loves us and because He wishes to save us. We can respond, as did Nephi, with humility and gratitude (verse 16), or as did his brothers, with anger, pride, and resentment. One needs only read the story to know which approach brought happiness and which brought suffering and sorrow.

In this miracle Nephi exemplifies the truth that we should not murmur or question God when we have trials. The budding prophet was physically injured during this ordeal—to say nothing of what he suffered emotionally. However, the moment he was freed from the cords that bound him, he fell to his knees and did praise God "all the day long" (verse 16). He did not murmur; he expressed gratitude. The Lord has said, "And he who receiveth all things with thankfulness shall be made glorious" (D&C 78:19). Commenting on this verse, Truman G. Madsen said, "Notice the 'all' in that: difficulties, strains, disaster, setbacks"—we must praise God through and for all of them.[6] This is certainly an attribute to be developed; but Nephi demonstrates that such a grateful heart *can* be acquired.

> One of the great teachings of life is that everyone is going to have afflictions, trials, and tribulations. Adversity is part of life. The righteous are not spared, for this is a testing time. Our test is how we respond to adversity. Adversity also allows God to show forth His power. Nephi did not murmur in his affliction—and neither should we. He praised God, and so should we. Again, since the hearts of Laman and Lemuel were not sensitive to the Lord, only external means could be used to effect a change: they were about to be swallowed up in the depths of the sea, so they repented. We learn a great lesson in regard to our spiritual wellness: Are we subject to the Spirit and the will of God by being easily entreated or do we too need external means to bring us to humility so as to bring about change?[7]

Who among us enjoys time spent with those who are negative, with those who murmur? Elder Neal A. Maxwell pointed out that "too many of us seem to expect that life will flow ever smoothly, featuring an unbroken chain of green lights with empty parking places just in front of our destinations!"[8] Were this possible, life would be pointless. Ogden and Skinner commented, "To remain loyal to God, especially through trials clearly not of our own making, and [to] resist the temptation to become bitter over the Lord's nonintervention is the great test and lesson of life—'to serve Him at all hazards,' thus guaranteeing our exaltation."[9]

It seems significant that as soon as Laman and Lemuel stop their unrighteous deeds, the storms stop and "a great calm" comes (verse 21). So it is in our own lives. When we sin, the winds of life blow fiercely and the waves toss us to and fro. However, when we repent—I mean sincerely repent and change our hearts—"a great calm" often comes into our lives, and the storms typically dissipate. Most certainly, God turns to us as soon as we return to Him. (Of course, the residual effects of our trials may last for a time, but God will immediately be near if our hearts are right.)

One commentary on the Book of Mormon points out that the brothers were quite harsh with Nephi, even resorting to physical violence in their dealings with him. Yet, no one else stood up for him, "meeting violence with violence." Why the lack of response by the others on the boat? One text suggests, "The answer to that is given in the sentence beginning this paragraph [verse 11]. It was the conviction of Nephi and his friends, that, 'The Lord did suffer it, that he might show forth his power.' . . . The object the Lord had in view was their conversion and not vengeance; hence his patience and long-suffering. Nephi understood this by the Spirit within him. (See v. 16.) Non-resistance was his duty at this time."[10] Similarly, in the book of Alma we read, "For the Lord suffereth the righteous to be slain that his justice and judgment may come upon the wicked; therefore ye need not suppose that the righteous are lost because they are slain; but behold, they do enter into the rest of the Lord their God" (Alma 60:13). At times God allows bad things to happen to good people, all in an effort to manifest His power and provide the wicked with opportunities to exercise their agency unto repentance. It was Nephi's conviction in this episode that God had not abandoned him, but that God was instead showing forth His power to those who doubted it—in the hopes of bringing them to repentance. Nephi had not been ignored or neglected. Rather, he was being used as a tool in God's hands. Occasionally you and I may have similar opportunities to be used by God in such a manner.

One last application seems worth noting. Laman and Lemuel may not have liked whom God had chosen as their leader, but that was not their choice to make. What they *did* have a right to decide was whether or not they would respect and obey their younger brother. Whom God places in positions of leadership is not ours to decide. Binding Nephi did not give Laman and Lemuel more freedom. Rather, binding their leader actually placed them and their families in peril. An experience from the life of the Joseph Smith is instructive. The Prophet had a dream in which he saw two members of the Church— men who had struggled to sustain him in his leadership as president. In the dream, these two men (William and Wilson Law) had thrown Joseph into a hole so deep that there was no way for him to jump or climb out. Shortly after imprisoning the Prophet in the pit, poisonous serpents appeared and began to attack the Law brothers, biting them and threatening to take their lives. William and Wilson cried out to Joseph, "Help us, Joseph! Help us!" to which the Prophet rejoined, "I would help you if I could, but *you* have made it impossible for me to help."[11] Though this was but a dream, it is instructive. The Law brothers ended up seeking the life of the Prophet. Similarly, Laman and Lemuel sought to put Nephi in a position wherein his hands were also bound—metaphorically and literally. When you and I bind those who hold the keys of leadership and revelation over us, we place ourselves in danger. We "bind" them when we reject their council or challenge their leadership. In rejecting Nephi's authority and admonitions, Laman and Lemuel nearly lost their lives—and put others' lives in jeopardy too. We must learn the lesson of Lehi's eldest sons and sustain the prophets so that they can protect us in our journey to the promised land—even the celestial kingdom of our God.

NOTES

1. Reynolds and Sjodahl (1955–1961), 1:186.
2. Boyd K. Packer, *Mine Errand from the Lord*, Clyde J. Williams, compiler (Salt Lake City: Deseret Book, 2008), 192.
3. McConkie and Millet (1987–1991), 1:142.
4. Nibley (2004), 1:185.
5. See Packer in Williams (2008), 193.
6. Truman G. Madsen, *Joseph Smith the Prophet* (Salt Lake City: Bookcraft, 1989), 104.
7. Ed. J. Pinegar and Richard J. Allen, *Commentaries and Insights on The Book of Mormon: 1 Nephi—Alma 29* (American Fork, UT: Covenant Communications, 2007), 94.

8. Neal A. Maxwell, cited in Bassett (2007–2008), 1:84.

9. Ogden and Skinner (2011), 1:82–83. See also Pinegar and Allen (2007), 93. Ogden and Skinner are drawing from the following statement by the Prophet Joseph: "When the Lord has thoroughly proved him, and finds that the man is determined to serve Him at all hazards, then the man will find his calling and his election made sure, then it will be his privilege to receive the other Comforter, which the Lord hath promised the Saints, as is recorded in the testimony of St. John, in the 14th chapter, from the 12th to the 27th verses" [Smith, in Smith (1976), 150].

10. See Reynolds and Sjodahl (1955–1961), 1:186, 187. See also Gardner (2007), 1:317.

11. See Madsen (1989), 42–43; emphasis added. The *History of the Church* account of this story is as follows: "In the evening I . . . related a dream which I had a short time since. . . . I was overtaken and seized by William and Wilson Law and others, saying, 'Ah, ah! we have got you at last! We will secure you and put you in a safe place!' and, without any ceremony dragged me out of my carriage, tied my hands behind me, and threw me into a deep, dry pit, where I remained in a perfectly helpless condition, and they went away. While struggling to get out, I heard Wilson Law screaming for help hard by. I managed to unloose myself so as to make a spring, when I caught hold of some grass which grew at the edge of the pit. I looked out of the pit and saw Wilson Law at a little distance attacked by ferocious wild beasts, and heard him cry out, 'Oh Brother Joseph, come and save me!' I replied, 'I cannot, for you have put me into this deep pit.' On looking out another way, I saw William Law with outstretched tongue, blue in the face, and the green poison forced out of his mouth caused by the coiling of a large snake around his body. It had also grabbed him by the arm, a little above the elbow, ready to devour him. He cried out in the intensity of his agony, 'Oh, Brother Joseph, Brother Joseph, come and save me, or I die!' I also replied to him, 'I cannot, William; I would willingly, but you have tied me and put me in this pit, and I am powerless to help you or liberate myself'" [*History of the Church* (1978), 6:461–62; Smith, in Smith (1976), 368–69].

Nephi *Is* Warned That His Brothers Seek *to* *Take* Away His Life

2 Nephi 5:1–11

The Miracle

Lehi had passed away (2 Nephi 4:12) and Nephi became the leader of the deceased prophet's posterity. Of course, Laman and Lemuel struggled with this—though it was clearly the will of both the Lord and many of the people.

Lehi's eldest sons had murmured, saying, "Let us slay him, that we may not be afflicted more because of his words" (2 Nephi 5:3). Concerned that these were more than idle threats, Nephi prayed fervently to the Lord, aware that for many years Laman and Lemuel had plotted to kill both him and their father. Through the intervention of God and angels, their attempts had always been foiled. Nephi pled that such might be the case this time also.

In response to his prayer, the Lord warned Nephi, telling him that he and his family should depart into the wilderness to escape the evil plot of his eldest brothers. Consequently, the families of Nephi, Zoram, and Sam, along with Jacob, Joseph, and Nephi's sisters, gathered their possessions and traveled some distance into the wilderness that they might permanently separate themselves from Laman, Lemuel, and those who chose to follow them.

Nephi recorded that "those who would go with me were those who believed in the warnings and the revelations of God; wherefore, they did hearken unto my words" (verse 6). Once separated from the blood-thirsty older brothers, Nephi and those who followed him did strictly obey the commandments of the Lord, and God greatly prospered them for their faithfulness.

BACKGROUND

This was not Laman and Lemuel's first threat to kill Nephi, nor was not their first attempt (see 1 Nephi 17:48). However, this time there may be a more pressing reason. As one source postulates, "Laman and Lemuel now feel that they must take action against the threat they have feared for years: that Nephi will rule over them. Nephi says as much. This fear/hatred dates back at least to obtaining the brass plates and perhaps before as Nephi's righteousness made him his father's natural ally and, in their eyes, his heir."[1] This heightened motivation to kill their prophet-brother may explain why this time God requires Nephi to flee, whereas before He always simply dissuaded the two older brothers.[2]

It has been suggested that Nephi's group (at this point) may have only consisted of some eleven adults and thirteen children—twenty-four people in all.[3] Perhaps. However, a curious point of background commentary was offered by the twentieth-century LDS exegetes George Reynolds and Janne M. Sjodahl. Suggesting that Nephi's phrase "all those who would go with me" likely implied a fairly large group, they reasoned,

> [Nephi] was accompanied by Zoram, Sam, Jacob, Joseph and their families, his sisters and all those who would go with him. Nephi explains that "all those who would go with him" were those who believed in the warnings and revelations of God. But were they only the children and grandchildren of Lehi and his company, who less than thirty years previously had left Jerusalem? (v. 28) Were these as numerous already at this time as the expression, "all those who would go with me," seems to imply? Or, is it possible that Lehi and his family had established their first settlement in a locality where they found aborigines . . . who had identified themselves with the newcomers, as the Mulekites did with the immigrants led by Mosiah (Omni vv. 12–19)?[4]

While we have no way of knowing, and Reynolds and Sjodahl were certainly speculating, it is certainly possible that Nephi's followers at this point in their history consisted of a larger group than one would think (some thirty years into their trek).

Nephi mentions that the families of Zoram and Sam accompanied him into the wilderness, along with his brothers Jacob and Joseph. However, when he mentions his sisters who accompanied him, he doesn't speak of their families. We know that Nephi had at least two sisters—perhaps more. We also know that he had two sisters who married the sons of Ishmael. If the sisters mentioned here (2 Nephi 5:6) are those same sisters, then it is quite possible that Nephi's brothers-in-law did not accompany the party of believers into the wilderness, as they had occasionally sided with Laman and Lemuel before (see 1 Nephi 7:6; 16:20, 37; 18:9, 17; 2 Nephi 4:13). Thus, it is possible that Nephi's married sisters followed their prophet-brother, leaving their rebellious husbands behind.[5] On the other hand, it is also possible that the sisters mentioned in 2 Nephi 5 are younger sisters who had been born after Nephi's younger brothers, Jacob and Joseph, were born. If that were the case, then perhaps these younger sisters did not have husbands yet. In this latter scenario, Nephi's older sisters (those married to Ishmael's sons) must have stayed behind with their husbands, who supported Laman and Lemuel. The text is not clear. But what seems clear is this: aside from Laman and Lemuel, a number of other members of Nephi's family also rejected his patriarchal and prophetic leadership.[6]

SYMBOLIC ELEMENTS

One commentary points out a symbolic correspondence between this miracle and the miracle of the life of Joseph of Egypt being preserved:

> Again, the brothers seek the life of Nephi. As a parallel to the life of Joseph of Egypt, his brothers "conspired against him to slay him" (Genesis 37:18). As Zoram, Sam, Jacob, and Joseph stood by Nephi (2 Nephi 5:6 . . .), so Reuben, the older brother of Joseph of Egypt "delivered him out of [the older brother's] hands" (Genesis 37:21). . . . Joseph of Egypt recognized that it was God "that sent me hither" (Genesis 45:8). We will now see how God intervened in the life of Nephi.[7]

APPLICATION AND ALLEGORIZATION

One of the great messages of this miracle is that God is able and willing to warn his faithful Saints when they are in danger—and when it is His will and desire that they continue to labor on His behalf on *this* side of the veil. The Prophet Joseph had numerous experiences wherein the Father warned him of impending danger. Truman G. Madsen shared the following story:

> A man acting, as it were, as an undercover agent came to Nauvoo, tried to work his way into the good graces of the Prophet, then invited him out for a walk. On the crest of a hill the Prophet stopped, called him by name, and said, "You have a boat and men in readiness to kidnap me, but you will not make out to do it." It was true. The man had planned to kidnap him, but instead he went away cursing. Joseph once wrote in a letter, "It is in vain to try to hide a bad spirit from the eyes of them who are spiritual, for it will show itself in speaking and in writing, as well as in all our other conduct. It is also needless to make great pretensions when the heart is not right: the Lord will expose it to the view of faithful Saints."[8]

Such miraculous acts of warning and preservation are not reserved for the life of the President of the Church. Wilford Woodruff shared an experience where the Lord warned a group of Latter-day Saints who were in imminent danger:

> It took me two years to gather up everybody [who was a member of the Church] . . . in New England and Canada . . . (there were about one hundred of them). We arrived at Pittsburgh one day at sundown. We did not want to stay there, so I went to the first steamboat that was going to leave. I saw the captain and engaged passage for us on that steamer. I had only just done so when the spirit said to me . . . very strongly, "Don't go aboard that steamer, nor your company." Of course, I went and spoke to the captain, and told him I had made up my mind to wait. Well, that ship started, and had only got five miles down the river when it took fire, and three hundred persons were burned to death or drowned. If I had not obeyed that spirit, and had gone on that steamer with the rest of the company, you can see what the result would have been.[9]

One commentary on Nephi's experience, pointed out, "In countless instances, such warnings have been given to protect the faithful. Relative to his enemies, Joseph Smith was promised that bounds were set beyond which they could not pass and that his days were known to the Lord and they would not be 'numbered less' by the evil designs of the wicked (D&C 122:9). In principle, the same applies to all who are true and faithful to the covenants they have made with the Lord."[10] So long as it is not our time to serve beyond the veil, the Lord promises us His warning voice and His protecting hand—*if* we are living in such a way as to be guided by His Spirit.

Another obvious message of this miracle is the simple reality that God hears and answers prayers. "That is an eternal truth, solid as the everlasting hills."[11] Nephi prayed in faith, and God answered. The response he received was likely not the one he desired—for in the past God had always intervened, causing Laman and Lemuel to abandon their murderous designs. However, in this case the divine guidance received was much less convenient for Nephi and those who sided with him. This time they would have to uproot themselves, leave behind almost all they possessed, and head into the wilderness for safety. Nevertheless, God answered when Nephi cried out. And He will ever answer our prayers too. As with Nephi, that answer may not be what we desire—but it will certainly be what's best.

I have occasionally had in my own life promptings that came that I did not immediately act upon. In each case, the consequences were unfortunate and, I hope, the lesson has been learned. The warnings and promptings of the divine are only helpful to us if we obey them, and if we do so promptly. An important point in Nephi's miracle was his act of obedience to the prompting when it came (2 Nephi 5:5–7), and his continued obedience to the commandments afterward (verse 10).

Finally, the experience of Nephi reminds us of the importance of trusting the prophets, in believing that they receive revelation for our lives today. One commentary on the Book of Mormon offered the following symbolic application of this miracle narrative:

> Following the death of Lehi, the ... Nephites and the Lamanites become separate nations. The latter embrace an idle and uncivilized lifestyle; the former establish a Christ-centered lifestyle based on industry, self-reliance, and temple worship. Thus these peoples become a

parable, as it were, for the doctrine of free agency and the consequences of choices in life—the obedient harvesting rich blessings of enduring joy, and the rebellious harvesting the dire and empty outcomes of a self-centered and anchorless existence, devoid of the fruits of the gospel of Christ and separated from the blissful fold.[12]

Some did not follow Nephi into the wilderness, choosing instead to remain behind with Laman and Lemuel.[13] Others, fortunately, exercised faith in the Lord's anointed, did what Nephi counseled them, and—though amid great sacrifice and inconvenience—escaped the murderous hands of Nephi's older brothers. One text reminds us, "As with Nephi and his brothers, so with Joseph Smith and those who oppose him—they refuse to accept the warnings and revelations of God. Today virtually every anti-LDS argument reduces itself to a rejection of modern and continuing revelation."[14] Even today there are those in the Church who trust only the convenient counsel of the prophets, seers, and revelators. But when hard things are asked of them, like Laman and Lemuel of old, they murmur, saying, "[Oh] that we may not be afflicted more because of his words" (verse 3).

NOTES

1. Gardner (2007), 2:87.
2. See Gardner (2007), 2:87.
3. See John L. Sorenson, cited in Gardner (2007), 2:87–88.
4. Reynolds and Sjodahl (1955–1961), 1:272–73. See also Gardner (2007), 2:88, who also conjectured that "these 'others' are New World peoples who joined with the Nephites."
5. Nibley assumes the sisters' families did come along—though the text doesn't mention them [Nibley (2004), 1:226].
6. See Ludlow, Pinegar, Allen, Otten, and Caldwell (2007), 1:65.
7. Nyman (2003–2004), 1:436.
8. Madsen (1989), 441. See also Matthew C. Godfrey, et al, *The Joseph Smith Papers Documents—Volume 2: July 1831–January 1833* (Salt Lake City: The Church Historians Press, 2013), 364–68.
9. Wilford Woodruff, in G. Homer Durham, editor, *The Discourses of Wilford Woodruff* (Salt Lake City: Bookcraft, 1998), 294–95.
10. McConkie and Millet (1987–1991), 1:221.
11. Reynolds and Sjodahl (1955–1961), 1:272.
12. Pinegar and Allen (2003), 95.
13. One text points out, "With Nephi's departure, Laman and Lemuel lose the anchor of Gospel strength. They are in effect separated from God, which is the

ultimate consequence of sin. We separate ourselves from God, in effect, when we reject His word and fail to follow the living prophet" [Pinegar and Allen (2007), 142].

14. McConkie and Millet (1987–1991), 1:221.

Israel Is Healed of the Poison of Fiery Flying Serpents

2 Nephi 25:20
Alma 33:19–21
Helaman 8:13–15
Numbers 21:8–9
2 Kings 18:4
John 3:14–17

The Miracle

Because the Edomites would not allow the Israelites to pass through their land, the Israelites were traveling around Edom when this miracle took place. But, as usual, the Israelites became impatient because of the inconvenience of having to backtrack, and so they began to murmur against God and Moses. "Have you brought us here to die, without bread or water? We detest this monotonous manna!" (see Numbers 21:4–5).

As a consequence of their attitude, the Lord sent poisonous snakes, which bit the Israelites, and many died. This provoked fear in, and apologies from, the Israelites—who begged Moses to have God take the snakes away. So Moses prayed to God on their behalf.

In response, the Lord commanded Moses to make a snake out of brass and place it atop a pole, and those who had been bitten need only look upon it in faith and they would be healed. So Moses did as the Lord commanded.

BACKGROUND

Nephi (the son of Lehi), Zenock, Nephi (the son of Helaman), Moses, and John the Beloved, as well as the author of 2 Kings, all testified of this miracle. Indeed, it is one of the most widely attested miracles in holy writ. All of the Book of Mormon authors use it as a teaching device and assume their readers are well acquainted with the miracle.

While the Numbers account of this miracle tells us what Israel had to do to be saved from the poison of the snakes—namely look with faith upon the brass serpent—what it does not tell us is whether or not the Israelites complied with Moses's instructions. In the book of Alma, however, we are given a bit of additional information regarding this miracle—facts that are not recorded in the Pentateuch.

> Behold, [Christ] was spoken of by Moses; yea, and behold a type was raised up in the wilderness, that whosoever would look upon it might live. And many did look and live. But few understood the meaning of those things, and this because of the hardness of their hearts. But there were many who were so hardened that they would not look, therefore they perished. Now the reason they would not look is because they did not believe that it would heal them. (Alma 33:19–20)

Nephi confirms the words of Alma in his commentary on the miracle and then adds an additional insight that neither Moses nor Alma record. He tells us, "And the Lord . . . sent fiery flying serpents among them; and after they were bitten he prepared a way that they might be healed; and the labor which they had to perform was to look; and because of the simpleness of the way, or the easiness of it, there were many who perished" (1 Nephi 17:41). Thus, from the book of Numbers we learn what the Israelites needed to do in order to be saved, but from the Book of Mormon we learn that many did not have faith sufficient to obey the prophet's simple instructions. Consequently, many died. Nephi tells us that the Israelites thought the way to be saved was "too simple." While this seems almost incomprehensible, perhaps many of us are equally guilty of making things harder than they really are.

Nephi also speaks of the serpents not just as "fiery serpents" (meaning snakes whose venom makes one's body burn[1]) but as "fiery *flying* serpents" (meaning snakes that could lunge quite a distance in order to strike their victims). The implication is that there would be no escaping the bite of these lunging venomous vipers. Everyone was in danger.

An obvious incongruity appears in the Old Testament version of the miracle. One commentator noted, "The description of the plague seems to be of something that was spreading quickly; yet Moses had to take the time to fashion, or direct the fashioning of, a metal image of one of the poisonous snakes."[2] How long it would take to make such a statue or image we can only guess. But one would think hours, not minutes. Anyone bitten would surely die before such an image could be crafted. Jewish Midrash offers a plausible explanation as to how Moses could come by a brass snake so quickly. It suggests that just as Moses turned his staff into a serpent in Pharaoh's court, he likely turned it into a brass snake during this miracle.[3] Thus, the need for a brass image could almost instantaneously be met. Conjectural, but curious!

The serpent fashioned out of brass was not discarded once this miracle was accomplished. Indeed, it was retained by Israel for some five hundred years, and eventually inappropriately became an object of worship for them. Thus, when King Hezekiah saw that the Israelites were burning incense to it, he broke it into pieces so as to end their idolatrous behavior (2 Kings 18:4).[4]

SYMBOLIC ELEMENTS

As noted already, manna was a symbol of Christ.[5] Since Jesus is typified by this heaven-sent bread, "a rejection of the heavenly manna is tantamount to one spurning the grace of God in the Savior."[6] Thus, for the Israelites to say to Moses and to God, "We're sick of manna!" (see Numbers 21:4–5), was equivalent to saying we're sick of Christ, who, like this manna, sustains us from day to day.

The snake is a curious symbol. In contemporary Christian thinking it is often associated with Satan and temptation. However, originally it symbolized healing, resurrection, and immortality.[7] It was a symbol of Christ long before it was a representation of Satan![8] Thus, when the devil appeared to Adam and Eve in Eden in the form of, or through the use of, a serpent, he was actually seeking to appear as an "angel of light" (2 Nephi 9:9). In other words, he chose that symbol because he knew the snake represented the Messiah, and that was what he wished to be viewed as.[9] Curiously, the Hebrew word for

Messiah (*mashiyakh*) totals 358 in gematria.[10] Likewise, the Hebrew word for serpent (*nakhash*) has the numerical value of 358.[11] Thus, by the gematria employed in Numbers 21, it is confirmed that the serpent lifted up by Moses upon his staff was indeed a type for the Savior, Jesus Christ. Satan had attacked Israel via getting them to worship false gods, such as the cravings of the flesh. But in this miracle the true Messiah appears, retaking His serpent symbol and offering covenant Israel healing—something only He had the power to give.

On a related note, the snakebites spoken of in this miracle were believed by the early Christian Church to represent "evil actions, idolatries, and other sins."[12] One Church Father wrote,

> The wounds caused by the fiery serpent [symbolize] the poisonous enticement of the vices, which afflict the soul and bring about its spiritual death. . . . The sins which drag down soul and body to destruction . . . are appropriately represented by the serpents, not only because they were fiery and poisonous and artful at bringing about death but also because our first parents were led into sin by a serpent.[13]

Just as every one of the Israelites was in danger of being bitten by these fiery flying serpents,[14] so also each of us are bitten by sin (Romans 3:19, 23). Consequently, we each need Christ and His healing power, as found in His Atonement.

Brass and copper are typically symbols of judgment.[15] Thus, when Moses raised the brazen snake upon the pole in an attempt to destroy the effects of the fiery flying serpents, the Christocentric typology is deepened via the employment of brass; for Christ will be the judge of all mankind (John 5:22).[16] Similarly, in Daniel 10:6 and Revelation 1:15 (see also 2:18) Christ is described as having feet of brass. In both cases, it appears that the message is that (beyond the image of strength, stability, and permanence) Christ's life was such that He could serve as the perfect judge because He lived the perfect life.[17]

APPLICATION AND ALLEGORIZATION

While there are a number of symbols present in this miracle, the most important is its representation of Christ's Atonement as being necessary for the salvation of all of God's creations. Said one commentator,

In the cross is our only hope, since none of us have failed to bellyache when we have not liked the direction in which God has sent us. . . . None of us fails to be affected by moral or spiritual failure, so all of us need to look to the cross for our salvation. It will not stop sin from biting us, but it will bring us to the gracious Father, through the sacrifice of His only Son.[18]

Similarly, in Helaman 8:14–15 we find the following application of this miracle: "Yea, did [Moses] not bear record that the Son of God should come? And as he lifted up the brazen serpent in the wilderness, even so shall he be lifted up who should come. And as many as should look upon that serpent should live, even so as many as should look upon the Son of God with faith, having a contrite spirit, might live, even unto that life which is eternal" (see also John 3:14–15). Moses pointed the attention of ancient Israel to the symbol of Christ's Atonement (as our attention is pointed that direction each week during the sacrament), but too many looked elsewhere for relief, and thus they died. In this there is an important lesson for all. We each desperately need Christ. He is the only source of relief. This miracle highlights that fact, while it also emphasizes the dangers of not trusting Him or in looking elsewhere for salvation.

When this miracle took place, the Israelites found themselves surrounded by these leaping venomous vipers. In the midst of all of the chaos this surely caused, Moses told them to just keep looking at the serpent on the staff he had affixed and raised up. That was hard for most, as what was happening around them was such a distraction. As Spurgeon wisely noted, "The healthiest way of living where serpents swarm is never to take your eye off the brazen serpent at all."[19] With no desire to sound like a pessimist, I believe we live in a world absolutely teaming with satanic influences. If we keep our eye on Christ (as Moses encouraged the Israelites to), the adversary will have no access to us.[20]

While this miracle reminds us of what Israel needed to do to be saved—namely "look to God and live" (Alma 37:47)—it also tells us a bit about what Christ needed to do to save us—namely, offer His life as a ransom for sin. "The fashioning of the brazen serpent alone was not enough!" one commentator noted. "It had to be lifted up! The coming of Jesus into the world alone was not enough. He must needs have been lifted up!"²¹ Christ lived the perfect life and, in so doing, showed us the way to live. However, He also needed to die the perfect death or His perfect life would have been in vain. This miracle highlights the importance of His death and the power resident in Christ's sacrifice to heal and to save!

One commentator has suggested that there is also a message about proper repentance in this miracle. She wrote,

> It would have been no use for the bitten Israelites to bathe their wounds, or to put ointments or plasters on them, or to bandage them up; but there are many who try to get rid of their sins in this way. They bathe their wounds with tears of repentance; they put on the ointment of good words, or plasters of good resolutions, and bandage themselves with doing their best; but the bites of sin get no better with this sort of treatment; a look at the Crucified One is what they need.²²

Though we must certainly do our part in the process of repentance, we must be cautious about relying more on our own merits than we do on Christ's. (Those guilty of serious sins will sometimes try to "take care" of such things themselves—without enlisting the aid of their priesthood leaders.) This miracle seems to emphasize that there was nothing those bitten could do to save themselves from the poison coursing through their veins. Indeed, those who refused to look in faith upon the brazen serpent died, no matter what they tried to do for themselves. And thus they were wonderful symbolic representations of those who are willing to work but are not willing to trust! We must do all that we can to change, repent, be holy, and cease sinning. However, in the end we must also remember that it is Christ's Atonement, and not our feeble works, that will save us from Satan, sin, and death.

Finally, Elder A. Theodore Tuttle of the Seventy offered this modern-day application of Moses's miracle of the fiery flying serpents:

> When they came among the flying serpents, Moses fashioned a brazen serpent, raised it, and all they had to do was look at that serpent, and they would be healed. The account says that many perished because they wouldn't even look (see 1 Ne. 17:32, 41; see also Num. 21:8–9). He was trying to do what you and I as parents need to do with our families today—to develop [in them] faith in the Lord. And the way to do it is to recount the examples of faith that have happened in our history and in our heritage and with our people. That's the value of

history. It contains accounts of faith of our own blood and ancestry and of our own people and our children. . . . We cannot go one generation without losing faith if we do not do this. And to rear a generation of faith for what we must do in these [latter] days, you and I simply must develop and increase faith in the Lord Jesus Christ.[23]

Just as Book of Mormon prophets shared this miracle from their peoples' past—as a means of building the faith of those in the present—you and I should tell our own posterity the stories of faith and miracles from our lives and the lives of our ancestors. Nephi (the son of Lehi), Zenock, Nephi (the son of Helaman), and John all saw the benefit of telling this story to their modern-day counterparts as a means of teaching faith. Do we have our own stories of how we have overcome the "bites" of the adversary through focusing our eyes of faith on Christ? And does our posterity know of these miracles the Lord has performed for us?

NOTES

1. The Hebrew can quite literally be translated "the snakes that produce burning" [Allen, in Gaebelein (1976–1992), 2:876].
2. Allen, in Gaebelein (1976–1992), 2:877.
3. See Ginzberg (1967–1969), 6:116n658.
4. One source states, "Hezekiah found it necessary to destroy the relic, that he might put an end to the idolatry. History repeats itself, and men would still worship, if they could, the sacred wood [of Christ's cross]; and, failing that, are obliged to be content with pictured or carved crosses and crucifixes" [Habershon (1975), 143].
5. See "God Fed Israel Manna in the Wilderness" above, and as recorded in Exodus 16:14–36; Numbers 11:7–9; and as cited in 1 Nephi 17:28; Mosiah 7:19.
6. Allen, in Gaebelein (1976–1992), 2:876.
7. See Bruce Vawter, *On Genesis: A New Reading* (New York: Doubleday, 1977), 78.
8. See Andrew Skinner, "Savior, Satan, and Serpent: The Duality of a Symbol in the Scriptures," in Stephen E. Ricks, Donald W. Parry, and Andrew H. Hedges. *The Disciple as Scholar: Essays on Scripture and the Ancient World in Honor of Richard Lloyd Anderson* (Provo, UT: FARMS, 2000), 359–84; Wilson (1999), 363.
9. On a related note, the Hebrew word translated as "serpent" in the Genesis account of the Fall is related to the Hebrew word for "luminous" or "shining." Thus, some have suggested that the Genesis account should not read "serpent" but rather "angel of light" [See, for example, Victor P. Hamilton, *Handbook on the Pentateuch* (Grand Rapids, MI: Baker Book House, 1982), 42. See also "Revelation of Moses," in Alexander Roberts and James Donaldson, editors, *Ante-Nicene Fathers*, ten volumes (Peabody, MA: Hendrickson Publishers, 1994), 8:566]. Ginzberg records,

"Satan assumed the appearance of an angel" [Ginzberg (1967–1969), 1:95; "Life of Adam and Eve," Latin version 9:1 and Greek version 17:1–2; 29:15, in James H. Charlesworth, *The Old Testament Pseudepigrapha*, two volumes (New York: Doubleday, 1983, 1985), 2:260, 261, 277; Robert Jamieson, Andrew Fausset, and David Brown, *Jamieson, Fausset and Brown One Volume Commentary* (Grand Rapids, MI: Associated Publishers and Authors Inc., 1974), Old Testament page 19; Clarke (1846), 1:48]. Some commentators on this miracle argue that the reason Moses is commanded to make a "brazen serpent" for Israel to exercise faith in is because Jesus, "who knew no sin," became sin for us, "that we might be made the righteousness of God in him" (2 Corinthians 5:21). While it is true the Jesus took upon Him flesh that He might help us to overcome the flesh, the symbolism of the serpent in this miracle is likely not about how Jesus took upon Himself the appearance of that which is human. Rather, it is more likely that the symbolism is centered on Jesus's role as healer and provider of resurrection.

10. The word *gematria* means literally "to reckon by numbers." In most ancient societies, letters and numbers were used interchangeably. Each letter of an alphabet had a numerical value. Technically speaking, gematria is a mode of interpretation in which the numerical value is substituted for each letter in a word. By so doing, a word's numerical value could be determined and compared for potential relationships with other words possessing the same numerical value.

11. Alan F. Johnson, "Revelation," in Gaebelein (1976–1992), 12:533; William Barclay, *Revelation of John*, two volumes (Norwich, England: St. Andrew Press, 1959), 2:295; Fontana (1994), 152; John J. Davis, *Biblical Numerology* (Grand Rapids, MI: Baker Book House, 2000), 143; Georges Ifrah, *The Universal History of Numbers* (New York: John Wiley & Sons, 2000), 253.

12. Justin Martyr, "Dialogue with Trypho," 94, in Lienhard (2001), 242.

13. Bede the Venerable, "Homilies on the Gospels," 2:18, in Lienhard (2001), 241.

14. See Trent (1960), 107.

15. Habershon (1974), 97; Wilson (1999), 56–57; Trent (1960), 107; Conner (1992), 131.

16. See our discussion of the "brass serpent" as a symbol for Christ (Numbers 21:4-9) above.

17. Leon Morris, *Tyndale New Testament Commentaries: Revelation*, revised edition (Grand Rapids, MI: Eerdmans, 1999), 70; Wilson (1999), 58; J. Massyngberde Ford, *The Anchor Bible: Revelation* (New York: Doubleday, 1975), 383.

18. McQuade (2008), 61.

19. Charles H. Spurgeon, cited in Habershon (1982), 93–94.

20. The Prophet Joseph is said to have taught, "The devil has no power over us only as we permit him; the moment we revolt at anything which comes from God the Devil takes power" [Andrew F. Ehat and Lyndon W. Cook, *The Words of Joseph Smith* (Provo, UT: Religious Studies Center, 1980), 60. See also Smith, in Smith (1976), 181].

21. Trent (1960), 108. See also John 12:32–22.

22. Habershon (1982), 90–91.

23. A. Theodore Tuttle, "Developing Faith," *Ensign*, November 1986, 72.

SHEREM *the* ANTI-CHRIST DIES

JACOB 7:1–23

THE MIRACLE

Jacob, the fifth son of Lehi, had a cerebral and yet miraculous encounter with a self-proclaimed (Jacob 7:9) anti-Christ named Sherem.[1]

Sherem had been using his gifts of rhetoric and flattery to overthrow the doctrine of Christ and to dismantle the testimonies of those who were believers in the gospel. Now he sought an audience with the prophet Jacob in the hopes that he might also dissuade him from believing: something unlikely, owing to Jacob's spiritual endowments (having seen angels and heard the voice of the Lord).

Sherem's approach to Jacob appears to have been filled with condescension. He employed snarky lines, such as, "Show me a sign by this power of the Holy Ghost, *in the which ye know so much*" (verse 13; emphasis added), and seemingly sarcastically referred to the prophet as "Brother Jacob" (verse 6) when he felt no brotherhood toward Jacob, only animosity.[2]

In the process of their interaction, Sherem denied Christ (verses 2, 9), employed flattery to manipulate Jacob and others (verses 2, 4, 6), utilized his gift at language to intimidate (verse 4), accused Jacob of teaching blasphemy (verse 7), denied the gifts of prophecy and revelation (verse 7), and sought for a sign (verse 13).

In response to Sherem's request to see a sign, Jacob first acknowledged that it was not his place (even though he was a prophet) to "tempt" or "test" God by promising people proof of God's existence. Jacob even went so far as to say, 'Sherem, if God *did* show you a sign, you would deny it—because you're of the devil!' But Jacob added, 'If it is God's will to show you a sign, then let that sign be Him smiting you' (see verse 14). No sooner had Jacob said this, Sherem fell to the earth, and "he was nourished for the space of many days" (verse 15).

Recognizing he was on his deathbed, Sherem requested that the people be gathered together that he might say a few things to them before he passed. His message was simple: 'The things I taught you were false'; 'I know Jesus is the Christ, the Holy Ghost is real, and that angels minister to people on the earth today'; 'I was deceived by Satan'; and 'I fear I am going to be a Son of Perdition' (see verses 17–19).[3]

After confessing his wrongs and acknowledging the reality of God and Christ, Sherem died, and the multitude who watched "fell to the earth" in a spirit of reverence for this significant manifestation of God's power (verse 21).

Jacob recorded that, upon the death of Sherem, "peace and the love of God was restored again among the people; and they searched the scriptures, and hearkened no more to the words of this wicked man" (verse 23).

BACKGROUND

Nibley suggested that the name Sherem means "pug nosed" or "snub nosed."[4] While such a name could have been given to him as an infant because of his physical appearance, it seems the ideal title for one who manifests such an arrogant and "stuck-up" demeanor.

One commentator described Sherem as an outsider—a non-native of the region in which he seeks to stir up trouble and seeks to damage faith:

> The fact that Sherem comes "among the people of Nephi" tacitly acknowledges that he is not genealogically a Nephite or a citizen of the town of Nephi. He must ask to find Jacob, something that would be unusual had he been a resident in the city of Nephi. No matter how large the city of Nephi would have been at this point in history, it is unlikely that it had grown so large that major political and religious figures would be unknown.[5]

The *Book of Mormon Reference Companion* points out that Sherem made some explicit accusations against Jacob: "Sherem made specific charges from the law of Moses against Jacob, accusing him of blasphemy, false prophecy, and causing public apostasy. . . . All three crimes were punishable by death under the law of Moses (Lev. 24:10–16; Deut. 18:20–22; 13:1–18). . . . It becomes obvious that Sherem himself was guilty of the three charges that he made against Jacob."[6] And, ultimately, Sherem received the penalty of death from the very giver of the law he had used to falsely accuse and condemn God's prophet.

Of anti-Christs in their various dispensations, McConkie and Millet pointed out that they have some commonly employed techniques:

> Prior to the meridian of time the anti-Christ contended that there would be no Christ and that no man had the ability to speak authoritatively concerning things future. The anti-Christ contends that there is no need for a Savior; that man is perfectly capable of securing his own happiness and well-being; and that any trust in or allegiance to things beyond human reach or reason is futile. Clever ploys of the modern anti-Christ include an insistence upon the preeminence of man; an exaggerated stress upon man's self-reliance; an emphasis upon Jesus as the great moral teacher and community leader, with a corresponding deemphasis upon the necessity for spiritual regeneration through a blood atonement.[7]

Sherem's theological position was what we today call "secular humanism." Man is god, and therefore, God is not needed, nor can He actually exist. Why worship the Creator when you can worship the creature? Man is the center of creation—the center of the universe. For one to speak beyond humanity's rational capacities is foolishness; thus, all religion must be a lie, gibberish, or the ravings of scared madmen.[8] The condescension (toward people of faith) oozes from those who take this position.

Sherem's request to see a sign was a mistake that ultimately cost him his life. One text describes the anti-Christ's motivations as follows:

> Sherem calls what he believes to be a bluff and demands that Jacob prove his prophetic identity. Sherem asks for a proof, not because he

wants one, but because he is certain that Jacob cannot provide one. Jacob's failure will allow Sherem to deny Jacob's prophetic calling for lack of evidence, and the hollowness of Jacob's prophetic calling will likewise cast doubt on Jacob's scriptural interpretations. It is a masterful move, but it is a fatal mistake.[9]

As to the medical condition associated with Sherem's collapse, one commentary on the Book of Mormon suggested that he "had, evidently, a paralytic stroke in the sight of all present."[10] Nibley makes this same claim.[11]

After Sherem's collapse, he is said to have been "nourished for the space of many days" (Jacob 7:15). While this is traditionally interpreted to mean that he was so incapacitated that he had to be fed and cared for upon his deathbed, this has never struck me as the primary message of the verse. I resonate with the following commentary on this passage: **"He was nourished for the space of many days.** That is, Sherem was taught and instructed in the ways of truth and righteousness—he was 'nourished by the good word of God' (see Jacob 6:7; Alma 39:10)."[12] While Sherem was certainly fed and cared for physically upon his deathbed, it seems that more is intended by the declaration that he was "nourished." Significantly, it isn't upon his collapse that he requests to speak to the people. Rather, it is after he had been "nourished for many days" that his heart changes and he seeks to confess the error of his ways.

Upon the death of Sherem, the people engage in *proskynēsis*—willful prostration (7:21).[13] In other words, they do not fall to the earth unconscious (as at other times in the Book of Mormon). Rather, their prostration is a symbol for their having been "overcome" with feelings of awe at the manifestation of God's power. It is an act of astonishment.

When Sherem offers his confession (verses 17–19), he mentions that he has a testimony of the ministry of angels. However, we know nothing of such an experience in the life of Sherem. Was this an experience in the past (prior to his confrontation of Jacob), or could it have been something more recent? One text suggests that during his period of incapacitation (prior to his death), Sherem may have had an experience akin to Alma the Younger's: "Sherem . . . testifies to the power of the Holy Ghost and the ministering of angels, almost certainly an allusion to his experience during the time when he lay under the influence of the Spirit. Assuming that it also parallels Alma's experience, such ministering was for Sherem's salvation (Mosiah 27:24–27)."[14]

SYMBOLIC ELEMENTS

As noted above, in this particular miracle, the act of falling to the earth is a symbol of awe and reverence—of worship. It is a physical manifestation of an inward awareness that God's hand has been manifest in a supernatural manner.[15]

Being "nourished" here implies two things. It certainly reminds us of the need to be loving to our enemies. But the act of "nourishing" also symbolizes feeding someone spiritually.[16]

The death of Sherem is an apt symbol for spiritual death. Just as he lost his life fighting against the truth, one who fights against God's gospel will surely die spiritually.[17]

APPLICATION AND ALLEGORIZATION

The most obvious application of this miracle is that Sherem is a prototype for the various disgruntled and misguided folks who seek to destroy the Church and challenge the testimonies of its members.[18] Our antagonists are often aggressive and confident, as Sherem was. They, like this Book of Mormon anti-Christ, don't just challenge the meek and humble followers of Christ. Sometimes they even seek to take on the presiding Brethren. McConkie and Millet noted,

> The devil and his disciples are neither shy nor hesitant about the accomplishment of their purposes. While some among the legions of Beelzebub are subtle and cunning, the approach of the anti-Christ is aggressive and direct.
>
> Why the confrontation with one such as Jacob? The devil would always rather capture a spiritual general than one of lesser rank. Such would be a monumental victory to be celebrated by the hordes of hell. And be it remembered that the Lord himself was not immune from personal confrontation with the evil one (see Matthew 4), and that he in turn said to Peter, the chief Apostle, "Behold, Satan hath desired to have you, that he may sift you as wheat" (Luke 22:31).[19]

The devil always gives his followers confidence. It is unfounded, but he fills them with it. Confucius wisely noted, "Those who are virtuous always take caution to speak appropriately, but those whose speech is appropriate may not always be virtuous. Men of principle tend to be bold, but just because someone is bold does not mean that he is necessarily a man of principle."[20] Sherem exemplified this truth—as do many who fight against the Church and kingdom of God.

On a related note, this miracle reminds us that—though there will always be those who challenge the Church—their reign will not last. For a time they may act with great sophistry and success. They may shake the faith of many. However, eventually God will expose their wrongs and lies, in due course they will have to acknowledge that what they have said and taught was false, and they will finally be destroyed for their pernicious ways. This is the case not only for those who attack the doctrines and history of the Church but also for those who falsely attack our character. I'm reminded of a man I know—a man who is by no means evil but who loathes the Church and can't stop criticizing it. He feels he knows its doctrines better than the members themselves. The spirit he radiates is one of animosity toward the Saints and their beliefs. He looks for every opportunity to "poke us in the eye," *per se*. I wish no harm on this brother, and I have every hope that God will be merciful to him at the judgment bar. However, I do believe the day will come when this friend of mine will "be brought to stand before God" and will have "a bright recollection of all [his] guilt" (Alma 11:43). He will know at that point that he spent much of his life fighting against God and the truths of His divinely restored gospel. God will love him and, like Sherem, forgive him, I hope. Nevertheless, that day will come, and it will bring him a measure of discomfort, I have no doubt.

An important lesson we can draw from this miracle is the reality that "Sherem was able to deceive the people because their love of God and understanding of the scriptures was seriously deficient (Jacob 7:10–11, 23; Alma 33:14)."[21] Had they been better versed, the anti-Christ would have been much less effective.

It is inconceivable how an individual could hope to dislodge a prophet of God from his station of certainty in the faith. But Sherem brazenly makes the attempt. How might we apply this encounter to our own situation? Are we unshakable in our faith? Is the foundation upon which we stand as sure as the foundation upon which the prophets of the Lord stand? Through faith, devotion, continually studying and pondering the word of God, constant prayer, and the cultivation of a service-minded love for our fellowmen, we can also become unshakable so that no anti-Christ or evil influence can dislodge us from our spiritual moorings. The Lord said to Oliver Cowdery: "Wherefore, if you shall build . . . upon the foundation of my gospel and my rock, the gates of hell shall not prevail against you" (D&C 18:5). Yet Oliver failed to secure himself upon the rock of the Savior and fell away from his high office. We can learn a lesson from that. . . . We can follow the counsel of the Lord's prophets.[22]

Are we where we need to be spiritually so that we can withstand attacks on the Church or upon our personal testimonies? Such attacks are sure to increase in the last days as the world grows more and more wicked and, thus, the Church appears to be more and more at odds with the trends of society. Are you doing what is necessary to insulate and inoculate yourself? Do not be naïve, for even the very elect shall fall if they neglect to daily do the basics (Matthew 24:24).

While in graduate school I had a professor—once the dean of the divinity school at Yale—who informed our class that no one in the Old Testament—no prophet or patriarch—had any idea that Jesus was coming or that their rites and sacrifices were types of Him. Rather, he said, we Christians just like to read Jesus back into the Hebrew Bible. We see Him in places that the authors of Old Testament books never intended Him to be seen. We have inappropriately Christianized the books of the Hebrew Bible, he said. I remember being shocked that a man who professed to be Christian would also deny that prophets in the pre-Christian era had any clue as to what all of this is really about. In this miracle, Jacob informed Sherem that "none of the prophets have written, nor prophesied, save they have spoken concerning this Christ" (Jacob 7:11). One author pointed out, "The Lord gave the law of Moses as a type to cause the children of Israel to look forward to the redemption of Christ. . . . Satan makes every effort to strip Christ out of the lives of God's children, including removing Christ from the very types, shadows, and the likenesses that are designed to draw God's children to Him."[23] Lucifer doesn't want us to see Jesus in the scriptures or the temple. He doesn't want us to recognize Him in our lives or in the faces of those around us. He wants us to forget Him or, at least, neglect Him every chance we get. That's what Sherem was trying to get the Nephites to do, and that's what our modern culture is doing to us. Are you watching? Are you seeking His face constantly?

I'll mention one final application. I find touching the statement that after Sherem was struck down, the members of the Church "nourished [him] for the space of many days" (verse 15). Whether you perceive that nourishing as spiritual or physical or both, there is something beautiful about how they rallied around a man who sought to destroy them and their faith, and "nourished" him, tending to his every need. Speaking to those who did not embrace the restored gospel, the Prophet Joseph once said, "If ye will not embrace our religion, accept our hospitality."[24] Translation? The Latter-day Saints should be hospitable, even to their enemies. And not just in dire circumstances such as that depicted in this miracle, but in *all* circumstances.

NOTES

1. The LDS Bible Dictionary defines what an anti-Christ is in this way: "One who would assume the guise of Christ, but in reality would be opposed to Christ (1 Jn. 2:18, 22; 4:3–6; 2 Jn. 1:7). In a broader sense it is anyone or anything that counterfeits the true gospel or plan of salvation and that openly or secretly is set up in opposition to Christ. The great anti-Christ is Lucifer, but he has many assistants both as spirit beings and as mortals. See 2 Thes. 2:1–12; Rev. 13:17: Jacob 7:1–23; Alma 1:2–16; 30:6–60" [*LDS Bible Dictionary* (1979), 609].
2. Nibley speaks of Sherem as addressing Jacob "very benevolently" [Nibley (2004), 1:323. See also 1:325]. In addition, see Ogden and Skinner, who state, "Sherem approached 'Brother Jacob' in a false spirit of brotherhood" [Ogden and Skinner (2011), 1:283]. See also Gardner, who suggested "Sherem's addressing him as 'Brother Jacob' creates the illusion of shared belief and [that] their discussion [is] as one between believers, not as an attack from the outside" (which it really is) [Gardner (2007), 2:569].
3. The suggestion that Sherem feared that he might become a "son of perdition" comes from footnote 19b (in Jacob 7:19). There it explicitly interprets Sherem's fear of having committed the "unpardonable sin" as a fear of becoming a "son of perdition."
4. Nibley (2004), 1:329.
5. Gardner (2007), 2:565.
6. Largey (2003), 720. See also Gardner (2007), 2:570–71.
7. McConkie and Millet (1987–1991), 2:82–83.
8. See McConkie and Millet (1987–1991), 2:85.
9. Gardner (2007), 2:572–73.
10. See Reynolds and Sjodahl (1955–1961), 1:486.
11. Nibley (2004), 1:325.
12. McConkie and Millet (1987–1991), 2:89; emphasis in original.
13. Nibley (2004), 1:325–26.
14. Gardner (2007), 2:574.
15. See Nibley (2004), 1:325. See also Ryken, Wilhoit and Longman (1998), 522.

16. See Kevin J. Todeschi, *The Encyclopedia of Symbolism* (New York: A Perigee Book, 1995), 106; Cooper (1982), 112.

17. Wilson (1999), 112. See also Ryken, Wilhoit and Longman (1998), 198.

18. See Pinegar and Allen (2007), 294.

19. McConkie and Millet (1987–1991), 2:83.

20. Confucius, *The Analects*, Book 14:4.

21. Largey (2003), 720.

22. Pinegar and Allen (2007), 293.

23. Largey (2003), 720.

24. See Ehat and Cook (1980), 162; Madsen (1989), 31.

MOSIAH INTERPRETS *the* WRITING *on the* STONE

OMNI 1:19–22

THE MIRACLE

The people of Zarahemla were a large nation who had many wars and contentions and who had experienced the corruption of both their language and their religion because "they had brought no records with them" when they first set out to the Americas.

Over time, Mosiah "caused that they should be taught his language" (Omni 1:18), and consequently, the people of Zarahemla (the Mulekites) united with the people of Mosiah and he was appointed their king.

During his reign, a large stone was brought to him, which had some engravings upon it. By the gift and power of God, Mosiah interpreted the writings, which gave an account of Coriantumr (the last of the Jaredites) and recorded a few details about the confounding of the languages of the people when they built their "tower" and also regarding their ultimate destruction (verse 22).[1]

BACKGROUND

One commentator pointed out that "Mesoamerica is unique in the Western hemisphere for its writing systems. . . . Part of that tradition includes inscriptions on stelae, or large stones."[2] In this miracle a stela carved during the latter years of the Jaredites is discovered and translated. The content of the stela is primarily an account of the last days of the Jaredite people.

Owing to the fact that the stela appears to speak of things very near the end of the Jaredite nation, Brant Gardner suggested that Mosiah may have given an "inspired" translation of the stone rather than a word-for-word translation.

> Carving a stela takes time and resources to support the carvers. Without a kingdom, Coriantumr would have had no means of providing support, would not likely have been himself a carver, and most certainly would not have wanted to memorialize his defeat [in writing]. . . .
>
> Since the information [regarding] Coriantumr comes through Mosiah's inspired (but perhaps not literal?) reading of the stone, the explanation may be a prophetic/seeric "reading" of the stone, supplying information that does not appear in its inscription. Mosiah would be using the stone as a base text but expanding it with information about the Jaredite destruction [received through revelation].[3]

In the end, there is no way of saying. However, the likelihood that Coriantumr was the carver of the stone seems remote; as does the suggestion that whoever carved it had the details of the destruction of the people before they happened. Thus, it makes sense the Mosiah may have been giving a "springboard" translation wherein the writing on the stone stela inspired him with revelation beyond its contents— whatever those may have been.

Regarding exactly how King Mosiah translated the stone brought to him, one commentary on the Book of Mormon explains,

> Mosiah translated the engravings on the large stone discovered by the people of Zarahemla (the Mulekites) through the Urim and Thummim. . . . It was done "by the gift and power of God" (v. 20), the power by which [the Urim and Thummim] worked. His grandson, Mosiah son of Benjamin, had possession of the "two stones which were fastened into the two rims of a bow. Now these things were prepared from the beginning, and were handed down from generation to generation, for the purpose of interpreting languages" (Mosiah 28:13-14). . . . While there is no record given of where Mosiah had obtained the Urim and Thummim, it is not mentioned as being with the records found by Limhi's people in searching for the land of Zarahemla (Mosiah 21:25–27). Nor was it with the large stone brought to Mosiah. We do know that Joseph Smith used the one "given to the brother of Jared on the mount" (D&C 17:1). We will have to wait for the larger plates of Nephi to come forth to know where Mosiah obtained them.[4]

SYMBOLIC ELEMENTS

Perhaps the most important symbol in this miracle narrative is the stone brought to King Mosiah. Stones are used in a number of ways in scripture, but one symbolic meaning often associated with them is permanence, immortality, imperishability, eternal, and so on.[5] The stone King Mosiah translated carried an immortal story with an eternal truth behind it: namely, when we cease to trust in the Lord and instead place our trust in the arm of flesh, we will surely lose the protection and direction of our God (D&C 1:19). Just as the Jaredites were destroyed as a society, we too run the risk of our utter ruin—as a nation or as individuals—if we do not keep the Lord central to all that we do.[6]

APPLICATION AND ALLEGORIZATION

The importance of Lehi's sons being sent back to Jerusalem to get the plates of brass (1 Nephi 3:2–4) is highlighted by the story of the Mulekites—who "brought no records with them" (Omni 1:17). Because they had no written records, their language became corrupted, as did their doctrine (Omni 1:17). Thus, "the Lord . . . sent . . . the plates of brass which contained the record of the Jews" (verse 14) as a means of teaching the people of Mulek the Nephite language and the true doctrine, thereby facilitating the uniting of the two people under the leadership of King Mosiah. The backstory to this miracle reminds us that to be without or to not use scriptures can equate to not knowing God. Just as the Mulekites did not know their God because they didn't have scriptures in their lives, so also you and I run this risk if scripture isn't central to our daily lives. Elder L. Lionel Kendrick of the Seventy stated, "The pattern" of the Mulekites "is the same for individuals as it is for nations. Without searching the scriptures, they cease to know the Savior."[7] Indeed, one of the great benefits of reading scriptures each *morning* (as one begins the day) is that the Spirit of God's words can temper us throughout the day as frustrating encounters arise with coworkers, customers, or family members. Minus that influence in our lives, we are prone to "forget" God and allow the natural man to reign. However, if we begin the day with the scriptures at the forefront of our minds, the odds of their spirit tempering our own in the hour of temptation is greatly enhanced.

This miracle also reminds us that prophets, seers, and revelators can know things the laity do not. God has endowed them with gifts beyond their own so they may receive and convey the messages He would have His children hear. We need not worry ourselves about the humanity of those who preside over the Lord's Church specifically *because* they have a mantle that makes them more than "good men." It makes them prophets of the Most High!

Finally, in this miracle we are reminded that, where God needs us to be instruments in His hands, He can endow us with spiritual gifts that will enable us to be His instruments. The Book of Mormon is certainly a testament to the existence of prophets, seers, and revelators. But it is also a witness to the fact that God takes normal men and women and uses them in extraordinary ways. He certainly wishes to make you and me a part of this great work. Are we living our lives in such a way that we can be His tools?

NOTES

1. Nibley has suggested that this may not have been the Tower of Babel, as we always assume. He stated, "Notice that it doesn't say the Tower of Babel. That's very important. As a matter of fact, we learn from the book of Ether in the Book of Mormon that the name isn't Babel, but it's Nimrod, which is exactly what it was. Remember it went north in the valley of Nimrod. Now we know through tradition and everything else that the tower was called 'Nimrod's Tower,' because Babel didn't come in until later. That was determined from the philological events, etc. And so they came out from the tower. It's careful not to say the 'Tower of Babel,' which was later. But Nimrod's Tower was that one, and it tells us in the first verse of the second chapter of the book of Ether that they went up into the valley northward where there never had men been, and it was the valley of Nimrod. Nimrod was the big name at that time" [Nibley (2004), 1:345].
2. Gardner (2007), 3:64.
3. Gardner (2007), 3:65. See Garner 3:64–65.
4. Nyman (2003–2004), 2:164. See also Joseph Fielding Smith, *Doctrines of Salvation*, three volumes in one (Salt Lake City: Bookcraft, 1998), 3:223–24.
5. See Cooper (1982), 160; Tresidder (2000), 115.
6. While the Lord will not allow the Church (as a whole) to fall into apostasy again, as individuals we can fall—and, as a nation, we may collapse if we ignore the commandments of God.
7. L. Lionel Kendrick, cited in Bassett (2007–2008), 2:28.

ABINADI CANNOT *Be* SLAIN *until* HE DELIVERS HIS MESSAGE

MOSIAH 13:1–7

THE MIRACLE

Abinadi had come before the court of King Noah to testify against him and his priests for their wickedness. So angered were they at his words that they threw him in prison. However, after he languished for a time in a cell, the priests requested of the king permission to question Abinadi, "that they might cross him, that thereby they might have wherewith to accuse him" (Mosiah 12:19).

After listening to the Lord's prophet chastise them a second time, King Noah said, "Away with this fellow. . . . Slay him . . . for he is mad!" (13:1). As the servants of Noah sought to lay hands upon Abinadi, he withstood them, saying, "Touch me not, for God shall smite you if ye lay your hands upon me, for I have not delivered the message which the Lord sent me to deliver; neither have I told you that which ye requested that I should tell; therefore, God will not suffer that I shall be destroyed at this time. But I must fulfil the commandments wherewith God has commanded me. . . . But I finish my message; and then it matters not whither I go, if it so be that I am saved" (verses 3–4, 9).

We are told that Abinadi spoke "with power and authority" and "his face shone with exceeding luster" (verses 5, 6). The people dared not lay their hands on him because they feared the power that seemed to radiate from the person of Abinadi.

Once again, he rebuked them and condemned them because they were angry with him for speaking the truth. Ultimately Abinadi testified that whatever they chose to do with him (after he had delivered the message God had sent him to convey) would be but a type and shadow of what God would do to them.

BACKGROUND

Who was in the crowd that sought to arrest God's prophet? While we may typically imagine the priests of Noah making up the bulk of the throng, Reynolds and Sjodahl suggest that it was likely more than just the king's wicked clerics: "At the King's command, the unfriendly throng that had gathered in Noah's counsel chamber, including among them his wanton priests, attempted to seize Abinadi to carry out the dread decision of the wasted king."[1]

Noah uses the phrase "away with this *fellow*" (verse 1). In Joseph Smith's day, the word *fellow* was not a term of endearment. Rather, it meant "a man without good breeding or worth; an ignoble man."[2] Thus, King Noah's language reveals the disdain he had for the Lord's prophet, one whom he considered undeserving to stand in his presence.

The book of Mosiah tells us that when the crowd sought to lay hands on Abinadi, he "withstood" them. One commentary on the Book of Mormon suggested that the prophet was given "strength . . . from on high" to physically push back those who sought to restrain him.[3]

The glowing of Abinadi's face evidences the reality that he was transfigured.[4] "*Transfiguration* is a special change in appearance and nature which is wrought upon a person or thing by the power of God. This divine transformation is from a lower to a higher state; it results in a more exalted, impressive, and glorious condition."[5] This state of transfiguration was also the means by which Abinadi's enemies were prevented from arresting him.

SYMBOLIC ELEMENTS

As with all prophets of God, Abinadi was a type for Christ. Not only did what he taught mirror the teachings of the Savior, but his very life—in many ways—also foreshadowed Christ's.

> Abinadi's life can be seen as a type or a foreshadowing of several details of the life of Christ. Abinadi, like Christ, faced questioning by corrupt priests whose efforts were to "cross him, that thereby they might have wherewith to accuse him" (Mosiah 12:17; cf. Matt. 26:59–66). Both Abinadi and Christ answered questions to the astonishment of their audience (Mosiah 12:19; cf. Matt. 22:46; Luke 2:47). The charge against Abinadi was for teaching that "God himself should come down among the children of men, and take upon him the form of man" (Mosiah 13:34; 17:7–8). The charge against Christ was that he "being a man, makest [himself] God" (John 10:33; Matt. 26:63–65). King Noah, like Pilate, was willing to let him go, yet the voice of the crowd objecting, "He has reviled the king," would not permit it (Mosiah 17:11–12; cf. John 19:4–15). Neither Abinadi nor Christ was taken and executed until his mortal mission was completed (Mosiah 13:2–3; cf. John 10:18; 19:11; Matt. 26:53–54).[6]

The transfiguration of Abinadi, though a physical reality, also served as a significant symbol. The change that came upon him was as a mantle, testifying of God's support and power, with which Abinadi had been endowed.

> Abinadi's warning not to touch him echoes Nephi's experience in building the ship when he warns off his angry brothers. The brothers received that message just as clearly as Noah's court (1 Ne. 17:47–49). Moses's face, after he descended from Mount Sinai, shone so brightly that he veiled himself (Ex. 34:30). Heavenly beings are frequently described in terms of "light" (see, for instance, JS—History 1:16, 30). Manifestations from the spiritual realm may be accompanied by what we perceive as light, and the powerful presence of the Spirit with Abinadi transformed and lighted his face. Possibly the light extended to his entire person but was most evident in his face as that would be where the priests would naturally concentrate their vision.[7]

The transfiguration of Abinadi places him in good company. The glow that radiated from his countenance was a symbolic testament that he was a man of God, and one who spoke (with power and authority) the words of God.

APPLICATION AND ALLEGORIZATION

This miracle is a testament to the fact that God's servants are endowed with power and the promise of protection in order to accomplish the mission the Father has for them. For all of his efforts, Satan cannot defeat God's work. He may successfully hinder this or that for a time. However, the purposes of the Lord will ultimately triumph, and His faithful servants will come off victorious. The Lord has promised, "The works, and the designs, and the purposes of God cannot be frustrated, neither can they come to naught" (D&C 3:1). This promise applies as much to the laity as it does to those foreordained to preside over this work. As President Spencer W. Kimball noted, "It has been said that the death of a righteous man is never untimely because our Father sets the time. I believe that with all my soul."[8] When God calls any of us to do His work and will, He can protect us to accomplish it. And through His Spirit, He can ensure that those to whom we minister will feel of our power, sense God is with us, and recognize His influence upon us.[9]

McConkie and Millet gave the following application of this miracle: "We . . . note with interest the verity that purity and truth can tolerate the existence of wickedness and falsehood, while the reverse never seems to be the case. Wickedness and falsehood, like weeds, seek to exclude, retard, and strangle that which produces good food, raiment, beauty, and fragrance."[10] If we are filled with the Spirit of Christ, we can have compassion on, and love for, those who see the world differently than we do. Nevertheless, Satan will continually stir up to anger those who serve him—and they will ever seek to destroy that which is of God. As Truman Madsen once noted, "Light always stirs up darkness. That is an eternal law."[11] And so it is. If we're not experiencing this, perhaps we're batting for the wrong team.

NOTES

1. Reynolds and Sjodahl (1955–1961), 2:137. See also Gardner (2007), 3:277.
2. See Don Norton, cited in Gardner (2007), 3:277.
3. See Reynolds and Sjodahl (1955–1961), 2:137.
4. See McConkie and Millet (1987–1991), 1:139; Odgen and Skinner (2011), 1:335; Rust (1994): 42.
5. Bruce R. McConkie, *Mormon Doctrine*, second edition (Salt Lake City: Bookcraft, 1979), 803.

6. Robert J. Matthews, "Abinadi," in Largey (2003), 23.

7. Gardner (2007), 3:278. See also Ogden and Skinner (2011), 1:335.

8. Spencer W. Kimball, cited in Bassett (2007–2008), 2:64.

9. McConkie and Millet pointed out, "As it was with Joseph Smith, so it was with Abinadi, and, for that matter, so it is with all of the household of faith" [McConkie and Millet (1987–1991), 2:213].

10. McConkie and Millet (1987–1991), 2:212.

11. Madsen (1989), 56.

THE BURDENS *of* ALMA *and* HIS PEOPLE *Are* MADE LIGHT

MOSIAH 24:14–15

THE MIRACLE

More than twenty years after Alma had fled the court of King Noah, he and his people found themselves living under the dominion and authority of Amulon, who had been appointed a "king and a ruler" over them by the king of the Lamanites (Mosiah 23:39).

Amulon despised Alma for his defection from their priestly quorum and, thus, aggressively persecuted him and his people. They were forbidden to pray, were greatly afflicted, and were threatened with death. But, in faith, they pled with the Lord for intervention, and the voice of the Lord came to them, saying,

> Lift up your heads and be of good comfort, for I know of the covenant which ye have made unto me; and I will covenant with my people and deliver them out of bondage. And I will also ease the burdens which are put upon your shoulders, that even you cannot feel them upon your backs, even while you are in bondage; and this will I do that ye may stand as witnesses for me hereafter, and that ye may know of a surety that I, the Lord God, do visit my people in their afflictions. (Mosiah 24:13–14)

The scripture informs us that the Lord did strengthen Alma and his people so that they could "bear up their burdens with ease," and do so with "cheerfulness" and "patience." And "they poured out their thanks to God because he had been merciful unto them, and eased their burdens" (verse 21).

BACKGROUND

Alma and Amulon had served as priests under King Noah. While both heard the testimony and stinging rebuke of Abinadi, only one allowed it to change his heart and, thus, his life. Alma repented and sought the forgiveness of the Lord. Amulon, however, hardened his heart and continued to live a riotous life while he persecuted the righteous.

SYMBOLIC ELEMENTS

Burdens and bondage are standard symbols for the distractions of life, which keep us from fully consecrating ourselves to the Lord, because we are addicted to or weighed down by some other god or some other thing.[1] Jesus indicated that He had come to give us the truth, and that truth would make us "free" (John 8:32). He added that the Father had sent Him "to proclaim release to the captives and . . . to let the oppressed go free" (*NRSV* Luke 4:18).[2] Time and again the Apostle Paul equated sin with spiritual bondage and burdens (see Galatians 5:13; Romans 6:16–18, 20–22; Ephesians 3:1; 4:1). Sometimes that bondage or burden comes because of our own choices and sins. But at other times we find ourselves burdened or in bondage because of the sins and actions of others—or simply because of the fallen nature of the mortal condition.[3] Either way, Christ is the answer. He is the one, and only one, who can free us from the burdens of the mortal experience.

APPLICATION AND ALLEGORIZATION

God will not always remove the burdens that confront us, but—*if we are faithful*—He will make them bearable. He will visit us in our afflictions, and He will give us the strength necessary to endure with cheerfulness and patience those things we are called to bear. But we, like Alma and his people, must turn to Him in faith.

In the economy and omniscience of God, it was intended that mortality be a time of trial, a place of struggle. And it is in his extremities, in the fiery flames of adversity, that man often finds the needed motivation to search out and come to know his God. It is not to be supposed that gospel covenants and promises shelter man from the winds and storms which come to all; indeed, acceptance of the responsibilities of mortality and the agreement to be in the world but not of the world presuppose that the Saints of the Most High will "suffer for well doing" (1 Peter 3:17), will undergo "tribulation in their Redeemer's name" (D&C 138:13). Since the Saints have been called upon to bear greater burdens, a merciful God endows them with a power from on high, with vision and strength that they, even in suffering, might have dominion over all things. The promise is sure that "whosoever shall put their trust in God shall be supported in their trials, and their troubles, and their afflictions, and shall be lifted up at the last day" (Alma 36:3).[4]

Elder Neal A. Maxwell pointed out, "We may feel 'put upon' by events and circumstances. . . . And yet these things which we feel 'put upon' with actually constitute the customized curriculum needed for our personal development. Too often we push away the necessary and prescribed courses of 'spiritual calisthenics,' as if we could withdraw from all of life's courses and still remain enrolled in school."[5]

As the old colloquialism goes: "Pain is inevitable. [However,] misery is optional."[6] For those of us not strapped with the cross of clinical depression (or other mental health factors), our faith in and faithfulness to the Lord determines the degree to which our burdens weigh us down.

As a related application, Alma and his people didn't simply bear their burdens with ease; they did so "cheerfully." Elder Jeffrey R. Holland shared what he termed "one of Elder Holland's maxims for living." He said, "No misfortune is so bad that whining about it won't make it worse."[7] For all of our trials and suffering in this life—and we will *all* have trials and suffering!—cheerfulness and hopefulness will do more to carry us through than will murmuring, doubting, and nurturing fears. Faith, not fear, allows us to ride out the storms of life. Fear is paralyzing. Faith is empowering. As Nibley said, "The most powerful form of thought is faith."[8] Again, these are choices we can and must make. But they will make all the difference in the heaviness of the burdens we bear.

It should be remembered, if God doesn't remove the burdens we are carrying, that does not mean that our prayers have gone unanswered. As has been said, "Sometimes he calms the storm, and sometimes he calms the sailor."[9] God's answer to our petitions may be to remove our trial. However, it may instead be to equip us for the storm. Either way, the prayer has been heard and God has intervened. The ungrateful will not see that. The faith-filled, however, will perceive and know.

Finally, Elder Maxwell suggested the importance of being willing to say not only "Thy will be done, O Lord" but also "Thy timing be done" as well.[10] This miracle can remind us of the importance of "waiting upon the Lord" (Psalm 37:9). Sometimes He requires that we trust His choice to not remove our burdens—believing that such must be what's best for us and all involved, even when we can't see the "whys" of His decision (Isaiah 55:8–9).

NOTES

1. See Ryken, Wilhoit, and Longman (1998), 112–13.

2. While the context of this verse is Christ's ministry to the spirit world, it seems evident that He did this as much for those still in mortality as He did for those who have passed beyond the veil.

3. One Latter-day Saint scholar noted the following: "The question may be asked why Alma's group was put into bondage since they had repented, had made covenants, and had served the Lord for some time. The answer seems to go back to Abinadi's prophecy. When he first came to the Nephites in the land of Nephi, he warned that they would be brought into bondage if they did not repent (see Mosiah 11:21). This warning went unheeded until Abinadi returned two years later. His warning then proclaimed that they would be brought into bondage, and if they still refused to repent they would be destroyed (see Mosiah 12:2, 8). It was at this time that Alma was converted and began to teach the words of Abinadi secretly to those Nephites who would listen. Thus, even though Alma and his people had repented, it was still necessary that Abinadi's first prophecy be fulfilled—as the majority had *not* repented.

"A great principle we can learn from this portion of the book of Mosiah (chapters 19–24) is that the longer we wait to repent and forsake our sins, the more serious the consequences will be. Elder Melvin J. Ballard reiterated this principle: 'Every man and woman who is putting off until the next life the task of correcting and overcoming the weakness of the flesh are sentencing themselves to years of bondage, for no man or woman will come forth in the resurrection until he has completed his work, until he has overcome, until he has done as much as he can do' (242).

Sadly, for many this bondage has already begun in this life. As with Limhi and his people, if we are slow to hearken to the counsel of the Lord, we only make our transformation to freedom more difficult and increase the degree of our bondage."

[See Clyde J. Williams, "Deliverance From Bondage," in Monte S. Nyman and Charles D. Tate, Jr., editors, *Mosiah: Salvation Only Through Christ* (Provo, UT: Religious Studies Center, 1991), 272]

4. McConkie and Millet (1987–1991), 2:286–87.

5. Neal A. Maxwell, Friday, February 2, 2001, CES, *Evening with a General Authority*, broadcast live from the Tabernacle on Temple Square in Salt Lake City, UT. See also See Neal A. Maxwell, *The Promise of Discipleship* (Salt Lake City: Deseret Book, 2001), 80–81. Elder Hartman Rector Jr. offered an example of the important principle of submission: "My dad was smarter than I was when I was seven years old. Of course, I was smarter than he was when I was seventeen, but that changed later, too. He said to me one time, 'You are not big enough to milk the cows.' Now, I knew I was. I was seven years old, and I knew I could milk the cows. So I proved to him that I could. My dad said, 'You know, I believe you can milk. You've got the job.' For the next ten years I milked eight to twelve cows night and morning. You may rest assured I got to the place where I did not want to milk, and once I said to Dad, 'Dad, I don't want to milk.' He said, 'That's all right. You don't have to want to—as long as you do it.' This seems to be what the Lord says to us at times when the going gets rough and we feel—'I really don't want to go to the temple,' or 'It is inconvenient to pay tithing,' or 'I don't want to go home teaching'" [Hartman Rector Jr., "The Gospel," *Ensign*, November 1985, 74–75].

6. See Hyrum W. Smith, *Pain Is Inevitable, Misery Is Optional* (Salt Lake City: Deseret Book, 2004).

7. Jeffrey R. Holland, "The Tongue of Angels," *Ensign*, May 2007, 18.

8. Nibley (2004), 129.

9. *The Other Side of Heaven*, cited in Ogden and Skinner (2011), 1:370.

10. Neal A. Maxwell, "Plow in Hope," *Ensign*, May 2001, 59.

GOD FREES ALMA
and HIS PEOPLE *from*
LAMANITE BONDAGE

MOSIAH 24:16–24

THE MIRACLE

Alma and his people had been living in bondage to the Lamanites and were grievously persecuted by them. They had pled for the Lord's intervention and had "submitted cheerfully and with patience to all the will of the Lord" (Mosiah 24:15).

Having seen their faith and patience, the Lord spoke to them, promising them freedom from their captors: "Be of good comfort, for on the morrow I will deliver you out of bondage" (verse 16).

With the promise of God—and surely with limited perspective as to how His hand would be manifest—Alma and his people secretly prepared themselves to depart, trusting in the Lord's promise of freedom.

"And in the morning the Lord caused a deep sleep to come upon the Lamanites, yea, and all their task-masters were in a profound sleep. And Alma and his people departed into the wilderness" (verses 19–20). So deep and universal was the sleep that Alma and his people were enabled to take with them their flocks, grain, and other needed supplies.

Once they arrived in the valley of Alma, they "poured out their thanks to God because he had been merciful unto them . . . and had delivered them out of bondage." They "gave thanks to God, yea, and . . . lifted up their voices in the praises of their God" (verses 21–22). And as they continued on in their journey, they had the promise of the Lord that He would stop the Lamanites in the valley of Alma, that they would pursue them no farther.

BACKGROUND

As it relates to the cause of the drowsiness that came upon the Lamanites guarding Alma and his people, one commentary suggested this:

> Both the Limhites and the Almaites leave with their belongings past sleeping guards. However, Limhi's guards were sleeping because of extra wine [Mosiah 22] while Yahweh himself caused a deeper sleep to come upon the Lamanites guarding [the land of] Helam. Perhaps this detail suggests that Alma's group had relied almost entirely on their new faith throughout their existence as a people, while the Limhites, who were in the process of repentance, were more used to relying upon themselves rather than Yahweh. In each case, Yahweh causes a miracle; but perhaps the more active role of the Limhites reflects that, though strong of faith, they still saw themselves as an important part of their own destiny.[1]

The nature of our spiritual experiences is certainly governed by the level of faith we are able to muster at a given time in our lives.

SYMBOLIC ELEMENTS

The "deep sleep" that came upon the Lamanite guards carries a *slightly* different symbolic connotation than the "deep sleep" that is said to have come upon Adam during the creation. Adam's sleep represented the veil of forgetting, which we each receive when we enter mortality. (Thus, our lives seem mirrored in their lives.) The "deep sleep" of the guards can also be seen as a symbol for "forgetting"—but not a forgetting caused by the placement of the premortal veil. Instead, the sleep of the guards well represents the reality that God had intervened—causing them to "forget" their duties and obligations—so that Alma and his people might escape.[2] As one commentator put it, sleep is "associated with being unconscious to the external environment."[3] And this the guards absolutely were.

The act of naming the valley "Alma" has been seen by commentators as a symbolic gesture. One text highlighted the implications of this act. "The naming of the valley Alma is certainly symbolic, since the Almaites are only a single day away from their oppressors and they certainly would not have considered putting down permanent roots. Nevertheless, the naming reconfirms Alma's leadership."[4]

APPLICATION AND ALLEGORIZATION

Humans are prone to plead with the Lord when they need something, or when some trial is upon them. As the old saying goes, "There are no atheists in foxholes." However, when life is good and when our trials are abated, it is the natural tendency of man to forget his God (Helaman 12:2). In this miracle, Alma and his people set an example for us to follow. Upon their escape, and even before they had reached a place of safety, they knelt down and thanked God for their deliverance, praising Him for their many blessings—past and present.[5] We too should be more prone to gratitude, more aware of how much the Lord blesses us each and every day. And we should express that gratitude constantly in our prayers and through living lives faithful to Him.

Though Alma's people did not know how the Lord would free them, nevertheless, they exercised their faith by making preparations to leave. We too must have sufficient faith in the Lord to act when He makes us promises—whether those promises come in the form of a patriarchal blessing, counsel from a priesthood leader, words of living prophets, or even promptings of the Holy Spirit. When the Lord promises us blessings, it is our duty to act so that those blessings may come to fruition.

Offering a modern application of the narrative of this miracle, BYU's Dr. Monte Nyman explained,

> One of the purposes of the Book of Mormon is to warn us of the situations and experiences that were among the Nephites so that we may [know how to] avoid like situations and experiences. There are many other kinds of bondage in addition to physical bondage. A person may be bound by intellectual pursuits, financial extensions, social customs, or others. The formula is essentially the same for deliverance from all these conditions, and there is none but the God of Abraham, Isaac, and Jacob who can and will deliver his people (see Mosiah 7:19; 23:23 . . .). However, much more important is the admonition to prevent such bondage from occurring in our lives. The Book of Mormon suggests some preventions.[6]

In addition to the intellectual pursuits, financial extensions, social customs that can bind us, there are a host of other enticing and enslaving elements: pornography, drug addictions, alcohol, tobacco, eating disorders, pride, dishonesty. The list of Satan's tools is nearly endless. The scriptures and the words of the prophets hold the keys both to free us and to prevent us from becoming entangled in such satanic snares.

Finally, there is this obvious application of this miracle. God can cause our enemies to fall into a "deep sleep" so that they neglect to notice us or the activities in which we are engaged—which seem so prone to stir them up to anger and animosity. He can make them unaware of that which they might otherwise attack. Where necessary, our Father can blind them to our activities so that the work can move forward. As a singular example, we cite the experience of Nicholas Owen, an English contractor during the reign of Elizabeth I. Queen Elizabeth was the Protestant daughter of Henry VIII, and during her reign Catholics in England were aggressively persecuted. Owen, himself a Roman Catholic, determined to do what he could to save the lives of his brothers and sisters in Christ. Thus, he spent years designing countless hiding places for endangered Catholics. He built secret rooms between the walls of homes, quarters under the floors of houses, hiding places inside stone fences, underground passageways, and a variety of nooks and crannies that looked like anything but a hiding place. Owen viewed what he was doing as divinely inspired. Before he began one of his secret building projects, he would receive the sacrament of the Lord's Supper. He would also fervently pray throughout the building project. And once the hideaway was completed, he would dedicate it to God. It is said that "no one saved the lives of more Catholics in England during those days than Nicholas Owen."[7] Like Alma and his people, Nicholas Owen also experienced God's ability to hide his work from those who would seek to thwart it—even though Owen was but a commoner. And so it is with us. What God did for Alma and Nicholas, God can do for you and me as we faithfully do His work and keep our covenants. Our circumstances may be different, but God's need to use us is no less important today than it was centuries ago; and thus we, like they, have His promise.

Notes

1. Gardner (2007), 3:412–13.

2. Sleep is often a euphemism for death, though that connotation seems less applicable here [see Joseph Fielding McConkie and Donald W. Parry, *A Guide to Scriptural Symbols* (Salt Lake City: Bookcraft, 1990), 100].

3. Todeschi (1995), 238. See also Wilson (1999), 375.

4. Gardner (2007), 3:413.

5. It will be recalled that they thanked Him not only for their released but also for lightening their burdens during the time of their bondage (see Mosiah 24:21–22).

6. Nyman (2007), 2:456.

7. Robert J. Morgan, *On This Day in Christian History* (Nashville, TN: Thomas Nelson, 1997), s.v., March 22.

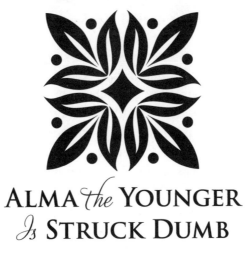

ALMA *the* YOUNGER
Is STRUCK DUMB

MOSIAH 27:8–24
ALMA 36:6–24

THE MIRACLE

Alma the Younger and the four sons of Mosiah (Ammon, Aaron, Omner, and Himni) had set out to destroy the Church of God. They were living lives of wickedness and idolatry, and because of their intellectual gifts, many were drawn away from the Church through their sophistry.

Alma the Elder and many of the members of the Church had prayed fervently that God would intervene, not only that Alma the Younger and the sons of Mosiah might each be stopped in their hindrance of the Church, but also that they might be brought to a knowledge of the truth. In response to the prayers of many, an angel of the Lord appeared to these five wayward souls and rebuked them—more particularly Alma the Younger. The angel's presence caused the earth to shake and caused the five of them to fall to the ground, trembling in fear.

Perhaps rhetorically, the angel asked Alma (in essence), Can you dispute God's power? Can you not feel how my voice causes the earth to shake? Can you not see me standing before you? He then commanded Alma the Younger, "Go thy way, and seek to destroy the church no more" (Mosiah 27:16). Alma was left unable to speak, and also so physically weakened that he had to be carried by his companions to the feet of his father, Alma the Elder.

When the Younger's father saw his wayward son's condition, he rejoiced, knowing that his prayers had been answered. Having fasted and prayed for the young boy to be "brought to a knowledge of the truth" (Mosiah 27:14), Alma the Elder and others now began to fast and pray that God would enable the boy to recover.

Again, the senior Alma's prayers were heard and answered with a blessing upon the head of his son. After three days of unconsciousness, Alma the Younger regained both his strength and his voice; and he also regained the Spirit of God, long absent from his life. Alma had repented and accepted the Lord and had been "born of the Spirit" and "redeemed of the Lord" (Mosiah 27:24).

The junior Alma and the repentant sons of Mosiah went about "zealously striving to repair all the injuries which they had done to the Church" (Mosiah 27:35), suffering many persecutions themselves and yet "bringing many to the knowledge of the truth, yea, to a knowledge of their Redeemer" (Mosiah 27:36).

BACKGROUND

Alma the Younger and the sons of Mosiah experienced a life-changing encounter with the Lord, one few in mortality have been privileged to have. In response to the question of why they were allowed this angelic "call to repentance" when so many others who have left the Church—and fought against it—have not been granted such a privilege, Joseph Fielding McConkie and Robert L. Millet wrote,

> First, . . . if all rebellious souls were accorded a personal visit from an angel assuring the reality of the world to come with its rewards and punishments, there would be little need for faith on anyone's part.
>
> Second, such appearances of angels would create the temptation to obtain a testimony by negative behavior rather than through righteousness. . . .
>
> Third, it could be that some appreciable number of people have had such an experience and have rejected the divine counsel and chosen not to repent, and thus we have no record of the experience.[1] . . .
>
> Fourth, the Savior explained that those who reject the testimony of scripture and living prophets would also reject the testimony of angels were they to appear to them (see Luke 16:31).
>
> Fifth, we have the testimony of scripture that "some have entertained angels unawares" (Hebrews 13:2), and we might suppose that

in many instances angels have sought to entice transgressors from their course in unobserved or less dramatic ways than this appearance to Alma and the sons of Mosiah.

Sixth, the prayers of the righteous cannot go unheard. Alma the Elder and Mosiah were both men of great faith who no doubt implored the heavens night and day with a plea of help to save their wayward sons. Nor did they pray alone, for their pleadings were joined by those of all the faithful of the Church in and around Zarahemla.

Seventh, . . . the Lord, who can manifest his power in a great variety of ways, is hardly limited to angelic ministrations or open visions. Many have had conversion experiences of spiritual impact and consequence equal to Alma's, experiences which are the result of a coalescence of circumstances divinely contrived: life-changing experiences involving such things as a confrontation with death, an inspired sermon, a caring parent or relative, or a sensitive priesthood leader.[2]

It seems noteworthy that Alma's conversion did not come about because he saw an angel. Rather, we are told it was the consequence of fasting and prayer, and because of what happened to him during his three days of unconsciousness. It was at least in part the suffering he endured for his sins and his willingness to accept Christ that brought about his conversion and his change of heart.[3]

When Alma the Younger speaks of his "eternal torment," this does not have reference to the duration of his suffering. Rather, it has reference to the nature of it. Thus, the Doctrine and Covenants informs us,

Nevertheless, it is not written that there shall be no end to this torment, but it is written endless torment. Again, it is written eternal damnation; wherefore it is more express than other scriptures, that it might work upon the hearts of the children of men, altogether for my name's glory. Wherefore, I will explain unto you this mystery, for it is meet unto you to know even as mine apostles. I speak unto you that are chosen in this thing, even as one, that you may enter into my rest. For, behold, the mystery of godliness, how great is it! For, behold, I am endless, and the punishment which is given from my hand is endless punishment, for Endless is my name. Wherefore—Eternal punishment is God's punishment. Endless punishment is God's punishment. (D&C 19:6–12)

God's names are "Eternal" and "Endless" (Moses 1:3; 7:35). Thus, His type of punishment is called "eternal" and "endless." It is called this because it comes from Him, and not to convey the idea that it has no end.

Commentators have pointed out that the book of Alma records that Alma the Younger "was racked . . . with the pains of a damned soul . . . for three days and for three nights" (Alma 36:16); while Mosiah 27:23 uses the language "two days and two nights." This has been seen by some as a contradiction between the two accounts.[4] However, since the statement in the book of Alma is in reference to the length of Alma's torment, and the reference in Mosiah is to the length of the fast on Alma's behalf, there is no obvious contradiction. Alma the Younger suffered for three days, but his family and friends fasted for two of those days.

One text on the Book of Mormon suggests that Alma and the sons of Mosiah were not the only rabble-rousers in their apostate group. Though the story focuses on these five, apparently others had engaged along with them in the anti-Church movement of which the famed five were a part.[5]

SYMBOLIC ELEMENTS

One commentator summarized the overarching symbolic message of Alma the Younger's conversion in this way:

> Alma has been fighting against the teaching of the Atoning Messiah who, according to prophecy, will die and be resurrected. Dramatically, Alma becomes a visual symbol of (spiritual) death and resurrection. As the Messiah before death was mortal and subject to the world (as Alma had proved to be), after resurrection, the Messiah (and Alma) would belong to Yahweh. While Alma was certainly not resurrected as a god, his tremendous transformation revealed him as new person, a powerful advocate for the church he had once persecuted.[6]

Certainly any type or symbol can be taken to the extreme—this one included. Nevertheless, the overarching idea of Alma's life as a symbol for death and resurrection is appealing.

Of the nature of the angel's appearance to Alma and the sons of Mosiah, Brant Gardner wrote, "The angel explicitly reminds Alma of three indubitable markers of divinity: the cloud, the voice as thunder, and the shaking of the earth."[7] Each of these signs were traditional symbols of God. The cloud reminds us of the way in which the

Lord led Israel through the wilderness after their exodus from Egypt (Exodus 13:21–22). The voice of thunder is a common symbol for the divine (Psalm 77:18; Revelation 14:2). And the shaking of the earth was often understood as a symbol of God's power manifest (Psalm 18:7; 60:2; Isaiah 2:19, 21).

As we have mentioned earlier in this text, falling to the earth is a traditional sign of awe and reverence for the divine. It is also a manifestation of fear—including holy fear (though these young men had less "holy fear" and more "fear of the holy"). This act of prostration is traditionally called *proskynēsis*,[8] and it evidences the overwhelming terror Alma and his friends were experiencing at the appearance of the angel.

The fact that Alma was struck "dumb" is the perfect symbol for what God was doing to his ministry of mayhem: silencing it. Alma had been using his gifts as a "man of many words" (Mosiah 27:8) to destroy the Church and the testimonies of many. Now God would take that gift from him, that he no longer used it for evil—returning it only when he was committed to use it for good.

The number three is the traditional scriptural number for that which is of God or that which comes from God. Thus, when the number three is associated with an act or person, the traditional implication is that whatever is associated with that number is divine in its origin or works. For example, there are three members of the First Presidency, symbolically reminding us of whose errand they are on. Jesus's body lay in the tomb three days, suggesting that the Atonement was God's will—a fulfillment of His eternal plans for Jesus and for each of His children (who would be blessed by it). Alma the Younger's three days of unconsciousness (Alma 36:10, 16) may well also be a symbolic depiction that God was behind his collapse and his conversion. As an additional symbolic application of the number three, one commentary offers this insight:

> These "three days" may be symbolic. . . . Jonah's three days in the belly of the beast would also serve as a model tying three days to a salvation theme (Jonah 1:17). Certainly a modern reader, armed with the understanding of the relationship of three days to Christ's death and resurrection can see an important parallel to Alma. Symbolically, Alma dies and is resurrected. . . . The repetition of the three days and three nights has a strong dramatic effect and centers Alma's symbolic death and resurrection on the Messiah.[9]

On a related note, the regaining of strength by Alma has also been seen as a symbol—a representation of "returning to life after literally being thought dead."[10] For all intents and purposes, Alma the Younger was dead. Because of his life of sinfulness, he was spiritually dead. Because of the path he was pursuing, his family and friends may have had every expectation that he would ultimately inherit eternal death (at the judgment bar of God). However, as this narrative suggests, God revived him, bringing him back to life spiritually and offering him the hope of eternal life.

APPLICATION AND ALLEGORIZATION

Few of the miracles of the Book of Mormon have more obvious life applications than does this account of the conversion of Alma the Younger. The following are but a few examples of lessons we can draw from this miraculous story.

God does not desire the pain or punishment of any of His children, including those who are living wicked lives. He seeks our happiness, and for that reason alone, He commands our obedience to Him. However, His purpose in commanding us to live in accordance with His law is not that He might control us. Rather, He desires that we be recipients of His blessings and happiness. Just as our nervous system gives us pain when we touch something hot—all in an effort to protect us—so also God allows or sends us discomfort in our wickedness in an attempt to protect and bless. There was nothing punitive about what happened to Alma. It was fully a manifestation of love, not an attempt at forcing compliance or obedience. God may allow us to experience trials to correct us and to bring us back to Him (when we have strayed); however, trials are often a blessing from God—as this one was in the life of Alma the Younger.[11]

Alma informs us that after he was "born again," he had an intense desire for others to "taste" of the joys he had "tasted" (Alma 36:24). When we are truly converted to Christ, we too have a desire to share that with which the Lord has blessed us. Indeed, for those who are fully converted, keeping such things locked within their heart is very difficult. They feel compelled to share with others the joy that is theirs—just as Father Lehi, once he had tasted of the fruit of the tree of life, desperately desired to share his blessing with others (1 Nephi 8:12).

Nibley applied this miracle as follows: "The experience of Alma the Younger and his friends is our experience. We must all decide how seriously we are going to take this side or the other side. He laughed at the other side and took it lightly. He wanted to make fun of it and have his fun here."[12] Alma's experience invites us to assess our own. To what degree do we have access to the truth but don't appreciate it? In what ways do we rebel against the things of God?

In his six-volume commentary on the Book of Mormon, Brant A. Gardner drew the following application of this miracle story:

> From this story, many modern parents take comfort and hope. Mosiah and Alma [the Elder] certainly taught their children the gospel. They provided homes that were probably above standard both spiritually and economically, since Mosiah was king and Alma the chief priest. Nevertheless, both families had at least one child who rejected parental teachings and followed ideas antithetical to their parents' beliefs. Many modern parents experience the same ordeal. Even when miraculous conversion does not await their children, the parents can at least take some comfort in understanding that even the best parents cannot fully prevent such departures from faith.[13]

We each have agency. Even parents who are faithful to their covenants and who rightly raise their children can yet have a wayward child or two. Such is the divine plan. To wish otherwise would be to side with the adversary in the great war in heaven. With Alma the Elder, it is our place to trust in God and pray for His intervention. But regardless of what happens, if we have faithfully taught our children, we cannot blame ourselves for their bad choices.

On a related note, this miracle testifies loudly to the influence parents can have over their children and, for that matter, to the influence a ward can have over a wayward child—if they will fervently pray for God's intervention on behalf of the one who is struggling or has strayed. As the New Testament informs us, "The effectual fervent prayer of a righteous man availeth much" (James 5:16).

It seems a lesson can also be drawn from this narrative regarding what our obligation is if we have failed to live up to what we know is true. In other words, if we are blessed with a "second chance"—as Alma the Younger and the sons of Mosiah were—we must do all we can to repair what damage we have done by our inactivity or through our raucous living. Indeed, whenever we sin we have a divinely given

obligation to do all that we can to repair the damage we have caused—
to the Church, to its image, to others, and to testimonies. One commentary pointed out, "There is a zeal and devotion that attends true
repentance."[14] If we are *truly* repentant, we should feel zealous about
repairing any damage we have caused, and we should anxiously seek to
bless those whom we may have harmed.

Another observable message in this story is the reality that sin
brings suffering. When we consciously choose to do wrong, we certainly cause Christ to suffer in His act of atonement on our behalf.
But additionally, even if we repent, we too suffer because of our sinful
choices. We suffer the loss of the Spirit for a time. We may suffer from
addictions. Often we suffer a loss of respectability in the eyes of others.
We may also experience a loss of quality of life. There can be no sin
without suffering. Those who sin casually, seeking to repent later,
clearly do not see the far-reaching implications of their choices.

The difference between Alma before and after his conversion is
instructive. Initially he is angry and cannot do enough to destroy the
Church, which he hates (Mosiah 27:8–10). After being born again,
his "soul did long" to be with God (Alma 36:22), and his only desire
was to build the kingdom of God. True conversion has the power to
change the nature, desires, demeanor, countenance, behaviors, motivations, and work of even the vilest of sinners. If one has truly been born
of God, the Lord has the ability to accomplish a complete 180-degree
change. "Is any thing too hard for the Lord?" (Genesis 18:14; Jeremiah
32:27). "Alma's experience dramatically illustrates the power that is in
Christ to bear our sins, to lift the burden of sin from the souls of those
who have been properly cleansed by their own suffering, granting them
a newness of life."[15]

Finally, this story reminds us that when the Lord deems it necessary, He can strike down those who challenge or hinder His work.
Exemplary of this is the experience of Wilford Woodruff, who had an
interaction with a former member of the Church while serving a mission in Arkansas:

> The spirit of the Lord came upon me like a rushing mighty wind and
> the voice of the spirit said to me go up again and visit Mr. Akeman and
> again bear testimony unto him of the truth of the Book of Mormon
> and the work of God. . . . I told him I had come to again bear testimony

unto him of the truth of the Book of Mormon and the work of God, in the danger of opposing that work. He soon was filled with wrath and indignation and he opposed me in the strongest terms, and raged against the leaders of the Church. . . . I felt that the house was filled with devils and awful darkness. I felt Horribly. I did not understand why the Lord should send me into the midst of such spirits. . . . I felt very strange [and] my tongue was glued to my mouth. I could not speak. I arose to my feet to leave the house. I felt . . . like fleeing as Lot did when He went out of Sodom, without looking behind me. Mr. Akeman followed me out the door close to my heels about 8 rods without either of us speaking. I know he was following close to me when about 8 rods from the House this strange feeling left me in a twinkling of an Eye and when Mr. Akeman got to the place where this feeling left me he fell dead at my feet as though he had been struck with a thunderbolt from Heaven.[16]

NOTES

1. "We know, for example, that Laman and Lemuel were rebuked by an angel and that they disregarded it (1 Nephi 3:29). And there is no evidence that they ever recorded such things" [McConkie and Millet (1987–1991), 2:305].

2. McConkie and Millet (1987–1991), 2:304–05. See also Nibley (2004), 2:151; Gardner (2007), 3:452.

3. See McConkie and Millet (1987–1991), 3:263–64.

4. See Reynolds and Sjodahl (1955–1961), 2:275. See also Gardner (2007), 3:456, 4:500. Gardner reads the "two days and two nights" as total four—a number "particularly auspicious" in Mesoamerican culture and representative (among ancient Mesoamericans) of "perfection." Thus, for Gardner, this may imply that Alma "experienced a 'perfect rebirth'" [Gardner (2007), 3:456].

5. See Gardner (2007), 3:448.

6. Gardner (2007), 3:455.

7. Gardner (2007), 3:453.

8. Nibley (2004), 1:325.

9. Gardner (2007), 4:500, 501.

10. See Gardner (2007), 4:502.

11. It is important to realize that trials come from many sources—not *just* from God. Elder Neal A. Maxwell pointed out, "Some things happen to us because of our own mistakes and our own sins, as contrasted with suffering brought on because we are Christian. Peter makes this distinction very well: 'But let none of you suffer as a murderer, or as a thief, or as an evildoer, or as a busybody in other men's matters. Yet if any man suffer as a Christian, let him not be ashamed; but let him glorify God on this behalf.' (1 Peter 4:15–16.) Even indecision—about whether or not to be a believer—can produce its own unnecessary trial and sorrows, as President Brigham

Young observed: 'As to trials, why bless your hearts, the man or woman who enjoys the spirit of our religion has no trials; but the man or woman who tries to live according to the Gospel of the Son of God, and at the same time clings to the spirit of the world, has trials and sorrows acute and keen, and that, too, continually.' (*Journal of Discourses*, 16:123.) . . . Still other trials and tribulations come to us merely as a part of living, for, as indicated in the scriptures, the Lord 'sendeth rain on the just and on the unjust.' (Matthew 5:45.) We are not immunized against all inconvenience and difficulties nor against aging. This type of suffering carries its own real challenges, but we do not feel singled out" [Neal A. Maxwell, *All These Things Shall Give Thee Experience* (Salt Lake City: Deseret Book, 1979), 29–30].

12. Nibley (2004), 2:151.

13. Gardner (2007), 3:447. Did their privileged lifestyles play any role in their rebelliousness? One can only conjecture. Nibley, speaking somewhat tongue-in-cheek, said, "And notice that the sons of no less than the great King Mosiah and the oldest son of Alma joined the hell-fire club, the smart-aleck club, and rejected the gospel completely. . . . These kids were rich, sophisticated, and cynical; they spoiled a lot of things" [Nibley (2004), 2:138]. Agency, rather than upbringing, seems to be their downfall.

14. McConkie and Millet (1987–1991), 3:268.

15. McConkie and Millet (1987–1991), 3:265.

16. Wilford Woodruff, in Thomas G. Alexander, *Things in Heaven and Earth: The Life and Times of Wilford Woodruff, a Mormon Prophet* (Salt Lake City: Signature Books, 1993), 40; spelling and punctuation as in Woodruff's original journal entry.

GOD PROVIDES *for* ALMA *the* YOUNGER

ALMA 8:18–22; 10:5–11

THE MIRACLE

Alma the Younger had been preaching the gospel in the city of Ammonihah. However, "Satan had gotten great hold upon the hearts of the people" (Alma 8:9), and thus, they rejected his message—reviling him, spitting upon him and, ultimately, casting him out of their city.

Alma left, as the citizens of Ammonihah had demanded, but he continued to fast and pray for the people of that community. The prophet felt great sorrow and anguish of soul over their faithlessness. In the midst of being "weighed down with sorrow" (Alma 8:14), an angel of the Lord appeared to him, encouraging him to lift up his head and rejoice because of his own faithfulness to God. Alma also received the command (through the angel) to return to Ammonihah and again preach repentance to the people, informing them that "except they repent the Lord would destroy them" (Alma 9:19).

Alma immediately returned to the city, entering "by another way" (Alma 8:18). Having fasted for several days, he was hungry. He met a man by the name of Amulek, who had himself left the Church. Alma said to him, "Will ye give to an humble servant of God something to eat?" (Alma 8:19). To which Amulek responded, "I know thou art a holy prophet of God, for thou art the man whom an angel said in vision: Thou shalt receive. Therefore, go with me into my house and I will impart unto thee of my food" (Alma 8:20).

Alma went with Amulek, was fed, and blessed him and his entire family. Amulek later testified to the people of Ammonihah that "he hath blessed mine house, he hath blessed me, and my women, and my children, and my father and my kinsfolk; yea, even all my kindred hath he blessed, and *the blessing of the Lord hath rested upon us according to the words which he spake*" (Alma 10:11; emphasis added).

BACKGROUND

Amulek was a descendant of Nephi and was a prominent citizen in Ammonihah. "A blueblood," as Nibley called him.[1] Lapsed in his faithfulness to the gospel, through his personal affluence, he lived a worldly lifestyle—even though earlier in his life he had witnessed "much of [God's] mysteries and his marvelous power" (Alma 10:5). It was the appearance of an angel, and the visit of Alma, that drew Amulek to Christ and turned him into a faithful missionary. In time, Amulek would sacrifice everything—home, family, friends, wealth, and even freedom—for his rediscovered faith in God.[2]

When Alma first entered Ammonihah, the people recognized him, saying, "We know that thou art Alma; and we know that thou art high priest over the church which thou hast established in many parts of the land, according to your tradition" (Alma 8:11). One commentary on the Book of Mormon suggested of the residents of that city:

> Many of the people of Ammonihah had known Alma in Zarahemla during the early days of the Republic. They had founded Ammonihah to have a place far away from those who strictly kept the Law of Moses, and where they could revel, unmolested, in their queer belief that all men unmindful of their wicked ways would be saved. They rejoiced in what they called liberal doctrines, they forgetting that the doctrines of the Lord's Salvation are the most liberal of all, and the most forgiving of any.[3]

Alma 14:16 indicates that in Ammonihah the "order of the Nehors" was present and, perhaps, prevalent. Thus, the "great hold" of Satan upon the people of this community (Alma 8:9) may have been this same apostate version of religion Nehor taught, "with all of the associated ideological and economic trappings."[4]

The angel who appeared to Alma in this miracle is the same angel that helped him to course-correct during his period of rebelliousness some twenty years earlier (Alma 8:15). The angel's original message to Alma the Younger was one of chastisement and repentance. Now his comments are of comfort and consolation. Some have seen in the fact that the same angel has appeared to Alma evidence that you and I have guardian angels—or those assigned to us to help us accomplish what God needs of us.[5]

Several commentators have picked up on Amulek's use of the phrase "my women," suggesting that the verse has reference to the practice of polygamy among the Nephites.[6] Perhaps; though Brant Gardner suggests that this would not have been divinely sanctioned plural marriage but instead evidence of the prevalence of Nehorism, which seemed to allow for multiple wives.[7] Thus, Amulek's reference to his "women" might be evidence of how far he had strayed from the path of true religion during his period of apostasy.

SYMBOLIC ELEMENTS

The story of Alma being sent to Amulek, and Amulek being prepared to receive him, has significant symbolic merit. One commentator pointed out:

> The story of Alma meeting Amulek is intentionally cast to remind the reader of Elijah (ca. 875 B.C.) and Zaraphath, a reminder that Yahweh deals with his children in similar ways, even on different continents. Alma may well have been familiar with this story from the brass plates. Just as Elijah was commanded to enter a city and find someone who would give him food (1 Kgs. 17:8–16), so Alma is commanded to find a person in the same way.
>
> The point of both stories is that the Lord performed the miracle of matching two complete strangers in a strange city when he wanted them to meet. It is not surprising that the sign of that match would involve food, for sharing food is a very intimate experience, an important ritual in virtually all societies. Even in modern America, the invitation to share a meal implies some kind of accepting and well-intentioned relationship.
>
> So it was with both Elijah and Alma. The act of asking for and offering food not only identified both prophet and disciple, but also identified the disciple's sympathy with the prophet and openness to inspiration. He was not just a charitable person, but a companion in the gospel. This important connection is part of what was symbolized by the offer of food.[8]

Just as the lives of all prophets mirror the life of Christ,[9] by default, the lives of prophets and apostles also often mirror each other.[10] Here the lives of Alma and Elijah appear to demonstrate that truth.

APPLICATION AND ALLEGORIZATION

When Alma is called by the Lord (through the angel) to return to Ammonihah to again preach the gospel to the hard-hearted residents of that city, surely the idea was an unpleasant one to him. However, the account tells us that—unlike Jonah—Alma "returned speedily" (Alma 8:18). This is evidence not only of his great faith in God but also of his sincere desire to place his own will and wants behind those of his Heavenly Father.[11] When you and I are asked by our bishop, stake president, or quorum or class leader to do that which is less than palatable to our tastes, do we act more like Jonah did? Or are we prone to respond as did the prophet Alma, with an anxious desire to please our Father through our faithfulness to the requests of those whom *He* has placed to preside over us?

In this miracle, God sent an angel to prepare Amulek to receive Alma. The story is a brilliant testament to how God prepares the way for His servants. Behind the scenes, God is ever orchestrating the details of what needs to happen to bless our lives and further His purposes. As one commentary pointed out, "Before Alma had even returned to town, an angel had appeared to Amulek with specific instructions as to how he was to meet and care for Alma."[12] President Boyd K. Packer shared a similar experience from his own life.

> Over 30 years ago I was assigned with then-Elder Thomas S. Monson to organize a servicemen's stake in Europe. . . .
>
> After we had finished setting apart and completing that organization, we were assigned to go to Berlin for a stake conference. . . .
>
> The elders [who were serving their missions in that area] took us to the train station, helped us buy our tickets, and saw us aboard the train, which would take from about midnight until about 10:00 the next morning to arrive in Berlin.
>
> As the train was pulling out, one young elder said, "Do you have any German money?"
>
> I shook my head no.
>
> He said, "You better have some," and, running alongside, pulled from his pocket a 20-mark note. He handed that to me.

At that time the Iron Curtain was very "iron." The train . . . set out across East Germany toward Berlin.

The U.S. government had just begun to issue five-year passports. I had a new passport, a five-year passport. Before our trip, we went to have my wife's passport renewed, but they sent it back saying that the three-year passports were honored as a five-year passport. She still had more than two years left on her passport.

At about two o'clock in the morning, a conductor, a military-type soldier, came and asked for our tickets, and then, noting that we were not German, he asked for our passports. I do not like to give up my passport, especially in unfriendly places. But he took them. I almost never dislike anybody, but I made an exception for him! He was a surly, burly, ugly man.

We spoke no German. In the train compartment, there were six of us: my wife and a German sitting to the side of her and then almost knee to knee in a bench facing us were three other Germans. We had all been conversing a little. When the conductor came in, all was silent.

A conversation took place, and I knew what he was saying. He was denying my wife's passport. He went away and came back two or three times.

Finally, not knowing what to do, I had a bit of inspiration and produced that 20-mark note. He looked at it, took the note, and handed us our passports.

The next morning when we arrived in Berlin, a member of the Church met us at the train. I rather lightly told him of our experience. He was suddenly very sober. I said, "What's the matter?"

He said, "I don't know how to explain your getting here. East Germany right now is the one country in the world that refuses to honor the three-year passport. To them, your wife's passport was not valid."

I said, "Well, what could they have done?"

He answered, "Put you off the train."

I said, "They wouldn't put us off the train, would they?"

He said, "Not us. Her!"

I could see myself having someone try to put my wife off the train at about two o'clock in the morning somewhere in East Germany. I am not sure I would know what to do. I did not learn until afterwards how dangerous it was and what the circumstances were, particularly for my wife. I care a good deal more about her than I do for myself. We had been in very serious danger. Those whose passports they would not accept were arrested and detained.

All of this comes to this point: the elder who handed me the

20-mark note was David A. Bednar, a young elder serving in the South German Mission, who is now a member of the Quorum of the Twelve Apostles.

So why was it that this young elder from San Leandro, California, handed me the 20-mark note? If you understand that and understand what life is about, you will understand really all you need to know about life as members of the Church. You will understand how our lives are really not our own. They are governed—and if we live as we should live, then we will be taken care of. I do not think he knew the consequences of what he was doing. That 20-mark note was worth six dollars, and six dollars to an elder is quite a bit!

As you go through life, you will find that these things happen when you are living as you ought to live.[13]

Regardless of who we are, God has a plan for our lives. And if we are living faithfully to the dictates of His Spirit, the details of that plan will be taken care of by Him. He will intervene in little ways to make sure we encounter those we need to and experience what He needs us to. As we are obedient to commandments, we have the assurance that God will be in the details of our lives.

Joseph Fielding McConkie and Robert L. Millet reasoned that Amulek "had not been a bad man." He had simply chosen to live a life "beneath his spiritual privileges, to exist in twilight when he could have been basking in the glory of the noonday Son."[14] Amulek put it this way: "I did harden my heart, for I was called many times and I would not hear; therefore I knew concerning these things, yet I would not know" (Alma 10:6).

> The voice of the Lord calls to us regularly. It is not wickedness or carnality alone which keep us from feeling and hearing the word; it is preoccupation. We need not be guilty of gross sin to be unready for the impressions of the Spirit; we need only have our minds and hearts focused upon other things, to be so involved in the thick of thin things that we are not taking the time to ponder or meditate upon matters of substance. Excessive labor in secondary causes leads to a lessening of spiritual opportunities.[15]

Can you hear the voice of the Lord calling you? Or is your life so filled with the mundane that the sacred is getting edged out? Making time for meditation and contemplation is necessary if the Lord is going to use us to the degree that He would, and in the ways He wishes. Banking on the intervention of an angel (as Amulek did) is unwise. Are we, like him, "called" and yet do not hear? Do we "know" and yet "would not know" because of what it might require of us? How many spiritual experiences and divinely offered blessings are lost because members of the Church choose to live far beneath their privileges spiritually?

As members of the Church, we love to share stories of missionary successes. However, not all missionary encounters have the positive outcome one would hope. "Missionary success is measured less by numbers of baptisms than by the missionary's obedience and diligence."[16] The backstory of this miracle is a testament to that fact, and to the reality that not all those we teach are of equal preparation and receptivity. As one commentary pointed out:

> Alma's experience is a marvelous example of a pertinent but often painful reality—that the righteousness and personal power of the preacher is only one factor in the conversion of a people. The listeners must open their hearts, be willing to acknowledge and confess their weaknesses, and ponder and pray about what is spoken. Alma labored with all the faith he could muster. But faith is built upon evidence, and in this case (as in the case with Mormon in Mormon 3:12 or with Jesus in Mark 6:1–5) the intransigence of the Ammonihahites precluded the miracle of conversion at that time.[17]

Just as bad soil can prevent a good seed from growing, so also the gospel planted in the hearts of those who are not spiritually ready will not develop and grow. The pupil must prepare the soil of his heart for the seed of truth. Otherwise the seed cannot germinate. As much as we wish this were not the case, this principle is eternal. So Alma and Amulek discovered, and so learns many a Mormon missionary when he sets out to share the gospel with the world.

Another missionary application is to be found in the fact that Alma had taught the people of Ammonihah and had been rejected. However, when the Lord directed him to return, while most rejected him a second time, he *did* find a convert, a powerful member and missionary—Amulek. Had Alma not returned, Amulek's conversion would not have taken place, nor would he have served his many missions. And all those whom Amulek converted would have never heard the gospel from his mouth. Thus, in the details of this miracle we find a message about the importance of missionaries—full-time and member missionaries—being willing to be persistent (in accord with the Spirit's dictates). Rejection and, sometimes, even persecution will come. But if the Spirit says "persist," we must so do, knowing that the Lord has souls prepared to hear the word from our mouths.[18]

Alma's discouragement at the lack of interest and belief on the part of the Ammonihahites teaches us a lesson about discouragement when engaging in the work of the Lord. President James E. Faust taught missionaries, "You must know that Lucifer will oppose you, and be prepared for his opposition. Do not be surprised. He wants you to fail. Discouragement is one of the devil's tools. Have courage and go forward. Recognize that the gospel has been preached with some pain and sorrow from the very beginning. Do not expect that your experience will be otherwise."[19] Not many missionaries are able to escape the occasional feeling of discouragement and disappointment. However, so long as we recognize those feelings for what they are, we can dispel them and move forward in our work.

When he invited Alma into his home, Amulek did so stating, "I know that thou wilt be a blessing unto me and my house" (Alma 8:20). "It is indeed a blessing to house and care for the servants of the Lord. Their presence and personal power proves an unspeakable blessing to the home in which they reside temporarily."[20] This blessing can be had by the stake president who houses a General Authority over a stake conference weekend visit. But it can also be had by the member of the Church who chooses to open up his or her home to the full-time missionaries, so that they can have a spiritual place to lodge during their missions. Even an act as simple as feeding the elders or sisters provides promised blessings to those who render this needed service. Truly, they can be a blessing to you and your house if you will open up your door to them.

Amulek's choice to go out with Alma and testify of the gospel—in city after city, and town after town—is really an example of the Lord's declaration and command that "it becometh every man who hath been warned to warn his neighbor" (D&C 88:81). If we have experienced the blessing of receiving a witness of the restored gospel of Jesus Christ, we have a covenant-bound duty to share that testimony with the world. Amulek did that amid great opposition and loss. The Lord expects us to be no less committed than was Amulek. That might mean a full-time mission at eighteen or nineteen years of age. It might require that we serve as senior missionaries once we have retired and our children are grown. It might mean that we labor diligently as member missionaries during our years of gainful employment. But it will surely require that we give of our time, our talents, and our energies. And it will undoubtedly mean that we will have to leave behind loved ones for a season: parents, children, grandchildren, girlfriends or boyfriends, and so on. Amulek gave all for the kingdom. Those of us who have entered the holy temple and made covenants have promised to give no less.

In frustration over the people of Ammonihah—and in seeking to know what he should do—Alma the Younger "labored much in the spirit, wrestling with God in mighty prayer" (Alma 8:10). Of this verse, Nibley pointed out:

> Wrestling with God? Does God resist you? Do you have to resist him? No, you have to put yourself into position, in the right state of mind. Remember, in our daily walks of life as we go around doing things, we're far removed. If you're bowling, or if you're in business, or if you're jogging or something like that, doing the things you usually do, and then you have to go from there to prayer, it's quite a transition. It's like a culture shock if you really take it seriously. You have to get yourself in form. . . . You're not wrestling with the Lord; you're wrestling with yourself. Remember, Enos is the one who really wrestled. And he told us what he meant when he was wrestling; he was wrestling with himself, his own inadequacies. How can I possibly face the Lord in my condition, is what he says. So this is what we're doing.
>
> In the world we operate on a different level. It takes great mental effort to confront the Lord in all seriousness. We do it at various shallow levels, by routine. We have a prayer here because we feel we should. If we're going to make it really serious, we have to work on it harder. We couldn't do it cold. In other words, you can't just come in cold. It's like an artist, a cellist, or a pianist. I have lots of relatives who are musicians. You can't just come in cold and begin a concert. Or even a tenor has to warm up and get his voice ready. But you have to warm up your fingers. My wife plays the cello, and she has to warm up her fingers and her instrument. It takes at least 15 minutes to warm up. Then you're in the mood. Then you have to take a while to think about it, and then you're ready to go. Now if it comes to confronting the Lord, you have to be very serious about that sort of thing. It's quite a preliminary exercise, which is called wrestling with the Lord, wrestling with yourself. He's at

a distance. That's what he had to go through here, and very few people are willing to do it, but it really pays off because you know exactly what you want and where you stand.[21]

Nibley's point is an important one. Asking the heavens to part, and revelation to be given, is no small request. If we wish so great a blessing, we must—like the concert pianist—be willing to pay the price. We must practice, practice, practice the art of prayer, and we must warm ourselves up as we anticipate a greater need of revelatory assistance. Through "laboring much" and "wrestling with God" in prayer, Alma demonstrated both his awareness of his dependence upon heaven, and also his willingness to work to obtain his holy desires. Sometimes we expect personal miracles all too cheaply.

NOTES

1. See Nibley (2004), 2:245. See also Nyman (2003–2004), 3:128.
2. See Randall L. Hall, "Amulek," in Largey (2003), 52–54; Pinegar and Allen (2007), 518.
3. Reynolds and Sjodahl (1955–1961), 3:148.
4. See Gardner (2007), 4:143.
5. See Nibley (2004), 2:240; Nyman (2003–2004), 3:105; Brigham Young, *The Complete Discourses of Brigham Young*, Richard S. Van Wagoner, compiler, five volumes (Salt Lake City: The Smith-Pettit Foundation, 2009), 5:2607. While there have certainly been some who have called into question the existence of guardian angels, many of the Brethren have also spoken of them as a reality [see, for example, David O. McKay, in Conference Report, October 1968, 86; Hyrum G. Smith, in Conference Report, October 1928, 81–82; Joseph Smith, in George Q. Cannon, *The Life of Joseph Smith, the Prophet* (Salt Lake City: Deseret Book, 1986), 494–95; Joseph Fielding Smith, *Doctrines of Salvation*, three volumes (Salt Lake City: Bookcraft, 1998), 1:54; Orson Pratt, in *Journal of Discourses*, 2:344; Daniel H. Ludlow, *A Companion to Your Study of the Doctrine and Covenants*, two volumes (Salt Lake City: Deseret Book, 1978), 1:558. Many other examples could be given].
6. See, for example, Gardner (2007), 4:169–70; Reynolds and Sjodahl (1955–1961), 3:169.
7. See Gardner (2007), 4:170.
8. Gardner (2007), 4:146–47.
9. See Alonzo L. Gaskill, *The Lost Language of Symbolism* (Salt Lake City: Deseret Book, 2003), 172–90.
10. See Gaskill (2003), 199–215.
11. See Pinegar and Allen (2007), 517, who see this as a lesson in obedience for us to emulate.
12. McConkie and Millet (1987–1992), 3:61.

13. Boyd K. Packer, "The 20-Mark Note," *Liahona*, June 2009, 20, 22.

14. See McConkie and Millet (1987–1991), 3:68, 69. This is but one view of Amulek. Those who believe he had been practicing unauthorized plural marriages might hold a more harsh view of his past practices.

15. McConkie and Millet (1987–1991), 3:68.

16. Ogden and Skinner (2011), 1:404.

17. McConkie and Millet (1987–1991), 3:59.

18. See Pinegar and Allen (2003), 267.

19. James E. Faust, cited in Bassett (2007–2008), 2:127.

20. McConkie and Millet (1987–1991), 3:61.

21. Nibley (2004), 2:239–40.

ALMA *and* AMULEK CANNOT *Be* CONFINED *or* SLAIN

ALMA 8:30–31

THE MIRACLE

After his conversion back to the faith he had been reared in, Amulek served as a missionary companion to Alma the Younger. The two of them unitedly called the people of Ammonihah to repentance, though with limited success.

While the Book of Mormon does not give us all of the details, we are informed that these two missionaries "had power given unto them, insomuch that they could not be confined in dungeons; neither was it possible that any man could slay them" (Alma 8:31).

Alma is quick to point out that though they had been given this miraculous power by God—as Ammon would be later (see Alma 19:22)—they only used it in extreme circumstances, and solely for the purpose "that the Lord might show forth his power in them" (Alma 8:32).

BACKGROUND

Alma tells us that they were "filled with the Holy Ghost" (Alma 8:30). Certainly the source of their miraculous protection and power was the Spirit of God. Whether via gifts of the Spirit or simply through the transfiguring power of the Spirit, these men were made unconquerable to their mortal enemies, until they had finished the work the Lord had given them.

Of the vagueness of Mormon's account of this miracle,[1] one commentary on the Book of Mormon states: "Verse 31 gives a fascinating synopsis of what must have been several events. It is not likely that Mormon was merely speculating when he said 'they could not be confined in dungeons.' Likewise, there must have been at least one historical event behind the statement that 'neither was it possible that any man could slay them.'"[2]

SYMBOLIC ELEMENTS

In this narrative, Amulek can well represent members of the Church and the role they need to play, alongside of the full-time missionaries, in the conversion process. Alma the Younger, on the other hand, is a good symbol of those who have been called and set apart to travel from town to town and village to village preaching the gospel of repentance. The combination of these two members reminds us of the synergy that comes when the members do their job (finding and inviting friends and family to be taught) so that missionaries can do theirs (teaching by the Spirit as authorized messengers of the Lord).

APPLICATION AND ALLEGORIZATION

One obvious message of this miracle is the truth that God can preserve His servants when they are on His errand. He sometimes does so in rather miraculous ways, as the following true story demonstrates.

On June 7, 1994, I was returning home by ferry with five other missionaries after a zone conference in Eastern Samar, Philippines. The night air was humid and heavy. After stowing our travel bags at our cots on the second level, four of us went to the front deck to escape the heat. Elders Dunford and Bermudez, however, stayed and went to sleep.

I was conversing with Elder Kern when we heard a firecracker-like explosion from the starboard side. Suddenly flames, fed by fuel from the engine room, were consuming the back of the ship. Smoke filled the passageways, followed by a power outage that left the panicked passengers in the dark.

The four of us on deck gathered together, praying for calm and clear thinking and for the Spirit to guide us. Immediately afterward, Elder Valentine walked quickly back inside the ship looking for life jackets. . . . By this time the bow was crowded with passengers, and the flames were coming close. There was no other choice except to jump. We put on our life jackets and said a short prayer before plunging in. . . .

The area around the boat was well lit because of the fire, and we could hear the screams of people around us. The four of us regrouped a short distance from the boat, amid the crowds that had also jumped, and swam to get away from the burning three-level vessel. We prayed again, thanking our Father in Heaven for the protection we had received and asked for help in finding our companions, Elder Dunford and Elder Bermudez. . . .

As the fire went out, the night became completely dark, and the waves were rolling, making it difficult for us to stay afloat even with the life jackets. . . .

After 30 minutes the wind picked up, rain started falling, and the already-large waves grew. We were still not sure what had happened to the other elders and knew the storm would halt any rescue efforts. Elder Kern, acting as a voice for the group, prayed for the storm to calm and that the other elders would be protected. Within a few minutes, the storm was gone.

We waited, awed by what we had witnessed, then heard Elder Dunford yelling out to Elder Kern. We shouted and swam towards them. Elders Dunford and Bermudez had managed to jump off the ship by climbing out a window, and they had two women, without life jackets, clinging to their backs.

We stayed together for some time, then caught sight of fishing boat lights leaving the Guiuan shore area. It was not long until one boat discovered us, but it was almost full, so we placed the two women in it and waited.

We had been in the water for two hours when another boat found us and took us to shore. . . . We prayed for the safe rescue of others still out in the sea and again gave thanks to our Heavenly Father for the protection we had received.

I will never forget this experience, and I hope never to forget the feeling of security we had throughout the whole ordeal. The Lord truly protected us. From this experience, I gained a greater testimony that the Lord is with His children always and grants us the peace and help we need during our trials.[3]

Though this kind of miraculous preservation has happened from time to time throughout the history of the Church, often the preservation (though miraculous) comes in more natural ways—as part of the program, *per se*. President Gordon B. Hinckley gave an example of this. He said,

Each of you has a companion. Why? Well, for one reason because the

Savior said, "In the mouth of two or three witnesses [shall all things] be established" (Matthew 18:16). Another is for your mutual protection—so that you can protect one another. When you are together, it isn't likely that both of you will go wrong. One of you might be tempted to. The other will pull him up and straighten him out and give him strength to resist. Subtle are the ways of the world. Clever are the designs of the adversary. Be careful. You want to go home in honor.[4]

The Lord certainly protected Alma the Younger and his companion, Amulek, and so He does His missionaries today. However, the dangers in our day are rarely dungeons and death. Rather, today missionaries face temptations of a moral nature, or in association with disobedience to mission rules. Like Alma and Amulek of old, the Lord has endowed His missionaries with the gifts and power necessary to remain aloof from temptation. One of the ways He does that is by giving elders and sisters companions. As He protected His missionaries of old, so He does today—but the dangers are often different, so the protection usually comes in a different form.

The Lord paired Amulek with Alma, not because of any inadequacy on the part of Alma. Rather, God saw that Amulek's connections with the community would simply bring something Alma did not have as an "outsider."

> What did Amulek bring to their partnership? First, he was a local man; and second, he also had tremendous faith. While Alma might be dismissed as a stranger whose belief may have been "put on" with his title, Amulek was among his neighbors. His belief could not be dismissed as either foreign or insincere. He had social connections that Alma lacked, and thus he increased Alma's effectiveness. Together, Alma and Amulek became more powerful than either one by himself.[5]

This is a testament to the importance of missionaries involving local members in the teaching and conversion process.

One element this miracle highlights is the fact that Alma and Amulek had powers they did not exercise, except when circumstances necessitated it (Alma 8:31). In other words, while they may have had times when a little miracle performed would please the crowd and potentially court converts, Alma and Amulek held this God-given power sacred, and they did not allow it to be consumed upon the lusts of those whom they taught (see D&C 46:9). The power to perform miracles should never be used as some sort of a circus sideshow. Nor should accounts of personal miracles be freely and casually told. Such experiences are for the recipients (and a select few that the Spirit indicates should be informed of such events). Generally speaking, sacred experiences are not to be shared publicly, or with numerous people. To do so grieves the Spirit and decreases the likelihood that further encounters with God will be provided. As Joseph Smith said, "Let us be faithful and silent, brethren, and if God gives you a manifestation, keep it to yourselves."[6] Brigham Young similarly counseled,

> There is one principle that I wish the people would understand and lay to heart. Just as fast as you will prove before your God that you are worthy to receive the mysteries, if you please to call them so, of the kingdom of heaven—that you are full of confidence in God—that you will never betray a thing that God tells you—that you will never reveal to your neighbour [sic] that which ought not to be revealed, as quick as you prepare to be entrusted with the things of God, there is an eternity of them to bestow upon you. Instead of pleading with the Lord to bestow more upon you, plead with yourselves to have confidence in yourselves, to have integrity in yourselves, and know when to speak and what to speak, what to reveal, and how to carry yourselves and walk before the Lord. And just as fast as you prove to Him that you will preserve everything secret that ought to be—that you will deal out to your neighbours all which you ought, and no more, and learn how to dispense your knowledge to your families, friends, neighbours, and brethren, the Lord will bestow upon you, and give to you, and bestow upon you, until finally he will say to you, "You shall never fall; your salvation is sealed unto you; you are sealed up unto eternal life and salvation, through your integrity."[7]

NOTES

1. This "vagueness" may simply be the result of the fact that this is an abridgement.
2. Gardner (2007), 4:150.
3. Kevin D. Casper, "The Lord Truly Protected Us," *Liahona*, March 2010, 16–17.
4. Gordon B. Hinckley, cited in Bassett (2007–2008), 2:129.
5. Gardner (2007), 4:150.
6. *History of the Church* (1978), 2:309.
7. Brigham Young, *Journal of Discourses*, 4:371–72.

AMINADI INTERPRETED
the WRITING *on the* WALL

ALMA 10:2

THE MIRACLE

As he taught the people of Ammonihah, Amulek explained to those listening that he was a descendant of a man named Aminadi. Though little is known of him, this same Aminadi was a descendant of Lehi, the father of Nephi.

Amulek informs his hearers that his predecessor, Aminadi, had "interpreted the writing which was upon the wall of the temple, which was written by the finger of God."

BACKGROUND

We know nothing about this miracle to which Amulek refers, though it apparently was well known among the people of Ammonihah.[1] One commentator said of this miracle, "It presumably finds a parallel in the Babylonian Empire of Belshazzar, recorded in Daniel 5:24–28."[2] While it is true that the footnote in Alma 10:2 cross-references the miracle of the appearance of handwriting on the wall of the palace of King Belshazzar (Daniel 5), we have no reason to necessarily assume that the two miracles parallel each other in *any aspects* beyond the fact that both record the interpretation of divinely given writing on a wall.

BYU's Monte Nyman reads Alma 10:2 to suggest that Aminadi was the great-grandfather of Amulek—and that this miracle had taken place only three generations earlier.[3] Were such the case, this would explain why Amulek could refer to them even in passing—knowing his audience would be very familiar with the famous wonder.

Because the Lehites left Jerusalem circa 600 BCE (prior to the Babylonian captivity), the account recorded in Daniel would not have been on the brass plates, nor would it have likely been a miracle familiar to Lehi and his posterity.[4] Thus, while there may appear to be surface parallels between Aminadi's miracle and Daniel's, Amulek's hearers would not have made the connection.[5]

SYMBOLIC ELEMENTS

The finger of God is a traditional symbol for God's power and divine activity. Sometimes it conveys His grace and mercy, other times His judgment. In all aspects—whether writing or not—it seems to covey God's efforts to communicate with His mortal children.[6]

Because of the episode with Daniel and King Belshazzar (in Daniel 5)—which is so often paired with this Book of Mormon miracle—the phrase "the handwriting on the wall" has become a symbolic euphemism for an "omen of impending calamity or imminent doom."[7]

APPLICATION AND ALLEGORIZATION

A basic application of this miracle (for which we have few details) is the broadly accepted truth that there are occasions when miraculous things *need* to be done. Nephi needed to build a ship. The Jaredites needed to have air and light in their barges. Moses needed to get the children of Israel across the Red Sea. Joseph needed to translate the plates. When God can accomplish His will through seemingly "normal" means, He typically does so. However, when the extraordinary needs to take place (plates in an entirely unknown language need to be translated into a known one), God can equip His servants with the power requisite to be His instruments in accomplishing those miraculous things—just as He did with Aminadi.

One commentary on the Book of Mormon offered this interpretation of the miracle: "We know nothing more about what was 'written by the finger of God' (Alma 10:2), or what interpretation was given by Aminadi, but it is a second witness from God that he could and does communicate to his people through this medium."[8] In short, while we have no idea what provoked the writing on the temple wall, what it said, or even why Aminadi was the man chosen by God to interpret it—we *do* know that "in the mouth of two or three witnesses shall every word be established" (2 Corinthians 13:1; D&C 6:28). Thus, at the very least, this miracle serves as a testament that this method of revelation, though rare, is of God.

NOTES

1. See Reynolds and Sjodahl (1955–1961), 3:167; Gardner (2007), 4:164. The account of this miracle may well have been recorded on the large plates. This is particularly likely if the event took place before Mosiah led his people out of the city of Nephi [see McConkie and Millet (1987–1991), 3:68; Gardner (2007), 4:164].

2. Ogden and Skinner (2011), 1:407.

3. See Nyman (2003–2004), 3:127.

4. See Gardner (2007), 4:165.

5. Brant Gardner wrote that "it is probable that, if we had a fuller version of Aminadi's story, we would see both similarities and differences" [Gardner (2007), 4:165].

6. See Ryken, Wilhoit, and Longman (1998), 286.

7. Lockyer (1965), 138.

8. See Nyman (2003–2004), 3:127.

AMULEK *and* ALMA DISCERN *the* THOUGHTS *of the* PEOPLE

ALMA 10:16–18; 11:21–25; 12:3, 7

THE MIRACLE

Alma and Amulek were preaching to the people of Ammonihah when the lawyers of that community sought to question Amulek in an effort to trip him up, or to find any contradiction they could in his words. These men were "learned in all the arts and cunning of the people" (Alma 10:16). Thus, they employed these corrupt skills in an attempt to discredit the Lord's anointed.

There was one among the people of Ammonihah whose name was Zeezrom. He was said to be "one of the most expert among them" (verse 15) in the employment of sophistry, and he "was the foremost to accuse Amulek and Alma" (verse 31).

As they were repeatedly challenged, God gave Amulek and Alma the ability to know the hearts, thoughts, and intents of their enemies, thereby exposing their evil designs and evidencing to both their accusers and various onlookers that the Spirit of the Lord was indeed upon His servants.

BACKGROUND

Zeezrom was a lawyer, or "legal official," in the city of Ammonihah. One commentary referred to him rather tongue-in-cheek as the "president of the Ammonihah Bar Association."[1] In other words, his stature was undeniable and his abilities unmatched. He argued with Amulek and Alma—challenging a number of their doctrines, but particularly the divinity of Christ. So perverted were his arguments and attempts, Amulek called him a "child of hell" (Alma 11:23). He sought to bribe Amulek (by offering him the equivalent of the salary for forty-two days of work) if he would deny the existence of a supreme being (Alma 11:3, 5–15, 22), but the missionary would not be enticed. Later, upon hearing the people employ his own arguments against Alma and Amulek, Zeezrom realized the consequences of his behavior. He publically admitted his manipulative words and works and embraced the teachings of these two representatives of the Lord. For this, he was cast out of Ammonihah (Alma 14:7). At one point he became very ill—apparently "overwhelmed with the realization of his iniquities"—but he was miraculously healed by Alma (Alma 15:11), who after healing him also baptized him. Seven years after his baptism, Zeezrom himself served a mission (Alma 31:6).[2]

It has been suggested that the primary motivation of those who challenged Amulek and Alma was not their difference in theological positions but, rather, money.[3] If what this prophet and his missionary companion taught was true, then these things would put an end to the lucrative careers of Ammonihah's lawyers. Thus, "armed with all the verbal paraphernalia of their trade these so-called defenders of truth and justice began to question Amulek about the things . . . of which he had testified."[4]

One commentary highlighted Amulek's financial situation at the time of this miracle. Alma 15:16 informs us that Amulek's conversion caused him the loss of all of his gold, silver, and precious things—and also the loss of his family and inheritance. Thus, the offer of six onties of silver—a very sizable amount of money in Amulek's day—would have been considerably enticing.[5] Yet, faithful as the day is long, Amulek did not flinch. The riches he sought were not of this world.

SYMBOLIC ELEMENTS

While this miracle has numerous potential applications, it isn't necessarily strong on standard symbolism. The one obvious component of the story that seems an archetype is the behavior of the lawyers of Ammonihah. Via their employment of sophistry, and because of their desire to use the law and their powers (both their legal authority and their powers of speech) to get gain, they well represent any class of citizens—within or without the Church—who have situational ethics.

They remind us of those who use their power in ways that are technically legal but ultimately immoral, and who, consequently, do harm to society by their behaviors.[6]

The fact that Zeezrom "trembles exceedingly" (Alma 12:7) at the testimony of Alma reminds us of the traditional symbolic meaning behind this behavior. In scripture, trembling often represents "realization" and "fear"—in this case, the realization of guilt and the fear of pending condemnation.[7]

APPLICATION AND ALLEGORIZATION

In this miracle of discernment God inspired Amulek and Alma with gifts beyond their own. They knew things they could not have known of themselves. The Lord has said that no one, "save God," knows the "thoughts and intents" of our hearts (D&C 6:16). However, as this miracle shows, the Father can give His servants (if they are worthy) the ability to discern the hearts and words of others for whom they have stewardship.[8] This is one of the gifts of the Spirit (D&C 46:27). Bishops should have this; stake presidents should have this; but so should other leaders in the ward or stake.[9] It is God's way of blessing both leaders (who have stewardship) and those for whom they have been given stewardship. Joseph Smith counseled: "Pray for . . . the Presiding Elder . . . that he may have this gift."[10] Indeed, who would want a bishop or stake president who didn't have this gift? Who would want someone leading the youth who didn't have this gift? Who would wish to be led by a quorum president or Relief Society president who didn't seek this gift? The Prophet added this: "It is in vain to try to hide a bad spirit from the eyes of them who are spiritual, for it will show itself in speaking and in writing, as well as in all our other conduct. It is also needless to make great pretensions when the heart is not right; the Lord will expose it to the view of His faithful Saints."[11] God gives worthy, seeking leaders this gift—and through that gift they can bless us (even in our sins), because God will reveal to and through them that which needs to come to light. He did this for Amulek and Alma, and He will do it for us.

Satan so often uses that which is potentially good as a means of spawning corruption and sin. He twists, distorts, perverts, and tempts so that good is used to accomplish his evil designs. In this miracle narrative we see exactly that. The adversary of all righteousness uses lawyers, who can have the ability to be a blessing to society, as a means of corrupting a society. McConkie and Millet wrote:

> One of the signs of moral decay, of apostasy and corruption within a society, is an emphasis on technicalities of law. This comes about when, in order to advance their cause, people seek to play the letter against the spirit of the law and in effect to legalize chicanery. Among the pure in heart God's laws are etched on the soul; they are found written in the countenances and inscribed on the inward parts. Among the perverse, however, law is a means of accomplishing the manipulation of others. Both anciently and in our own day, lawyers who seek to uphold the law, who strive to bring the lawless to account, who earnestly endeavor to protect the rights of all—these perform a valuable and appreciated service in society. On the other hand, when lawyers undertake to generate business for themselves by encouraging litigation in instances when patience and long-suffering would be more appropriate; when they cover up the truth; when their manipulations result in the guilty not being brought to justice, thereby penalizing and punishing the innocent; and when they employ the witchery of words or the sophistry of speech to deceive the unwary or the trusting—when they do such things they have become pawns in the hand of the Father of all lies. They have sold their souls. Amulek stated the matter simply: "The foundation of the destruction of this people is beginning to be laid by the unrighteousness of your lawyers and your judges" (verse 27).[12]

Owing to how litigious our own society has become, it is evident that this same thing is happening in our day. The law is used in "technical" ways to free the guilty and line the pockets of the corrupt. While this miracle certainly invites lawyers to introspection, it also requires that you and I ask of ourselves to what degree *we* are guilty of placing the "letter" over the "spirit" of the law—in any aspect of our lives and relationships.

Alma warns his dishonest and manipulative opponents, "Ye are laying plans to pervert the ways of the righteous, and to bring down the wrath of God upon your heads, even to the utter destruction of this people" (Alma 10:18). Have we any reason to assume, as a society, that we will be spared such consequences if we too allow—or, even worse, nurture—dishonest and manipulative behaviors? Any society that looks past sin is doomed to be consumed by it. If we do not stand up for that which is right, moral, and true, that which is wrong, immoral, and false will become the governing force in our society.

Zeezrom tried to force Amulek to answer certain questions—and asked him, quite pointedly, "Will ye answer the questions which I shall put unto you?" (Alma 11:21). Amulek's response is instructive: "If it be according to the Spirit of the Lord, which is in me; for I shall say nothing which is contrary to the Spirit of the Lord" (Alma 11:22). One commentary on this passage offered the following application:

> Those called to speak and act in the name of the Lord are careful in their ministry. They have no private agenda, no favorite doctrines, no special lessons they seek to put forward according to the whim of the moment. Rather, they strive earnestly to be in tune with that Spirit which teaches and shows a person what he or she must do at all times. They speak the words of Christ, meaning that they speak by the power of the Holy Ghost and thereby make known only that which the Lord would have made known (see 2 Nephi 32:3–5). Thus they answer only the questions that seem appropriate at the time, and deliver that "portion of the word" (Alma 12:9–11; D&C 71:1) which is needful for the edification of those they serve.[13]

This is a challenge for every leader and teacher in the Church—though it is the commission of God to all. Through personal righteousness and daily personal preparation, we can develop "the mind of Christ" (1 Corinthians 2:16), so that we think what He would think, say what He would say, and do what He would do.[14] Thus, our words and works are no longer our own. They are His; and they are directed by His Spirit, allowing us to be inspired in the very moment and beyond any native ability. Through those who have sought this process of personal development, God will bless His other children in quite miraculous ways.

This miracle reminds us of the truth: questions are not, of themselves, wrong or necessarily faithless. Initially Zeezrom asks questions to entrap and for no redeeming or holy purpose. Later, however, he questions because he sincerely wants to understand the things taught by the missionaries. As one commentator put it, "Something awakened in Zeezrom, something he either had not experienced or had not recognized. As a result, he relinquishes the role of the questioner-to-entrap and becomes a questioner-to-learn."[15] Asking questions about the Church—its doctrines, history, or ordinances—is not of itself a sign of faithlessness. Some questions are not asked in faith and, thus regardless of the answers given, will not receive a satisfactory response or result. Others, however, when asked in faith, can serve to allay doubts or confusion. The deciding factor is always to be found in the intent of the questioner. If our hearts are right, asking questions is not an act of unfaithfulness.

NOTES

1. See Ogden and Skinner (2011), 1:408.

2. See John W. Welch, "Zeezrom," in Largey (2003), 800–01 Reynolds and Sjodahl (1955–1961), 3:173–74.

3. See Gardner (2007), 4:186; Reynolds and Sjodahl (1955–1961), 3:170.

4. See Reynolds and Sjodahl (1955–1961), 3:170.

5. See Ludlow, Pinegar, Allen, Otten, and Caldwell (2007), 236.

6. See, for example, Bruce L. Rockwood, "The Good, the Bad, and the Ironic: Two Views on Law and Literature," in *Yale Journal of Law and the Humanities*, Volume 8, Number 2 (1996), 537, 539.

7. See Ryken, Wilhoit and Longman (1998), 892.

8. See Ogden and Skinner (2011), 1:410; Ludlow, Pinegar, Allen, Otten, and Caldwell (2007), 237.

9. See Pinegar and Allen (2007), 528–29; Elaine Jack, cited in Bassett (2007–2008), 2:134.

10. Smith, in Smith (1976), 162.

11. Joseph Smith, in *History of the Church* (1978), 1:317. Heber C. Kimball had an experience that illustrates this truth: "Being in charge of the Endowment House, while the Temple was in the process of construction, Heber C. Kimball met with a group who were planning to enter the temple for ordinance work. He felt impressed that some were not worthy to go into the temple, and he suggested first that if any present were not worthy, they might retire. No one responding, he said that there were some present who should not proceed through the temple because of unworthiness and he wished they would leave so the company could proceed. It was quiet as death and no one moved nor responded. A third time he spoke, saying that there were two people present who were in adultery, and if they did not leave he would call out their names. Two people walked out and the company continued on through the temple" [Spencer W. Kimball, *The Miracle of Forgiveness* (Salt Lake City: Bookcraft, 1989), 112].

12. McConkie and Millet (1987–1991), 3:71–72. See also Ogden and Skinner (2011), 1:407.

13. McConkie and Millet (1987–1991), 3:75. See also Nyman (2003–2004), 3:138; Pinegar and Allen (2007), 532.

14. See Bruce R. McConkie, *Doctrinal New Testament Commentary*, three volumes (Salt Lake City: Bookcraft, 1987–1988), 2:322.

15. Gardner (2007), 4:195.

THE LORD BREAKS
the CORDS BINDING
ALMA *and* AMULEK

ALMA 14:26

THE MIRACLE

Because of the things of which Alma and Amulek had testified, the people of Ammonihah were angry with them, "and the more part of them" desired the destruction of these two messengers of God (Alma 14:2). They bound Alma and Amulek, hauled them before the chief judge, and accused them of many things, including lying to the people and reviling against their laws and their leaders.

Observing all of this, Zeezrom was tormented by guilt because he knew he was—at least in part—responsible for the attitudes of the people toward Alma and Amulek. Thus, Zeezrom pled with the citizens of Ammonihah to let the prisoners go. However, the people reviled against him, declaring that he was possessed of a devil, spitting upon him and eventually casting him out of the city.

Because of their anger toward the Church and its representatives, these mobocrats and murderers began to burn to death believers in the Church—including women and little children. Alma and Amulek were forced to watch the death of the faithful, including the deaths by fire of many whom they had converted to the gospel.

Amulek, pained by what he was witnessing, cried out to Alma, saying, "Let us stretch forth our hands, and exercise the power of God which is in us, and save them from the flames" (verse 10). However,

Alma—no doubt equally as pained by what he was witnessing—said to Amulek, "The Spirit constraineth me that I must not stretch forth mine hand; for behold the Lord receiveth them up unto himself, in glory; and he doth suffer that they may do this thing, or that the people may do this thing unto them, according to the hardness of their hearts, that the judgments which he shall exercise upon them in his wrath may be just; and the blood of the innocent shall stand as a witness against them, yea, and cry mightily against them at the last day" (verse 11; see also Alma 60:13). Alma acknowledged that it was quite possible that they too might be burned—"be it according to the will of the Lord" (verse 13). However (he reminded Amulek), until they had completed their work, God would not permit the two of them to be burned or otherwise slain.

As their friends and family burned before their eyes, the chief judge slapped Alma's and Amulek's faces and said to them, "After what ye have seen, will ye preach again unto this people, that they shall be cast into a lake of fire and brimstone? Behold, ye see that ye had not power to save those who had been cast into the fire; neither has God saved them because they were of thy faith. And the judge smote them again upon their cheeks, and asked: What say ye for yourselves?" (verse 15). Like Christ before Pilate, Alma and Amulek "answered him nothing" (verse 17). The chief judge smote their faces again and had them thrown into prison.

For some three days, judges, lawyers, and many citizens of Ammonihah came to Alma and Amulek in prison and questioned them and smote them across their faces. But the two missionaries simply refused to respond to their captors and antagonists—even amid mockery and threats that they too would be burned, and even in the face of accusations that they had not that "great power" which they had professed to hold.

Over the time of their imprisonment—which lasted "for many days"—Alma and Amulek were beaten, verbally abused, forbidden food or drink, stripped of their clothing, and "bound with strong cords" (verses 22–23).

After many days had passed, the chief judge came to Alma and Amulek in their cell and, seeking a sign from them, said, "If ye have the power of God deliver yourselves from these bands, . . . then we will believe . . . according to your words" (verse 24). Many who had accompanied the chief judge made the same promise to Alma and Amulek—smiting them across the face as they declared that they would believe *if* they were shown a sign.

In what was most certainly an unexpected response (owing to their days of silence), Alma and Amulek suddenly stood, and Alma cried out in mighty prayer to God: "How long shall we suffer these great afflictions, O Lord? O Lord, give us strength according to our faith which is in Christ, even unto deliverance" (verse 26). Instantly they had the power to break their bands. And those of the mob who witnessed their divinely given strength feared and fled from before their presence. But so great was their fear of Alma and Amulek that they fell to the earth, not making their way out of the prison. Suddenly an earthquake struck the Ammonihah prison, causing the walls of the prison to shake and fall and slaying those who had smitten and tortured Alma and Amulek. However, our two prophetic preachers were preserved, unharmed.

When the people of the city arrived at the remains of the prison and found Alma and Amulek alive and well—but every other person who had been within slain—the citizens of Ammonihah fled from the presence of these divinely empowered missionaries.

BACKGROUND

While one might assume that an earthquake had struck the entire city of Ammonihah, Alma 14:29 suggests that the earthquake was not felt outside of the prison, only within. We are informed that those of the city "heard a great noise" and "came running together by multitudes" to the prison "to know the cause of it." Had the entire town been rattled by an earthquake, the sound of the prison crashing down would not have caused the questions or curiosity described in the text. Nibley offers a possible explanation for the trembling of the building and for its ultimate collapse. He suggests that perhaps "they all made a rush for the gate [of the prison], so naturally they crowded the exit. They jammed the exit, [and] nobody could get out, [so] the gate collapsed, and they were all killed there. The only safe people were Alma and Amulek who stayed behind. The people tried to get as far from them as they could."[1] While the scriptural account of this particular narrative is unclear whether this was the case, nevertheless, it is possible that this could explain how the prison could collapse because of shaking and yet no other part of the city was rattled.

It is worth noting that Alma and Amulek's antagonists were not simply the lawyers and judges but also the priests and teachers of Ammonihah. The land had reached a state of degradation, at least in part, because the church and the state were corrupt. What hope do a people have when both sources of ethics and law in society begin to side with the adversary rather than with the Advocate?

Brant A. Gardner points out numerous aspects of this miracle—particularly as it relates to the treatment and torture of Alma and Amulek—which parallel Mesoamerican customs in treating captives.[2] For apologists, Alma 14 has much to offer.

SYMBOLIC ELEMENTS

In this miracle, Alma and Amulek are obvious types for Christ—particularly as it relates to how they are treated by their enemies.

> It is difficult to avoid comment on the obvious parallelism between the events here related, and the appearance of the Savior of Men before Pontius Pilate. The two episodes abound in similarities. In each case, for example, wickedness had prejudged and foredoomed innocence, and was seeking only a legal pretext to accomplish its unholy purpose. In each case the accusers, in their ardor to establish their case, shamefully misquoted the words which had previously been spoken by the accused. Jesus, for example, was accused of "perverting the nation, and forbidding to give tribute to Caesar," (Luke 23:2) notwithstanding his previous public admonition to: "Render therefore unto Caesar the things which are Caesar's; and unto God the things that are God's." (Mat. 22:21)
>
> In the instant case Alma and Amulek were accused of preaching that the Son of God should "not save" his children. What they had actually said, of course, was that the Son of God should not save His children "in their sins," i.e., without repentance. (Alma 11:34) Between these two statements there is a world of difference, indeed. It would appear, however, that after evil men have decided upon the murderous destruction of him who thwarts the accomplishment of their aims, truth becomes expendable, and is willingly sacrificed upon the bloody altar of their ambition.[3]

The list of typological parallels goes on, but suffice it to say, the attentive reader will see much in this miracle narrative that points their minds and hearts to Christ—and reminds us of the truth that all prophets typify the Savior.[4]

The prison cell here seems an archetype. "Foul jails and prisons have furnished the stage-setting for many dramatic moments in sacred history: the Apostles released from prison by the power of an angel, (Acts 5:19) Paul imprisoned, converting his jailer, (Acts 16:30) and the Prophet Joseph Smith facing death in the Carthage Jail. (D. & C. 135:1)"[5] Alma and Amulek's cell reminds us well of the imprisonment of all those who have been in bondage for the truth of Christ. It reminds us that the consistent consequence of faithfulness to Christ is the solemn cell sponsored by Satan. So many, anciently and today, have languished in prison because they boldly bore witness of the truth.

APPLICATION AND ALLEGORIZATION

The first and most obvious application of this miracle is the eternal truth that God can endow us with the strength—through Him—to break whatever binds us: the cords of our enemies, but also the sins with which Satan binds us. Even the bonds of mental or physical illness can be tempered through the strength and intervention of the Lord. This is not to say that God will always take away our "chains of affliction." Sometimes He does. At other times He simply makes the bands bearable. In the case of Alma and Amulek, we saw both sides of this. Initially God did not remove their bands. Indeed, for a significant time they were required to endure them, though we doubt not that He comforted them in their afflictions. Eventually, however, those bands were broken and they were set free from their prison. And so it can be for each of us. "Weeping may endure for a night, but joy cometh in the morning" (Psalm 30:5). God can, and eventually will, free us from whatever binds us. Of course, this blessing can only be had through our faith in Him (Ether 12:13) and through our willingness to wait patiently upon the Lord (Psalm 37:7).

Another application can be found in God's willingness to allow wickedness to afflict His children—even when they are faithfully living the commandments. Alma and Amulek suffered, though they were completely faithful to the Lord. Their converts suffered, even though they had faith in the gospel and trusted in God. McConkie and Millet wrote,

God is not the author of evil, yet within limits and bounds he allows it to exist. This is done so that the righteous might merit the fulness of his glory and that the wicked, the workers of evil, might in like fashion merit the fulness of his wrath. Suffering sanctifies the souls of the faithful. The inflicting of that suffering soils all that is decent and makes the perpetrator a fit companion to the devil, to merit as he has merited and to be rewarded as he will be rewarded. Mocking and scourging, bonds and imprisonment, flight and refuge destitution and torment have been the common lot of Saints in all ages. Yet that God who is not unmindful of the sparrow that falls has witnessed it all—"having provided some better things for them through their sufferings, for without sufferings they could not be made perfect" (*JST*, Hebrews 11:40).[6]

The suffering of the righteous always has a purpose.[7] Of Jesus, it was said, "Though he were a Son, yet learned he obedience by the things which he suffered" (Hebrews 5:8). President Monson taught, "We cannot go to heaven in a feather bed. The Savior of the world entered after great pain and suffering. We, as servants, can expect no more than the Master."[8] Though we may not always see it in the midst of our trials, the Lord has a divine plan, and we are players in it. In dark times, such as those encountered by Alma and Amulek—and which will be experienced by us all—we must remember that there is a higher purpose to what God calls us to endure. If we can trust in that, like these two prophetic missionaries, we can find the faith to move forward, and we, like them, will eventually see God's hand manifest. As one commentary points out, "Suffering plays an indispensable role in the progress of the human soul through the valley of mortality. We must not conclude, because we pray for the alleviation of suffering, and yet suffer on, that our prayers have gone unheard. In such a posture, it is better to wrap about us more securely the reassuring garment of our faith, for it is precisely then that it can do us the most good."[9]

As with Abinadi, and now with Alma and Amulek, if we have a mission to fulfill, so long as we are living faithfully, we will be preserved from our enemies until we have accomplished that which we were foreordained to do.[10] Only our unfaithfulness can thwart that promise of God.

It is curious that the chief judge, the lawyers, and apparently other citizens of Ammonihah sought a sign from Alma and Amulek, promising belief if they got one (Alma 14:23–25). However, as one commentary on the Book of Mormon points out, their words were a lie. Such a promise of belief they would not keep. "Of one thing we have perfect assurance—the last thing wanted by those who demand signs is signs; the last thing wanted by those who demand evidence is evidence. A world of signs and evidences would not soften their hearts. The leaders of the Jews sought signs and Christ gave them signs sufficient to convince any people, yet they rejected him (see 2 Nephi 10:4)."[11] Those who do not believe, and who manifest a spirit of antagonism toward the gospel and kingdom, certainly cannot be converted through signs. Such, were it given, would only stir up their anger toward the faithful and the faith. And, for you and me (who profess to be believers), as our own spirituality increases and as our own faith develops, signs become less and less meaningful. Visions, angels, proofs, and evidences pale in comparison to the "still small voice" (D&C 85:6), which can and should be our constant companion. What more need those who are filled with faith?

Reynolds and Sjodahl bring up an interesting application of the background story of this miracle. We are told that the Ammonihahites were angry because of the words of Alma and Amulek—so much so that they wished to destroy them (Alma 14:2). These two missionaries taught something with which the Ammonihahites disagreed, and that filled them with rage. "It is difficult for those who have been oriented to the traditions of free speech and tolerance for others' beliefs to understand why the Ammonihahites became so infuriated, as shown by their conduct throughout all of Chapter 14, over the words of Alma and Amulek."[12] If we wish to be proponents of tolerance, then it *must* cut both ways. We must fight for tolerance not only for those with whom we agree, but also for those with whom we totally disagree. When we feel anger and animosity toward those with views opposite from our own, that anger and animosity reveals more about us and our positions than it does about the positions and character of our opponents. In the words of a hymn,

> School thy feelings, O my brother,
> Train thy warm, impulsive soul;
> Do not its emotions smother,
> But let wisdom's voice control.
> School thy feelings, there is power

In the cool, collected mind;
Passion shatters reason's tower,
Makes the clearest vision blind.

School thy feelings; condemnation
Never pass on friend or foe,
Though the tide of accusation
Like a flood of truth may flow.
Hear defense before deciding,
And a ray of light may gleam,
Showing thee what filth is hiding
Underneath the shallow stream.

Should affliction's acrid vial
Burst o'er thy unsheltered head.
School thy feelings to the trial,
Half its bitterness hath fled.
Art thou falsely, basely slandered?
Does the world begin to frown?
Gauge thy wrath by wisdom's standard,
Keep thy rising anger down.

Rest thyself on this assurance:
Time's a friend to innocence,
And the patient, calm endurance
Wins respect and aids defense.
Noblest minds have finest feelings
Quiv'ring strings a breath can move,
And the gospel's sweet revealings,
Tune them with the key of love.

Hearts so sensitively moulded,
Strongly fortified should be,
Trained to firmness and enfolded
In a calm tranquility.
Wound not willfully another;
Conquer haste with reason's might;
School thy feelings, sister, brother,
Train them in the path of right.[13]

Zeezrom's repentance, as described in the backstory of this miracle, is interesting. We are told of the pain he felt for his past and the

recognition he developed for the harms he had caused through his previously sinful life. Of this, Ogden and Skinner wrote,

> Zeezrom began the conversion process. He was "harrowed up." To harrow is to plow over hardened ground in order to break it up and make it receptive to planting. Zeezrom's heart was, in effect, plowed and broken. He felt godly sorrow and tried to repair what he had earlier wrought among the people. But the damage was not so easily undone. This is an important lesson: while true repentance guarantees that the Lord remembers it no more, sometimes it is not possible to reverse completely the consequences of past choices in mortality. On one occasion Brother Skinner interviewed a man for advancement in the priesthood. He had made very poor choices earlier in his life but had fully repented and was by then a stalwart. Yet the earlier choices had cost him his wife, his children, his home, and his employment. Even though he had fully turned to the Lord, he could not get back the things he had lost earlier. That would have to wait until a future day of restoration. Ironically, Zeezrom suffered the persecution he had earlier instigated. And he had to live with the knowledge that he had caused women and children to be cast into the fire.[14]

God forgives us for that of which we sincerely repent. However, choices have consequences. And, as the life of Zeezrom attests, even when we are forgiven, some of those consequences remain with us—or others we have harmed—throughout mortality. Of course, Satan would love to see you and me sin so egregiously that he could saturate us in an unrelenting guilt, which would give him the ability to hold our sins over our heads forever. But such is not God's way or will. Rather than bemoaning the past, we must earnestly repent, offer our sincere apologies to those whom we have harmed or offended, do what we can to fix the fallout of our sins, and then move forward with faith and confidence in God.

NOTES

1. See Nibley (2004), 2:278.
2. See Gardner (2007), 4:230–42.
3. Reynolds and Sjodahl (1955–1961), 3:216–17.
4. See Nibley (2004), 2:277–78; McConkie and Millet (1987–1991), 3:113; Ogden and Skinner (2011), 1:422; Nyman (2003–2004), 3:201.
5. Reynolds and Sjodahl (1955–1961), 3:223.

6. McConkie and Millet (1987–1991), 3:109.

7. Elder Maxwell expounds on this principle, and on the various sources of our trials, in "Willing to Submit," *Ensign*, May 1985, 70-73.

8. Thomas S. Monson, as cited in Bassett (2007–2008), 2:145.

9. Reynolds and Sjodahl (1955–1961), 3:220.

10. See McConkie and Millet (1987–1991), 3:110.

11. McConkie and Millet (1987–1991), 3:113.

12. Reynolds and Sjodahl (1955–1962), 3:214.

13. Charles W. Penrose, "School They Feelings," *Hymns of the Church of Jesus Christ of Latter-day Saints*, second revised edition (Salt Lake City: Intellectual Reserve, Inc., 2002), hymn number 336.

14. Ogden and Skinner (2011), 1:420–21.

ZEEZROM *Is* HEALED *by* ALMA

ALMA 15:3–12

THE MIRACLE

After being freed from the prison, Alma and Amulek traveled to the land of Sidom, where Zeezrom and their other converts had sought refuge from the persecutions taking place in Ammonihah.

Upon their arrival, they learned that Zeezrom lay sick with a "burning fever" (Alma 15:3), which was caused by the distress he felt over his previous wickedness and how his personal sins had harmed many of the believers. What made things worse was Zeezrom's assumption that Alma and Amulek had perished with of the others who had been thrown into the fires set by the judges, lawyers, priests, and teachers of Ammonihah. Zeezrom was sickened physically, spiritually, and mentally at the thought of all that he had done and caused.

Then news arrived that Alma and Amulek were in Sidom and Zeezrom took heart. He sent for them, supplicating them to come to his bedside immediately. When they arrived, he pled for a blessing that he might be healed. Alma, in response to the request, asked this desperately sick man, Do you believe in the power of Christ unto salvation? In earnestness, Zeezrom replied, I do. I believe *everything* you've taught! (verse 6). Then Alma informed him: If you believe in the redemption of Christ, then you can be healed (verse 8). And Alma, perhaps looking heavenward, prayed: "O Lord our God, have mercy on this man, and heal him according to his faith which is in Christ" (verse 10). Zeezrom was immediately healed. He leapt from his bed and began to walk about. And the story of his healing spread throughout Sidom, causing great astonishment among the people.

Alma then baptized this new convert, and Zeezrom "began from that time forth to preach unto the people" (verse 12).

BACKGROUND

As noted above, Zeezrom had been a lawyer, or "legal official," in the city of Ammonihah. His stature in the community was great, because his corrupt gifts were so honed. He had argued with Amulek and Alma—challenging a number of their doctrines—but eventually felt convicted by the Spirit when he realized that Alma and Amulek could read his thoughts. This caused him to stop debating and to start sincerely listening to the message of these two missionaries. Later, upon hearing the people employ his own arguments against Alma and Amulek, Zeezrom realized the consequences of his behaviors. He publically admitted his manipulative words and works and embraced the teachings of these two representatives of the Lord. For this, he was cast out of Ammonihah (Alma 14:7). Other believers followed as he and they made their way to Sidom.

In James 5, Jesus's half-brother counsels, "Is any sick among you? let him call for the elders of the church; and let them pray over him, anointing him with oil in the name of the Lord: and the prayer of faith shall save the sick, and the Lord shall raise him up; and if he have committed sins, they shall be forgiven him" (James 5:14–15). Of this passage, Elder Bruce R. McConkie wrote:

> The relationship between the bearing of testimony by the power of the Holy Ghost and the forgiveness of sins illustrates a glorious gospel truth. It is that whenever faithful saints gain the companionship of the Holy Spirit they are clean and pure before the Lord, for the Spirit will not dwell in an unclean tabernacle. Hence, they thereby receive a remission of those sins committed after baptism.
>
> This same eternal verity is illustrated in the ordinance of administering to the sick. A faithful saint who is anointed with oil has the promise that "the prayer of faith shall save the sick, and the Lord shall raise him up; and if he have committed sins, they shall be forgiven him." (James 5:14–15.) The reasoning of the ancient apostle James, in this instance, is that since the miracle of healing comes by the power of the Holy Ghost, the sick person is healed not only physically but

spiritually, for the Spirit who comes to heal will not dwell in a spiritually unclean tabernacle.[1]

Elsewhere we read that "the faith required for healing the body is apparently also simultaneously sufficient for healing the soul."[2] If this be true, we can assume that Zeezrom was healed not only physically but also spiritually. His physical restoration is evidence of the fact that God had expunged him of accountability for those sins over which he so grievously agonized.

As for Alma's unique means of healing Zeezrom, one commentary suggests: "We would assume that we are given but a glimpse of the whole story here. Surely Alma did more on this occasion than offer a sincere prayer; we would suppose that he laid his hands on the head of Zeezrom and (assisted by Amulek) in behalf of this faithful person exercised the powers of the priesthood he held."[3]

The fact that Zeezrom "leaps" to his feet after receiving a blessing makes it clear to the reader that this was no gradual healing. His recovery was instantaneous.[4]

Nibley brings up an obvious yet interesting insight into this miracle. It is Alma, not Amulek, who is the voice in this blessing (though Amulek likely assisted and, if oil was used, most probably would have performed the anointing). Nibley wrote, "Alma was just as guilty as Zeezrom was. Alma, who saved him, had been just as guilty [because of his sordid past]. He had done just as dirty [of] things, and he had less reason to, as a matter of fact, because his father was the head of the church. Zeezrom's father wasn't."[5] That being said, it makes sense that Alma would be the one to act as voice in this blessing. If anyone could exercise faith in such a setting it was he, for he too had been on the brink of destruction. He too had experienced these "fires" of the soul. He too had known the torments of a damned soul. Thus, of all men, he was most suited to bless this repentant son of God. Oh that we had the full text of the blessing. My suspicion is that Alma spoke words of great power, comfort, and compassion.

SYMBOLIC ELEMENTS

Of the archetypal nature of this story, McConkie and Millet note: "Though the cast changes, the story is universal. The great cities of men (the Ammonihahs) war against God and are destroyed, while some few of their number (the Zeezroms) humble themselves and reach forth their hand to God and his servants and are saved with an everlasting salvation."[6]

The act of healing generally is a symbol for the healing acts of Christ. Priesthood holders who lay hands on the sick or afflicted, and who invoke the name of Jesus ("by the authority of the Holy Melchizedek Priesthood, and in the sacred name of Jesus Christ"), are acting in Christ's stead. They are saying what He would say and doing what He would do. Thus, the blessing is not from Alma (or Elder So-and-so), but from Christ Himself. The one who vocalizes the blessing is but a surrogate, a symbol of the Lord, through whom all blessings come (D&C 36:2).

Zeezrom's burning fever also has some symbolic merit. Brant Gardner explained: "Zeezrom . . . is 'scorched with a burning heat.' Although fever is a physical manifestation, Mormon attributes it to a spiritual, rather than a physical cause. At the very least, Mormon presents it as symbolic of the burning of the wicked—the lake of fire and brimstone of which Alma preached."[7] The fever reminds us of the consequences and accountability for unresolved sin. Though Zeezrom was on the road to repentance, he had not yet completed it and, thus, continued to harbor those feelings that rack the soul of the damned—and those who expect to be damned. He suffered from a "fever of his soul" *per se*—as much for his lack of understanding as for his previous sins.[8] But Alma and Amulek were sent by God with the authority to teach him and the priesthood power to bless him (that he might access the healing Atonement of Christ).

APPLICATION AND ALLEGORIZATION

An overarching application of this narrative is the reality that, through faith in Christ and by means of the priesthood of God, you and I *can* be physically healed—if the Lord so wills it. Miracles such as this have happened thousands upon thousands of times in the history of the Church. I, myself, have seen unspeakable things via the priesthood of God. As a singular example, Wilford Woodruff shared the following experience:

> Mary Pitt . . . had not been able to walk a step for fourteen years, and confined to her bed nearly half that time. She had no strength in her

feet and ankles and could only move about a little with a crutch or holding on to a chair. She wished to be baptized. Brother Pitt and myself took her in our arms, and carried her into the water and I baptized her. When she came out of the water I confirmed her. She said she wanted to be healed and she believed she had faith enough to be healed. I had had experience enough in this Church to know that it required a good deal of faith to heal a person who had not walked a step for fourteen years. I told her that according to her faith it should be unto her. It so happened that on the day after she was baptized, Brother Richards and President Brigham Young came down to see me. . . . I told President Young what Sister Pitt wished, and that she believed she had faith enough to be healed. We prayed for her and laid hands upon her. Brother Young was mouth, and commanded her to be made whole. She laid down her crutch and never used it after, and the next day she walked three miles.[9]

God's priesthood is real. He has the power to heal. If we have faith, and if He does not deem otherwise, we can receive the blessing that ancient Zeezrom and modern Mary received. Do *you* have the faith to be healed?

In addition to the promise that God can heal us from physical sickness, this miracle is also a testament to the reality that we can be healed from our spiritual ailments too. God is the source, but He has placed around each of us those (like Alma and Amulek) who are His servants, who have His authority, and who have been sent by Him to walk us through the process of repentance. In addition to his physical cure, Zeezrom received spiritual healing because he reached out in faith to God's authorized servants. As we struggle with temptation and sin, if we will but reach out to those whom God has appointed, we too can receive that spiritual cure. While ours *may not* be as instantaneous as Zeezrom's was, it can be. (Sometimes the biggest stumbling block to overcoming sin is our unwillingness to confess it.) Regardless, the Lord can heal us—however long it takes—if we reach out to His authorized servants.

One application of this miracle reminds us that guilt can be a blessing. Zeezrom was sorely racked with it—and it caused him a great deal of pain, including (apparently) a sickness that was nigh unto death. That being said, his guilt also brought him to a state of humility, which brought sincere repentance. As much as we may hate feelings of guilt and the loss of the Spirit, these function as divine devices for change. Were it not for such feelings, you and I would have no regrets about sin because we would have no sense of sorrow. God be praised for this glorious gift we call guilt!

Alma's question, "Believest thou in the power of Christ unto salvation?" is instructive. Alma the Younger didn't ask Zeezrom if he believed in the priesthood's power to heal. He asked if he believed in Christ's power to save. Our faith—our trust—must always and ever be in Christ Jesus and His power to heal and to save.[10] Trusting in the priesthood, *minus faith founded in Christ*, is the equivalent of trusting in the man who wields that priesthood; and we can never place our faith in fallible men—even righteous men. I appreciate the following story, shared by President Gordon B. Hinckley:

> I have on my wall a painting that was given to me by a woman here in Hong Kong. On the back it says, "To Elder Gordon B. Hinckley, with gratitude for the restoration of my eyesight," and then her name is signed. *I did not restore her eyesight; the Lord did.* But she says that that administration saved her eyesight, and the doctors could not believe what happened to her. She was going blind, and they told her she would be blind in a matter of a few months. It was faith in the power of the priesthood and, *most important of all*, the goodness of the Lord which made possible that miracle.[11]

If we don't believe in the power of the priesthood, we may limit the blessings of the Lord available to us through it. However, as President Hinckley and Alma both emphasized, our faith must be based in Christ, and it must be He to whom we look for healing. Men cannot heal—and even priesthood, without our trust in the Savior, has no power to restore us.

The reformation of Zeezrom over the course of what appears to have been a fairly small window of time is dramatic, to say the least. He goes from being a chief antagonist to becoming a missionary and defender of the faith. By way of application, one commentary asks:

> Do we have a Zeezrom element within us that needs to be reformed and converted into an element of strength in building the kingdom of God? We can learn from Zeezrom by placing our trust in the Lord and seeking to divest ourselves of worldly entanglements that detract from

heavenly commitments, or worse, that enchain us to a life of sin. "O Lord our God," prayed the prophet, "have mercy on this man" (verse 10). In the same way we can ask our leaders and friends to pray for us, and we can pray for ourselves, that our lives may become kinder, gentler, and holier.[12]

Each of us has those elements within that keep us from fully consecrating our lives to the Lord. If we, like Zeezrom, are willing to open ourselves up to the dictates of the Spirit, the Lord can reform us too. And like Zeezrom, we can become powerful instruments in the hands of the Lord.

NOTES

1. Bruce R. McConkie, *The Mortal Messiah*, four volumes (Salt Lake City: Deseret Book, 1980–1981), 3:40–41n1.
2. Gardner (2007), 4:245. See also Matthew 9:2–7.
3. McConkie and Millet (1987–1991), 3:116.
4. See Gardner (2007), 4:245.
5. Nibley (2004), 2:279.
6. McConkie and Millet (1987–1991), 3:114.
7. Gardner (2007), 4:243–44.
8. See Gardner (2007), 4:244.
9. Wilford Woodruff, in *Journal of Discourses*, 15:344.
10. See Reynolds and Sjodahl (1955–1961), 3:227. See also Gardner (2007), 4:244.
11. Gordon B. Hinckley, cited in Bassett (2007–2008), 2:147; emphasis added.
12. Pinegar and Allen (2007), 556.

Ammon Cuts Off *the* Arms *of the* Lamanites

Alma 17–18

The Miracle

Ammon and his brothers (Aaron, Omner, and Himni) spent some fourteen years preaching the gospel to the Lamanites. As they began their individual ministries, they "separated themselves and departed one from another, trusting in the Lord that they should meet again" (Alma 17:13). Ammon determined that his field of labor would be the land of Ishmael—a region inhabited by "a wild and a hardened and a ferocious people; a people who delighted in murdering, . . . and robbing and plundering; . . . whose hearts were set upon riches; . . . yet they sought to obtain these things by murdering and plundering, that they might not labor for them with their own hands" (verse 14).

Arrested as soon as he entered the land, Ammon was taken before King Lamoni, where he declared his desire to live among the people of Ishmael "perhaps until the day" he died (verse 23). Flattered by Ammon's attitude toward his people, Lamoni offered him one of his daughters as a wife. Running the risk of offending the king and thereby endangering his own life, Ammon responded to the king's offer: "Nay, but I will be thy servant. Therefore Ammon became a servant to King Lamoni. And it came to pass that he was set among other servants to watch the flocks of Lamoni, according to the custom of the Lamanites" (verse 25).

There had been some recurring problems between Lamoni's servants and other Lamanites in the region—specifically at the communal watering hole known as "the waters of Sebus" (verse 26). Three days after Ammon began his service watching the flocks of the king, this tension manifest itself again. The Lamanite antagonists "scattered the flocks . . . of the king . . . insomuch that they fled many ways" (verse 27). Once the flocks of the king were dispersed, Lamoni's servants reasoned: "Now the king will slay us, as he has our brethren because their flocks were scattered by the wickedness of these men. . . . Now they wept because of the fear of being slain" (verse 28). Clearly King Lamoni had put other seemingly incompetent servants to death when (on previous occasions) the adversarial Lamanites had scattered his flocks (Alma 19:20). Knowing this, Lamoni's servants felt they were able to predict how this episode would end—and the conclusion was not a positive one for them.

At the scattering of the flocks, Ammon, apparently seeing a potential missionary opportunity in all of this, quickly sprang into action. At his insistence, he and Lamoni's other servants gathered all of the scattered animals, at which point Ammon ordered the others to "encircle the flocks" that they not be scattered again (verse 33). Mosiah's son then turned his attention to the rather large group of antagonistic Lamanites who had intentionally dispersed Lamoni's herd. Though he was greatly outnumbered, Ammon took his nemeses to task.

He began to cast stones at them with his sling and, in doing so, slew "a certain number of them," thereby astonishing and angering his enemies (verse 36). Determined that he should fail (because he had slain six of their brethren), the Lamanites used their slings in an attempt to pelt Ammon with stones, but they were unable to hit him. Therefore, they "came forth with clubs to slay him" (verse 36).

As the mob lifted their clubs to smite Ammon, one by one he "smote off their arms with his sword" (verse 37). Indeed, he deflected blow after blow in this manner—again leaving his antagonists "astonished" (verse 37). The number of "arms" Ammon "smote off" were "not few in number," and his strength and skill was such that "he caused them to flee" (verses 37, 38).

The account informs us that Ammon killed six men with his sling, killed one with his sword,[1] "and smote off as many of their arms as were lifted against him, and they were not a few" (verse 38).

Once the king's enemies had been driven "afar off" Ammon went back to watering the flocks and then returned the herd to its pasture (verse 39). Meanwhile, the king's servants when into the king, "bearing the arms which had been smitten off by the sword of Ammon," and showed them to the king "as a testimony of the things which they had done" (verse 39).

BACKGROUND

We are informed that there had been some recurring problems between Lamoni's servants and other Lamanites in the region. The reason for the tension is not entirely clear. It may simply have been because of what the Book of Mormon refers to as the violent and plundering nature of the Lamanites in that region. Or the hostilities may have surfaced because of a degree of prejudice against Lamoni's servants—who apparently were not full-blooded Lamanites. The text refers to them as "Lamanitish" rather than Lamanite (Alma 17:26), potentially suggesting that they were of a mixed race—something prone to provoke hostilities and prejudice.[2]

While one might assume that the flocks were scattered as a means of stealing them, the text suggests that a much more heinous purpose was the motivation. For, of the villains in this episode, the book of Alma informs us, "They delighted in the destruction of their brethren; and for this cause they stood to scatter the flocks of the king" (verse 35). Thus, they had apparently learned through past experience that scattering the flocks stirred up the wrath of the king and resulted in the death of his domestics. The text suggests that these heartless Lamanites reveled in their power to bring to pass the death of Lamoni's servants through such a simple act. And, thus, they scattered the king's flocks.

As this background section will suggest, there may be things about this story that we have traditionally misinterpreted. For example, we customarily interpret this story to be about how Ammon was able to miraculously cut off dozens of arms with his sword—and how a bag of bloody human limbs was dragged into the king's palace as evidence of Ammon's almost supernatural skills and strength.[3] While it is quite possible that this is exactly what happened in this narrative, consider the following points, which may suggest a slightly different interpretation of the miracle.

- The narrative informs us that six men died by the sling, and only one by the sword. If Ammon cut off the arms of many men, why the lack of loss of life in this episode? Medical science would suggest that an individual who had his arm or hand amputated—thereby severing the brachial artery (of the upper arm) or radial and ulnar arteries (below the elbow)—would most likely bleed to death in a matter of minutes.[4] The rate of bleeding, and the likelihood of a swift death, would be increased by the physical exertion of the fight and the flight. Yet, the Book of Mormon informs us that *all* of the Laminate aggressors whose arms Ammon removed (presumably amputated) escaped alive even after the violent exchange. In the language of the text, Ammon "slew *none* with the sword *save it were their leader*; and he smote off as many of their arms as were lifted against him, *and they were not a few*" (Alma 17:38; emphasis added).[5] From a medical standpoint, it seems highly unlikely that a large mob of attackers could each suffer the amputation of a limb and yet not a single one die from the injury sustained. One commentator reasoned: "The amputees were severely injured, but probably they could recover. Mesoamericans were well used to battle injuries and were doubtless capable of arresting the blood loss."[6] *Perhaps!* However, there seems to be two potential problems with this explanation. First, the Book or Mormon dates this event to approximately 90 BCE.[7] The earliest date we have for the use of anything akin to a tourniquet is circa 199 BCE[8]—and on the Eastern Hemisphere, for snake bites (*not* for hemostatic purposes). The suggestion that this technique made its way to the Americas, and became common knowledge, only a hundred years later seems highly unlikely. A second problem is that the text speaks of the injured as fleeing "afar off" for their lives (Alma 17:37). As noted, this would not only increase the rate of blood loss, but it implies that the injured did not lie down to receive medical attention. Rather, they and those who *could* have attended to their wounds ran for their lives. Even if a *few* of those injured could have been fortunate enough to receive a tourniquet at the hands of a friend, the idea that *every single amputee* received one goes against reason.[9] At that point in history, a tourniquet would be the only possible way to have saved the life of one whose arm had been cut off. Yet, the text is clear: not a one of those who had their arms cut off died.

- We are told that those who "lifted" their "club to smite Ammon" were astonished as he consistently "smote off their arms" as they lifted them. Indeed, he "smote off as many of their arms as were lifted against him, and they were not a few." Is it possible that, when the text speaks of "arms" it means weapons (their clubs and swords) rather than the arms of their bodies? The term "arms" appears repeatedly in the Book of Mormon, but its usage is usually not how we traditionally interpret it in Alma 17. Together with its derivatives, the word *arm* is used in three distinct ways in the Book of Mormon, as shown in the following chart.

ARMS AS WEAPONS	ARMS AS GOD'S MANIFEST POWER	NON-WEAPON USES OF ARMS	UNCLEAR USES OF ARMS
1 Nephi 14:14; 1 Nephi 16:23; Jacob 7:24–25; Mosiah 9:16; Mosiah 10:8–9; Mosiah 20:24–26; Alma 2:10, 12, 14; Alma 24:2, 6; Alma 26:25, 34; Alma 27:3; Alma 27:23, 28; Alma 35:14; Alma 43:11; Alma 47:3, 5; Alma 48:23; Alma 50:26; Alma 51:9, 13, 17, 20; Alma 53:11, 13, 16; Alma 54:12; Alma 54:18; Alma 55:22; Alma 60:2; Alma 61:6; Alma 62:9; Helaman 1:14; 3 Nephi 2:11–12; 3 Nephi 3:3; Mormon 3:1; Ether 7:9.	1 Nephi 20:14; 1 Nephi 22:10, 11; 2 Nephi 1:15; 2 Nephi 8:5, 9; 2 Nephi 28:32; Jacob 2:25; Jacob 6:5; Enos 1:13; Omni 1:13; Mosiah 1:14; Mosiah 12:24; Mosiah 14:1; Mosiah 15:31; Mosiah 16:12; Mosiah 29:20; Alma 5:33; Alma 19:36; Alma 29:10; Alma 34:16; 3 Nephi 9:14; 3 Nephi 16:20; 3 Nephi 20:35; Mormon 5:11; Mormon 6:17.	1 Nephi 11:20[10]; 1 Nephi 21:22, 26, 28 and 2 Nephi 6:6[11]; 2 Nephi 4:34, 28:31[12]; 2 Nephi 19:20[13]; Mosiah 11:11[14]; Ether 14:12.[15]	Words of Mormon 1:13[16]; Alma 17:37–39 and 18:16, 20[17]; Alma 20:20[18]; Alma 24:25[19]; Alma 43:44[20]; Alma 44:5.[21]

It will be noted that the most common use of the term *arm* in the Book of Mormon is as a weapon: "They would take up arms against their brethren" (Alma 26:34). The second most common meaning of the term is as a representation of God's power being manifest: "The Lord hath made bare his holy arm" (3 Nephi 16:20). There are also a few examples where the word *arm* is employed to mean an appendage of a body: "And I looked and beheld the virgin again, bearing a child in her arms" (1 Nephi 11:20). Finally, there are a half dozen or so examples of the word *arm* being used in a way that could mean either a weapon or the arm of one's body, but where the passage is not entirely clear. The passage under discussion seems to be a prime example of this.

Is it possible that the Book of Mormon's reference to Ammon cutting off the arms of his Lamanite antagonists is actually a reference to him divesting them of their weapons—and not to amputating the limbs of their bodies? This interpretation seems to make sense on a number of fronts. First, it is harmonious with the language of the passage. For example, if one inserts "weapons" or "clubs" for "arms," the result is significant, in that Ammon is no longer doing something largely impossible (from a medical perspective). Likewise, if one replaces "smote" and "smite" with their equivalent meanings in early nineteenth-century English ("throwing," "casting," or "flinging"[22]) the following results:

> But behold, every man that lifted his club to *hit* Ammon, he *cast* off their *weapons* with his sword; for he did withstand their blows by *striking* their *clubs* with the edge of his sword, insomuch that they began to be astonished, and began to flee before him; yea, and they were not few in number; and he caused them to flee by the strength of his *weapon*.
>
> Now six of them had fallen by the sling, but he slew none save it were their leader with his sword; and he *cast* off as many of their *weapons* as were lifted against him, and they were not a few.
>
> And when he had driven them afar off, he returned and they watered their flocks and returned them to the pasture of the king, and then went in unto the king [one of his other servants], bearing the *weapons* which had been *cast* off *or flung to the ground* by the sword of Ammon, of those who sought to slay him; and they were carried in unto the king for a testimony of the things which they had done. (Alma 17:37–39)

Significantly, Alma 44:12 seems to support this reading of "smote"/"smite" as a reference to "knocking" or "casting" something to the earth. It states: "And now when Moroni had said these words, Zerahemnah retained his sword, and he was angry with Moroni, and he rushed forward that he might slay Moroni; *but as he raised his sword, behold, one of Moroni's soldiers smote it even to the earth, and it broke by the hilt*" (emphasis added). Here *smote* does not mean to "cut off" but to knock it to the earth—which is how Alma appears to be using the term in Alma 17:37–39. Each of Webster's 1828 synonyms for *smote* ("throwing," "casting," "flinging," "kicking," "striking" with a "blow," "colliding" with, or "destroying") seems to work in Alma 44, much as they do in Alma 17.

When we read the word *arms* in the way it is most commonly used in the Book of Mormon—as a weapon—it seems to agree with the language of the text. For example, Alma 17:38 reads: "He smote off as many of their *arms* as *were lifted* against him" (emphasis added). Typically, one would say he "raises" his arms but "lifts" his weapon. But verse 38 describes the Lamanites as "lifting" their "arms." Thus, our reading of the verse—"he *cast* off as many of their *weapons* as were *lifted* against him"—makes more sense in light of the verb employed.

Again, it makes no sense that every one of the men who raised the limbs of their bodies could have had those cut off and yet not a single one die because of the wound received. But it does make sense that every one of them could have had their weapons broken or knocked out of their hands in a way that seemed beyond the strength or ability of a normal mortal—thereby causing them to flee. Similarly, the image of a servant dragging a blood-soaked bag across the floor of the king's palace in order to show him the gory amputated limbs of his enemies seems somewhat fanciful. However, the idea that a servant would bring in a bag of captured weapons to show the king how many clubs or swords one man was able to take away from the king's enemies seems more likely.

In the end, this specific passage is unclear and we are left to conjecture. We simply do not have the ability to do a proper linguistic word study of the Book of Mormon, such as we might do when examining a passage from the Hebrew Old or Greek New Testament. The most we can do is offer an educated guess as to the intended meaning of the word *arms* in this specific story.[23] That being said, logic, combined with the most common use of the term *arms* in the Book of Mormon, suggests that perhaps a better interpretation of Alma 17 would be that Ammon "cut off" or took away the armaments of his enemies—rather than the limbs of their bodies.[24]

SYMBOLIC ELEMENTS

The most significant symbol in this story appears to be the "arms" Ammon "smites off" (Alma 17:37). The *Book of Mormon Reference Companion* points out: "Many of the references [in the Book of Mormon] to swords and perhaps other weapons are probably metaphorical rather than literal. Thus to 'take my sword' (Alma 60:28) might mean simply to go to war rather than actually picking up a sword; to 'fall by the sword' (2 Ne. 13:25) is probably a metaphor for dying in battle."[25] This being the case, it seems that the reverse can also be said to be true: when the Book of Mormon speaks of "arms" it *may* well be referring to weapons rather than the arms of one's body. Weapons are standard symbols for "warfare" or "violence"—and the word *arm* generally carries the connotation of manifest "power."[26] Thus, in this miracle "arms" can be representative of war, manifest power, and antagonism. The "smiting off" of "arms" then functions well as a symbol of Ammon's victory over the corrupt—even evil—powers and antagonism of his enemies.

Describing the Christocentric symbolism present in this narrative, Joseph Fielding McConkie and Robert L. Millet wrote, "Ammon becomes a messiah figure—humble servant, good shepherd, hope to the distraught, protector and defender of the king's flock. . . . Ammon, whose power was heaven-sent, sought no honor for himself save it were that of teaching the doctrines of his Father to King Lamoni and his people."[27] Thus, as with any prophet or faithful missionary, we see in Ammon's life an emulation of the Son of God.

APPLICATION AND ALLEGORIZATION

Ammon's purpose in serving King Lamoni and his people was their conversion to Christ. The miracle in this episode—whether you believe it to be about the removal of human limbs or the disarming of enemies—demonstrates that, through His servants, God manifests

His own power in astonishing ways. By application, for the purpose of His missionary work, God can make the Saints stand out, and thus bring them to the attention of those not of our faith. In the process, the gospel can be shared (see Alma 18:9–10). Elder Neal A. Maxwell pointed out: "God does not begin by asking us about our ability, but only about our availability, and if we then prove our dependability, he will increase our capability!"[28] President Hinckley said, "Live for the opportunity when you may go out as a servant for the Lord and an ambassador of eternal truth to the people of the world."[29] The key for us is that we must live in such a way that our lives truly are exemplary and a testament to the truthfulness of the gospel, rather than a distraction from the message we bear.

On a related note, one commentary on the Book of Mormon pointed out: "Ammon made quite a first impression on Lamoni, the king, that he would want Ammon to marry one of his daughters."[30] Missionaries must be beyond reproach in their behaviors—both public and private. Recently the *Salt Lake Tribune* highlighted an episode from the 1970s that caused the Church a great deal of embarrassment—and that greatly harmed missionary work in Thailand for a number of years: "In 1972, a Mormon missionary in Bangkok climbed on a statue of Buddha to have his picture taken. It was a huge embarrassment for the church and the missionary was sentenced to a year in prison, but released after six months when the king of Thailand pardoned him. Now all missionaries are instructed in cultural sensitivity."[31] Ammon's example drew the attention of those not of his faith—but in a positive way. Missionaries must ensure that their example draws attention, but the right kind of attention. One commentary pointed out, "As we live righteously, the power of God is made manifest in us. If we are willing, the Lord will provide the opportunity and give us the strength as well as the words to say to bless peoples' lives."[32] The reverse is also true: if our behavior is not holy, those who observe us will not recognize us as true messengers of God.

It is interesting that Ammon's teaching opportunity came only after his service to the king and his people. One source points out: "Ammon's approach to missionary work was simple and effective. The first thing he told the king was, 'I will be thy servant'—in other words, he was willing to serve. While serving, he would show forth God's power in order to win some hearts and to lead them to believe in his words."[33] Elsewhere we read: "The formula is simple: first a servant, and then a teacher."[34] One of the most effective forms of missionary work is service.[35] Those whose hearts are hardened against the Church are often softened when they are served in sincerity and love.

As a final application, it has been suggested that Ammon can be seen as a type for Christ in this narrative. Like Jesus, he stands between his people and their enemies to protect (defense) and disarm (offense). As Ammon did this for King Lamoni's people, Christ does this *for* us—and *against* our greatest enemy, Satan! "What a comfort to envision the Lord that way, . . . standing against evil, even dying to rescue us from hell."[36] Ammon's actions certainly remind us of the Lord's power and devotion to us as we daily face our enemies.

NOTES

1. The only one he killed with the sword was their "leader" (Alma 17:38).

2. See John Sorenson, "When Lehi's Party Arrived in the Land, Did They Find Others There?" in *Journal of Book of Mormon Studies*, Volume 1, Number 1 (Fall 1992): 31. See also Gardner (2007), 4:273.

3. As an example of how we typically interpret this passage, one commentator wrote: "The servants of King Lamoni . . . took the bloody stumps of the attackers' arms cut off by Ammon to the king 'for a testimony of the things which they had done' (Alma 17:39)" [John W. Welch, "Why Study Warfare in the Book of Mormon," in Stephen D. Ricks and William J. Hamblin, editors, *Warfare in the Book of Mormon* (Salt Lake City: Deseret Book, 1990), 21. See also Bassett (2007–2008), 2:162]. Another described the scene as follows: "While defending the flocks of King Lamoni, Ammon was attacked by a band of brigands who had been marauding in the region. He killed a number of them at long range with his sling, after which 'they came forth with clubs to slay him. But behold, every man that lifted his club to smite Ammon, he smote off their arms with his sword; for he did withstand their blows by smiting their arms with the edge of his sword' (Alma 17:36–37). . . . Ammon's sword technique deserves some attention. The text reads, 'Every man that lifted his club to smite Ammon, he smote off their arms with his sword.' Actually severing an enemy's forearm or hand with a sword is a difficult task. What will generally occur is that the sword will cut into the flesh until it reaches the bone, partially severing or cracking it. However, since the victim's arm is free to rotate at the shoulder, the sword will simply push the limb away in the direction of the blow rather than cut deeper into the limb. Thus, in most situations one would expect a sword to make a deep gash but not actually to sever the arm. In order to sever an arm with a sword, the sword must be extremely sharp, must be swung swiftly, and must strike against a limb that is either somehow fixed, or that is moving toward the sword blade. Thus Ammon's sword technique makes perfect military sense. He waits for the enemy to attack

him with his club. As the club is raised and brought down swiftly toward Ammon, Ammon swings his sword in a fast powerful blow aimed at the forearm. The combination of the attacker's swing toward Ammon and the force of Ammon's own swing is sufficient to sever the forearm. Thus, according to the Book of Mormon, Ammon waited for precisely the right moment to initiate his arm-severing sword technique with maximum efficacy against his enemy" [William Hamblin and Brent Merrill, "Swords in the Book of Mormon," in Stephen D. Ricks and William J. Hamblin, editors, *Warfare in the Book of Mormon* (Salt Lake City: Deseret Book, 1990), 335–37]. Elsewhere we read: "He smote off their arms with his sword. This detail of the narrative may be read in connection with Deut. 33:20. In this verse and the following verses, Moses prophesied concerning the Tribe of Gad, among other things, 'He dwelleth as a lion and teareth the arm with the crown of the head.' That means, according to Hebrew commentators, that the warriors of that Tribe had learned to disarm, and kill an antagonist by smiting the crown of his head and his arm with one stroke, or one movement of the sword's blade. Ammon seems to have learned this manner of swordplay, in which the warriors of Gad excelled, and which inspired Moses to compare that Tribe to a lion having its lair in the wilderness" [Reynolds and Sjodahl (1955–1961), 3:251–52.] The preceding commentary is an example of the traditional interpretation of this pericope. In this reading, Ammon accosts the king's enemies first with his sling and then with his sword. He kills six men with his sling, after which he kills their leader with his sword. And, using unusual—but feasible—swordplay, he cuts the hands or forearms off numerous men who, in astonishment, "began to flee" after receiving a wound that would normally cause one to bleed to death (Alma 17:37).

4. In his widely cited article, Dr. Donald Trunkey indicates that death from the traumatic severing of a limb can take place in as little as a few minutes. Dr. Trunkey suggests that severe cases of hemorrhaging require surgical intervention within twenty minutes of the injury [see Donald Trunkey, "Trimodal Distribution of Death" in *Scientific America*, volume 249, number 2 (1983), 20–27. See also Justin Sobrino and Shahid Shafi, "Timing and causes of death after injuries," in *Baylor University Medical Center Proceedings*, volume 26, number 2 (2013), 122].

5. See Royal Skousen, editor, *The Book of Mormon: The Earliest Text* (New Haven, CT: Yale University Press, 2009), 342–43. See also Skousen (2006), 1972–1976. Nyman conjectures that Ammon cut off the arms of "at least . . . fifteen or twenty" men [Nyman (2003–2004), 3:241].

6. Gardner (2007), 4:280.

7. See parenthetic date on the bottom of pages 252–53 of the 1981 LDS edition of the Book of Mormon. Of course, these dates are approximations. Nevertheless, their general accuracy is assumed.

8. See Jai Prakash Shama and Rashmi Salhotra, "Tourniquets in Orthopedic Surgery," in *Indian Journal of Orthopedics*, Volume 46, Number 4 (July–August 2012), 377; Stephen L. Richey, "Tourniquets for the Control of Traumatic Hemorrhage: A Review of the Literature," in *World Journal of Emergency Surgery*, Volume 2 (2007), 28. The earliest use of tourniquets was for snakebites, *not* to stop bleeding. The latter

use developed much later [see Richard A. Gabriel and Karen S. Metz, *A History of Military Medicine*, 2 vol. (Westport, CT: Greenwood Press, 1992), 1:130]. One text placed the beginning of the use of tourniquets among Native Americans at around AD 1000 [see Emory Dean Keoke and Kay Marie Porterfield, *Encyclopedia of American Indian Contributions to the World* (New York: Facts On File, 2002), 271]. While no one is certain exactly when the first hemostatic tourniquet was used, what is certain is that it was too late to have been known by the Lamanites of Ammon's era [see David R. Welling, Patricia L. McKay, Todd E. Rasmussen, and Norman M. Rich, "Historical Vignettes in Vascular Surgery," in *Journal of Vascular Surgery*, Volume 55, Issue 1 (January 2012), 286; John F. Kragh Jr., et al., "Historical Review of Emergency Tourniquet Use to Stop Bleeding," *The American Journal of Surgery* (2012), 242–52].

9. Without speaking in hyperbole, it seems fair to say that the friend who would have applied this tourniquet would have to have been inspired, as it appears quite certain that no one on the Western Hemisphere in the pre-Christian era could have known about this technique for preventing an amputee from bleeding to death.

10. Mary holds Jesus in her arms.

11. The Gentiles shall carry their children in their arms.

12. Do not trust in the arm of flesh.

13. Men will eat their own flesh.

14. Rest one's arm upon the chair.

15. Coriantumr received a wound on his arm during a fight with Lib.

16. King Benjamin fought with the strength of his arm. This can certainly imply his physical arm, but it could also imply his weapon (which the passage implies he is using).

17. Ammon cuts off the arms of the Lamanites. This can be interpreted as physical arms or weapons. The latter interpretation makes the most sense in light of the claims of the passage that no one died from this injury.

18. Ammon "smote" the "arm" of Lamoni's father. Since Lamoni's father didn't die from this "smiting," it would seem reasonable that it was his weapon that was "smitten" or knocked out of his hand rather than his arm being cut off.

19. We read of weapons of war and arms lifted to slay enemies. The word *arms* here can refer to the hands that held the weapons or the weapons themselves. The passage is simply unclear on the matter.

20. The Lamanites did "smite in two" the Nephite's "head-plates," and did "pierce" their "breastplates," and did "smite" their "arms." As the description here is of the lack of protection of the Nephites' armor, it is quite possible that the "smiting" of the "arms" was a reference to the Lamanites' knocking weapons from the hands of the Nephites—or breaking the weapons of their opponents. The passage does not say that the Nephites' heads were split open or that their chests were pierced. Thus, it may not mean that the arms of their bodies were injured.

21. God strengthened the "arms" of the Nephites, that they gained power over Zerahemnah and his armies. While they may have gained physical strength from

God, the passage can quite readily be seen to be implying that God made their weapons powerful against their enemies.

22. See *Noah Webster's First Edition of an American Dictionary of the English Language—Facsimile [1828] Edition* (San Francisco, CA: Foundation for American Christian Education, 1967), s.v., "Smite." Webster is not alone in using *smite* as a synonym for "throwing," "casting," "flinging," "kicking," "striking" with a "blow," "colliding" with, or "destroying." A survey of texts contemporary with Joseph Smith suggests that this use of the word is commonplace [see, for example, Daniel P. Thompson, *The Adventures of Timothy Peacock, Esquire, or, Freemasonry Practically Illustrated* (Vermont: Knapp and Jewett, 1835), 210; Lydia Howard Sigourney, *Sketches* (Philadelphia: Key & Biddle, 1834), 15; Achsa W. Sprague, *The Poet and Other Poems* (Boston: William White and Co, 1865), 170]. Each of these texts uses *smite* as a synonym for the aforementioned words.

23. I am not calling for an entire rereading of all passages of the Book of Mormon in which "arms" are mentioned, or in which warfare is depicted. I am only suggesting that *this particular periscope* may need to be re-examined because the description of the event, when traditionally interpreted, requires the reader to assume things largely impossible (that a dozen or more people could have their arms cut off, run as hard and fast as they can into the wilderness to escape their enemy, and yet never bleed to death). The aforementioned alternate reading simply seems to make more sense in context of the details of the chapter, and in light of what modern medicine tells us the human body is capable of enduring.

24. For a more systematic treatment of this story, see Alonzo L. Gaskill, "Ammon and the Arms of the Lamanites: Have We Been Misreading the Book of Mormon?" in *Restoration Studies*, Volume 15 (2014): 82–94.

25. William J. Hamblin, "Weapons," in Largey (2003), 783–84.

26. See Ryken, Wilhoit, and Longman (1998), 44–47, 43–44.

27. See McConkie and Millet (1987–1991), 3:130.

28. Neal A. Maxwell, *The Neal A Maxwell Quote Book*, Cory H. Maxwell, compiler (Salt Lake City: Bookcraft, 1997), 1.

29. See Hinckley (1997), 345.

30. Ogden and Skinner (2011), 1:424.

31. See "Mormon Missions: Did You Know . . . ?" in *Salt Lake Tribune*, September 30, 2011. See also http://www.freerepublic.com/focus/f-religion/1991107/posts. Another source added: "Relations with Thailand's immigration office became troubled in 1972. For 20 years missionaries were limited to numbers under 100, and visas were issued for only brief periods. In 1992 the government created a new visa policy for LDS missionaries that allowed 100 missionaries to remain for 2 years with only one renewal. Growth expanded rapidly after that action" [http://globalmormonism. byu.edu/?page_id=68].

32. Pinegar and Allen (2003), 568.

33. Ogden and Skinner (2011), 1:424.

34. Pinegar and Allen (2003), 567.

35. McConkie and Millet wrote: "The ambassadors of the Lord Jesus are called upon

to do that which their Master does best-love and serve. Selfless service sanctifies both giver and receiver" [McConkie and Millet (1987–1991), 3:131].

36. Debbie Parker, in review of *Miracles of the Book of Mormon*.

King Lamoni *and* Others Collapse *as* Though They Were Dead

Alma 18–19

The Miracle

Having learned of Ammon's miraculous recovery of the king's flocks and his disarming of the king's enemies, Lamoni assumed that Ammon was "more than a man" (Alma 18:2). Indeed, the king said to his servants, "I know that" he "is the Great Spirit . . . of whom our fathers have spoken" (verse 4). Believing as he did that Ammon was a divine being, Lamoni began to fear, owing to the fact that he had slain many of his own servants who had failed to adequately protect his flocks.

The king inquired as to where Ammon was. When he learned that Ammon was feeding his horses and preparing his chariot, the king was astonished at the faithfulness of his servant. Puzzled and yet filled with a desire to understand who or what Ammon was, the king sent for him.

When Ammon arrived he asked the king what he wanted of him. But rather than answering, for the space of an hour Lamoni just looked at Ammon. Having asked more than once what the king desired, Ammon received (through the Spirit) a knowledge of the thoughts of the king and explained to him that he knew the king had called him forth because of what had happened with his enemies. Ammon explained that he was but a man, and not "that Great Spirit, who knows all things" (verse 18).

Ammon then asked the king a question: "Wilt thou hearken unto my words, if I tell thee by what power I do these things?" (verse 22). Lamoni replied that he would, at which point Ammon began to teach him about God, the plan, the creation, the Fall, the Atonement, and even the history of the descendants of Father Lehi. Lamoni "believed all his words" (verse 40) and cried out to God: "O Lord, have mercy; according to thy abundant mercy which thou hast had upon the people of Nephi, have upon me, and my people" (verse 41). After the king had offered this prayer, "he fell unto the earth, as if he were dead" (verse 42). Lamoni was carried to his wife, where he lay for some two days and two nights, while the queen and her children mourned over the loss of their husband and father, assuming he was deceased.

As they were about to place Lamoni's body in the sepulcher, the queen sent for Ammon and, upon his arrival, indicated that her servants had told her that he was a "prophet of a holy God, and that" he had "power to do many mighty works in his name" (Alma 19:4). Lamoni's wife implored Ammon to go in unto her husband and to do whatever he had power to do on his behalf. Ammon informed her that Lamoni indeed was not dead and that on the morrow he would rise again—thus she should not bury him. Ammon then asked the queen if she believed what he had said. She replied that she had no witness save his word and that of her servants. Nevertheless, she believed. Therefore, Ammon said to her, "Blessed art thou because of thy exceeding faith; I say unto thee, woman, there has not been such great faith among all the people of the Nephites" (verse 10).

According to the words of Ammon, on the morrow the king arose and announced to his wife: "Blessed be the name of God, and blessed art thou. For as sure as thou livest, behold, I have seen my Redeemer; and he shall come forth, and be born of a woman, and he shall redeem all mankind who believe on his name" (verses 12–13). When Lamoni had spoken these words, "his heart was swollen within him, and he sunk again with joy" (verse 13). The queen was then also "overpowered by the Spirit," and she too fell to the ground unconscious. Ammon immediately fell to his knees and thanked God for the miracle He had performed. Then Ammon was "overpowered with joy; and . . . sunk to the earth" (verse 14).

Seeing the king, his wife, and now Ammon all unconscious upon the earth, Lamoni's servants began to fear, and they too collapsed—all save it were one: a female servant named Abish. She "knew that it was the power of God" and, therefore, "ran forth from house to house, making it known unto the people" (verse 17). Though she apparently expected this miracle would convert others to her cherished faith, "to her disappointment the assembled group contended about the meaning of the spectacle before them."[1]

BACKGROUND

Abish was a "Lamanitish" woman—a servant in the household of King Lamoni and his wife. While we cannot say for certain, it has been suggested by commentators that the phrase "Lamanitish" (as opposed to "Lamanite") suggests that Abish may have been of a mixed race (not a full-blooded Lamanite but perhaps half Lamanite and half Nephite).[2] Or this unique descriptor may simply suggest that she was a Lamanite who had rejected the religion of the Lamanites and, thus, lived among them while not subscribing to their culture and beliefs (hence, "Lamanitish" or "kind-of-Lamanite"). The text is clear that Abish had been converted to the Lord years earlier (Alma 19:16), though she had hidden that fact from others. Her conversion is said to have come through "a remarkable vision of her father" (Alma 19:16). Some have interpreted that to mean that her father had a vision, shared it with her, and it converted her to Christ. However, it has also been suggested that Abish had a vision of her deceased father—appearing to her from the spirit world—which resulted in her conversion to the Lord.[3] It is unclear which is the case, though the former is probably most likely. Daniel H. Ludlow pointed out that "she is one of only three women in the entire Nephite-Lamanite-Mulekite-Jaredite records to have her name in the Book of Mormon. The other two are Sariah, the wife of Lehi (1 Nephi 2:5), and Isabel, the harlot (Alma 39:3)."[4] Abish's gift of healing (see Alma 19:29–30) highlights her spirituality. Her being named here caused one commentator to suggest, "Abish must have played a more significant role in the original record than she does in Mormon's account."[5]

Of King Lamoni, the *Book of Mormon Reference Companion* states that he was a

Lamanite king over the land of Ishmael, a descendant of Ishmael (Alma 17:21), and the first Lamanite convert of Ammon. Although an enemy of the Nephites and a king of an apostate people, Lamoni was still a man of reason and conscience. He eventually became a man of great faith and an example of the joy and dedication that accompanies spiritual rebirth, as well as a tremendous tool in the hand of the Lord that led to thousands of Lamanites coming to a knowledge of the truth (Alma 17–21).[6]

We also know that sometime after his conversion he set out with Ammon to free his brethren who were imprisoned in Middoni (see Alma 10:1–8). Lamoni stood up to his father, who commanded him to slay the Nephite Ammon and who also sought to take Lamoni's life. Lamoni "built synagogues, taught his people the gospel, granted them religious liberty"—and he also refused to take up arms along with the other Anti-Nephi-Lehies when their unconverted brethren determined to slay them (Alma 24:1–5).[7] Thus, though initially an ardent disbeliever, Lamoni became a great missionary and an example of faithfulness to covenants and conscience.

It seems fair to say that Ammon is not as disturbed by Lamoni's collapse as those around him are, at least in part because he has experienced this before. It will be recalled that he was present when his friend Alma the Younger collapsed and lay unconscious for two days and two nights (Mosiah 27). Thus, for Ammon, the similarity between these two experiences may have actually given him hope where others were provoked to despair and doubt by the experience.[8]

One commentary on the Book of Mormon pointed out: "Some have been critical of Ammon's response to Lamoni, knowing that God is a corporeal being and, thus, more than just 'a Great Spirit.' In fact, Ammon's statement is technically correct. The God of the Old Testament was Jehovah, who had not as yet obtained a body of flesh and bones."[9] Ammon is clearly using the language familiar to Lamoni to convey foreign ideas in a meaningful way. The missionary is hardly guilty of teaching false doctrine when he refers to "that Great Spirit"— of which Lamoni had spoken—as the true God.

SYMBOLIC ELEMENTS

In his six-volume commentary on the Book of Mormon, Brant A.

Gardner conjectures that the number of days King Lamoni is seemingly dead before the family buries him (two days) may have some symbolic significance. He wrote, "Apparently the two days and two nights had a symbolic significance in Ishmaelite culture, since otherwise, given the climate, burial would have been required within a matter of hours or certainly by the next day. Alma had also lain unconscious for two days and two nights."[10] Another commentator likewise explained, "Alma was struck down and carried to his father, who gathered the priests together. They then fasted and prayed for two days and two nights, the total time being about three days (Mosiah 27:19–23). King Lamoni was unconscious for two days and two nights, and then Ammon said he would rise on the morrow. While there may be some symbolism with Christ being in the tomb for three days, there is no scriptural mention of it in either case."[11]

For Lamoni and his wife, the "sleeping in God" (Alma 19:8) they suddenly experienced reminds us somewhat of the ordinance of baptism, in that the king and his companion were of one persuasion before their "sleep" and of another after. It will be recalled that the Apostle Paul spoke of baptism as the death of the old man and the birth of a new (Romans 6; Colossians 3:8–17). The king and queen of the land of Ishmael had a conversion experience that was well symbolized by their "sleep," just as baptism for you and me serves as a token of our own conversion experience. The old person is dead and gone, and a new one now lives and reigns—or so it should!

APPLICATION AND ALLEGORIZATION

There is an interesting lesson to be learned from Abish's experience. She had secretly been a believer, but she had hidden that fact from most everyone she knew. Suddenly a miracle took place, and in her excitement and love for the gospel, she went about telling everyone, thinking they would be converted by what she knew was a sign from God. Much to her surprise, however, people were not converted by witnessing the miracle. Rather, they reasoned it away. The Prophet Joseph Smith noted: "The dawning of the morning makes its appearance in the east and moves along gradually. So also will the coming of the Son of Man be. It will be small at its first appearance and gradually become larger until every eye shall see it. . . . Shall the wicked understand? Oh no. They [will] attribute it to a natural cause. They will probably suppose it is two great comets coming in contact with each other."[12] Joseph's point was that even the miracle of the Second Coming itself will be explained away by those who do not have faith. Miracles simply do not have the power to convert. As a testament to this truth, the *History of the Church* records:

> Ezra Booth, of Mantua, a Methodist preacher of much more than ordinary culture, and with strong natural abilities, in company with his wife, Mr. and Mrs. Johnson, and some other citizens of this place, (Hiram) visited [Joseph] Smith at his home in Kirtland, in 1831. Mrs. Johnson had been afflicted for some time with a lame arm, and was not at the time of the visit able to lift her hand to her head. The party visited Smith partly out of curiosity, and partly to see for themselves what there might be in the new doctrine. During the interview the conversation turned on the subject of supernatural gifts, such as were conferred in the days of the apostles. Someone said, "Here is Mrs. Johnson with a lame arm; has God given any power to men now on earth to cure her?" A few moments later, when the conversation had turned in another direction, Smith arose, and walking across the room, and taking Mrs. Johnson by the hand, said in the most solemn and impressive manner: "Woman, in the name of the Lord Jesus Christ, I command thee to be whole," and immediately left the room. The company were awe-stricken at the infinite presumption of the man, and the calm assurance with which he spoke. The sudden mental and moral shock—I know not how better to explain the well-attested fact, electrified the rheumatic arm—Mrs. Johnson at once lifted it with ease, and on her return home the next day she was able to do her washing without difficulty or pain.[13]

Through witnessing this miracle, Ezra Booth was "converted" to the Church. A few months later he left for a mission to Missouri (D&C 52:3, 23). However, Booth was upset to have to walk and preach the entire journey. He thus began to criticize and find fault with the Church and its leaders. And in September of that same year, he was excommunicated.[14] The miraculous experience of seeing Joseph Smith instantly heal Alice "Elsa" Johnson provided no staying power, because miracles have not the power to convert (D&C 63:9–11). Only sincere faith, coupled with prayer, holds the seeds of true conversion. Abish's intent (in inviting others to witness the miracle) was pure. Nevertheless, sacred things are to be kept sacred for a reason. And what seems so obviously miraculous to believers is ever the focus of scorn and ridicule for those who disbelieve.

Perhaps another lesson we can learn from Abish is this: though her efforts seemed to fail miserably (Alma 19:28), nevertheless, God was able to look past her failings and accomplish good. So it is with each of us. We are all inadequately equipped to do the work of God. We make mistakes, regardless of what our calling is. However, in spite of our weakness, God is able to move the work forward. And just as he turned Abish's less-than-ideal activities into fruitfulness, He can do the same for you and me as we seek to faithfully serve Him.

Another message resident in this miracle is the eternal truth that we should never "write off" any of God's children. King Lamoni was not a likely convert. He and his people had largely embraced a pagan religion. He was filled with racial prejudice against Nephites. He was comfortable putting to death those who worked for him when they fell short of expectations. However, Ammon saw a son of God in this corrupt king. Through the missionary's example and the workings of the Spirit, Lamoni was changed in his heart and his beliefs. He repented of his violent ways. He embraced the doctrine of Christ. He rejected his former prejudices. And he served as a mighty missionary. No one is beyond God's reach. You and I should look optimistically at every soul—at every one of God's children. They may choose to reject our message, but all have a right to hear it, and conversion often comes in the lives of those we would never expect.

It seems that this miracle is also a testament to the reality of the gifts of the Spirit and the fact that they are manifest in different ways in various individuals' lives.

> In this simple ability to believe based upon another's testimony, the queen is laying claim to one of the most powerful of the gifts of the Spirit: "To some it is given by the Holy Ghost to know that Jesus Christ is the Son of God, and that he was crucified for the sins of the world. To others it is given to believe on their words, that they also might have eternal life if they continue faithful" (D&C 46:13–14). . . .
>
> Those who know certainly have a gift, but others have the gift of the ability to believe. They apparently do not need the Spirit's personal confirmation [through a voice or vision] but, like this Lamanite queen, may sincerely believe because of faith in other's words.[15]

Not all need the same kind of spiritual experiences—or necessarily the same caliber of experience—to believe and hold faithfully to the gospel and their covenants. "For all have not every gift given unto them; . . . to some is given one, and to some is given another, that all may be profited thereby" (D&C 46:11, 12). This miracle reminds us that spiritual experiences are really Spirit to spirit. In other words, the Spirit—when necessary—may take our spirit to a place where God can commune with us unfettered by worldly or external influences. At other times, it may not. However, the Prophet Joseph Smith taught: "All things whatsoever God in his infinite wisdom has seen fit and proper to reveal to us, while we are dwelling in mortality . . . are revealed to us in the abstract, and independent of affinity of this mortal tabernacle, but are revealed to our spirits precisely as though we had no bodies at all."[16] Thus, spiritual encounters are actually the experience of the Holy Spirit speaking to your personal spirit. And how my spirit will connect with God's Spirit may not be how yours will. Regarding the uniqueness of this particular miracle, one commentary states: "This remarkable story sheds considerable light on a number of biblical texts. In both the Old and New Testaments we have instances in which the bodily functions of prophets were suspended as part of a revelatory experience."[17] Balaam had such an experience (Numbers 24:4, 16), as did Saul (1 Samuel 19:20–24). Ezekiel (Ezekiel 3:14–17), Peter (Acts 10:10–11; 11:5), and Paul (Acts 22:17, 21; 2 Corinthians 12:1–4) each experienced this sort of miracle—that included a period of time in a state of trance.

> From what we can deduce from scriptural writ, it appears that a trance is a state in which the body and its functions become quiescent in order that the full powers of the Spirit may be centered on the revelations of heaven. Freed from the fetters of a mortal body, man's spirit can be ushered into the divine presence; it can hear what otherwise could not be heard and see what otherwise could not be seen—even the visions of eternity and even the Almighty himself. . . .
>
> The story of Ammon and Lamoni affirms religious trances as a legitimate revelatory device. Lamoni, as already noted, came forth from his trance testifying that he had seen the Redeemer and then prophesied relative to the Savior's birth and the necessity of all mankind believing on his name. . . . The test of the legitimacy of the religious trance, like that of tongues is the efficacy of its purpose. Its genuineness

must be ascertained by the same standards that determine the verity of revelation in all other forms—that is, by the asking of such questions as: Does it teach faith in Christ, repentance, sacrifice, obedience to the laws and ordinances of the gospel, and loyalty to the Lord's current and constituted Church and his anointed servants?[18]

Ammon, along with Lamoni and his wife, spoke sacred truths after their spiritual encounter—and their lives, along with those whom they taught, were changed because of this spiritual experience. Such attests to its divinity. While encounters such as this one are rare, nevertheless, we sense in this miracle a truth: namely, that the Spirit operates in a variety of ways in the conversion process. Some see visions while others simply feel the sweet confirming witness of the Holy Spirit (1 Corinthians 1:6). Some are healed, while others simply experience a healing of their hearts. One conversion is not more real—more meaningful—than another.[19] But the Lord, in his infinite wisdom, provides what you and I individually need. The converting power of His Spirit is available to all who seek it—and in the form and manner specifically best for the earnest seeker.

As an additional application, the reader will recall Nephi's exhaustion after testifying with force to Laman and Lemuel (1 Nephi 17:47). As one commentator noted, "An unusual outpouring of the Spirit of the Lord is typically followed by physical exhaustion (see 1 Nephi 1:7; Moses 1:10; Joseph Smith—History 1:20; Daniel 8:27; *Teachings*, pp. 280–81)."[20] Many men who have faithfully exercised the priesthood have had the experience of being physically drained after a powerful priesthood blessing. The Prophet Joseph testified that "a man who exercises great faith in administering to the sick, blessing little children, or confirming, is liable to become weakened."[21] Such seems to be the case here also. Ammon, Lamoni, and the queen, along with others in the house, had a significant spiritual encounter, and each was left physically drained because of it. While the Spirit is primarily concerned with the changing of our souls, it also tends to have a powerful physiological effect on us from time to time. Joseph Smith taught:

[The] Holy Ghost has no other effect than pure intelligence. It is more powerful in expanding the mind, enlightening the understanding, and storing the intellect with present knowledge, of a man who is of the literal seed of Abraham, than one that is a Gentile, though it may not have half as much visible effect upon the body; for as the Holy Ghost falls upon one of the literal seed of Abraham, it is calm and serene; and his whole soul and body are only exercised by the pure spirit of intelligence; while the effect of the Holy Ghost upon a Gentile, is to purge out the old blood, and make him actually of the seed of Abraham. That man that has none of the blood of Abraham (naturally) must have a new creation by the Holy Ghost. In such a case, there may be more of a powerful effect upon the body, and visible to the eye, than upon an Israelite, while the Israelite at first might be far before the Gentile in pure intelligence.[22]

Finally, in this miracle we see Ammon exercising a gift we have seen exercised by others who wear the prophetic mantel, namely the ability to know the thoughts and intents of the heart. Regarding this gift and its symbolic merit, see our earlier discussion of Amulek and Alma discerning the thoughts of the people (Alma 10:16–18; 11:21–25; 12:3, 7).

NOTES

1. See Largey (2003), 24–25. See also Pinegar and Allen (2007), 574.

2. See Sorenson (Fall 1992), 31.

3. See Gardner (2007), 4:302–03. See also Daniel H. Ludlow, *A Companion to Your Study of the Book of Mormon* (Salt Lake City: Deseret Book, 1976), 207.

4. See Ludlow (1976), 207. Though she is not a Nephite or a Lamanite (or one of the other "ites" of the Book of Mormon), nevertheless, Mary, the mother of Jesus, is also mentioned by name in that sacred text (Alma 7:10; Mosiah 3:8). See also Nyman (2003–2004), 3:255.

5. Gardner (2007), 4:303.

6. Jack R. Christianson, "Lamoni," in Largey (2003), 498. See also Reynolds and Sjodahl (1955–1962), 3:271.

7. Christianson, in Largey (2003), 499.

8. See Gardner (2007), 4:299.

9. McConkie and Millet (1987–1991), 3:136.

10. Gardner (2007), 4:298.

11. Nyman (2003–2004), 3:252n6.

12. Joseph Smith, in Ehat and Cook (1980), 181; spelling and punctuation standardized.

13. *History of The Church* (1978), 1:215–216, note †.

14. See *Church History in the Fulness of Times*, second edition (Salt Lake City: The Church of Jesus Christ of Latter-day Saints, 2000), 113–14.

15. Gardner (2007), 4:300.

16. See Smith, in Smith (1976), 355.

17. McConkie and Millet (1987–1991), 3:139.

18. McConkie and Millet (1987–1991), 3:140, 141.

19. Nibley pointed out, regardless of the nature of the divine experience, "They are all communication beyond your control" [Nibley (2004), 2:306].

20. McConkie and Millet (1987–1991), 1:139. See also Gardner (2007), 1:308.

21. Smith, in Smith (1976), 281.

22. Smith, in Smith (1976), 149.

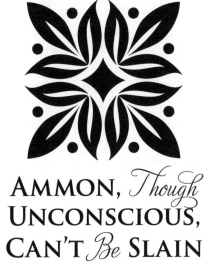

AMMON, *Though* UNCONSCIOUS, CAN'T *Be* SLAIN

ALMA 19:22–24

THE MIRACLE

In the process of their conversion experience, King Lamoni and his wife—along with Ammon and the servants of the king—fell to the earth, unconscious, as though they were dead. Indeed, so much was their state akin to death that Lamoni's family had prepared to bury him, sensing no respirations or circulation in their fallen father.

As Ammon lay unconscious upon the ground and those whom Abish had gathered gawked at the scene, one man stepped forward—approaching the body of the motionless missionary. He who approached with weapon drawn was the brother of the only man Ammon had slain with his sword at the waters of Sebus. (Ammon, in an attempt to defend the king's flocks, slew six with his sling, but only the leader of the mob was killed via Ammon's sword.) This brother of the now deceased leader of terrorist Lamanites perceived an opportunity at hand. Mormon informs us that he was "exceedingly angry" at Ammon for killing his brother and sought now to capitalize on this opportunity to "slay him" (Alma 19:22).

However, much to the surprise of all present, as the unnamed villain raised his weapon to smite Ammon, the man with murder in his heart suddenly dropped dead. Mormon does not record for us the specific cause of death, but the implication is "death by divine." In other words, in an act of preservation, God saved the missionary and killed the mercenary.

Mormon informs us that, though unconscious and incapable of defending himself, Ammon could not be slain. Indeed, Mormon suggests his divine protection was the fulfillment of the promise God made to Ammon's father, King Mosiah, when He informed the monarch: "Let them go up [on their missions], for many shall believe on their words, and they shall have eternal life; and I will deliver thy sons out of the hands of the Lamanites" (Mosiah 28:7). God always keeps His promises, and here a divine assurance to Mosiah is recorded as having been kept.

Those who witnessed the unexpected death of the Lamanite vigilante were overcome with fear and "durst not put forth their hands to touch him or any of those who had fallen" (verse 24).

BACKGROUND

One commentator on this miracle highlighted the fear that came upon those who saw Ammon's life preserved—and the consequences of this miracle on their view of Ammon. "Those present have literally seen a marvel. An armed man, about to kill a helpless one, had just fallen dead. No wonder no one dared touch any of the unconscious bodies. . . . This experience reinforced the already prevalent possibility that Ammon was 'more than a man.'"[1]

The preservation of Ammon's life in a miraculous manner—when all circumstances would suggest that he should have been slain in this scenario—makes a significant doctrinal point. We have been told time and again that "the righteous are not taken before their time."[2] While it is common to hear at funerals individuals say things like, "What a tragedy!" or "She was too young!" yet the doctrine seems to suggest otherwise. In the Doctrine and Covenants we read: "Thy days are known, and thy years shall not be numbered less" (D&C 122:9). Elsewhere in the Doctrine and Covenants we are told, "For there is a time appointed for every man, according as his works shall be" (D&C 121:25). President Joseph Fielding Smith stated, "No righteous man [or woman] is taken before his [or her] time."[3] President Spencer W. Kimball taught, "I am positive in my mind that the Lord has planned our destiny. We can shorten our lives [by living recklessly and unrighteously], but I think we cannot lengthen them very much."[4] Elsewhere

President Kimball wrote, "Just as Ecclesiastes (3:2) says, I am confident there is a time to die. . . . [We] seldom exceed our time very much. . . . God controls our lives . . . but gives us our agency."[5] Elder Neal A. Maxwell also taught that "no righteous individual dies an untimely death."[6] In President Kimball's famous talk "Tragedy or Destiny?" we find this statement about deaths that come about through seemingly tragic circumstances:

> The daily newspaper screamed the headlines: "Plane Crash Kills 43. No Survivors of Mountain Tragedy," and thousands of voices joined in a chorus: "Why did the Lord let this terrible thing happen?"
>
> Two automobiles crashed when one went through a red light, and six people were killed. Why would God not prevent this?
>
> Why should the young mother die of cancer and leave her eight children motherless? Why did not the Lord heal her?
>
> A little child was drowned; another was run over. Why?
>
> A man died one day suddenly of a coronary occlusion as he climbed a stairway. His body was found slumped on the floor. His wife cried out in agony, "Why? Why would the Lord do this to me? Could he not have considered my three little children who still need a father?"
>
> A young man died in the mission field and people critically questioned: "Why did not the Lord protect this youth while he was doing proselyting work?" . . .
>
> If all the sick for whom we pray were healed, if all the righteous were protected and the wicked destroyed, the whole program of the Father would be annulled and the basic principle of the gospel, free agency, would be ended. No man would have to live by faith. . . .
>
> If we say that early death is a calamity, disaster, or tragedy, would it not be saying that mortality is preferable to earlier entrance into the spirit world and to eventual salvation and exaltation? If mortality be the perfect state, then death would be a frustration, but the gospel teaches us there is no tragedy in death, but only in sin. . . . In the face of apparent tragedy we must put our trust in God, knowing that despite our limited view his purposes will not fail.[7]

We trust that the Lord receives our loved ones home when they have fulfilled their mission here upon the earth.[8] As much as we might wish it to be otherwise, it seems that no medical attention or human intervention can change the Lord's will when the appointed hour of one's passing arrives.

SYMBOLIC ELEMENTS

The man who stepped forward to slay Ammon reminds us of the many enemies Satan sends to do his bidding. We ought not to be "pickle suckers"—but we should be realists.[9] In many ways the world has changed, and the enemies of righteousness are increasing. There are more today than ever before who are looking to destroy the Church and kingdom of God.

The sword raised in this miracle can well symbolize the many armaments in the arsenal of Satan, weapons he uses to destroy us spiritually and even physically. He regularly equips his soldiers with the arms necessary to inflict mortal and eternal wounds upon you and me. Some of his favorite vices with which he hopes to slay us include situational ethics or dishonesty, verbal or physical abuse, hatred and anger, the abuse of alcohol or drugs, and immorality and pornography. The list is lengthy, and his success rate is increasing as the world becomes less and less conscious of their own desensitization to sin.

APPLICATION AND ALLEGORIZATION

When there is a mission to be filled or a work to be done, God's servants are promised His protection. That comes in a number of ways—the Ammon example only illustrating one such means of divine intervention. Nevertheless, if we are faithful, we have the assurance that God will be involved in the details of our lives. As a modern example, Elder Dallin H. Oaks shared the following story from his own life:

> During my life I have had many experiences of being guided in what I should do and in being protected from injury and also from evil. The Lord's protecting care has shielded me from the evil acts of others and has also protected me from surrendering to my own worst impulses. I enjoyed that protection one warm summer night on the streets of Chicago. I have never shared this experience in public. I do so now because it is a persuasive illustration of my subject.
>
> My wife, June, had attended a ward officers' meeting. When I came to drive her home, she was accompanied by a sister we would take home on our way. She lived in the nearby Woodlawn area, which was the territory of a gang called the Blackstone Rangers.
>
> I parked at the curb outside this sister's apartment house and accompanied her into the lobby and up the stairs to her door. June remained in the car on 61st Street. She locked all of the doors, and I left

the keys in the ignition in case she needed to drive away. We had lived on the south side of Chicago for quite a few years and were accustomed to such precautions.

Back in the lobby, and before stepping out into the street, I looked carefully in each direction. By the light of a nearby streetlight, I could see that the street was deserted except for three young men walking by. I waited until they were out of sight and then walked quickly toward our car.

As I came to the driver's side and paused for June to unlock the door, I saw one of these young men running back toward me. He had something in his right hand, and I knew what it would be. There was no time to get into the car and drive away before he came within range.

Fortunately, as June leaned across to open the door, she glanced through the back window and saw this fellow coming around the end of the car with a gun in his hand. Wisely, she did not unlock the door. For the next two or three minutes, which seemed like an eternity, she was a horrified spectator to an event happening at her eye level, just outside the driver's window.

The young man pushed the gun against my stomach and said, "Give me your money." I took the wallet out of my pocket and showed him it was empty. I wasn't even wearing a watch I could offer him because my watchband had broken earlier that day. I offered him some coins I had in my pocket, but he growled a rejection.

"Give me your car keys," he demanded. "They are in the car," I told him. "Tell her to open the car," he replied. For a moment I considered the new possibilities that would present, and then refused. He was furious. He jabbed me in the stomach with his gun and said, "Do it, or I'll kill you." . . .

When I refused, the young robber repeated his demands, this time emphasizing them with an angrier tone and more motion with his gun. . . .

"Give me your money." "I don't have any." "Give me your car keys." "They're in the car." "Tell her to open the car." "I won't do it." "I'll kill you if you don't." "I won't do it."

Inside the car June couldn't hear the conversation, but she could see the action with the gun. She agonized over what she should do. Should she unlock the door? Should she honk the horn? Should she drive away? Everything she considered seemed to have the possibility of making matters worse, so she just waited and prayed. Then a peaceful feeling came over her. She felt it would be all right.

Then, for the first time, I saw the possibility of help. From behind the robber, a city bus approached. It stopped about twenty feet away. A passenger stepped off and scurried away. The driver looked directly at me, but I could see that he was not going to offer any assistance.

While this was happening behind the young robber, out of his view, he became nervous and distracted. His gun wavered from my stomach until its barrel pointed slightly to my left. My arm was already partly raised, and with a quick motion I could seize the gun and struggle with him without the likelihood of being shot. I was taller and heavier than this young man, and at that time of my life was somewhat athletic. I had no doubt that I could prevail in a quick wrestling match if I could get his gun out of the contest.

Just as I was about to make my move, I had a unique experience. I did not see anything or hear anything, but I knew something. I knew what would happen if I grabbed that gun. We would struggle, and I would turn the gun into that young man's chest. It would fire, and he would die. I also understood that I must not have the blood of that young man on my conscience for the rest of my life.

I relaxed, and as the bus pulled away I followed an impulse to put my right hand on his shoulder and give him a lecture. June and I had some teenage children at that time, and giving lectures came naturally.

"Look here," I said. "This isn't right. What you're doing just isn't right. The next car might be a policeman, and you could get killed or sent to jail for this."

With the gun back in my stomach, the young robber replied to my lecture by going through his demands for the third time. But this time his voice was subdued. When he offered the final threat to kill me, he didn't sound persuasive. When I refused again, he hesitated for a moment and then stuck the gun in his pocket and ran away. June unlocked the door, and we drove off, uttering a prayer of thanks. We had experienced the kind of miraculous protection illustrated in the Bible stories I had read as a boy.

I have often pondered the significance of that event in relation to the responsibilities that came later in my life. Less than a year after that August night, I was chosen as president of Brigham Young University. Almost fourteen years after that experience, I received my present calling [as an Apostle].

I am grateful that the Lord gave me the vision and strength to refrain from trusting in the arm of flesh and to put my trust in the protecting care of our Heavenly Father. I am grateful for the Book of Mormon promise to us of the last days that "the righteous need not fear," for the Lord "will preserve the righteous by his power." (1 Ne. 22:17.) I am grateful for the protection promised to those who have kept their covenants and qualified for the blessings promised in sacred places.[10]

Like Ammon of old, God protected Elder Oaks—who had a mission from God to fulfill. Every week mothers and fathers send their sons and daughters into the mission field, placing them in the watchful care of a loving Father in Heaven and His heavenly hosts (D&C 84:88). While knowing you won't see them again for many, many months always makes emotionally difficult the act of sending a child away, nevertheless, for some parents this divine duty is even harder because the call to serve is to a land or location that is filled with unrest and danger. Of the miracle of Ammon's preservation, and what it means for the parents of missionaries today, one commentary noted:

> This story instills in us the motivation to increase our faith and trust in the Lord. All missionary parents who send their sons and daughters into the mission field understand the feelings of faith and trust that accompany such a sacrifice. We can assume that King Mosiah was given to constant prayer on behalf of his four sons who were laboring such a long time in dangerous territory—but his prayers would have been prayers of faith and hope, for the Lord had promised that his sons would be preserved in safety.[11]

As we exercise faith in the Father's plan, we have the assurance that He will watch over His own—and over our missionary sons and daughters.[12] (This promise applies as much to senior missionaries as it does to single adults called to serve.) That does not mean that all come home safe and healthy. Such was never part of God's plan. But it does give us the assurance that if the missionary is faithful, he or she will be watched over by the Father—and, thus, God's perfect plan will be fulfilled in the way He deems best. Could we ask for more than that?

NOTES

1. Gardner (2007), 4:305.
2. See McConkie and Millet (1987–1991), 3:143.
3. Spoken at the funeral of Richard L. Evans, cited in McConkie and Ostler (2000), 960.
4. Edward L. Kimball, editor, *The Teachings of Spencer W. Kimball* (Salt Lake City: Bookcraft, 1998), 37.

5. Spencer W. Kimball, *Faith Precedes the Miracle* (Salt Lake City: Bookcraft, 2001), 103, 104, 105.

6. Neal A. Maxwell, *But For a Small Moment* (Salt Lake City: Bookcraft, 1986), 116.

7. Kimball (1972), 95, 97, 101, 106.

8. By "home" I do not mean into the celestial kingdom. Rather, upon death they are received into paradise.

9. See Gordon B. Hinckley, "Let Not Your Heart Be Troubled," BYU Lecture delivered October 29, 1974.

10. Dallin H. Oaks, "Bible Stories and Personal Protection," *Ensign*, November 1992, 39–40.

11. Pinegar and Allen (2007), 574.

12. See Matthew Cowley, in Conference Report, October 1948, 160.

ABISH TOUCHES *the* QUEEN, *the* QUEEN TOUCHES *the* KING, *and* THEY *Are* RAISED *from* THEIR COMATOSE STATE

ALMA 19:29–30

THE MIRACLE

After Ammon, Lamoni and his wife, and many of the servants had collapsed as a result of the Spirit's influence upon them, Abish had gathered many in the land to witness the miracle. Much to her disappointment, rather than being converted, they contended about the cause; and nearly universally, they denied the miraculous nature of the event. When Abish "saw the contention which was among the multitude she was exceedingly sorrowful, even unto tears" (Alma 19:28).

In what can only be interpreted as an act of faith, Abish approached the queen—whom she may well have been the personal servant to—and took her by the hand in an effort to "raise her" from her comatose state (verse 29). The queen immediately recovered, stood upon her feet, and bore testimony of Jesus Christ and His saving power!

Shortly after this miracle at the hand of her servant, Lamoni's wife then took her husband's hand and, like Abish manifesting faith in God's power, sought to raise him up. Again, instantaneously the unconscious gained consciousness. King Lamoni stood, rebuked the people for their contention, and then taught them "the words which he had heard from Ammon; and as many as heard his words believed, and were converted unto the Lord" (verse 31).

BACKGROUND

The fact that Abish grasps the hand of the queen (rather than the culturally or politically more powerful king) has been highlighted as significant. One commentator explained: "The fact that Abish, a woman, first touched the queen rather than Lamoni confirms the plausible patriarchal structure to Lamanite society. The woman servant would have been attached to the queen's service, possibly prohibited from even touching Lamoni."[1] Such makes sense, as does the suggestion that—if Abish was in the service of the queen—she may have felt an emotional bond to the queen she would not necessarily have had for the king.

In this miracle, it indicates that upon being revived, the queen "clasped" her hands (verse 29). Though perhaps insignificant, in the original manuscript of the Book of Mormon, Oliver Cowdery had written that she "clapped" her hands. The typesetter of the Book of Mormon apparently misinterpreted Oliver's notes, typesetting it instead as "clasped."[2]

SYMBOLIC ELEMENTS

Anciently the hand was often a symbolic representation of one's actions, or that which one chose to do or pursue.[3] But it was also a symbol of power, probably because the Hebrew root for *hand* can mean either "power" and "strength," or it can mean literally one's "hand."[4] Hence, one source on biblical and Semitic symbols records: "By stretching out the hand towards a person . . . one symbolized the transference of power from one party to another."[5] The actions of Abish may be illustrative of this. She reaches out and touches the queen and thereby transfers to her power and revitalization. The queen then does the same for her husband, Lamoni. Hands are valued symbols because they "speak more eloquently than our words, since the actions of the hands come from the heart. Through hands come blessing and healing."[6] In a very real sense, Abish's subtle act was a testament of the nature of her heart—something not discussed in the narrative but clearly taught by her simple act.

APPLICATION AND ALLEGORIZATION

The miraculous element in this particular portion of the narrative is Abish's grasping of the hand of the queen—which resulted in the reviving of Lamoni's wife. Also highlighted is the identical act by the queen on behalf of her husband, with the exact same result. There is no evidence in the text that the two women did anything akin to what we would call in the Church today the "laying on of hands." Thus, it would be an error to try to interpret this passage as implying that these women offered a "priesthood blessing" to those whom they raised. However, Mormon's description of the miracle suggests that something more was taking place than a simple act of "awakening" a "sleeping" person. Abish and the queen each acted in faith—and two people who were void of *any* signs of life instantly rose up and bore fervent testimony. Thus, Mormon clearly expected his readers to see these actions as miraculous—and as representing some conveyance of power on the part of Abish and her matron. In Doctrine and Covenants 46, we find a modern recitation of the gifts of the Spirit (verses 11–26). There we have listed many spiritual endowments available to members of the Church, including the gift of "the working of miracles" (verse 21), the "faith to be healed" (verse 18), and the "faith to heal" (verse 20). The scriptures do not limit these gifts to men but, rather, suggest that they are available to members of the Church generally—"for the benefit of the children of God" (verse 26). Latter-day Saint women do not perform the same priesthood functions as men within the Church; however they have every right to the same gifts of the Spirit. And, as the Apostle James testified, "The prayer of faith shall save the sick" (James 5:15). We can only suppose that it was by that "prayer of faith" that Abish and the queen performed their respective miracles. And it is by that same manifestation of faith that you and I can lay hold on the gifts of the Spirit, thereby enabling the accomplishment of miracles in our own lives and in the lives of those whom we serve.

NOTES

1. Gardner (2007), 4:308.

2. Oliver misspelled "clapped" as "claped" and the typesetter apparently thought Oliver had inadvertently dropped the s in "clasped." Hence the erroneous statement in our current edition of the Book of Mormon [see Gardner (2007), 4:308].

3. Nadia Julien, *The Mammoth Dictionary of Symbols* (New York: Carroll & Graf Publishers, 1996), 191; Todeschi (1995), 128. Hands can also invoke images of strength, providence, authority, or blessings [McConkie (1985), 261; Cirlot (1971), 137].

4. Francis Brown, S. R. Driver, and Charles A. Briggs, *The Brown-Driver-Briggs Hebrew and English Lexicon* (Peabody, MA: Hendrickson Publishers, 1999), 388, 1094; Tresidder (2000), 22; McConkie (1985), 261.

5. Farbridge (1923), 274–75.

6. Ryken, Wilhoit, and Longman (1998), 362.

THE QUEEN SPEAKS
in TONGUES

ALMA 19:30

THE MIRACLE

After being raised from her comatose state, King Lamoni's wife stood up on her feet and exclaimed in a loud voice, "O blessed Jesus, who has saved me from an awful hell! O blessed God, have mercy on this people!" Then, filled with the joy that accompanies the Spirit of the Lord, she spoke "many words which were not understood" (Alma 19:30).

BACKGROUND

In this miracle, King Lamoni's wife manifests one of the most provocative gifts of the Spirit—namely, the gift of tongues. One source points out: "It is difficult to tell whether she is preaching in the language of God, the Adamic (see Moses 6:5–6), or simply speaking with the tongue of angels, that is, speaking the words of Christ by the power of the Holy Ghost (see 2 Nephi 32:2–3)."[1] In the end, it matters little. The fact is, under the influence of the Holy Spirit, she is utilizing a divinely given gift.

Regarding this gift and its use in the Church, the Prophet Joseph taught:

- Its primary purpose is to teach the gospel in the language of the investigator. In other words, it is a gift designed primarily for the advancement of missionary work and spreading the gospel.[2]

- It is the least significant of *all* of the gifts of the Spirit, and yet the most sought after.[3] Joseph went so far as to say that it is "not necessary for tongues to be taught to the Church."[4]

- It is one of the gifts of the Spirit that Satan uses to deceive people, as he too can speak in tongues—he knows all languages.[5]

- Joseph said: "We have also had brethren and sisters who have had the gift of tongues falsely; they would speak in a muttering unnatural voice, and their bodies be distorted; . . . whereas, there is nothing unnatural in the Spirit of God."[6]

- This gift should not be exercised unless the one speaking in tongues or another person present has the gift of the interpretation of tongues and, therefore, someone present offers an interpretation. If no intelligence is communicated through the experience of tongues, it is simply vain babbling.[7]

- This gift should never be used to govern or lead the Church.[8]

- Joseph added, "If anything is taught by the gift of tongues, it is not to be received for doctrine."[9]

Owing to the rules governing this gift of the Spirit, one commentator pointed out: "Although the words of the queen were not understood, there was probably someone who received the message. When someone is given the gift of speaking in tongues, which the queen apparently received, there is usually someone else who is given the interpretation of tongues. . . . The Prophet Joseph Smith admonished: 'do not speak in tongues except there be an interpreter present' (*TPJS.* 247)."[10]

SYMBOLIC ELEMENTS

The manifestation of the gift of tongues is a physical act that implies a symbolic message. One text on biblical symbolism noted:

Speaking in tongues ([known as] glossolalia) can refer to human languages ("tongues of men," Acts 2:11) or ecstatic speech ("tongues of angels," 1 Cor 12–14). Glossolalia is a sign both of prophetic inspiration by the Spirit (Acts 2:4, 18; 19:6; "speaking mysteries in the Spirit," 1 Cor 14:2 NRSV), and of direct revelation from God (1 Cor 14:6). Tongues . . . [as manifest] in the church symbolizes God's intention to speak to his people.[11]

Thus, the queen's manifestation of this gift in this miracle narrative symbolically testifies to her hearers that she is being used by the divine, that she has heard God's voice, and that He has a message for His children. Whenever God gives the full-time missionaries this gift—through enabling them to speak a language other than their native tongue—He is symbolically stating, "These are my authorized messengers; harken unto their words, for the words which they speak are mine."

APPLICATION AND ALLEGORIZATION

This miracle is a testament to God's ability and willingness to endow each of us—male and female—with manifestations of His power and support. Curiously, Lamoni's wife exercised faith in Ammon's words and promises, received a spiritual manifestation of the truthfulness of his message, bore witness of Jesus and His saving grace, and then immediately (upon her conversion) manifest the gift of tongues and a form of the gift of healing. This story stands as a witness that spiritual endowments are not given solely based on office or longevity in the Church. While certain gifts are promised to the worthy in association with their calling (see D&C 46:27), nevertheless, Lamoni's wife's experience shows that even those who are new to the gospel, if worthy, have a right to the gifts of God and abundant spiritual manifestations.

As we have already alluded to above, the fact that this spiritual outpouring—coupled with a gift to raise the comatose—came to and through a woman is a strong reminder that God is not a respecter of persons (Acts 10:34; D&C 1:35). He loves and works through His faithful daughters just as much as He does His sons. President Brigham Young said that when women "carry out the instincts of their nature, they . . . effect a revolution for good."[12] The queen of the land of Ishmael epitomizes this power and promise—and is an example to all women of God.

NOTES

1. McConkie and Millet (1987–1991), 3:144.

2. *History of the Church*, 2:162, 3:379, 5:31–32, cited in Dahl and Cannon (1998), 670–71.

3. Ibid., 5:30, cited in Dahl and Cannon (1998), 671.

4. Ibid., 3:379, cited in Dahl and Cannon (1998), 670.

5. Ibid., 1:369, 3:392, 4:580, 4:607, cited in Dahl and Cannon (1998), 670–71.

6. Ibid., 4:580, cited in Dahl and Cannon (1998), 670.

7. Ibid., 3:392, 5:31–32, cited in Dahl and Cannon (1998), 670–71.

8. Ibid., 2:162, cited in Dahl and Cannon (1998), 670.

9. Ibid., 4:607, cited in Dahl and Cannon (1998), 671.

10. Nyman (2003–2004), 3:257–58.

11. Ryken, Wilhoit, and Longman (1998), 876.

12. Brigham Young, in *Journal of Discourses*, 12:194.

King Lamoni's Father
Is Overcome *by the* Spirit *and* Collapses, *but* Aaron *Raises* Him

ALMA 22:18–23

The Miracle

King Lamoni's father—who was "king over all the land" (Alma 22:1)—inadvertently ran into Ammon and Lamoni as they journeyed toward the land Middoni. When Lamoni's father saw that his son was traveling with a Nephite—already frustrated that his son had not shown up when he had held a feast for his boys—he became enraged. He forbade Lamoni from fraternizing further with Ammon and commanded him to turn around and accompany him to the land of Ishmael. The king then commanded his son to slay his Nephite companion. However, Lamoni refused to do any of what his father ordered.

Furious at his son's apparent insubordination, the king drew his sword and attempted to slay Lamoni; however, Ammon stepped forward and prevented him. Indeed, the Nephite missionary injured the king's arm so that he could not harm Lamoni. Our Nephite hero then commanded the king to release his brethren from prison, grant that Lamoni could retain his kingdom, and allow the king's son to do what he believed best—threatening, "I will smite thee to the earth" if you don't comply (Alma 20:24).

Seeing that Ammon had no desire to harm him and conscious of the tremendous love this missionary had for his son, Lamoni's father was moved. He promised all that Ammon asked of him and expressed a desire to learn from Ammon and his brethren.

Sometime later, after Ammon's brother Aaron had been freed from his captors in Middoni, "he was led by the Spirit to the land of Nephi, even to the house of the king which was over all of the land; . . . and he was the father of Lamoni" (Alma 22:1). Disappointed that Ammon had not accompanied him, but receptive to the message Aaron bore because of his previous interaction with Ammon, the king accepted an invitation to be taught. Aaron then instructed him regarding the creation, the Fall, the great plan of redemption, and the doctrine of grace. Feeling the spirit of this missionary's teachings, the king earnestly desired to know what he would need to do in order to have eternal life—in order to be born of God. Lamoni's father expressed a sincere desire to have the "wicked spirit rooted out" of his breast, that he might be "filled with joy" (verse 15). He told Aaron that he would give up all he possessed if he could receive that joy.

Aaron's instruction to the penitent potentate was simple: "Bow down before God," "repent of all" of your "sins," "call on his name in faith," and "believe," and you will "receive the hope which thou desirest" (verse 16).

The king immediately prostrated himself and prayed: "O God, Aaron hath told me that there is a God; and if there is a God, and if thou art God, wilt thou make thyself known unto me, and I will give away all my sins to know thee, and that I may be raised from the dead, and be saved at the last day." No sooner had Lamoni's father uttered these words then "he was struck as if he were dead" (verse 18).

Seeing this, his servants ran to tell the queen, and upon her arrival, she assumed that Aaron and his brethren were the cause of the king's apparent demise. She ordered her servants to slay him. Having witnessed the miracle and fearing that his power was greater than all theirs combined, they refused. Seeing their alarm, the queen began to fear also. So she commanded her servants to call together the people of the land that they might slay Aaron and his brethren. Sensing the potential danger if a "multitude should assemble themselves together," Aaron immediately "put forth his hand and raised the king from the earth" (verse 22). The king stood, receiving back his strength.

Having been raised from his state of unconsciousness, the king began to minister to those who had witnessed the miracle, and "his whole household were converted unto the Lord" (verse 23).

BACKGROUND

The attentive reader cannot help but notice how similar this story is to the conversion of the same king's son Lamoni. Of this, one text on the Book of Mormon offers the following possible explanation:

> The conversion stories of Lamoni and of his father are remarkably parallel. Both cases involve being overcome by the Spirit in such a way that witnesses assume that they are dead and attempt to kill the righteous messenger or issue orders to that effect. . . . These experiences also parallel much of Alma's conversion and . . . the Book of Mormon records a particular conversion "form." . . . The question is what these parallels mean.
>
> Of course, it is possible that they are completely accurate descriptions of precisely what happened. It is also important to remember, particularly in the case of Lamoni and his father, that Alma is telling the story. Even in the case of historical information, certain literary forms might inform the way a particular author shapes a tale.
>
> One important literary form that appears to underline many biographies is the set of traits . . . described as "The Hero." . . .
>
> When biographies and stories are written down, structural patterns embedded in society tend to dictate the form in which we prefer to see those stories. . . .
>
> Combining all of this information on the literary structures of folklore and remembering that we have both a common tradition and a common redactor in the conversion stories of Lamoni and his father, there is every reason to see the commonalities as preferred structures. . . . The stories are parallel because they are made to appear as parallel as possible—not because they were invented, but because the literary expectation was to link such conversion events into an understandable and acceptable pattern.[1]

One can hardly say with certainty, but such an explanation *may* shed light on the common parallels between conversion stories in the book of Alma.

SYMBOLIC ELEMENTS

As we have noted elsewhere in this text, prostration is an act of submission and self-effacement. "To prostrate oneself, or fall to the earth, before *The Majesty on High* is an act of humble devotion. It recognizes the greatness of God and the nothingness of man. It expresses the soul's deepest humility."[2] Kings, so often treated as gods, would never be found manifesting such humility. It was to them that others traditionally bowed. However, by this act the king of the land of Nephi showed his repentance, his faith, his meekness, and his sincere belief in the God of Aaron.

APPLICATION AND ALLEGORIZATION

Perhaps an obvious application of this miracle is this: the miraculous actions of God's servants can *sometimes* convert those who witness them. We should not seek for signs for the sake of conversion—or perform them for that same reason. However, sometimes God uses such things to convert people. One is reminded of the famed 1844 transfiguration of Brigham Young, when he appeared and sounded like the recently deceased Prophet Joseph. This event certainly served to convert those who were confused to the path of the prophet, and away from the road of the rogue. Occasionally God sends us similar signs as a means of directing our steps or bolstering our faith.

The king's prayer during this miracle is instructive—regarding both his personal character and the process of gaining a testimony of truth:

> This short prayer is one of the most remarkable recorded in any scripture. It is a model of faith moving to action with divine result. Later, Alma will tell seekers: "If ye will awake and arouse your faculties, even to an experiment upon my words, and exercise a particle of faith, yea, even if ye can no more than desire to believe, let this desire work in you, even until ye believe in a manner that ye can give place for a portion of my words" (Alma 32:27).
>
> How weak may faith be and still be faith? The over-king's prayer answers that question. Alma suggests that the lowest form of faith is simply the desire to believe coupled with an action based upon that belief. Lamoni's father prays: "O god, Aaron hath told me that there is a God," This God is not one he understands. It is not his god, but Aaron's. He is honest in saying so, not claiming more than he knows. In fact, he expresses his very real skepticism by adding, "and if there is

a God . . ." Here is faith so small that it is only the desire to believe! Not yet convinced of God's existence, still the king prays.[3]

What a perfect example of that which Alma would later teach us about the value of a simple seed of faith (Alma 32). How often could God bless us if we were willing to exhibit this kind of faith in circumstances where we had this little knowledge? Not just in questions about the gospel, but in every facet of our lives.

It also seems significant that the king is willing to give up all that he has—his entire kingdom and all of his sins—to know God. One commentator wrote, "This humble and awe-inspiring offer separates mere curiosity from a true desire to believe."[4] The curious want to know but don't want to sacrifice *to* know. "Curiosity requires no fundamental change of being—faith does."[5] Lamoni's father was more than curious. He was completely sincere; and God was able to answer that sincerity with the blessing of a lifetime.

One additional and important lesson that can be drawn from this miracle is to be found in the king's response to his conversion. He immediately began to preach what he had found to those around him. McConkie and Millet wrote: "It is characteristic of those who are truly converted to seek to share the fruit of the tree of life with family and other loved ones (see 1 Nephi 8:12; Enos 1:9)."[6] If you and I are truly converted, we will have this same desire. Even those who labor under the burden of shyness, if truly converted, will have a desire to testify to others of the gospel, its truths, and its influence upon their personal lives.[7]

In highlighting the influence of the king upon his household, Ogden and Skinner offered this simple application: "Where the father ministers in the home, the household is converted and blessed."[8] Too many Melchizedek Priesthood holders seem to miss this important point.

Perhaps an application can be drawn from the actions of the queen's servants. She ordered them to kill Aaron and his brethren. She certainly had the power to order her domestics' death for their insubordination. However, they stood their ground. They refused to do the immoral act demanded of them—and at the risk of their own lives. Of course, we should never act out of fear (as they did). But surely we can draw a parable from their decision to refuse to act, reminding each of us that there will be times when those who have power over us may demand of us that which is not right. Will we follow the example of the queen's servants and refuse to act unrighteously—regardless of the personal cost?

For a discussion of the symbolism and application of one who falls into a state of unconsciousness or trance, see our previous discussion of the miracle of King Lamoni and others collapsing as though they were dead (Alma 18–19).

NOTES

1. Gardner (2007), 4:334–35, 336. BYU's Monte Nyman similarly stated: "This eight verse account is probably brief because it is basically the same as the previous experience of King Lamoni and his wife and servants" [Nyman (2003–2004), 3:291].
2. Reynolds and Sjodahl (1955–1961), 3:305.
3. Gardner (2007), 4:333.
4. Ibid., 4:334.
5. Ibid.
6. McConkie and Millet (1987–1991), 3:161.
7. The *Book of Mormon Reference Companion* highlights the spirit of missionary work that continued with the father of King Lamoni after his conversion: "He sent a proclamation throughout the land granting the Nephite missionaries freedom to preach anywhere (Alma 22:27; 23:1–4). As a result, 'thousands were brought to the knowledge of the Lord' (Alma 23:5) and were greatly blessed" [W. Jeffrey Marsh, "Lamoni, Father Of," in Largey (2003), 500].
8. Ogden and Skinner (2011), 1:431.

Korihor *Is* Struck Dumb

ALMA 30:6–60

THE MIRACLE

A man by the name of Korihor—an anti-Christ—went about seeking to destroy the faith of those who believed in God. His indictments against the Church and its leaders included the claims "that there should be no Christ" and that "there could be no atonement" (verses 12, 17). He testified that life after death was a myth and believing in Jesus was utter "foolishness" (verses 13–14). According to Korihor, "Prophecies . . . are foolish traditions" (verse 14). No one can know of that which is to come. He ridiculed the religious, saying that their manifestations of faith—and their belief that Jesus would save them from their sins—were "the effect of a frenzied mind" (verse 16). He told them that this "derangement" of their minds had come because of foolish "traditions" and corrupt leaders (verse 16). Indeed, he claimed that the only reason their religious leaders sought to instill faith in the people was so that the populace would be afraid of offending God and, thus, would be obedient to the leaders, leaders who then would glut themselves on the labors of the naïve people. According to Korihor's thinking, we each fare in this life according to the "management of [our] creature" and we prosper "according to [our] genius"—but not because of what some god does for us (verse 17). This anti-Christ taught relativism. He said that there are no "crimes"; right and wrong are hardly absolute. "Foolish ordinances . . . are laid down by ancient priests to usurp power and authority over" the people and "to keep them in ignorance" (verse 23). The Church, according to Korihor, only placed the people in bondage.

This hardened preacher of disbelief gave his faith-destroying spiel in the land of Zarahemla, then Jershon, and then in the land of Gideon. Finally, he was bound and taken back to Zarahemla to be brought before Alma (the high priest) and Nephihah (the chief judge and governor over all the land).

In a seeming battle of wits, Alma challenged Korihor's claims, point by point. Having heard enough to know the anti-Christ's heart, the prophet declared, You are "possessed with a lying spirit, and . . . the devil has power over you" (verse 42).

Korihor told Alma, "Show me a sign and I will believe" (verses 43–44, 48). To which Alma responded, You have plenty of signs. You have the testimony of all of your brethren and all of the holy prophets. In addition, "all things denote there is a God; yea, even the earth, and all things that are upon the face of it, yea, and its motion, yea, and also all the planets which move in their regular form do witness that there is a Supreme Creator" (verse 44). What more could one need as evidence that God exists?

Korihor's response to Alma was no different. Again, he demanded a sign or he would not believe the testimony of the various witnesses to which the prophet had pointed.

Grieved at Korihor's hardness of heart, Alma nevertheless concluded that it would be better that he be lost than he be allowed to continue to act and thus "be the means of bringing many souls down to destruction" (verse 47). Alma gave him one last chance: If you deny God again, He will smite you that you will become dumb, thereby preventing you from deceiving the people any more.

This final plea from the prophet affected Korihor. He appears to have felt the Spirit and power of Alma's words and testimony against him, because he suddenly changed his line of reasoning. Now he qualifies his claims: "I do not deny the existence of a God, but I do not believe that there is a God" (verse 48). If you don't show me a sign, I simply can't believe. Suddenly the rhetoric is softer—though Korihor still stands his ground.[1]

Alma simply reiterated what he had already prophetically declared: "This will I give unto thee for a sign, that thou shalt be struck dumb, according to my words; and I say, that in the name of God, ye shall be struck dumb, that ye shall no more have utterance." No sooner had Alma said these words, than "Korihor was struck dumb, that he could not have utterance" (verses 49, 50).

Seeing that Korihor could no longer speak nor hear, the chief judge wrote the anti-Christ a note asking him if he believed in God *now*. You asked for a sign and Alma gave you one, he said; "now will ye dispute more?" (verse 51).

Korihor, no doubt shocked at this sudden disability, wrote back saying he knew that it was God who had struck him deaf and dumb—and that nothing but the power of God could cause such a miracle. And then he added this sad note: "*I always knew that there was a God*" (verse 52; emphasis added). Amazingly, he claimed that the devil had deceived him, appearing to him as an angel and telling him "there is no God" (verse 53). (It is one of the most puzzling realities that a man could argue that a being from the *other side* appeared and convinced him that *there is no other side*. Yet, this is Korihor's reasoning: Satan appeared to me and told me that supernatural beings do not exist. And I believed him!)

In writing, Korihor informed Alma and the chief judge that he taught what the devil told him to because the words were pleasing to the carnal mind—and he spoke and taught them enough that he, himself, began to believe that they were true.

The deaf-mute anti-Christ then scribed a note to Alma, begging him to pray to God for him, that this curse might be taken from him. Alma, however—under the influence of the Spirit, we suppose—declared that were this curse taken from Korihor, he would simply resume his awful ways. Thus, "the curse was not taken" from him, and he was cast out, spending the remainder of his days seemingly homeless, going "from house to house, begging for his food" (verse 56).

Those who had believed the anti-Christ, seeing the wrath of God upon him, repented of their ways and returned to the Church—"and were converted again unto the Lord" (verse 58).

Sometime later, as Korihor was out among the Zoramites, he was "run upon and trodden down, even until he was dead" (verse 59).

BACKGROUND

While the text only explicitly states that Korihor was "dumb," it is evident that he was also struck "deaf" as those who sought to communicate with him had to write down what they wanted to convey. If he had only been made mute, he could have still heard their questions—but, we are told, he could not.[2] While Korihor's ability to write might seem to make his plight of being deaf and dumb more bearable, owing to the fact that he likely lived in a largely illiterate population, we would assume that this skill was not of much help—and Korihor was basically cut off from any form of meaningful communication.[3]

Alma's warning that Korihor was liable to be struck dumb by God seemed to give the anti-Christ a moment's pause. He seemed to soften his argument, stating, "I do not deny . . . but I do not believe" (Alma 30:47–48). This change in language could have been provoked by feelings of fear or may have only been "a clever appeal to Nephite law" which declared "that one could not be punished for his personal belief (Alma 30:11)."[4]

When Alma offers his repeated warnings to Korihor—informing him of the thin ice upon which he treads—and when Alma feels grieved at the anti-Christ's continued sinfulness, his pain for Korihor may be empathy and understanding rather than frustration or disdain. Remember, Alma the Younger had skated on that same "thin ice" some years earlier and had learned firsthand what it felt like to be "racked . . . with the pains of a damned soul" (Alma 36:16). He may be less angry at our anti-Christ and more filled with empathy and even love for him, knowing intimately what he's about to go through.[5]

Korihor, living hand-to-mouth among the Zoramites, was trampled to death as he went from house to house seeking his daily maintenance. We are given no details of the circumstances in which a crowd of sufficient size overran the famed anti-Christ. We do not know if his death was intentional or a tragic accident. All we are told is that the one who could not cry out for help lay silently upon the ground as others trampled him to death. Ignominy has its cruel way with its victims, as Korihor's experience attests.

SYMBOLIC ELEMENTS

The fact that Korihor—an apparently eloquent orator—is struck mute is symbolically meaningful. In this narrative the villain's inability to speak well represents God's act of silencing His enemies. They may for a time have their voice and their platform, but in the end, all who raise their voice against God will be silenced.[6]

Korihor's loss of his ability to hear seems symbolically appropriate since he had refused to listen to anything the prophets or scriptures testified of.[7]

Being trampled under the feet of another is "an effective image of triumph": he who tramples is empowered over he who has been trampled.[8] Mormon's description of Korihor's trampling is made all the more poignant by the fact that he is crushed by the Zoramites—a "self-righteous and inhospitable" people who, in many ways, mirrored the behaviors and attitude of their victim.[9] The irony of Korihor's death is hard to miss. It illustrates the scriptural maxim that "it is by the wicked that the wicked are punished" (Mormon 4:5).[10]

An additional symbolic insight into this miracle is to be found in the following comment by Brant Gardner:

> Looked at realistically, Korihor probably has little impact on Nephite history. Unlike Nephi, he creates no organized movement. He may have influenced some in the first city where he preached, but failed utterly in Jershon and Gideon. Korihor's greatest value comes in Mormon's use of his story. Literarily, Korihor serves two functions. First, the failure of his mission to teach false doctrine contrasts with Yahweh's power in strengthening the missionaries who taught true doctrine and reaped an impressive harvest. Second, and more important, Mormon juxtaposes Korihor, the anti-Christ, to Alma, the Messiah's defender and prophet. Mormon uses the encounter of these individuals as emblematic of the more universal conflict between the gospel and its detractors. He thereby shows Yahweh's superiority over those who would claim he does not exist.[11]

Gardner adds this:

> Both Alma and Korihor were believers in something, both had received an angelic visitation, both were converted by that experience, and both preached the gospel learned in that experience. Korihor and Alma are too similar to be accidental. They have only one fundamental difference: Alma is converted to truth and Korihor to error. That conclusion is powerfully underlined in Korihor's curse because of his continued demand for a sign.[12]

APPLICATION AND ALLEGORIZATION

President Ezra Taft Benson taught that the Book of Mormon was written for our day: "They saw our day, and chose those things which would be of greatest worth to us."[13] He added that the Book of Mormon exposes the enemies of Christ. It confounds false doctrines and lays down contention (see 1 Nephi 3:12). It fortifies the humble followers of Christ against the evil designs, strategies, and doctrines of the devil in our day. The type of apostates in the Book of Mormon are similar to the type we have today. God, with His infinite foreknowledge, so molded the Book of Mormon that we might see the error and know how to combat false educational, political, religious, and philosophical concepts of our time.[14]

It has been said, "The Book of Mormon is everlastingly relevant."[15] And so this miracle attests. Korihor capitalized on the right to exercise freedom of conscience under the Nephite legal system as a means of harming the religious beliefs, practices, and freedoms of others (Alma 30:11).[16] In our own day there are those who similarly seek to use the legal system to their advantage—even when that advantage, though technically "legal," is decidedly immoral. Korihor's free reign certainly did some measure of damage to the people of Jershon and Gideon. We must ever be supportive of the rights of all to enjoy the free exercise of conscience. However, we must also be vigilant to oppose any attempt by one group to use their "rights" as a means of curtailing the freedoms of another group. Religious freedoms are slowly being eroded by those whose "freedom of conscience" motivates them to fight the faithful so that they personally can live in a world without God or moral restraints. As one author stated: "Korihor's teachings echo many latter-day debates and challenges to religious faith."[17] Like Alma, we must be willing to stand up against such challenges and their influences upon our society and families.

On a related note, McConkie and Millet pointed out: "Few things are more threatening to a people than to suggest that they are blindly obedient or, worse yet, that they are slaves to their religious way of life."[18] Korihor plays on this fear, while he seeks to make his hearers self-conscious or embarrassed about being naïve believers in that which the "intellectually superior" can readily see through. How often are these same arguments employed against those with believing blood today? We *must* see them for what they are, lest they become powerful instruments in the hands of the adversary.

Korihor demands a sign! Alma retorts that there are plenty of signs (Alma 30:41). God certainly gives us signs. However, sign seekers want more. They want to determine for themselves what "signs" are acceptable evidence and which ones are not. The problem isn't the desire for some evidence of the truth. The problem is, minus the Spirit of God, sign seekers can't see the signs. "Korihor is not without witness from Yahweh, he is simply without the Spirit to believe them."[19] If we have the Spirit of the Lord with us, we'll recognize those signs the Father has given. If we do not have His Spirit, it will not make any difference what He shows us.

This miracle reminds us that if we tell a lie long enough, we can convince ourselves that it is the truth. Fabricate only ever so slightly some detail, and before long it will be difficult to remember what reality is. Korihor bears testimony that he is the poster child for this reality (Alma 30:53). Too many, when asked if they are "honest in their dealing with their fellow men" reply, "I try." Such a reply does not qualify one as honest. Either we are truthful or we are not. And when one becomes comfortable "trying" to be honest—rather than feeling an obligation to be honest—one opens one's self up to the very sin to which Korihor fell prey.[20]

Mormon concludes his account of this miracle with the phrase "and thus we see." He is offering us the moral of the story—the point of why he has retained a record of this miracle. And what is the truth behind the tale? Satan intends to dump you in the end. He is not your friend. He is committed to no one, and he keeps none of his promises. Such has been the case from the very beginning—as Cain could bear fervent witness. From this miracle Mormon drew a poignant point: "And thus we see the end of him who perverteth the ways of the Lord; and thus we see that the devil will not support his children at the last day, but doth speedily drag them down to hell" (Alma 30:60). One commentary on these verses explained:

> One who in Faustian fashion sells his soul to Satan need not expect in times of difficulty any sense of fraternal or familial attachment, any type of protection or support from the archdeceiver. He who knows no love knows no family. He who was willing to promise salvation before the world was made will have no power to raise his own out of perdition. He is not one to be trusted. Indeed, he "rewardeth [his subjects] no good thing" (Alma 34:39).[21]

In every temptation Satan promises his victims some reward, some measure of pleasure or gain. But know this: he *will not* provide what he has promised you. He has no power to do so. All he has authority to give is pain and heartache. The disciplinary councils of the Church are filled with those who tested these words, those who trusted the "father of all lies" (2 Nephi 2:18). In the words of Jacob, "O be wise; what can I say more?" (Jacob 6:12).

As a final application of this miracle, note that Nephite law protected a person's right to believe as he wished. Korihor was hauled before a judge on more than one occasion, not for what he believed, but for "fomenting social contention and division."[22]

> This Book of Mormon division between belief and overt attempts to prompt division is echoed in the modern LDS Church's typical position on members' differences of opinion. It is no crime to hold beliefs that differ from those of the main body of the Church. Many active and fully contributing members of wards and stakes may have differing views of such fundamental concepts as faith. Not allowed, however, is the effort of people with different ideas to attempt to convert others to their own ideas with the purpose of creating division among the Saints. Divisiveness is the crime, not the idea.[23]

As with Korihor, so it is with us today. We may believe as we wish, think as we may. However, when we seek to destroy the faith of others, or to challenge the teachings of those whom the Lord has appointed to teach and protect the doctrines and ordinances of the Church, then we have crossed a line. One is never punished in the Church for what he or she believes—only for what one does *with* that belief.

NOTES

1. One commentator suggested that Korihor here goes "from atheist to agnostic" [Todd Parker, review of *Miracles of the Book of Mormon*].
2. See McConkie and Millet (1987–1991), 3:211–12; Gardner (2007), 4:426; Nibley (2004), 2:338.
3. See Gardner (2007), 4:428.
4. Dennis L. Largey, "Korihor," in Largey (2003), 484.
5. See Gardner (2007), 4:424–25.
6. The Psalms sometimes use silence as a symbol for defeat or destruction (Psalm 101:5; 143:12. See also Isaiah 47:5). See Ryken, Wilhoit, and Longman (1998), 791.
7. See Gardner (2007), 4:426.
8. See Ryken, Wilhoit, and Longman (1998), 896.
9. See Gardner (2007), 4:430.

10. See Ogden and Skinner (2011), 2:4.

11. Gardner (2007), 4:418.

12. Ibid., 4:427.

13. Ezra Taft Benson, *Teachings of Ezra Taft Benson* (Salt Lake City: Bookcraft, 1998), 59.

14. Benson (1998), 56.

15. McConkie and Millet (1987–1991), 3:202.

16. See Largey in Largey (2003), 483.

17. Largey in Largey (2003), 484.

18. McConkie and Millet (1987–1991), 3:203.

19. Gardner (2007), 3:424. See also Gardner (2007), 4:423.

20. To quote Yoda: "Try not. Do, or do not. There is no try" [in *The Empire Strikes Back* (Lucasfilm Ltd. and 20th Century Fox, 1980)].

21. McConkie and Millet (1987–1991), 3:214.

22. See Gardner (2007), 4:414.

23. Gardner (2007), 4:414.

God Provides *for* His Missionaries

ALMA 31:38

THE MIRACLE

Alma, Ammon, Aaron, Omner, Himni, Amulek, Zeezrom, Shiblon, and Corianton all headed to Antionum, where they encountered the apostate Zoramites and their strange and arrogant worship practices (Alma 31:3, 6–8).

Perceiving the apostate nature of these former believers, and on the eve of their own missionary journeys, Alma expressed sorrow over what he had seen and heard. He repeatedly petitioned God for comfort for his "pained soul." After which he blessed each of his fellow missionaries, and as a result, "they were filled with the Holy Spirit" (verse 36).

The nine missionaries then began their next mission, separating themselves "one from another" and "taking no thought . . . what they should eat, or what they should drink, or what they should put on." Miraculously, "the Lord provided for them that they should hunger not, neither should they thirst; yea, and he also gave them strength, that they should suffer no manner of afflictions, save it were swallowed up in the joy of Christ. Now this was according to the prayer of Alma; and this because he prayed in faith" (verses 37–38).

BACKGROUND

Alma was the high priest over the Church. He held the priesthood keys. He, and he alone, was authorized to receive revelation regarding the broad-scope work of the Lord, and only he had the power necessary to set them apart to serve as "authorized" messengers of the Lord. [1] While we cannot say whether the blessings he gave his eight friends were "setting apart" blessings or simply ones of comfort and direction, the fact that it was he, and not others, who pronounced the blessing speaks to his presiding authority.

The phrase "clapped his hands" upon them is traditionally interpreted to mean he performed the "laying on of hands."[2] Nibley said it meant to place one's hands "firmly" on the head of the blessing recipient.[3] Brant Gardner, however, offered an interesting and slightly different interpretation of this verse. He suggested that the "clapping" meant that Alma made some sort of a noise as he placed his hands upon their head—perhaps swinging his hands hard enough to make a clapping sound as he moved to place them on their heads. Gardner's reasoning is that in Mesoamerican culture sound is very important and is often linked to deity. The "clapping" of thunder, for example, is associated with the divine. In Gardner's view, therefore, Alma may have made a sound in order to underscore "the divine aspects of the blessing he conferred upon them and the Spirit he was summoning to their aid."[4] While I am not completely convinced by Gardner's argument, it is an interesting proposition.

The statement that, as a result of the blessing, "they were filled with the Holy Spirit" (Alma 31:36) should not be taken as suggesting they were being confirmed members of the Church, or that they were receiving the gift of the Holy Ghost (at this time).[5] They were already members of the Church, and this statement only describes what any inspired priesthood blessing would do—namely, cause an outpouring of the Lord's Spirit.

It has been pointed out that, in an agrarian society—such as the one in which these nine missionaries lived—the rules of hospitality made going without purse or scrip much easier to do than it would be today. Even in the early days of the Restoration, missionaries approached their work much as the missionaries described in this miracle—without having arrangements for their necessities. However today, in our urbanized and technological world, such an approach is less feasible. Nevertheless, by so approaching the work, Alma and his brethren invited their potential investigators to feel the Spirit of the Lord (through their generosity), which may have made those same potential proselytes more receptive to the message the missionaries bore.[6]

SYMBOLIC ELEMENTS

The laying on of hands is the standard symbol in antiquity for the transference of power, authority, or blessings. Thus, Alma's act here would have been understood as more than just an authorization to preach, and also as an act that equipped his eight brethren for their work.

Going without purse or scrip (Mark 6:8; D&C 24:18) is a symbol of one's faith in God. To embark on a mission without a means of providing food or taking extra clothing or sufficient money symbolically evidences one's trust in God to provide.

APPLICATION AND ALLEGORIZATION

The Nephite nine went out with no significant supplies, trusting in the Lord, and He provided *all* they needed. Jesus asked the Twelve: "When I sent you without purse, and scrip, and shoes, lacked ye any thing? And they said, Nothing" (Luke 22:35). One of the obvious messages of this miracle is that, just as God provided for His missionaries in the Book of Mormon and the Bible, He does so for us today.[7] The Lord has said:

> And any man that shall go and preach this gospel of the kingdom, and fail not to continue faithful in all things, shall not be weary in mind, neither darkened, neither in body, limb, nor joint; and a hair of his head shall not fall to the ground unnoticed. And they shall not go hungry, neither athirst. Therefore, take ye no thought for the morrow, for what ye shall eat, or what ye shall drink, or wherewithal ye shall be clothed. . . . Neither take ye thought beforehand what ye shall say; but treasure up in your minds continually the words of life, and it shall be given you in the very hour that portion that shall be meted unto every man. (D&C 84:80–81, 85)

If we prepare ourselves, the Lord will prepare the rest. Such an approach to missionary work—or life—takes faith. But it also provides blessings that can be had *in no other way*. Missionaries today may prepare themselves temporally—by working and saving. However, they are still very dependent upon the Lord for the more miraculous things they will need in order to accomplish His work and will. Many missionaries fear their field of labor because of the unknowns and because of those things that will be beyond their control. However, this miracle invites us to trust that the Lord will take care of *all* things. We need not fear, "but be believing" (Mormon 9:27).

Mormon records that, amid all of their sacrifice and suffering, these nine missionaries found that their "afflictions" were "swallowed up in the joy of Christ" (Alma 31:38). Of this, Elder Neal A. Maxwell taught:

> Why is non-endurance a denial of the Lord? Because giving up is a denial of the Lord's loving capacity to see us through "all these things"! Giving up suggests that God is less than He really is. . . . So much of life's curriculum consists of efforts by the Lord to get and keep our attention. Ironically, the stimuli He uses are often that which is seen by us as something to endure. Sometimes what we are being asked to endure is His 'help'—help to draw us away from the cares of the world; help to draw us away from self-centeredness; attention-getting help, when the still, small voice has been ignored by us; help in the shaping of our souls; and help to keep the promises we made so long ago to Him and to ourselves. . . . Whether the afflictions are self-induced, as most of them are, or whether they are of the divine tutorial type, it matters not. Either way, the Lord can help us so that our afflictions, said Alma, can be "swallowed up in the joy of Christ" (Alma 31:38). Thus, afflictions are endured and are overcome by joy. The sour notes are lost amid a symphony of salvational sounds. Our afflictions, brothers and sisters, may not be extinguished. Instead, they can be dwarfed and swallowed up in the joy of Christ. This is how we overcome most of the time—not the elimination of our affliction, but the placing of these in that larger context.[8]

The "joy of Christ" can help us to shoulder any burden life brings—and even the best of us live a life filled with burdens. This is not a negative declaration but a resounding endorsement of God's plan. As a professor, I will often have students ask if they can audit my course—so that they won't have to do any of the assignments or commit to attending. I always tell them, "You won't have the experience this course was designed to provide if you do that—as you won't experience any of the challenges of the course." Too many of us wish to "audit" life: flying over the hills and speed bumps we would otherwise encounter. Doing so will certainly allow us to take in the occasional bird's-eye view, but it will not allow us to have the experience this "course of morality" was designed to provide. What a blessing are our trials—and how easily they can be endured if we will *allow* the "joy of Christ" to swallow them up! That requires that we jump in with both feet, ill equipped as we are, and trust Him with our whole souls.

NOTES

1. See McConkie and Millet (1987–1991), 3:221; Reynolds and Sjodahl (1955–1962), 4:78.
2. See Gardner (2007), 4:442; McConkie and Millet (1987–1991), 3:221.
3. See Nibley (2004), 2:344–45.
4. See Gardner (2007), 4:443.
5. See Nyman (2003–2004), 3:399; Gardner (2007), 4:443.
6. See Gardner (2007), 4:444.
7. By this I do not mean that the missionaries today go out without "purse or script." Rather, I mean that God provides spiritually for them. Sometimes that's temporal, but more often it is physical, spiritual, protective, inspirational, and so on.
8. Neal A. Maxwell, cited in Bassett (2007–2008), 2:190.

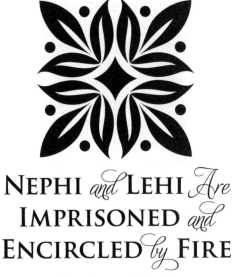

NEPHI and LEHI Are IMPRISONED and ENCIRCLED by FIRE

HELAMAN 5:21–52

THE MIRACLE

Nephi and Lehi—the sons of Helaman—were preaching in the land of Nephi when they were arrested by an army of Lamanites and cast into prison. The prison in which they were incarcerated was the same facility in which King Limhi imprisoned Ammon and his brethren.

For many days these preachers of righteousness were forbidden food, and ultimately, the Lamanites sought to take their lives. However, at the moment they were about to be slain, Nephi and Lehi were miraculously encircled "as if by fire"—thereby preventing their executioners from laying hands upon them (Helaman 5:23).

Mormon informs us that the Lamanites were not only frightened by the miracle but also "struck dumb with amazement" (verse 25). Realizing that the Lamanites could not harm them gave Nephi and Lehi courage so that they could stand forth and boldly declare their message. As they spoke "the earth shook exceedingly, and the walls of the prison did shake" also—though they did not fall (verse 27).

Suddenly, Nephi and Lehi's Lamanite captors were "overshadowed with a cloud of darkness" and filled with a "solemn fear" (verse 28). A voice—still and perfectly mild—was heard coming from above the cloud, warning them to repent and to seek no more to destroy the servants whom God had sent. As the voice spoke, "the earth shook exceedingly, and the walls of the prison trembled again" (verse 31).

A second time, the voice commanded Nephi and Lehi's enemies to "repent" and "seek no more to destroy [God's] servants" (verse 32). And again the earth shook and the walls of the prison trembled.

Then for the third time, the missionaries' captors heard the voice, this time speaking "unto them marvelous words which cannot be uttered by man" (verse 33). And the walls trembled and the earth shook again.

Because of the influence of the cloud (which hovered over them), Nephi and Lehi's captors were incapacitated to the degree that they could not flee. Additionally, Mormon tells us that their fear had a paralyzing effect on them, making it impossible for them to even move.

Aminadab, a Nephite by birth (who had "dissented" or apostatized from the Church), noticed that Nephi and Lehi had been transfigured[1]—"they did shine exceedingly" (verse 36)—and that they were looking heavenward, speaking to some being whom the two missionaries beheld. Grasping the significance of what was taking place, Aminadab told his Lamanite comrades to look at Nephi and Lehi. When they did so, not understanding what they were seeing, they entreated him to explain to them what was happening. Aminadab explained that Nephi and Lehi were talking with the angels of God.

Desirous to have the cloud of darkness removed from above them, the Lamanites asked Aminadab what they should do. He counseled them, "Repent, and cry unto the voice . . . until ye shall have faith in Christ" (verse 41). Trusting in his words, they did so, and the cloud dispersed.

At the withdrawal of the cloud, the Lamanite captors of Nephi and Lehi found themselves also encircled by a pillar of fire, and they were filled with "joy unspeakable" (verse 44). The Holy Ghost entered their hearts, they spoke "marvelous words," the heavens were opened, angels descended—ministering unto all of them (verse 45).

The Lamanites were so fully converted by what they had experienced that they went out and ministered to the other Lamanites—testifying to what they had experienced—and "the more part . . . were convinced" and converted; and their hatred toward the Nephites ended (verse 50).

BACKGROUND

Aminadab was a Nephite by birth who had been a member of the Church, but who had apostatized and joined the Lamanites (Helaman 5:35). In this miracle, it is *his* understanding of the doctrines of the Church (to which he had formerly belonged) that ultimately makes it possible for the Lamanites to interpret the experience Nephi and Lehi had with the divine.[2] Indeed, though in a state of sin himself, it is Aminadab who walks his Lamanite friends through the process of repentance and conversion, facilitating their own spiritual experience. Of him, Reynolds and Sjodahl wrote:

> God made use of Aminadab as an instrument in explaining the meaning of the glorious manifestation of His power which then took place. We may therefore infer that Aminadab was not radically a bad man. Whether he was in the prison as an officer, prisoner, or a stranger led thither by curiosity or by sympathy for the two Nephites is not explained, but we find him there when the earth shook, when the voice of God was heard from Heaven, and the other wonderful and awful manifestations of His presence occurred.[3]

The land of Nephi was controlled by Nephites from the time of Nephi, Lehi's son (in the sixth century BCE), until Mosiah and his people left it (in the second century BCE). During the era of Kings Zeniff, Noah, and Limhi, the land of Nephi became a Lamanite-controlled region—and remained such throughout the remainder of the Book of Mormon.[4] One text points out, "With the exception of the city of Zarahemla, the city of Nephi is mentioned more often than any other city in the Book of Mormon. Any prominent people of the Book of Mormon lived all or a portion of their lives in the city of Nephi. Among them were Nephi, Jacob, Mosiah, Abinadi, Alma, Zeniff, Noah, Limhi, and Gideon."[5]

As the glowing of their countenance indicates, Nephi and Lehi were transfigured during this miracle. Elder Bruce R. McConkie explained: "*Transfiguration* is a special change in appearance and nature which is wrought upon a person or thing by the power of God. This divine transformation is from a lower to a higher state; it results in a more exalted, impressive, and glorious condition."[6] This state of transfiguration may explain why it was that the Lamanites could not lay hold upon Nephi and Lehi. It certainly explains how it was they were enabled to endure the presence of God. Consequently, when the Lamanites eventually also experience being encircled by fire—and being ministered to by angels—they too were transfigured.

SYMBOLIC ELEMENTS

Mormon tells us that during this miracle the Lamanites were "struck dumb with amazement" (Helaman 5:25). In other words, the awe-inspiring experience left them literally speechless. The Psalms sometimes employ silence as a symbol for defeat or destruction (Psalm 101:5; 143:12. See also Isaiah 47:5).[7] The experience here reminds us of the truth that God's enemies will ultimately be silenced. The Lamanites fought against the witness of Nephi and Lehi. However, their sudden loss of speech was but a foretelling of what was shortly to come. Through their encounter with the divine, their dissenting witness would be silenced and the truth of the gospel would go forth converting "the more part of the Lamanites" (verse 50).

The "pillar of fire" and the "cloud" are standard symbols for the presence of God, as one text points out: "The divine presence with Israel in the wilderness took the visible form of a . . . cloud (by day) and [a pillar] of fire (by night) . . . (Ex 13:21–22; Neh 9:19). [The] cloud and fire symbolize the divine presence."[8] The British typologist Ada R. Habershon noted that "the pillar went behind [ancient Israel] and remained there all night, between them and the Egyptians; enshrouding their enemies in darkness, but giving light to the children of Israel."[9] So it was in this miracle of Nephi and Lehi. The cloud brought their enemies darkness while the missionaries were surrounded by light.

In Moses 1:19 Satan's voice is described as "loud." He "rants" and "cries" and screams! One commentary described it in this way: "Lucifer's voice of wickedness is both loud and harsh and lacks the mildness and softness of a heavenly voice."[10] On the other hand, the "still voice of perfect mildness" described here (see also 1 Kings 19:11–12; 3 Nephi 11:3; D&C 8:2–3) is a symbolic reminder of the fact that God will not scream to get our attention. His promptings are gentle, and the voice of His Spirit is soft like a whisper.[11] Spiritually audible? Absolutely! However, if we do not prepare our hearts and control our environment, then we run the risk of not hearing God's voice when He speaks—and He will speak!

The trembling of the earth is a standard symbol for the manifestation of God's power.[12] Consequently, one expert on Mesoamerican religion pointed out that in this specific miracle the earth's trembling would have been seen (by those of a Mesoamerican culture) as a sign of the divine presence.[13] That is exactly how the Lamanites in this miracle perceive it.[14]

As in 3 Nephi 11:3–6, in this account the voice of God is heard three times. The number three is a standard scriptural symbol for that which is divine in its power or origin.[15] This number's symbolism was largely engrained into the psyche of the ancients. Thus, it is quite feasible that "triple repetition" of God's voice and seismic activity would have confirmed for the Lamanites their suspicion, namely that this miracle was of God and that Nephi and Lehi were indeed true prophets of the Lord.

APPLICATION AND ALLEGORIZATION

The most obvious application of this miracle is the reality that God protects His servants until their work is completed. To Joseph Smith, the Lord declared, "Thy days are known, and thy years shall not be numbered less" (D&C 122:9). So it could be said of each of us who have a calling and mission to which we have been foreordained. God is in control. If we are living faithfully, we should not fear that our enemies could shorten our lives or stop God's work. In whatever way necessary, God will protect the faithful who are engaged in His service until they have finished their work upon the earth.[16]

An additional application of this miracle to the modern world is to be found in the fact that the sinful Lamanites were—because of their sins—enveloped in an immovable darkness. During the time I was investigating the Church, I had a somewhat parallel experience.

> During my freshman year of college—and while still a member of the Greek Orthodox Church—I attended a social activity sponsored by the Campus Crusade for Christ. At one point during the evening, we were all gathered around, sitting in a large circle, talking casually about this and that. Someone made a passing reference to Mormonism, and I, without thinking anything about it, took that opportunity to insert

into the conversation a condescending joke about the Latter-day Saints. While I do not remember the joke, I do remember the hearty and sustained laughter that followed. Yet, more memorable for me was the feeling I had the very moment I articulated my unkind comment.

As those around me laughed, I noticed that I was immediately enveloped in a tangible darkness that seem to permeate every fiber of my person. I felt something physically withdraw from me. I sensed a loss of light. I felt in my heart that God was somehow not happy with what I had said—though I could not (at that stage of my life) grasp the meaning of the experience.

After my conversion to The Church of Jesus Christ of Latter-day Saints, and having learned about the Holy Ghost and the Light of Christ, I became convinced that what I experienced that day was the withdrawal of God's Spirit. I believe that the Light of Christ temporarily withdrew from me because I chose to say something that I knew to be unkind, untrue, and potentially hurtful—to the Latter-day Saints, but also to those evangelical Christians present (whom I had mislead about the Mormons).

One reason my words were particularly inappropriate—and potentially offensive to the Spirit—was that I knew several Latter-day Saints and knew them well. Indeed, my best friend at that time was LDS. In my high school there were several thousand students, but only a few Mormons; and those few stood out. They were noticeably better people than many of the non-LDS friends I had during those four years. Because I *knew* that the circle of Mormons I was acquainted with were a cut above the rest, my derogatory comment was a conscious choice to say something untrue and potentially hurtful. I did not sin out of ignorance. And the Spirit instantly let me know I had stepped over a line I should not have crossed.

The memory of the feelings I had that day have never left me. Neither has the lesson I learned. God's Spirit can be grieved. When you and I consciously choose darkness over light, we may experience a withdrawal of God's Light—and we will come to know intimately what spiritual darkness feels like. This darkness is not punitive but sent by God as a means of motivating us to repentance and change—just as it did for Nephi and Lehi's Lamanite captors. And as for them, so also for us: repentance is the only way to remove that enveloping cloud of darkness.

In this miracle, each time truth was testified of, and every time the divine voice spoke, the earth and those upon it were shaken. We are reminded of the beautiful verity that the power of the testimony of those who know God can "shake" the very being of those who hear their words. Some will not heed the warnings and witness of the Spirit—yet it is my conviction that none can remain indifferent. For when the Spirit of God brushes up against a human soul—even for a brief moment—it leaves its mark. Even those who reject the witness are left with that testimony engraved upon their souls—prepared to blossom when the beneficiary is ready, or capable of testifying against the recipient if he or she chooses to never repent.

On a related note, this miracle seems to testify that those who have fallen away (like Aminadab had) often retain a knowledge of the truth—even if they are not living up to it. Sometimes, when trials or the vicissitudes of life come, that latent belief, knowledge, or testimony will awaken, and the less-active Saint will become saintly again. It is commonly taught within the Church that the witness of the Spirit is stronger than seeing an angel.[17] This may very well be the reason why. Regardless, Aminadab's reconversion to Christ and His Church reminds us that we should give up on no one—no matter how long they have been gone or how hardened they may seem (Moroni 9:6). It also testifies to the fact that there is much missionary work to be done among the less-active members of the Church.

Mormon informs us that the Lamanites, as soon as they were converted to the Church, "did go forth, and did minister unto the people, declaring throughout all the regions round about all the things which they had heard and seen" (Helaman 5:50). When we are truly converted, our natural desire will be to seek out others who would be blessed by what we've found. We will feel both a desire and a need to testify of the power and influence of the gospel in our own lives. We see evidence of this with the Lamanites in this miracle, and we saw it with Enos in his life (Enos 1:9, 11). Indeed, in my own life I found that, after I had been converted and baptized, I had an insatiable desire to serve a mission—to tell the world of what great blessings had come into my life because of the restored gospel of Jesus Christ.

This miracle speaks of how Nephi's and Lehi's countenances "did shine exceedingly" and how they had "the face of angels" when the Spirit of the Lord was resting upon them (Helaman 5:36). While in this case they were being transfigured, it seems fair to say that those who commune with God (through lives of holiness) have a noticeable change in their countenances also. Each of us has likely known individuals who had a glow—a radiance about them. One cannot help but ask, To what degree do others sense this same radiance in you? Is your life such that there is a power about your presence and a light associated with your countenance? Do they see God in your face and hear God in your voice? (Alma 5:19). If not, why? President James E. Faust shared the following:

> I recently recalled a historic meeting in Jerusalem about 17 years ago. It was regarding the lease for the land on which the Brigham Young University's Jerusalem Center for Near Eastern Studies was later built. Before this lease could be signed, President Ezra Taft Benson and Elder Jeffrey R. Holland, then president of Brigham Young University, agreed with the Israeli government on behalf of the Church and the university not to proselyte in Israel. You might wonder why we agreed not to proselyte. We were required to do so in order to get the building permit to build that magnificent building which stands in the historic city of Jerusalem. To our knowledge the Church and BYU have scrupulously and honorably kept that nonproselyting commitment. After the lease had been signed, one of our friends insightfully remarked, "Oh, we know that you are not going to proselyte, but what are you going to do about the light that is in their eyes?" He was referring to our students who were studying in Israel.
>
> What was that light in their eyes which was so obvious to our friend? The Lord Himself gives the answer: "And the light which shineth, which giveth you light, is through him who enlighteneth your eyes, which is the same light that quickeneth your understandings." Where did that light come from? Again the Lord gives the answer: "I am the true light that lighteth every man that cometh into the world." The Lord is the true light, "and the Spirit enlighteneth every man through the world, that hearkeneth to the voice of the Spirit." This light shows in our countenances as well as in our eyes.
>
> Paul Harvey, a famous news commentator, visited one of our Church school campuses some years ago. Later he observed: "Each . . . young face mirrored a sort of . . . sublime assurance. These days many young eyes are prematurely old from countless compromises with conscience. But [these young people] have that enviable headstart which derives from discipline, dedication, and consecration."[18]

As a final application of this miracle, remember that through repentance the Spirit of the Lord is brought into our lives, and that Spirit has the power to change us from the inside out. Mormon informs us that after the obvious miracles of this narrative took place, the Lamanites "did lay down their weapons of war, and also their hatred and the tradition of their fathers" (Helaman 5:51). True conversion softens our hearts so that we hate no more, we anger no more, we seek the suffering of our enemies no more, and the false and harmful "traditions of our fathers" no longer tempt nor control our lives and beliefs. Such was true with the Lamanites in this miracle, and such can be true with you and me as we turn our hearts over to the Lord and allow His Spirit to fully operate in our lives.

NOTES

1. See Gardner (2007), 5:95; Andrew C. Skinner, "Nephi's Ultimate Encounter with Deity: Some Thoughts on Helaman 10," in Monte S. Nyman and Charles D. Tate Jr., editors, *The Book of Mormon: Helaman Through 3 Nephi 8, According To Thy Word* (Provo, UT: Religious Studies Center, Brigham Young University, 1992), 119, 115–127.

2. See Gardner (2007), 5:95; Nyman (2003–2004), 4:302.

3. Reynolds and Sjodahl (1955–1961), 5:245.

4. See Joseph L. Allen, "Nephi, land of and city of," in Largey (2003), 593.

5. See Allen, in Largey (2003), 594.

6. McConkie (1979), 803.

7. See also Ryken, Wilhoit, and Longman (1998), 791.

8. Ryken, Wilhoit, and Longman (1998), 646. See also McConkie and Millet (1987–1991), 3:358; Habershon (1974), 57, 148–52; Ogden and Skinner (2011), 2:88.

9. Habershon (1974), 149.

10. Ludlow, Pinegar, Allen, Otten, and Caldwell (2007), 379.

11. Elder Boyd K. Packer taught that "the Spirit does not get our attention by shouting or shaking us with a heavy hand. Rather it whispers. It caresses so gently that if we are preoccupied we may not feel it at all" [see Ludlow, Pinegar, Allen, Otten, and Caldwell (2007), 379].

12. See for example Ryken, Wilhoit, and Longman (1998), 225. See also Gardner (2007), 5:95.

13. See Gardner (2007), 5:93.

14. One commentary on the Book of Mormon suggested a natural explanation for this miracle: "The combination of an earthquake and an overshadowing cloud of darkness suggests a volcanic eruption. . . . Mesoamerica is an area of significant volcanic activity. . . . The 'cloud of darkness' could be the cloud of suspended particulates accompanying many volcanic eruptions. . . . The Lamanites would be immobilized, not only because of fear but because they could not see where to go or whether other structures had fallen" [Gardner (2007), 5:93, 94]. While this view is possible— and while admitting that God often works through natural means—nevertheless, I

remain unconvinced. This explanation doesn't explain the pillar of fire that encircled Nephi and Lehi (and eventually the Lamanites) without harming them. Nor does it harmonize (in my mind) with the description Mormon preserves, which seems to associate the trembling and the cloud not with a natural phenomenon that the Lamanites would have been familiar with but instead with something theretofore unknown by them.

15. See Gaskill (2003), 115–17.

16. Certainly God knows the timing of the death of each of us. He is truly omniscient. However, there is a divine protection afforded the faithful who have a work to do that is required by God and His holy plan. Thus, while any of His children may receive protection, such is particularly true of those who are on His errand.

17. See for example Joseph Fielding Smith, *Answers to Gospel Questions*, five volumes (Salt Lake City: Deseret Book, 1993), 2:151.

18. James E. Faust, "The Light in Their Eyes," *Ensign*, November 2005, 20.

Nephi Cannot *be* Captured *by* His Enemies, *and* He *Is* Conveyed *by the* Spirit *out of* Their Midst

Helaman 10:15–17

THE MIRACLE

Nephi had been pondering the wickedness of his people, the Nephites. In the midst of his contemplation, the voice of the Lord came to him, saying, "Blessed art thou, Nephi, for those things which thou hast done; for I have beheld how thou hast with unwearyingness declared the word, which I have given unto thee, unto this people. And thou hast not feared them, and hast not sought thine own life, but hast sought my will, and to keep my commandments. And now, because thou hast done this with such unwearyingness, behold, I will bless thee forever; and I will make thee mighty in word and in deed, in faith and in works; yea, even that all things shall be done unto thee according to thy word, for thou shalt not ask that which is contrary to my will" (Helaman 10:4–5). The Lord then gave Nephi the sealing power so that he could bind and seal as the Spirit directed him.

Having endowed him with power, the Lord then commanded Nephi to go forth and call the Nephites to repentance, lest they be destroyed. Nephi did so, but his message was not well received. Even though they knew from past experience that he had the gift of prophecy, they hardened their hearts and would not repent. Indeed, his preaching angered them, so that they reviled him and sought to cast him in prison. However, the "power of God was with him," and therefore, his enemies were not able to lay hands upon him because "he was taken by the Spirit and conveyed away out of the midst of them" (Helaman 10:16).

Mormon tells us that Nephi then went forth "in the Spirit" from "multitude to multitude" preaching the word of God, declaring it unto all, or sending it forth unto all the people (verse 17).

BACKGROUND

Commentators typically downplay the miraculous nature of the events in Helaman 10:15–17. However, something significant may be described herein. This miracle is reminiscent of a similar one in the life of Christ. The Gospel of John informs us that the Savior had condemned a group of scribes and Pharisees for an act of hypocrisy and blatant dishonesty. Having born His witness to them that He was the "light of the world" and Jehovah of old, His antagonists "took up stones to cast at him." However, John tells us that Jesus "hid himself" and left the temple "through the midst of them"—though they could not detect Him (see John 8:59. See also Acts 8:39–40). Nephi, like the Lord, was spirited away, "conveyed out of the midst of them" by the Holy Ghost (Helaman 10:16). This could simply mean that he followed the Spirit to his next destination. But the fact that they "could not take him . . . for he was conveyed away out of the midst of them" suggests something more miraculous is being described.

SYMBOLIC ELEMENTS

Like Jesus, Nephi imperceptibly slips away. This functions well as a subtle metaphor for the veil and how it conceals sacred things from the unworthy while also revealing holy things to those who are prepared and worthy to received them. Neither the Lord nor His prophet could be detected or retained by the wicked. Both were enabled to pass unmolested from their antagonistic attackers. Both were able to continue the work of the Father contrary to the will of their combative opponents. God can veil the eyes of our enemies that we might do His work unharmed and unhindered.

APPLICATION AND ALLEGORIZATION

An obvious application of this miracle is that those who are on the Lord's errand, as Nephi was, can be protected by Him—and sometimes in rather miraculous ways. Such protecting is not reserved for prophets. All who embark in the service of the Lord can expect His intervention and protection according to His will and needs.

In addition, just as Nephi was directed by the Spirit from one multitude to another, the Spirit can direct us to where we should go and what we should say. President Thomas S. Monson has taught: "When you are on the Lord's errand, you are entitled to the Lord's help."[1] Faithful bishops, stake presidents, Relief Society presidents, youth leaders, and others experience this in their ministries—as do dedicated and Spirit-directed missionaries. As a singular example of how God guides the faithful, I cite the following experience from my days as a young missionary in Europe. One of the ward mission leaders I worked with was a convert to the Church. When I enquired as to what had brought him to the restored gospel, he shared with me the following story:

I had been struggling for some time. My life was not going as I had hoped it would. I felt somewhat despondent, as my efforts to find meaning and happiness seemed to fail time and again. I had gotten to the point that I felt I could no longer endure the burdens I was carrying; and at that stage in my life, though religious, I did not understand enough about God to tap into His strength as a means of shouldering the weight I was being crushed by.

Finally, in desperation, I knelt in my living room one afternoon and pled with God to intervene or to just "take me." While I had never seriously contemplated suicide prior to this time, I felt the problems I was struggling with were of such a nature that I could not help but consider that as my most appealing option.

As I prayed, I simply told God, "I think this is my last chance. I cannot endure another day feeling lost and hopeless. If you are there, and if you do not want me to take my own life, you need to intervene now! Otherwise, I quit! I do not wish to live any longer."

The instant I uttered those words, my doorbell rang. Now that should not necessarily strike you as miraculous. However, it struck me as a miracle, as my doorbell had been broken for several years. It did not work! Ever!

Puzzled, to say the least, I got up and apprehensively walked to the door. When I opened it, there stood before me two LDS missionaries who informed me that they had a message for me. They literally saved my life—not only physically, but also spiritually. I was baptized a short time later.

No doubt the Lord directed those two missionaries to the door of this good brother on that particular day. God is in the details, and in this circumstance, timing was crucial. The Father appears to have orchestrated every detail: the circumstances that provoked the prayer, the exact time the missionaries rang, the miraculous working of the bell, even the day on which the missionaries visited (this brother would normally have been at work during the day, but had stayed home that particular occasion because he was feeling so poorly). God knows what we need. He knows what those for whom we have stewardship need. Like Nephi, we only need to "go forth in the Spirit" and He will take care of the rest.

Another potential application of this miracle is this: the powers of the prophets can be lost because of our personal wickedness. Just as Nephi's antagonists rejected him and, thus, could no longer see or hear his witness and words, so also you and I—through rejecting the counsel of the Lord's servants—can lose our personal awareness of their inspired status. You and I can become spiritually blind so that we cannot see the truth. If we reject Christ (or His authorized messengers)—or if we refuse to heed their council—we run the risk of no longer being able to perceive their divinely inspired voice. They can become indiscernible to us, and we may be left to ourselves. Doctrine and Covenants 93:39 wisely warns us: "And that wicked one cometh and taketh away light and truth, through disobedience, from the children of men." We must regularly assess whether we are doing things that cause us to lose "light and truth" and our ability to discern Christ and His will for us—as given through His living oracles. The power of the prophets will only be evident to us as we trust in their words and ways. However, if we revile them—as in this miracle—our testimonies of their inspired mantel may also be disappear.

NOTES

1. Thomas S. Monson, quoted in Neil L. Andersen, "The Spiritual Gifts," *Ensign*, December 2009, 48.

No Darkness *the* Night *before* Jesus *Is* Born

Helaman 14:3–4
3 Nephi 1:4–20

The Miracle

Five years prior to the birth of Jesus, Samuel the Lamanite prophesied that the night before Christ's birth there would be no darkness once the sun had set. Thus, as a sign that Jesus had been born (on the Eastern Hemisphere), in the Western Hemisphere there would be a day and a night and a day without any darkness.

As the approximate time for the miracle arrived, the antagonists of the believers began to persecute those with faith, saying that the time for the sign had passed—and Samuel had made a false prophecy (Helaman 14:4). The believers "began to be very sorrowful" (3 Nephi 1:7), many worrying that perhaps the sign would not come as prophesied. Others watched steadfastly for the sign, believing that their faith was not in vain.

The persecutors, perhaps in an effort to end what they believed was foolish faith, set a date by which the sign given by Samuel must manifest itself. If by that day it had not happened, those who persisted in their belief would be slain.

Nephi, the son of Nephi, prayed to God for intervention, and the voice of the Lord came to him saying that "the time is at hand" (3 Nephi 1:13–14). That night the sign would come, and on the morrow Jesus would be born into the world.

As promised, when the sun set that evening "there was no

darkness," and the people were greatly "astonished" (3 Nephi 1:15, 19). Those who had persecuted the believers "fell to the earth . . . as if they were dead"—fearing "because of their iniquity and their unbelief" (3 Nephi 1:16, 18). All things prophesied of by the prophets were fulfilled "every whit" (3 Nephi 1:20).

BACKGROUND

Nephi, the son of Nephi, succeeded his father in the office of high priest and prophet to the people of Nephi. On the occasion of the appearance of the Lord to the people of the Americas, Nephi was chosen and ordained the senior member of the Nephite Twelve. He enjoyed great spiritual endowments, including the ability to cast out evil spirits, heal the sick, and even raise the dead. It was said that "angels ministered to him daily."[1]

Samuel the Lamanite prophet was one of the most gifted seers in the Book of Mormon. His detailed prophecies of that which would take place at the birth, death, and Resurrection of Christ stand as a testament to the inspiration under which he spoke and taught. He was the recipient of a visitation of an angel (Helaman 13:7; 14:9, 26, 28) and also communication from the "voice of the Lord" (Helaman 13:3). His courage is evident in his boldness in calling the then corrupt Nephites to repentance—even at the threat of his own life. One commentator noted: "The proud, wicked, and prejudiced Nephites were offended by the presence of a Lamanite reproving them for their sins (Hel. 14:10). Historically, that was a Nephite prerogative, but now the roles were reversed."[2] Samuel manifest no fear—and while many rejected his witness, this did not deter him from speaking the words of the Lord and His angels.

In this miracle the "voice of the Lord" came to Nephi (3 Nephi 1:12). Owing to President Brigham Young's statement that "the spirit from the eternal worlds enters the tabernacle" being created in the mother's womb "at the time of . . . quickening" (at the point the mother begins to feel movement[3]), some have questioned how it is that Jesus could be speaking to Nephi the night before He was born.[4] The *Doctrinal Commentary on the Book of Mormon* explains:

> This is the day before Jesus is to be born to Mary in Bethlehem of Judea. We would assume that by this time the spirit of Jesus is within

that infant body which is housed within the womb of Mary. How, then, does the voice of Jesus come to Nephi? . . .

The words of God are often spoken through his servants by divine investiture of authority. To Adam the Holy Ghost spoke for and in behalf of the Only Begotten Son (see Moses 5:9). Such may have been the case here: The Spirit may have been commissioned by the Father to speak to Nephi in the first person for Christ, as though Jesus himself were speaking. Another possibility is that an angel, acting by that same investiture of authority, spoke to Nephi the words of Christ (see *Mortal Messiah* 1:349, note 1; compare Revelation 22:6–9). In any event, whether the Lord's words are spoken by himself or by his anointed servants, "it is the same" (D&C 1:38).[5]

When the text speaks of the "sign" being seen by "all the people upon the face of the whole earth" (3 Nephi 1:17), it is assumed that this is a bit of hyperbole. The Book of Mormon itself seems quite clear that those on the Eastern Hemisphere did not receive the exact same signs as those on the Western. Thus, one commentator explained that " 'whole earth' meant only the Nephites' whole earth—or known lands. . . . [This most likely was] a regionalized phenomenon, but one sufficiently widespread that it was visible in all Nephite lands."[6]

Helaman 14 contains a remarkably specific set of prophecies regarding the birth of Christ, each having very clear fulfillment (as recorded in the book of 3 Nephi).[7]

The prophecy in Helaman 14:2 is fulfilled in 3 Nephi 1:13.

The prophecy in Helaman 14:3 is fulfilled in 3 Nephi 1:15.

The prophecy in Helaman 14:5 is fulfilled in 3 Nephi 1:21.

The prophecy in Helaman 14:6 is fulfilled in 3 Nephi 2:1.

The prophecy in Helaman 14:7 is fulfilled in 3 Nephi 1:16–17.

SYMBOLIC ELEMENTS

Jesus is the Light of the World (Alma 38:9; John 8:12). Satan is its darkness (Moses 7:26; Acts 26:18).[8] "Why was there no darkness [on the occasion of Christ's birth]? Because the literal Light of the World was entering the physical world (D&C 88:5–12). Similarly, darkness would dominate at the death of Jesus because the Light of the World had left the physical world."[9] This miracle could not be clearer in its use of light and dark—and their symbolic implications. We have light *because* Jesus came. We lose the light when we (in any way) reject

Him—as those who took His life did. When Christ returns, once again the darkness will flee "that at evening time it shall be light" (Zechariah 14:7). This miracle's dichotomy between light and darkness reminds us that whenever and wherever Christ is present, there will be light.

We have mentioned above *proskynēsis*—the act of falling to the earth in a spirit of fear, awe, reverence, or submission.[10] It is a sign of humility. It evidences one's awareness of his own nothingness in comparison to the greatness of God. That is what those who "fell to the earth" (3 Nephi 1:16) were feeling—particularly in light of their previous attempts to destroy God's Church. They are deeply humbled by this miracle and fear that God will destroy them for the evils they have sought to bring to pass.

APPLICATION AND ALLEGORIZATION

At the birth of Jesus there was "no darkness" (Helaman 14:3). One source attests: "All things testify of Christ. . . . How appropriate and typical—with the coming of the Light of Life into the world there would be no darkness."[11] Jesus's presence has the ability to dissipate all darkness from our lives—that we may ever live in the light. One of the dangers of the mortal experience is that we become numb to the influences of the world. They are so prevalent, even in the best of communities, that we simply don't notice their influence swirling around us. We watch what we really should not. We ignore doing what we really should do. Darkness slowly creeps in, and thereby, the light is gradually chased away (D&C 93:39). I recently ran into a former student who had just returned from her mission. She shared the following:

> I grew up in an active LDS home—or so I thought. We always went to church, but prior to my mission I never considered the degree to which the gospel *really* influenced our day-to-day lives. Now that I have returned home and spend some time with my family, I've come to realize that they're all basically inactive. Yes, they go to church almost every Sunday. However, the Church isn't part of their lives outside of the three-hour block. They are going through the motions on Sundays, but our home is void of the Light the gospel should bring. The Spirit isn't there. Seemingly small, but spiritually dampening things, are readily accepted in the home and in their lives—and so there really is more darkness than there needs or should be. Of course, they can't

see that. When you're in the dark you can't see anything clearly. The Light is available to them, but they're too spiritually lazy to get up, walk across the proverbial room, and flip the switch.

Christ is the source of light. Those who know the gospel know that! Nevertheless, some linger in the darkness because of spiritual laziness—or because they "love darkness rather than light" (D&C 10:21). As this miracle suggests, if we invoke the presence of the Lord's Spirit, the darkness will dispel. But if we do that which douses the light, we will be left in deep darkness. The choice is ours, as is the power to invite the light or the darkness.

The non-believers in this miracle simply could not leave the believers alone. The disbelievers felt *compelled* to prevent the believers from peacefully living out their faith—even though doing so in no way infringed on the rights and lives of the non-believers. The signs, prophecies, and faith of the believers grated on the souls and hearts of those who did not believe. "The wicked who refuse to believe dare not allow others to believe. . . . To the impenitent, the unrepentant, the impure, and the spiritually insensitive—to these the signs of the times are laughable, inconsequential, and unconvincing."[12] Satan compelled the non-believers in this miracle to hate those who had faith; and so he does with many today. If faith is false, how are the atheists harmed by it? They can certainly go about their lives without any significant inconvenience. Yet some are stirred up to anger by the faith of those who believe. Christmas music, holiday TV specials, the erection of houses of worship—all these provoke anger in the heart of some. It seems that they cannot rest until they put a stop to the faith and faithfulness of those who profess a belief in God. (The devout atheist and anti-religion activist Madalyn Murray O'Hair was the poster child for such behaviors.) Satan is the source of such devout antagonism toward holiness and faith. 2 Nephi 28:20 warns us: "For behold, at that day shall he rage in the hearts of the children of men, and stir them up to anger against that which is good." Again, prophecy fulfilled!

In this narrative we learn that when the non-believers claimed that the prophecy of Samuel was "unfulfilled," some of the believers began to have doubts. "For the believers' part, they attempt to continue in faith; but given the real possibility that the prophecy has failed, they 'begin to be very sorrowful.'"[13] We can draw a lesson for our own lives from this portion of the miracle. Divine promises—whether made in a patriarchal or priesthood blessing—may take time to be fulfilled. We must trust not only in God's promises, but also His timing. We must not be like that smaller portion of Nephites who began to doubt. Indeed, doubting is the antithesis of faith and can lead to the loss of promised blessings (which are always contingent upon the recipient's faith). As Moroni wrote many centuries later, "And it came to pass that Ether did prophesy great and marvelous things unto the people, which they did not believe, because they saw them not. And now, I, Moroni, would speak somewhat concerning these things; I would show unto the world that faith is things which are hoped for and not seen; where-fore, dispute not because ye see not, for ye receive no witness until after the trial of your faith" (Ether 12:5–6). We must not forget that "faith precedes the miracle."[14] If we create limited windows of time in which we are willing to believe, we run the risk of never seeing the fulfillment of God's promises to us because we have sought to tie God's hands. Faith sets no parameters on God's will, ways, and timing. We must be willing to say, "Thy will be done" (Matthew 6:10)—not just to the nature of blessings, but also when it comes to their timing.

One commentary on the Book of Mormon highlighted the fact that in this miracle Nephi prayed to God and, thereby, provoked God's revelation and subsequent intervention. "Revelations are usually given because we ask with a sincere heart with faith in mighty prayer. The Lord is no respecter of persons and each of us has this right."[15] Among the many applications this miracle offers, the reality that we have the power to invoke personal revelation is central to this story. God is willing to speak to each of us—answering our sincere prayers and inter-vening in our lives. However, as this miracle demonstrates, "there must be a stirring below before there can be a stirring above."[16] In many cases, we must start the conversation. God is willing and waiting for our instigation, but the divine principle of agency requires that He allow us to initiate the miracle.

NOTES

1. See Reynolds and Sjodahl (1955–1961), 7:50.
2. Dennis L. Largey, "Samuel the Lamanite," in Largey (2003), 697.
3. This is typically around the beginning of the second trimester—or about the fourth month of the pregnancy.

4. See Brigham Young, in Van Wagoner (2009), 3:1477.

5. McConkie, Millet, and Top (1992), 6. See also Ogden and Skinner (2011), 2:110–11; McConkie (1987–1988), 1:85.

6. Gardner (2007), 5:239.

7. See Ludlow, Pinegar, Allen, Otten, and Caldwell (2007), 401.

8. Playing off of the contrasting themes of light and darkness, Brant A. Gardner highlighted the following symbolic motif in this miracle: "Samuel announced signs for both the birth and death. They form contrasting parallels: light at the birth versus darkness at the death: 'But behold, as I said unto you concerning another sign, a sign of his death, behold, in that day that he shall suffer death the sun shall be darkened and refuse to give his light unto you; and also the moon and the stars; and there shall be no light upon the face of this land, even from the time that he shall suffer death, for the space of three days, to the time that he shall rise again from the dead' (Hel. 14:20). Thus, dramatic light/darkness accompanied the birth/death" [Gardner (2007), 5:191].

9. Ogden and Skinner (2007), 2:112. One of my colleagues, Andy Skelton, pointed out: "A great cross-reference to this miracle is the story in 3 Nephi 8:21–23, where the narration does not put the emphasis on the darkness but instead on the lack of light: 'no light because of the darkness, neither candles, neither torches; neither could there be fire kindled. . . . [There] could not be any light at all; . . . nor any light seen, neither fire, nor glimmer, neither sun, nor the moon, nor the stars, for so great were the mists of darkness which were upon the face of the land. . . . There was no light seen; and there was great mourning and howling and weeping among all the people continually; yea great were the groanings of the people, because of the darkness and the great destruction.' After the description of the lack of light, we see what happens when the Light of the World goes out (see also D&C 88:6–13). Then in 3 Nephi 9:18 Christ speaks, saying, "I am the light and life of the world." This is one of the most dramatic object lessons teaching how He is "the Light" and how without Him darkness would reign—both spiritually *and* physically. Alonzo discusses this very concept later in this book, when he addresses 3 Nephi 8:5–25" [Andy Skelton, review of *Miracles of the Book of Mormon*].

10. See Nibley (2004), 3:299.

11. McConkie and Millet (1987–1991), 3:408.

12. Joseph Fielding McConkie, Robert L. Millet, and Brent L. Top, *Doctrinal Commentary on the Book of Mormon*, volume four (Salt Lake City: Deseret Book, 1992), 5.

13. Gardner (2007), 5:234.

14. See Spencer W. Kimball, *Faith Precedes the Miracle* (Salt Lake City: Deseret Book, 2001).

15. Pinegar and Allen (2003), 414.

16. Nibley (2004), 4:107. Nibley is quoting from the Talmud.

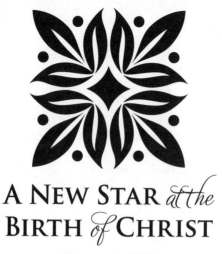

A New Star at the Birth of Christ

HELAMAN 14:5
3 NEPHI 1:21
MATTHEW 2:1–2

THE MIRACLE

Samuel the Lamanite prophesied to the people of Zarahemla that one of the signs that God would show forth—evidencing the birth of the Messiah—would be a "new star" in the heavens (Helaman 14:5; 3 Nephi 1:21). In fulfillment of that prophecy, Mormon records: "And it came to pass . . . that a new star did appear, according to the word" (3 Nephi 1:21). Matthew similarly testified of the fulfillment of this prophecy when he wrote: "Now when Jesus was born in Bethlehem of Judaea in the days of Herod the king, behold, there came wise men from the east to Jerusalem, Saying, Where is he that is born King of the Jews? for we have seen his star in the east, and are come to worship him" (Matthew 2:2).

BACKGROUND

There is some disagreement among commentators as to the exact nature of this star (what exactly did individuals like Samuel, Mormon, and Matthew intend their readers to understand by the phrase "new star"?) and who precisely was able to see it. One LDS commentator conjectured:

> There seems to have been in Jewish prophecy or legend the knowledge

that the Messiah's coming would be heralded by a special appearance of a star. Alfred Edersheim wrote: "There is . . . testimony which seems to us not only reliable, but embodies most ancient Jewish tradition. It is contained in one of the smaller *Midrashim*. . . . The so-called Messiah-Haggadah (*Aggadoth Mashiach*) opens as follows: "A star shall come out of Jacob. There is a Boraita in the name of the Rabbis: The heptad in which the Son of David cometh—in the first year, there will not be sufficient nourishment; in the second year the arrows of famine are launched; in the third, a great famine; in the fourth, neither famine nor plenty; in the fifth, great abundance and *the Star shall shine forth from the East, and this is the Star of the Messiah.*"[1]

The implication of this comment is that the "new star" was intended as a literal physical manifestation of the birth of the Jewish Messiah—a great sign that was expected to be rather universally seen and recognized. However, the inference of Herod's question to the Wise Men—"What time did the star appear?" (Matthew 2:7)—is that it was *not* seen by most, or even many people (at least not on the Eastern Hemisphere).[2] The Book of Mormon is a bit less clear, in that it doesn't drop the frequent hints the New Testament offers regarding the "star's" limited visibility.

It is commonplace for those commentators who interpret the "new star" to be a literal physical astronomical sign[3] to conjecture that it was one of three things: (1) some sort of planetary alignment, such as that of Saturn and Jupiter, which took place in 7 BCE; (2) a comet, such as Halley's, which appeared early in 12–11 BCE; or (3) a nova (a star that, owing to an explosion, appears with extraordinary brightness, but only for a short period of time). Even though two of these phenomena took place in the decade of Christ's birth, there are, nevertheless, two major problems with all three popular explanations. First of all, none of the theories account for the "new star's" ability to move and guide the Wise Men. Second, but more important, on the Eastern Hemisphere this "new star" is not noticed by Herod or the chief priests and scribes before or after the Wise Men approach Herod. Indeed, any of the three aforementioned standard explanations regarding what the "new star" was would have been noted quite universally. The early Christian "Protevangelium of James" states that Herod "examined the Magi, saying to them: What sign have you seen in reference to the king that has been born? And the Magi said: *We have seen a star of great size shining among these stars, and obscuring their light, so that the stars did not appear*; and we thus knew that a king has been born to Israel, and we have come to worship him."[4] The description is of a star that was so bright that it actually obscured the other stars in the sky, making them difficult to see. Yet the King, his astrologers, and the priests of the day seem unaware that this sign had been manifest. All of this suggests that there might be some alternate explanation as to what the "new star" was, or why most on the Eastern Hemisphere didn't notice it. It seems quite puzzling that a people whose lives were so heavily influenced by the stars (they used them for their calendaring, for their religious cycle, for their navigation or directions) would not notice a new star and the time of its first appearance. It also seems puzzling that the scribes (the very men who make all copies of the scriptures) and the priests (the religious leaders of the people) would not be reminded of the prophecy of the "new star" (in association with the Messiah's birth), if they indeed saw a new star in the heavens. Thus, it is believed by some scholars (and is implied by Matthew) that the "star" was not universally visible or recognizable among those of the Eastern Hemisphere[5]—and that, quite possibly, the "new star" was something other than some astrological phenomenon.

In one early Christian text we are told that this star appeared and disappeared (it was visible at times, but not at others).[6] It is quite possible that the Wise Men's receptivity to the Spirit enabled them to see and recognize the star for what it was—a herald of the Messianic age. Certainly Herod and the leadership of the Jews at that time had no such receptivity—and thereby may have missed both the star and its meaning.[7]

More important, it may well be that the reference to a "new star" (in the words of Samuel, Mormon, and Matthew) was somehow symbolic rather than literal—and that we (so removed from the culture and symbolism of the ancient Near East) are entirely missing their intended message behind their words.

SYMBOLIC ELEMENTS

It is feasible that Samuel, Mormon, and Matthew's reference to the "new star" was symbolic, for we know that stars were common symbols for angels. Indeed, this is exactly how many ancient prophets used the word *star*. For example, John the Revelator wrote: "The seven stars

are the angels of the seven churches" (Revelation 1:20. See also 9:1).
Joseph of Egypt saw his eleven brothers as represented by "stars" in the
prophetic dream God gave him (Genesis 37:9). Similarly, Abraham
used "stars" as symbols for Christ, angels, and the premortal spirits of
God's creations (see Abraham 3:17–18); and God used the metaphor
of "innumerable stars" to represent to Abraham his future posterity
(Genesis 15:5). Isaiah spoke of Lucifer as seeking to exalt himself above
the "stars" or "angels" of God (see Isaiah 14:12–13; Revelation 12:4)
and even calls him (in his pre-fallen state) the "morning star" (*NIV*
Isaiah 14:12). Job spoke of the "sons of God" as "morning stars" who
sang praises to the divine at the laying of the foundations of the earth
(Job 38:4). Even Jesus referred to Himself as "the bright and morning
star" (Revelation 22:16). Noting Samuel's prophecy that there would
be "great lights in the heavens" (Helaman 14:3), Ogden and Skinner
suggested, "Could these lights be the angelic hosts who were present at their Master's entrance into mortality, appearing in glory?"[8] In
other words, *perhaps* this elusive "star"—seen only by a few—actually
was a literal star.[9] However, it *may* also have been intended as a symbolic reference to a frequent visitation from some heavenly messenger
instructed by the Lord to guide the Wise Men (and others) on their
quest for Him.[10] In several of the early Christian infancy narratives we
are told, "There appeared to [the Wise Men] an angel in the form of
that star which had before been their guide in their journey; the light
of which they followed till they returned into their own country."[11]

APPLICATION AND ALLEGORIZATION

Just as God sent the "star" to guide the Wise Men (and others) to
Christ, He sends us divine messengers to direct our journey back to
His presence. And just as many among the Nephites were not moved
by the miracle, so also (in our day) many allow Satan "to harden their
hearts . . . that they might not believe in those signs and wonders" (3
Nephi 1:22). As has been suggested, there is reason to think that this
star may have been representative of one or more angels sent to draw
the receptive to Christ. God can send us angels in a variety of forms.
In Hebrews 13:2 we are warned: "Be not forgetful to entertain strangers: for thereby some have entertained angels unawares." How many
of our influential encounters in life have come to us through angels or
the angelic? How oft have we been the recipients of a divine visitor, yet

we were unaware? Beyond this potential promise, what of the Spirit's influence in our day-to-day lives? A number of years ago I sat in a fast and testimony meeting where a man stood and bore his humble witness. Part of his testimony, however, included this statement: "I've never had anything *big*, like an angel minister to me. I just have simple faith that God is real." I remember thinking, "You've had the repeated experience over a lifetime of feeling the Holy Ghost speak to your soul. You may not have seen a *lesser* angel, but you've had encounters with a member of the Godhead over and over again. That seems pretty '*big*' to me!" If we're seeking to draw near to Him, God will send us His "stars" when they are needed in our lives. These may be literal angels. They may come in the form of some spiritual giants in our ward or stake who appear just when we need them, speaking the very words we need to hear in the very hour we need them. Or that "star" may simply come as a manifestation of the Holy Ghost. Either way, as we exercise faith, God will send us "signs" of His reality and of His awareness of our personal circumstances and needs. And, like the Nephites—who were saved via this manifestation—each of us will have times when we recognize that through God's intervention we were "saved," spiritually, physically, or both.

A related question might be asked: What "stars" are we most prone to follow? The world's? Or heaven's? While expounding on these questions should be unnecessary, personal reflection is paramount.

Elder Neal A. Maxwell offered what strikes me as a relevant application of the "new star." He wrote: "The same God that placed that star in a precise orbit millennia before it appeared over Bethlehem in celebration of the birth of the Babe has given at least equal attention to placement of each of us in precise human orbits so that we may, if we will, illuminate the landscape of our individual lives, so that our light may not only lead others but warm them as well."[12] Are we able to see why we have been placed upon the earth at this time in the history of the world? Do we sense the potential scope of our influence? And are we seeking each day to use that influence to "lead" and "warm" those whom the Father has placed in our path?

God certainly manifests "signs" of His existence, Christ's divinity, the Restoration's reality, and the Book of Mormon's truthfulness. If we are in tune with the Lord's Spirit—living in harmony with His will and ways—those "manifestations" strike us as "bright" and "shining."

They are "signs" we cannot miss, neither can we deny. Sad and curious at the same time is the reality that so many cannot see those "signs." Just as Herod and his priests (on the Eastern Hemisphere) were unable to see the tokens of Christ's birth, but the Wise Men could, there are many around us who see no evidence of God's hand in the Restoration. They have read the Book of Mormon casually—if at all—and miss its internal complexity and profundity, assuming Joseph Smith readily wrote such a text. They have received their ordinances in the temple but seldom attend since the day of their endowment or sealing and miss the marvelous meaning in the symbolic details of those sacred rites. They get caught up in the humanity of the work and all the while miss its miraculous components that evidence God's hand in its day-to-day operations. Oh, yes, God shows His signs and wonders. But like the "new star" at Christ's birth, many simply miss them.

NOTES

1. Robert L. Millet, "The Birth and Childhood of the Messiah," in Kent P. Jackson and Robert L. Millet, editors, *Studies in Scripture Volume Five: The Gospels* (Salt Lake City: Deseret Book, 1986), 149.

2. Joseph Fielding McConkie wisely noted: "Whereas *some* among the faithful in the Old World were aware of a new star announcing the night of his birth, in the New World 'at the going down of the sun there was no darkness,' and throughout all the land *all* saw the star announcing his birth. (See 3 Nephi 1:14–17.)" [Joseph Fielding McConkie, *Witnesses of the Birth of Christ* (Salt Lake City: Bookcraft, 1998), 4; emphasis added].

3. See, for example, Nibley (2004), 3:291; Raymond E. Brown, *The Birth of the Messiah*, updated edition (New York: Doubleday, 1993), 170–73; R. T. France, *Tyndale New Testament Commentaries: Matthew* (Grand Rapids, MI: Eerdmans, 1997), 82.

4. "The Protevangelium of James," verse 21, in Roberts and Donaldson (1994), 8:366; emphasis added. This ancient document is attributed to James, Jesus's half-brother (the son of Mary and Joseph).

5. See McConkie (1998), 97.

6. See "The Gospel of Pseudo-Matthew," chapter 16, in Roberts and Donaldson (1994), 8:376.

7. Joseph Fielding McConkie wrote: "Apparently [the Wise Men] alone could see and follow the light that led from Jerusalem to the house in Bethlehem in which the Christ child was to be found. Were this not the case, Herod and those who did his bidding would have had no need of them" [McConkie (1998), 101].

8. Ogden and Skinner (2011), 2:105.

9. As noted above, it is puzzling that most simply didn't see or recognize this star.

The Book of Mormon also speaks of it but uses language that, again, could have very dualistic intentions. It notes that at the Lord's birth there were "great lights in heaven" (Helaman 14:3)—notice this is "lights" in the plural. The book of Helaman also states that "there shall a new star arise, such an one as ye never have beheld; and this also shall be a sign unto you" (Helaman 14:5). Such a statement does not preclude John or Abraham's use of the term *star* as a symbol for an angel, or the Son of God. Certainly Christ was "new" and "as one" they had "never beheld." The statement in 3 Nephi 1:21 that "a new star did appear, according to the word" also leaves open the possibility of a dualistic interpretation.

10. After all, Mary and Joseph both received angels regarding the matter—and the shepherds abiding in the fields were visited by angels that instructed them as to how to find the baby Jesus. It seems strange that these Wise Men would be treated so differently. However, as to why the text would call an angel a "star" only when speaking of the Wise Men is unclear.

11. "The First Gospel of the Infancy of Jesus Christ," 3:3, in *The Lost Books of the Bible* (New York: Bell Publishing, 1979), 40. See also "The Arabic Gospel of the Infancy of the Saviour," verse 7, in Roberts and Donaldson (1994), 8:406, which reads basically the same: "There appeared to them an angel in the form of that star which had before guided them on their journey; and they went away, following the guidance of its light, until they arrived in their own country."

12. Neal A. Maxwell, *That My Family Should Partake* (Salt Lake City: Deseret Book, 1974), 86. I express appreciation to Andy Skelton for bringing this source to my attention.

PHYSICAL UPHEAVALS
at the DEATH *of* JESUS

HELAMAN 14:20–28
3 NEPHI 8:5–25

THE MIRACLE

Samuel the Lamanite prophesied to the people of Zarahemla of many signs concerning the birth and death of Christ. Among other things, he indicated that at the death of Jesus the sun, moon, and stars would be darkened—refusing to give their light for a period of three days. According to Samuel, Jesus's death would bring darkness. In the end we see that His Resurrection would bring back the light.

The Lamanite prophet also predicted that Christ's passing would be accompanied by thundering, lightening, and the violent shaking of the earth. He testified of tempests that would also come, and resurrected beings that would be seen after Jesus had risen. "Many shall see greater things than these," he promised, "to the intent that they might believe" (Helaman 14:28).

Mormon recorded the fulfilment of Samuel's prophecies, attesting to the inspiration of this great seer who accurately predicted the exact details of what would take place.

BACKGROUND

Some commentators on the Book of Mormon are drawn to the assumption that God brought to pass all of the described upheaval through natural means, such as a divinely sent earthquake or volcanic eruption.[1] Such would certainly explain Mormon's claim that you "could feel the vapor of darkness" and you could not light a fire after the trembling (3 Nephi 8:20–22).[2] A seemingly natural cause to the upheaval would also explain how some, even after the fulfillment of Samuel's prophecy, could comfortably deny that God was the source of the miraculous occurrence. One commentator wrote: "Believers will have their belief confirmed. But verse 29 [of Helaman 14] suggests that there will still be unbelievers. How can they still refuse to believe? I hypothesize that, because the events are associated with natural phenomena, unbelievers will ascribe those signs to natural causes."[3]

The book of Helaman indicates that Samuel the Lamanite obtained that which he preached (regarding the signs of Christ's birth) from an angel (Helaman 14:9). Ogden and Skinner conjectured that this divine messenger may have been Gabriel (Noah), as he—by divine appointment—was the angel whom God sent to those upon the Eastern Hemisphere to announce Jesus's birth.[4]

Helaman 14 contains a remarkably specific set of prophecies regarding the death of Christ, each having clear fulfillment (as recorded in the book of 3 Nephi).[5]

The prophecy in Helaman 14:20 is fulfilled in 3 Nephi 8:19–23
The prophecy in Helaman 14:21 is fulfilled in 3 Nephi 8:6–7
The prophecy in Helaman 14:22 is fulfilled in 3 Nephi 8:12, 17–18
The prophecy in Helaman 14:23 is fulfilled in 3 Nephi 8:5–6
The prophecy in Helaman 14:24 is fulfilled in 3 Nephi 8:8–11, 13
The prophecy in Helaman 14:25 is fulfilled in 3 Nephi 23:9–14

SYMBOLIC ELEMENTS

Surveying the scripturally attested events that occurred at the death and Resurrection of the Lord, McConkie, Millet, and Top surmised: "These scenes are of value to us, not only because they detail the events on the American continent some two millennia ago but also because they typify what lies ahead. A study of 3 and 4 Nephi is of inestimable worth in our coming to understand how to prepare for the second coming of the Son of Man, and also what life will be like during the Millennium."[6] Elsewhere we read:

Typologically, the coming of the Messiah at the end of times will be preceded by great destructions, including burnings. . . . Mormon understands that the Atoning Messiah [of the first century] and the

Triumphant Messiah [of the Second Coming] are the same person; given Mormon's cyclical view of history, it is clear why he sees the two comings as typologically parallel. . . . The loss of life [during the upheaval accompanying Christ's death] was unavoidable. . . . Mormon would have seen these deaths typologically, paralleling the destruction of the wicked at the Triumphant Messiah's return. . . . Thus, the wicked (and Mormon has taken pains to establish their presence, even their dominance) must be destroyed at this first coming.[7]

The symbolism of this miracle reminds us that those who are privileged to be living upon the earth at the time of Christ's return—and those who, though physically dead, lived saintly lives during mortality—will experience the almost identical set of circumstances described in Helaman 14 and 3 Nephi 8, as will the wicked. These upheavals are but types and shadows of that which is to come. Though, the righteous in the last days have the additional promise that peace will reign supreme after Christ's return—a blessing the Nephites did not enjoy.

The darkness accompanying Jesus's death and the repeal of that extended night at His Resurrection has symbolic merit also. One commentary notes: "The coming of light each morning ought be a reminder to all of the manner in which our Redeemer brought to an end that long night of darkness we associate with death and ought also be a reminder of the promise granted us, through him, of a newness of life."[8]

Evidence of Mormon's literary gifts is found in how he describes the destruction in a rather symbolic way: "Verses 9 and 10 [of 3 Nephi 8] describe literal events that are juxtaposed for their rhetorical effect in showing extremes of destruction. One city sinks into the sea (v.9) while land is 'carried up' over the second (v.10). Both the elements (water/earth) and the motion (sinking/rising) form an antithetical parallel. This same set with its reverse parallel imagery is found in 3 Nephi 9:4–5."[9] Mormon is seeking to convey the history accurately while using his literary gifts to highlight the power of the juxtaposed phenomenon.

As we have suggested earlier in this text, the number three traditionally represents that which is divine in origin or purpose. One commentator pointed out: "Despite the apparent precision of 'three hours' and 'three days,' it would have been difficult if not impossible to determine either duration. There were no clocks for the hours, and the darkness would have made it impossible to differentiate day from night. I therefore interpret 'three' as symbolic."[10] Indeed, regardless of the duration of the darkness, the message seems clear: these signs were of divine origin. God was behind the miracle, and the Nephites would have perceived this.

APPLICATION AND ALLEGORIZATION

"It seems only natural," one commentary states, "that the earth should be in such tumult and turmoil after the death of Christ because it too is a living entity and was mourning the suffering of its Creator (Moses 7:39–40, 48)."[11] Similarly, according to the Gospel of Peter, the earthquake at Christ's death did not take place at the instant Jesus died. Rather, according to this early Christian text, it took place upon the removal of His body from the cross. We read: "[Having pulled down His cross] they drew out the nails from the hands of the Lord and placed him on the earth; and all the earth was shaken, and a great fear came about" (Gospel of Peter 6:21). According to one scholar, this symbolically testifies that Christ's body—although dead—retained its power.[12] This quaking of the earth when it came into contact with the body of the slain Lord is a testament to the fact that His death was not a defeat but instead an empowerment. *Now* the Atonement would have efficacy. *Now* Satan's work would be capable of being destroyed!

Mormon informs us that the death of Christ brought a distinct change to *everything*. The entire face of the land was altered (3 Nephi 8:5–23). One might draw an analogy with this historic fact and the gospel verity that Christ's death changed everything *for us*. For all of the faith of the ancients, until Jesus exited the holy sepulcher, salvation stood in a state of suspension. All faith and sacrifice was, to that point, merely hope without confirmation. However, when the Savior of all—"worlds without end" (Moses 1:33–35)—bled in Gethsemane, died on Golgotha's cruel cross, and stepped forth from His garden grave, "everything changed." Salvation was secured for all who found faith in the Son of God and the Father's holy plan. Nothing was as it had been—and praise be to God for that divine reality! Truly, Christ changes *everything*! At least for those who believe.

As suggested above, the "three hours" and "three days" highlighted in this miracle testify that God was in the details of this event. Tragic as it seemed, the destruction at Christ's crucifixion also served as a herald of truth: salvation had come to the world. One might rightly draw a parallel between the good news inherent in the upheavals the Nephites experienced and our own personal trials. Tragic as they often seem, they too can be the sign of better and brighter days. Among the Nephites the trial removed wickedness from the midst the people. In our own lives, tests and trials often similarly serve to help you and me overcome our sinful and weak selves. Trials—even devastating ones— are not always signs of the bad, but sometimes testify to the good. Such was the case for the Nephites; and such can be the case in our own lives.

Mormon records that "great were the mournings of the people, because of the darkness . . . which had come upon them" (3 Nephi 8:23). One commentary on the Book of Mormon explained: "Remorse, like a gnawing pain, excited by a sense of guilt, mingled with a repentant regret, took possession of each sufferer's conscience."[13] If, as a nation and as a people, we do not repent, the Lord will bring upon us that which He sent to humble the Nephites who, through their wickedness, brought down the wrath of God. Elder Orson Pratt explained:

> For the Lord has said in this book, (the Book of Mormon) . . . that if they will not repent He will throw down all their strongholds and cut off the cities of the land, and will execute vengeance and fury on the nation, even as upon the heathen, such as they have not heard. That He will send a desolating scourge on the land; that He will leave their cities desolate, without inhabitants. For instance the great, powerful and populous city of New York, that may be considered one of the greatest cities of the world, will in a few years become a mass of ruins. The people will wonder while gazing on the ruins that cost hundreds of millions to build, what has become of inhabitants. Their houses will be there, but they will be left desolate.[14]

What the Lord has in store, no one truly knows. But if the destruction in Zarahemla (at the time of Christ's death) is a type for what is to come—as commentators almost universally believe that it is—then you and I should quickly learn the lesson of the Nephites so that we do not have to take a "refresher course" in divine abasement. If we wish to avoid the "great groanings" the Nephites endured, we must avoid the behaviors in which they engaged. Sin always brings sorrow. Lives of obedience and faith are the only way to lay hold upon eternal joy.

NOTES

1. See, for example, Gardner (2007), 5:301–02, who argues that this darkness and upheaval was caused by "an explosive eruption of a volcano arising in a subduction zone. . . . At least three geologically attested volcanic events date to this basic period." See also Nibley, *Since Cumorah* (1988), 231–38; Nibley (2004), 3:331–34; Daniel C. Peterson, cited in Bassett (2007–2008), 3:32.

2. Beyond the dust and volcanic fall out [see Nibley (1988), 235–36.], one commentator noted: "The inability to light the wood in the Book of Mormon indicates that there was a concentration of volcanic gases (carbon dioxide and sulfur dioxide) that prevented ignition. This may be confirmed by 3 Nephi 10:13, which suggests that some died from suffocation" [Gardner (2007), 5:309].

3. Gardner (2007), 5:200.

4. See Ogden and Skinner (2011), 2:106.

5. See Ludlow, Pinegar, Allen, Otten, and Caldwell (2007), 402.

6. McConkie, Millet, and Top (1992), 36. President Ezra Taft Benson suggested that "in the Book of Mormon we find a pattern for preparing for the Second Coming" [Ezra Taft Benson, *A Witness and a Warning: A Modern-Day Prophet Testifies of the Book of Mormon* (Salt Lake City: Deseret Book, 1988), 20; see 20–21].

7. Gardner (2007), 5:301, 307. See also Nyman (2003–2004), 5:100.

8. McConkie, Millet, and Top (1992), 39. Highlighting the symbolic place of light, one of my reviewers wrote: "Joseph Smith was killed at the summer solstice—light leaving the world. Joseph was born at the winter solstice—light entering the world" [Todd Parker, review of *Miracles of the Book of Mormon*].

9. Gardner (2007), 5:305.

10. Gardner (2007), 5:308.

11. Ogden and Skinner (2011), 2:124.

12. Raymond E. Brown, *The Death of the Messiah*, two volumes (New York: Doubleday, 1994), 2:1137.

13. Reynolds and Sjodahl (1955–1961), 7:99.

14. Orson Pratt, in *Journal of Discourses*, 12:344.

SAMUEL *the* LAMANITE COULD NOT *be* HARMED, *nor* COULD HE *be* CAPTURED *by the* NEPHITES

HELAMAN 16:1–8

THE MIRACLE

Samuel the Lamanite had been directed by the Lord and an angel to call the people of the city of Zarahemla to repentance. As he stood upon the wall of the city, teaching and testifying, some believed his witness, repented of their sinful ways, and sought out baptism at the hands of Nephi. Others, however, were angered by his instructions and sought to take his life by stoning him or by shooting him with arrows.

Mormon informs us that because Samuel had the Spirit of the Lord with him, "they could not hit him with their stones neither with their arrows" (Helaman 16:2). This miracle caused some who had initially been angered by his words to soften their hearts and seek forgiveness through faith, repentance, and the ordinance of baptism. However, a percentage of the Nephites—seeing that they could not slay him with their weapons—sought to arrest him, insisting that he was possessed of a devil and that the power of the evil one was the means by which he had successfully avoided their stones and arrows.

As they moved to arrest Samuel, he jumped from the wall and fled out of the land of Zarahemla. He continued his ministry among his own people, but was never heard from again in the land of Zarahemla.

BACKGROUND

The fact that people in the crowd apparently had ready access to bows and arrows is a telltale sign of their potentially premeditated plot against Samuel. One commentary rightly notes: "Arrows were for either hunting or battle. They were not an item one would routinely carry around a city. Therefore, we can deduce a deliberate attempt at murder, possibly planned from the first moment Samuel made his reappearance. The archers had to leave the crowd, retrieve their weapons, and return. Samuel probably delivered the bulk of his message while they were gone."[1] This was no act of spontaneity. Either they brought weapons when they heard he was speaking or as soon as they saw him they went and collected what they would need to inflict the blows of death.

The Lamanite prophet received divine protection. Culturally speaking, to the theologically corrupt Nephites of Samuel's day, the "invincibility to arrows would . . . suggest [to those who viewed the miracle] that Samuel was at least touched by an other-worldly spirit (see v.6) and was possibly a demi-god himself. . . . Even unbelievers recognized something supernatural about Samuel but attributed it to 'a devil.'"[2]

SYMBOLIC ELEMENTS

Stoning was the most common means of execution in the Bible. Symbolically speaking, it represented a "communal sentence" typically carried out by "the common people." The represented meaning of stoning was that the victim had been "excommunicated" from the community "in the most dire sense."[3] The Nephite choice to stone Samuel is literally that—an excommunication or banishment from their community. What is curious is that stoning was traditionally used as a punishment for theological crimes—crimes against orthodoxy (blasphemy, idolatry, false prophecy, seducing others to forsake Jehovah). Yet, at this point in their history, the Nephites of Zarahemla were the ones who were heterodox, not Samuel.

The arrows in this episode remind us of "the fiery darts of the wicked" (Ephesians 6:16) about which the Apostle Paul warned us. One commentary on the symbolic nature of arrows stated: "The devil and his minions and human accomplices . . . employ the arrow. The devil's fiery darts (Eph 6:16) find their inspiration in the flaming arrows of Psalm 7:13. . . . In Psalm 91:5 [the] arrow parallels terror, pestilence and plague, [each of which are] read by some as demonic afflictions."[4] Whenever we seek to do good and holy things, we should expect "the fiery darts of the wicked" one to be hurled at us with such force. Satan will not stand by and watch us be and do good. He will hound and plague from the time we enter until the time we leave this mortal life. If we recognize his arrows for what they are, we, like Samuel, can avoid them. On the other hand, if we are not attentive to that which he does, we will surely receive a mortal wound. This is not a game. We are quite literally at war with the adversary. Our eternal lives hang in the balance.

Walls were largely used in ancient times as a means of protection, as a way to keep the enemy out. Thus they often symbolized invulnerability or the enemy's inability to conquer.[5] Samuel's stance upon the wall of the Nephite city, therefore, is suggestive of his power to surmount. Symbolically, he has overcome their false traditions and beliefs (as is evidenced by the converts he gained). The wall under his foot implies that the truths he preached would ultimately place all things in subjection. The God of Samuel would reign, and the false god of the Nephites of Zarahemla would be crushed.

APPLICATION AND ALLEGORIZATION

The most obvious application of this story is the truth that, like Samuel, if we are on the Lord's errand we can expect His protection. An extreme example of this is found in the life of President George Albert Smith. As a young man he was called on a mission. He and five other missionaries spent the night in the home of a member in Tennessee. In the middle of the night, they were each awakened by violent pounding on the door and the shouting of profanity. A mob had gathered, and they were demanding that the missionaries come out of the house. One of the missionaries, who had jumped up and was quickly dressing, noticed that Elder Smith was just lying in bed. He inquired of the future prophet, Aren't you "going to get up and dress?" To which Elder Smith replied, "No. I'm going to stay in bed. I am sure the Lord will take care of us." Momentarily the room was filled with splintering wood and flying bullets. The hailstorm of ammunition continued for some time, but the missionaries were protected, and ultimately the mob disbanded. Of that occasion, President Smith stated:

"I was very calm as I lay there, experiencing one of the most horrible events of my life, but I was sure that as long as I was preaching the word of God and following his teachings that the Lord would protect me, and he did."[6] Now, we ought not to be naïve. Though most come home safely, the tragic reality is, not every missionary does. However, again, the Lord's promise is divine protection. That may mean that your enemies can't physically harm you—as was the case with Samuel or George Albert Smith. Or it may mean that you are spiritually protected; remember, Jesus said not to fear those who could kill your body but rather those who were able to kill your soul (Matthew 10:28). Samuel was protected, we are told, because "the Spirit of the Lord was with him" (Helaman 16:2). The most important element in experiencing the blessing Samuel did—whether we are missionaries or lay members of the Church—is keeping the Spirit with us. If you have the Spirit of the Lord with you, God's will is certain to be done. If you keep the Holy Ghost operative in your life, even if you are physically taken, you will be spiritually saved. God does protect His servants, just as He protected Samuel, so long as they put on "the whole armor of God" (Ephesians 6:11–18).

Those who rejected Samuel's words were infuriated by what he had spoken. And yet the Spirit never provokes us to anger. Never! Whether one agrees with the words of another or not, one must remember: the Spirit of the Lord tempers us; the spirit of the adversary does the exact opposite. If we are feeling angry, most likely it is not God's Spirit that is inspiring us. "As the Spirit of the Lord brings peace and joy, so the spirit of the adversary is associated with anger and bitterness. . . . Wickedness acknowledges the weakness of its position by seeking the blood of those it makes its adversaries."[7] I recall an occasion where I was visiting with a man who had begun to lose his faith in the Church. Whenever he spoke about it, he became elevated and irate. I remember pointing out to him that the Spirit of the Lord does not make one angry and his rage over the small things he saw as errors within the Church was actually a testament to which spirit was driving him. The Apostle Paul rhetorically asked, "Be ye angry, and sin not[?]" (Ephesians 4:26). Those who were stirred up to anger by Samuel's testimony were harkening to the voice of the evil one. And what did Satan inspire them to do? Murder the prophet! When you and I find ourselves angry about *anything*, we should remember this miracle and recognize the adversary is gaining ground in our hearts and minds. The Lord Himself has declared that "the devil, who is the father of contention, . . . stirreth up the hearts of men to contend with anger, one with another" (3 Nephi 11:29). Our emotions are good litmus tests as to which spirit we have chosen to obey (Alma 3:26).

It is noteworthy that the Nephites who were converted by Samuel's teachings and testimony were sent to Nephi to be baptized, not to Samuel. One commentary suggested the following application of this:

> Nephi, the son of Helaman, was a man of great spiritual power. Signs, wonders, miracles, and prophecy were all common to his ministry. Nephi was presumably the local priesthood leader, and it would appear that those touched by the power of Samuel's message were sent to Nephi to receive the ordinances of salvation. This would be similar to a situation in which a nonmember attended a stake conference in which a visiting General Authority was present. If the investigator were to be moved by the message of the authority, he or she would be encouraged to be further taught by the missionaries and then to receive baptism at the hands of local legal administrators.[8]

Too often in the Church individuals go to the General Authorities for a priesthood blessing or for an answer to some long-held doctrinal question. However, as this miracle can suggest, we should go to our local leaders for such things—so that the presiding prophets can do their work.

Just as stones and arrows were shot and hurled at Samuel, but to no effect, the enemies of the Church will hurl their accusations and jeers—even going so far as to claim that we have a devil—as they said of Samuel. But, like the Lamanite prophet, these things will be of no effect. "The caravan moves on"—with or without them.[9] Helaman 16:22 informs us, "Satan did . . . go about spreading rumors and contentions upon all the face of the land, that he might harden the hearts of the people against that which was good and against that which should come." As the Saints are faithful, the fruits of the gospel will be manifest and the Spirit of the Lord will penetrate the hearts of all who are sincere. Prophets have a difficult job. Elder Richard L. Evans of the Twelve noted that

> a prophet is seldom popular, and the cost of being a prophet is always

great, for he may be called upon to say those things which are not pleasing, . . . and he may find himself fighting against a tide of mass misconception, and, as history records, be stoned, crucified, banished, ridiculed, shunned, or rejected. For the truth is not pleasing unto all men, and time has proved that majorities are not always right. . . .

It is not important that a prophet should say those things with which you and I are in full accord. But it is important that you and I should bring ourselves into full accord with those things which a prophet speaks by virtue of his office and calling.[10]

The enemies of the Church will ever hurl their stones and arrows at the prophets and apostles because of their conservatively moral and doctrinally unique stances. Such has ever been the case, and ever will be! It is not the calling of the prophet—or the Church—to be popular with the world.[11] It is their calling, and ours, to be popular with the Lord; and we can only accomplish that by standing up for and living His will and way. Those within the Church must themselves be cautious about seeking popular prophets. President Spencer W. Kimball wisely noted: "Many are prone to garnish the sepulchers of yesterday's prophets and mentally stone the living ones."[12] Even within the Church today, there are those who sing "We Thank Thee, O God, for a Prophet" and yet chafe whenever he offers a position that is contrary to their own worldview. Do we believe that they are inspired beyond that of normal men, or do we not? And if we do, we must never be found "stoning the prophets" for standing up on the wall and declaring to us God's words.

This miracle also bears witness that when we testify of truth, the sincere will feel the power of our words and repent—as many of the Nephites did (verses 1, 4–3). Sadly, this story also reminds us that those with hardened hearts will stand their ground, even in the midst of overwhelming spiritual evidence, just as the Nephites did with Samuel. God has endowed us with agency, and that agency allows us to make holy, life-changing choices. But it also authorizes us to make terrible, sinful, and spiritually destructive choices. God has given us so much power in our divinely decreed right to choose. May we ever use it wisely.

NOTES

1. Gardner (2001), 5:211–12.

2. Gardner (2001), 5:212, 213. Gardner's point is simply this: the religiously corrupt Nephites of Samuel's day would likely not have attributed this miracle to the God of Israel but rather to some supernatural power—"that great Spirit"—that appeared to be "touching" or "protecting" Samuel, preventing *them* from killing *him*.

3. See Ryken, Wilhoit, and Longman (1998), 816.

4. See Ryken, Wilhoit, and Longman (1998), 48. See also Wilson (1999), 20.

5. See Ryken, Wilhoit, and Longman (1998), 923–25. See also Todeschi (1995), 280.

6. George Albert Smith, *The Teachings of George Albert Smith*, Robert and Susan McIntosh, compilers (Salt Lake City: Bookcraft, 1998), 193–94.

7. McConkie and Millet (1987–1991), 3:422.

8. McConkie and Millet (1987–1991), 3:422.

9. See Bruce R. McConkie, "The Caravan Moves On," *Ensign*, November, 1984, 82–85.

10. Richard L. Evans, cited in Ogden and Skinner (2011), 2:108.

11. President Ezra Taft Benson taught: "The prophet will not necessarily be popular with the world or the worldly. As a prophet reveals the truth, it divides the people. The honest in heart heed his words, but the unrighteous either ignore the prophet or fight him. When the prophet points out the sins of the world, the worldly, rather than repent of their sins, either want to close the mouth of the prophet or else act as if they prophet didn't exist. Popularity is never a test of truth. Many a prophet has been killed or cast out. As we come closer to the Lord's second coming, you can expect that as the people of the world become more wicked, the prophet will be less popular with them" [Benson (1998), 133].

12. Spencer W. Kimball, cited in Bassett (2007–2008), 3:21.

LAMANITES' SKIN *Becomes* EXCEEDINGLY FAIR

3 NEPHI 2:14–16

THE MIRACLE

For all of their mutual loathing, as the influence of the Gadianton robbers increased, the Nephites and Lamanites determined that they would have to unite if they had any hope of defeating their shared enemy.

Mormon records that as these two former foes became friends, the Lamanites had "their curse . . . taken from them, and their skin became white like unto the Nephites; and their young men and their daughters became exceedingly fair" (3 Nephi 2:15).

BACKGROUND

A percentage of those who read the Book of Mormon interpret the passages having to do with the Lamanite "dark skin" as statements about race. In the minds of some, the Lamanites vacillated between Caucasian and brown skin, contingent upon the generation. McConkie and Millet rightly point out that the phrase "a white and a delightsome people" (in earlier printings of the Book of Mormon) was changed by the Prophet Joseph Smith (in 1840) to read "a pure" rather than "a white" people (2 Nephi 30:6).[1] The implications of that change seem significant, particularly in light of the following comments offered by Professor Hugh Nibley:

> It starts out by saying, "I, Nephi." You notice it is an autobiography, "I,

Nephi." Now, at this time the only style of writing was autobiographical. Everybody wrote autobiographies, and there's a great autobiographical literature in Egyptian. There are some famous autobiographies, and we will refer to some because they are so very close to the Book of Mormon. They take place in Palestine, even at this time. Well, I just picked up one from de Buck's *Reading Book* (p. 73–74). It's called *The Autobiography of Kai*. He lived a short time before Nephi. He was an important man, and he gave his titles. He started out by saying, "I, Kai was the son of a man who was *nehet* and *sᶜh* [who was worthy and wise]." And Nephi started out saying, "I, Nephi, having been born of goodly parents." Then Kai goes on to talk about himself here. Incidentally, I notice he referred to himself down here as *hd-hr* (white of countenance), *nfr bi·t* (excellent of character), *ph3 h·t* (clean of body and in moral habits). And he shunned everything that was *snk·wt*. The word is very interesting. It means "black of countenance," and it also means "greed or anything that is evil." Notice, in the Book of Mormon, that peculiar thing: "a white and delightsome people" and "a dark and loathsome people." It doesn't refer to skin color at all, but there's a lot about race in the Book of Mormon. That comes in here already; we can see that. But here, you notice he used those peculiar terms. He was *hd-her*. He has a picture of a white face (white of countenance). And he was clean of body, and he eschewed *snk·wt* (what is greedy or what is dark of countenance).[2]

Elsewhere Nibley wrote:

This amazing *coincidentia oppositorum* is the clash of black and white. With the Arabs, to be white of countenance is to be blessed and to be black of countenance is to be cursed; there are parallel expressions in Hebrew and Egyptian. And what of Lehi's people? It is most significant that the curse against the Lamanites is the very same as that commonly held in the East to blight the sons of Ishmael, who appear to the light-skinned people of the towns as "a dark and loathsome, and a filthy people, full of idleness and all manner of abominations, . . . an idle people, full of mischief and subtlety," etc. (1 Nephi 12:23; 2 Nephi 5:24). It is noteworthy that all the descendants of the Book of Mormon Ishmael fall under the curse (Alma 3:7), as if their Bedouin ancestry predisposed them to it. The Book of Mormon always mentions the curse of the dark skin in connection with and as part of a larger picture: "*After* they had dwindled in unbelief they *became* a dark, and loathsome, and a filthy people," etc. "Because of the cursing which was upon them they did become an idle people . . . and did

seek in the wilderness for beasts of prey" (2 Nephi 5:24). The statement that "*God* did cause a skin of blackness to come upon them" (2
Nephi 5:21) describes the result, not the method, which is described
elsewhere. Thus we are told (Alma 3:13, 14, 18) that while the fallen
people "set the mark upon *themselves*," it was none the less God who
was marking them: "I will set a mark upon them," etc. So natural and
human was the process that it suggested nothing miraculous to the
ordinary observer, and "the Amlicites knew not that they were fulfilling the words of God when they began to mark *themselves*; . . . it was
expedient that the curse should fall upon them" (Alma 3:18). Here God
places his mark on people as a curse, yet it is an artificial mark which
they actually place upon themselves. The mark was not a racial thing
but was acquired by "whosoever suffered himself to be led away by the
Lamanites" (Alma 3:10); Alma moreover defines a Nephite as anyone
observing "the tradition of their fathers" (Alma 3:11). Which makes the
difference between Nephite and Lamanite a cultural, not a racial, one.
Does this also apply to the dark skin? Note that the dark skin is never
mentioned alone but always as attending a generally depraved way of
life, which also is described as the direct result of the curse. When the
Lamanites become "white" again, it is by living among the Nephites
as Nephites, i.e., adopting the Nephite way of life (3 Nephi 2:15–16).
The cultural picture may not be the whole story of the dark skin of the
Lamanites, but it is an important part of that story and is given great
emphasis by the Book of Mormon itself. There is nowhere any mention of red skin, incidentally, but only of black (or dark) and white, the
terms being used as the Arabs use them.[3]

Finally, Nibley made this additional related point:

The dark skin is mentioned as the mark of a general way of life; it is a
Gypsy or Bedouin type of darkness, "black" and 'white" being used in
their Oriental sense (as in Egyptian), black and loathsome being contrasted to white and delightsome (2 Nephi 5:21–22). We are told that
when "their scales of darkness shall begin to fall from their eyes" they
shall become "a white and delightsome people" (2 Nephi 30:6; "a pure
and delightsome people," 1979 edition), and at the same time the Jews
"shall also become a delightsome people" (2 Nephi 30:7). Darkness
and filthiness go together as part of a way of life (Jacob 3:5, 9); we
never hear of the Lamanites becoming whiter, no matter how righteous they were, except when they adopted the Nephite way of life (3
Nephi 2:14–15), while the Lamanites could, by becoming more savage
in their ways than their brother Lamanites, actually become darker,

"a dark, filthy, and a loathsome people, beyond the description of that which ever hath been . . . among the Lamanites" (Mormon 5:15). The dark skin is but one of the marks that God places upon the Lamanites, and these marks go together; people who joined the Lamanites were marked like them (Alma 3:10); they were naked and their skins were dark (Alma 3:5–6); when "they set the mark upon themselves; . . . the Amlicites knew not that they were fulfilling the words of God," when he said, "I will set a mark on them. . . . I will set a mark upon him that mingleth his seed with thy brethren. . . . I will set a mark upon him that fighteth against thee [Nephi] and thy seed" (Alma 3:13–18). "Even so," says Alma "doth every man that is cursed bring upon himself his own condemnation" (Alma 3:19). By their own deliberate act they both marked their foreheads and turned their bodies dark. Though ever alert to miraculous manifestations, the authors of the Book of Mormon never refer to the transformation of Lamanites into "white and delight-some" Nephites or Nephites into "dark and loathsome" Lamanites as in any way miraculous or marvelous. When they became savage "because of their cursing" (2 Nephi 5:24), their skins became dark and they also became "loathsome" to the Nephites (2 Nephi 5:21–22). But there is nothing loathsome about dark skin, which most people consider very attractive: the darkness, like the loathsomeness, was part of the general picture (Jacob 3:9); Mormon prays "that they may once again be a delightsome people" (Words of Mormon 1:8; Mormon 5:17), but then the Jews are also to become "a delightsome people" (2 Nephi 30:7)—are they black?[4]

In Nibley's view, this miraculous removal of the Lamanite "dark-ness" is not about a change in race or skin color but is instead about a change in countenance as a result of personal righteousness. Like Nibley, Brant Gardner argued, "Their transformation into 'a pure and delightsome people' is not based on the alteration of a physical trait, but a spiritual one. This change depends on receiving the knowledge of Jesus Christ."[5] President Joseph Fielding Smith indicated that the "curse" was the withdrawal of the Spirit of the Lord from them when they were disobedient to the commandments.[6] Without question, there are numerous passages in the Book of Mormon that speak of "dark skin" as a result of the absence of spirituality, chief among them 2 Nephi 30:6 and Alma 19:6; 26:3.

SYMBOLIC ELEMENTS

It is impossible to fully grasp the symbolic meaning of light without seeing it in juxtaposition to darkness. Light is the "great antithesis and conqueror of darkness."[7] In this miracle "light" or "white" skin symbolizes purity, righteousness, faithfulness, and personal holiness. "Dark" or "black" skin, on the other hand, is employed by the Book of Mormon authors as a token of sin, disbelief, evil, and rebellion. As has been suggested above, these are not statements about the characteristics of race. Rather, they are symbolic depictions of how one's countenance takes on what one loves—light or darkness.

APPLICATION AND ALLEGORIZATION

This miracle reminds us of the eternal verity that when you and I embrace the gospel, reject sin, and align our lives with righteousness and light, our countenances change. The Spirit of the Lord radiates from us, and we too become "exceedingly fair" or "white" (see 3 Nephi 19:30; 4 Nephi 1:10; Mormon 5:15–18; Mormon 9:6).[8] We previously cited the Prophet Joseph's declaration about the influence of the Holy Ghost on one's countenance:

> This first Comforter or Holy Ghost . . . is more powerful in expanding the mind, enlightening the understanding, and storing the intellect with present knowledge, of a man who is of the literal seed of Abraham, than one that is a Gentile, though it may not have half as much visible effect upon the body; for as the Holy Ghost falls upon one of the literal seed of Abraham, it is calm and serene; and his whole soul and body are only exercised by the pure spirit of intelligence; while the effect of the Holy Ghost upon a Gentile, is to purge out the old blood, and make him actually of the seed of Abraham. That man that has none of the blood of Abraham (naturally) must have a new creation by the Holy Ghost. In such a case, there may be more of a powerful effect upon the body, and visible to the eye, than upon an Israelite, while the Israelite at first might be far before the Gentile in pure intelligence.[9]

President Ezra Taft Benson similarly taught: "There is an inner light manifested in the countenances of those who have sought and found truth, who have set standards and principles in their lives and have been enlightened by the light of the gospel—hence, the brightness and spiritual illumination of those who have learned of and accepted the gospel of Jesus Christ."[10] When we seek out truth and lives of personal holiness, it shows in our countenances. We radiate light. On the other hand, if our lives become steeped in sin—if we seek to hide our dark acts from those who are authorized to help and guide us—there will be a tangible darkness that comes into our lives and radiates from our person. As the Prophet Joseph declared: "It is in vain to try to hide a bad spirit from the eyes of them who are spiritual, for it will show itself in speaking and in writing, as well as in all our other conduct. It is also needless to make great pretensions when the heart is not right; the Lord will expose it to the view of His faithful Saints."[11]

NOTES

1. See McConkie and Millet (1987–1991), 1:355. See also Rodney Turner, "The Lamanite Mark," in Monte S. Nyman and Charles D. Tate Jr., editors, *The Book of Mormon: Second Nephi, the Doctrinal Structure* (Provo, UT: Religious Studies Center, BYU, 1989), 156n8; Gardner (2007), 2:427.
2. Nibley (2004), 1:11.
3. Nibley, *Lehi in the Desert* (1988), 73–74.
4. Nibley, *Since Cumorah* (1988), 216–17. See also Turner, in Nyman and Tate (1989), 133–57; Reynolds Sjodahl (1955–1961), 1:278.
5. Gardner (2007), 2:426. Elsewhere Gardner wrote: "The 'skin of blackness' was a social marker, differentiating Nephites and Lamanites so that they would not intermarry. . . . Black-becoming-white is a metaphor of political change, probably formally acknowledging that the groups may intermarry. It lifts the 'curse' in Nephi that ruled Lamanites out as legitimate sources of spouses. . . . This verse reinforces the interpretation that what was involved was not physiology but attractiveness based on availability for marriage" [Gardner (2007), 5:249].
6. See Smith (1993), 3:122.
7. Ryken, Wilhoit, and Longman (1998), 509.
8. See Nibley (2004), 1:228, 284, 306; Turner, in Nyman and Tate (1989), 133.
9. Smith, in Smith (1976), 149.
10. Benson (1998), 359.
11. Smith, *History of the Church*, 1:317.

NEPHI PERFORMS *Many* MIRACLES

3 NEPHI 7:18–20

THE MIRACLE

Nephi, one of the twelve disciples of Jesus chosen to preside over the work in the Western Hemisphere, was endowed with great spiritual gifts. Angels ministered to him, and his testimony was so powerful that it was hard for those who heard him to disbelieve his words. Among other gifts, he had the power to cast out unclean spirits and to raise the dead.

Many of the people who witnessed Nephi's miraculous powers were angered by them. The spirit of Satan stirred their wrath because of his holy works.

BACKGROUND

Nephi is described as having great force or power in his testimony and his words. He finds himself in good company with past prophets. Enoch, we are told, "spake the word of the Lord, and the earth trembled . . . and all nations feared greatly, so powerful was the word of Enoch, and so great was the power of the language which God had given him" (Moses 7:13). Of the sons of Mosiah, we read, "When they taught, they taught with power and authority from God" (Alma 17:2–3). As with Nephi, many other scriptural and modern prophets have qualified for such force of testimony. Of course, purity of soul and personal preparation are prerequisites. I have encountered a number of those who hold the apostolic office who also testify with an undeniable power and presence that evidences the Lord is with them.

In highlighting the power and position of Nephi in the Book of Mormon, Ogden and Skinner noted: "It appears that he served the same role as did Peter in the original Quorum of the Twelve Apostles—president of the quorum."[1]

One commentator on the Book of Mormon explained the anger manifest toward Nephi's power in this way: "Nephi went forth 'with power,' which, not surprisingly, brought him into conflict with the rulers of the various tribes 'because he had greater power than they.' Because of the combination of politics and religion, the tribal rulers were also its religious leaders. Nephi undermined their authority because he clearly had more religious power than they."[2] Nibley also commented on the anger of the "leaders" of the Nephite people:

> What was the mortal offense of Jesus? When the elders of the Jews, the high priests, and the Levites came together, they decided there was only one solution to the problem, and that was to put Jesus to death, get him out of the way. That was when he raised Lazarus. That was the thing that decided it. You go back and look there. They put up with everything, but when he raised Lazarus from the dead, that was too much. They decided that he would have to be put to death. The doctors came together then. And it's the same thing here. When the people saw it they "were angry with him because of his power."[3]

SYMBOLIC ELEMENTS

Nephi had been blessed by God with the power and gift to cast out evil spirits from those who had been possessed by them. The Prophet Joseph is said to have taught: "The devil has no power over us only as we permit him. The moment we revolt at anything which comes from God, the devil takes power."[4] The possessed are, therefore, potential symbols of the consequences of sin and rebelliousness. They well represent in a dramatic way the latent danger to all who choose to ignore God's counsels and commands.[5] The freeing of one possessed from his demonic captors can be seen as a symbol of the power Christ has to free each of us from *all* that binds us. Descriptions of demonic possession sometimes describe the devils leaving in rather dramatic and painful ways (Mark 1:21–28; Luke 4:31–37). The excruciating pain associated with freeing one from demonic possession is a symbolic testament to how difficult it can be to overcome the power of the devil once we have allowed it to gain footing in our lives.

In addition to casting out evil spirits, Nephi also had the power to raise the dead. The deceased in miracles, such as this, can signify those who are spiritually dead—those heading down a road that would make repentance difficult indeed. But, as with the story of Lazarus (see John 11), even once they are entombed in the grave, Christ can still raise the dead. Thus, even the worst of sinners can be redeemed through faith in Christ and sincere repentance. In this narrative we are told that Timothy was raised from the dead. Later this same brother of Nephi became an Apostle. Of course, we are all sinners (Romans 3:23). Yet, if we are healed from our sinful ways, God can find a place and use for each of us—as he did Nephi's brother.[6]

All prophets are types for the Lord (2 Nephi 11:4). Various elements of their ministries will always parallel Christ's—as that is the nature of their calling. Owing to this, Gardner points out:

> There is a powerful parallel in Nephi's preparation of the people for the Messiah's visit. In the New Testament, Jesus cast out devils and raised at least three people from the dead. In the New World at approximately the same time, Nephi functions as a Jesus-surrogate, performing the same types of miracles, including raising a dead person.
>
> The parallelism of these events suggests that they had a particular meaning that pointed to, and were fulfilled in, the resurrection of the Atoning Messiah. Although the post-resurrection appearance of the Messiah in both continents had some differences, the parallels are important. Mormon gives these preparatory parallels only passing notice, perhaps because he did not know about the similar events in the Old World or did not understand how Nephi functioned as a Jesus-surrogate just prior to the Messiah's visit to the New World.[7]

Gardner is not the only commentator to recognize that "Nephi's ministry had some similarities to Jesus' ministry in Jerusalem."[8] Not surprisingly, this is a common point of emphasis among commentators.

APPLICATION AND ALLEGORIZATION

One evident application of this miracle is that when we serve the Lord with faithfulness, we will be given power from on high. Indeed, the temple endowment promises us exactly that (D&C 38:32, 38; Luke 24:49). Faithfulness is key—not perfection, but faithfulness. Related to this, our miracle suggests that when we are faithful, and when we act in God's name, our enemies will sense that the Lord is with us (D&C 45:70), and we will be able to do things beyond our own natural strength. God will use us as an instrument in the accomplishment of His work, though potentially to the annoyance of the servants of Satan. Do you feel God's power in your life? More important, do those around you feel it? If not, why? Have the covenants you've made—at baptism and in the temple—become endowments of power in your life? If not, what must you do to make them such?

In this miracle those who observe Nephi's power are angered by it. We are told that it was not possible to "disbelieve his words" (3 Nephi 7:18), so powerful was his testimony and so miraculous his works. Some, nevertheless, chose anger as a means of dealing with what they had witnessed. One text suggests, "Those who had so given themselves up to the spirit of the adversary feasted upon anger and hatred and lost their appetite for the spirit of peace, joy, and love which accompany the gospel and the obedient spirit."[9] And so Satan seeks to inspire all of his followers. But those who fight against it will *never* thwart God's work. They will only seal their own fates. As the Psalmist has declared, "They that hate the righteous shall be desolate" (Psalm 34:21). As members of Christ's Church, we must never allow ourselves—as Laman and Lemuel did—to be angered by the righteous acts and words of others. If such a spirit enters our hearts and minds, we know what power is influencing us. God's Spirit does not stir us up to anger—and the concept of "righteous indignation" is a rare event largely reserved for God, but seldom given to His faithful followers.

Christ, and those whom He has authorized, have brought many a man back to mortal life after he has died; and in the resurrection Jesus will raise *all* from mortal death. However, the mortal experience is not about remaining upon this earth. Indeed, more powerful than being raised from physical death is the promise that Christ can raise us from spiritual death. Many will be brought forth from their graves to a resurrection of damnation (John 5:29; Mosiah 16:11). However, only those who have allowed Christ to raise them from spiritual death—only those from whose lives He has cast out Satan—will come forth to a resurrection of life and glory. Thus, just as Nephi raised Timothy from the dead here, and just as Jesus has raised many also, you and I must seek to be raised from our sins and spiritual sickness. We must seek a spiritual life now so that we can enjoy eternal life in the world to come.

NOTES

1. Ogden and Skinner (2011), 2:123.
2. Gardner (2007), 5:297.
3. Nibley (2004), 3:326.
4. See Ehat and Cook (1980), 60. See also Smith, in Smith (1976), 181.
5. This is not to say that disobedience always results in demonic possession, only that those possessed potentially symbolize the reality that rebellion against God opens us up to the influence of the adversary.
6. Of course, this is not to say that Timothy was a vile sinner prior to being raised from the dead. We know next to nothing about him. My only point here is to suggest that those raised from the dead remind us of how Christ can raise us from spiritual death—and if He does so, He will find a use for us in building His kingdom.
7. Gardner (2007), 5:298.
8. Nyman (2003–2004), 5:87.
9. McConkie, Millet, and Top (1992), 33.

THOSE WHO *Were* RECIPIENTS *of* NEPHI'S MIRACLES *Also* PERFORMED MIGHTY MIRACLES

3 NEPHI 7:22

THE MIRACLE

Nephi had performed many mighty miracles in the lives of the people. He had cast out evil spirits, entertained angels, and even raised the dead.

Mormon informs us that "as many as" had been the recipients of the miracles Nephi performed (via God's power and priesthood) "did show forth signs also and did do some miracles among the people" (3 Nephi 7:22).

BACKGROUND

Nephi raising Timothy is the only story of raising the dead recorded in the Book of Mormon (3 Nephi 7:19; 19:4). That is not to say that no one in the Western Hemisphere other than Timothy was ever raised, only that, unlike the Bible—which records a number of such experiences—the Book of Mormon has largely remained silent on them. One commentary suggests that "probably there were never such obvious manifestations of the Spirit as at this time." And then the text adds, "Yet the people did not believe." [1] Perhaps their lack of faith is why this type of miracle is not discussed in the Book of Mormon.

Miracles don't convert—and the raising of the dead in this narrative stands as proof of that fact!

SYMBOLIC ELEMENTS

The Lord declared, "And these signs shall follow them that believe; in my name shall they cast out devils; they shall speak with new tongues; they shall take up serpents; and if they drink any deadly thing, it shall not hurt them; they shall lay hands on the sick, and they shall recover" (Mark 16:17–18; Mormon 9:24; D&C 84:65–72. See also Ether 4:18). While the performance of miracles by those whom Nephi had healed are literal, they stand as a symbolic witness of the reality that these individuals truly were believers—that their conversions were real and deep. One with only casual faith will not experience miracles on this level. And while the Book of Mormon is somewhat vague on the exact nature of the miracles they performed, that same sacred text testifies generally to the types of miracles expected of believers. The faithless simply don't enjoy these same endowments.

APPLICATION AND ALLEGORIZATION

These miracles are a strong testimony to the reality that God's gifts are not reserved for prophets and apostles. All may know the Lord, and all may be the recipients and conveyers God's power and miracles—through faith and faithfulness. Just as all can qualify to receive the blessings of the temple, all can receive the "power from on high" that is promised.[2] McConkie, Millet, and Top describe the implications of this miracle in this way:

> There is no spiritual aristocracy. Those newly born to the faith are as entitled to the attentions and blessings of a loving Father as their older brothers and sisters. True it is that those more mature in spiritual things may be entrusted with greater authority and power, but this is not to say, as was the case in this instance, that the newly converted are without the power to dream dreams, see visions, prophesy, work miracles, and generally enjoy those signs that naturally follow faith and obedience.[3]

These miracles are a testament to the truth that those who are sincerely converted—and who fully function in the faith—will be endowed with gifts of the Spirit, because they will enjoy the gift of the Holy Ghost. If one is worthy of that Spirit, one will manifest its fruits. Such is an eternal law!

NOTES

1. Gardner (2007), 5:299.
2. See Smith, in Smith (1976), 237.
3. McConkie, Millet, and Top (1992), 34.

SIGNS *of* CHRIST'S CRUCIFIXION *Are* MANIFEST *in the* AMERICAS

3 NEPHI 8:5–25

THE MIRACLE

Samuel the Lamanite had been quite specific about the signs that would accompany Christ's death (see Helaman 14:20, 27). However, Mormon records that as the years passed, many began to doubt the likelihood of the signs being fulfilled—even though "so many signs had been given" previously (3 Nephi 8:4).

In time the miracles prophesied came to pass, including "thick darkness" (verse 20) and a complete void of any light for three days, and the wicked exhibited "great mourning and howling and weeping . . . continually" (verse 23). Indeed, "great were the groanings of the people, because of the darkness and the great destruction which had come upon them" (verse 23). Mormon informs us that the people, groping in darkness, cried out: "O that we had repented before this great and terrible day, and then would our brethren have been spared, and they would not have been burned in that great city Zarahemla" (verse 24). Elsewhere they lamented: "O that we had repented before this great and terrible day, and had not killed and stoned the prophets, and cast them out; then would our mothers and our fair daughters, and our children have been spared, and not have been buried up in that great city Moronihah" (verse 25). Thus were the cries of the damned souls in the day of destruction and darkness.

BACKGROUND

We examined this miracle previously, under the heading of "Physical Upheavals at the Death of Jesus" (Helaman 14:20–28). However, a brief return to the topic seems appropriate here, as there is an additional layer of symbolic meaning worth mentioning.

SYMBOLIC ELEMENTS

The presence of darkness is the absence of light. The juxtaposition of these two attributes—light and dark—are common scriptural symbols of the two powers ever fighting for our allegiance in time and throughout eternity. We have pointed out elsewhere that darkness is a symbol of sin and the withdrawal of the Spirit. The groping in the dark, and the howling (described herein) because of it, seem a good image of the status and pain of the sinful soul.

As mentioned previously, the number three traditionally represents that which is of God, or that which comes from God. Here the tangible darkness that causes the sinful to mourn is a perfect representation of what happens when we willfully sin: the Spirit of the Lord is grieved and withdraws from us, leaving us to grope in the dark.

APPLICATION AND ALLEGORIZATION

In the narrative of this miracle we are informed that "there began to be great doubtings and disputations among the people, notwithstanding so many signs had been given" (3 Nephi 8:4). By way of application, we remind the reader that having doubts is not a sin. Nor do doubts need to have an adverse effect on one's testimony. Doubting brings questions; and questions are often the source of personal revelation—as was so often the case with the Prophet Joseph. That being said, we must remember that not all doubts are equal in their nature or in their implications for our personal spirituality. One may run across some doctrine, teaching, or point of history that provokes a doubt or raises a question. However, that is much different than simply refusing to exercise faith and demanding empirical evidence prior to being willing to believe. This latter form of doubt is where the danger arises. Natural questions still allow a place for faith. However, doubts of the type described in this miracle—an unwillingness to believe even though "so many signs had been given" (3 Nephi 8:4)—do not allow for faith. Rather, they stand in opposition to faith. And this kind of doubt can bring trials and darkness into our lives, a darkness strong enough that we lose our way. Just as the darkness in this miracle caused the wicked to wish they had repented—and caused them to cry out in regret and sorrow—so also can our trials cause us to be humbled sufficiently that we turn to God (when otherwise we might not have). Of course, we cannot say how many of those lamenting their sins in this miracle sincerely changed their ways. However, we do know that God will sometimes allow us to encounter trials as a means of provoking change. This is not to say that all trials are the result of sin, nor are all divine in their source. However, we do know that this is one way the Father *sometimes* works in our lives as a means of saving the sin-bound soul.

An additional application is found in the fact that the righteous and the wicked all suffered through the same darkness. However, it is only the wicked who are described as crying out in desperation. The righteous in this miracle—though just as inconvenienced—waited patiently upon the Lord, believing His hand would be manifest in His due time. President Thomas S. Monson taught,

> Morality is a period of testing. . . . In order for us to be tested, we must face challenges and difficulties. These can break us, and the surface of our souls may crack and crumble—that is, if our foundations of faith, our testimonies of truth are not deeply imbedded within us. . . .
>
> If we do not have a deep foundation of faith and a solid testimony of truth, we may have difficulty withstanding the harsh storms and icy winds of adversity which inevitably come to each of us.[1]

Those who wailed during this season of darkness remind us that we must make sure, while times are still good, that we have sufficient spiritual strength and faith to endure when times are bad—*for surely bad times will come.* As Mother Teresa said, our "love for Jesus" is "proved by accepting little humiliations with joy."[2] Are you prepared to be joyful when the day of darkness arrives? And what if, as for the Nephites, it lasts for more than a brief "day"?

NOTES

1. Thomas S. Monson, in *Teachings of Thomas S. Monson*, Lynne F. Cannegieter, compiler (Salt Lake City, UT: Deseret Book, 2011), 11.

2. Mother Teresa, *Where There is Love, There is God*, complied by Brian Kolodiejchuk (New York: Image, 2010), 353.

A Voice *of* Warning *Is* Heard

3 Nephi 9:1–14

The Miracle

At the conclusion of the destruction that accompanied the crucifixion and death of Christ, a voice was heard "among all the inhabitants of the . . . land" (3 Nephi 9:1). As a warning to those who had survived, the Lord's voice announced the obliteration of many, many cities—and the death of the inhabitants of those locales.

Time and again during this miracle the voice of Jesus announced that the cause of this devastation was the wickedness of the people. He informed those who had survived that He had destroyed so many "to hide their iniquities and their abominations from before my face, that the blood of the prophets and the saints shall not come up any more unto me against them" (verse 5).

Christ's warning concluded with an invitation to the survivors: "O all ye that are spared because ye were more righteous than they, will ye not now return unto me, and repent of your sins, and be converted, that I may heal you? Yea, verily I say unto you, if ye will come unto me ye shall have eternal life. Behold, mine arm of mercy is extended towards you, and whosoever will come, him will I receive; and blessed are those who come unto me" (verses 13–14).

Background

The text states that "a voice [was] heard among all the inhabitants of the earth" (3 Nephi 9:1). Monte Nyman argues, "There is a difference between 'a voice was heard *among* all the inhabitants,' and '*all* the inhabitants hearing a voice.' Perhaps only the more righteous heard the voice, and they informed the others."[1] Perhaps; though the text makes no effort to highlight such a distinction, if one was indeed intended by Mormon.

The first city listed among the destroyed was Zarahemla—which, for some two hundred years, had been the Nephite capital. A little more than a half century prior to this destruction, the city was destroyed in a different way: infested with Gadianton robbers, whom the people had largely embraced (Helaman 6). Over time the people ousted the robbers and returned to faithfulness. However, a new secret combination among the judges of Zarahemla also brought down their government (3 Nephi 7:9–14). Now the government, people, and even physical environment were all destroyed through conscious wickedness. "The geographic shift northward begins in earnest after this point, with Bountiful apparently serving as the Nephite capital" from this point forward.[2]

SYMBOLIC ELEMENTS

Mass destruction is often a symbol of judgment.[3] That destruction can come in many forms, as it does in this miracle, but the message conveyed is often that of judgment.

> Perhaps the most astounding images of judgment are so-called natural disasters, the elements of the earth rising to overwhelm the wicked: floods, famines, earthquakes, fire, plagues and infestations. . . . The occurrence of such disaster does not necessitate that it happens as judgment. But Scripture details numerous occasions where the explicit cause behind natural disasters is the judgment of God.[4]

Commonly employed in scripture as a symbol, the fire in this miracle also has emblematic merit. The aforementioned source notes,

> Fire is another image of judgment. Inescapable and sudden like floods or plagues, fire consumes in judgment. . . . The final judgment of God will entail a fire that consumes the earth (Rev 16:8; 2 Pet 3:10) as well as a place of fire to which the unrepentant will go (Mt 3:12; 25:41; Rev 20:14–15).[5]

Fire, a subset of judgment, can sanctify the righteous while destroying the wicked. Thus, it is a positive and negative symbol at the same time—like the "great and dreadful day of the Lord" (3 Nephi 25:5).

The voice of God is a symbol of His power, person, and judgment.[6] This miracle is suggestive of God's involvement in the destruction, His revelation to the people, and His concern for their salvation (as evidenced by this warning).

Of the symbolic merit of the destruction, one commentary on the Book of Mormon pointed out:

> In addition to the literal reality [that many cities and peoples were destroyed], this catalogue [of leveled lands] stands as a type of the last-days' destruction. The same natural violence and destruction of the wicked will also accompany the Messiah's second and final coming. . . . Their burning fulfills Messianic prophecies of God's wrath in purging the wicked at his coming: "Upon the wicked he shall rain snares, fire and brimstone, and an horrible tempest: this shall be the portion of their cup" (Psalm 11:6). This verse must have been particularly significant for those who survived these events.[7]

APPLICATION AND ALLEGORIZATION

In this miracle, the sin for which the Lord says He has slain the wicked is curious and not what one would expect. One commentary explains: "While he could have recited an extensive listing of their abominations, the Lord simply cited their rejection of the living prophets whom he had sent unto them to 'cry repentance.' This phrase seems to be saying that most, if not all, of the wickedness of the world and individual iniquity could be averted through heeding the words of the Lord's living prophets (see Jeremiah 5:21; Acts 3:22–23; D&C 1:14)."[8] How true this is! Destruction comes because of sin: marriages are destroyed through infidelity; families are destroyed through the rebelliousness of children or the unrighteous dominion of parents; lives are destroyed through substance abuse; spirituality is destroyed through worldliness and pride. Of each of these destructive vices, we have received over and over again firm and clear warnings from prophets—ancient and modern. But humankind is so prone to ignore God's messengers. If we listen to the voice of the Lord—as given through His Spirit and through His living prophets and apostles—it will protect us.

If we ignore it, we will suffer and ultimately be destroyed. This miracle attests to that. Why can we not learn this lesson?

In several circumstances listed in this miracle, fire was used to destroy the wicked (3 Nephi 9:3, 9–11). Curiously, when we are wicked the Holy Ghost (which baptizes with "fire") has a negative—rather than positive—influence upon us. It convicts us and makes us feel uncomfortable. When Jesus returns, fire will destroy all those who do not have the Spirit or the Light of Christ with them. Thus, the Spirit and glory of God will be destructive, rather than positive, for those who are unrighteous—but positive and sanctifying for those who have sought to be faithful (3 Nephi 9:20). Like His word, the Holy Ghost (through which His word comes) truly is a "two-edged sword" (D&C 6:2).

We are told by the Lord that "the devil laugheth, and his angels rejoice because of the . . . iniquity and abominations" the people commit (3 Nephi 9:2; Moses 7:26). Satan is eternally miserable; and, thus, he desires the unhappiness of all humanity (2 Nephi 2:18). It is an unfortunate reality that so many of us, when we suffer, find solace in the suffering and misfortunes of others, particularly those who have hurt or offended us. This particular miracle reminds us that when we do so, we are really acting—in a very literal way—as Satan would. Because the devil rejoices in the misfortune of others, we must fight the temptation to do the same. Indeed, we must plead with the Lord for *all* who suffer, including our enemies.

The destruction that befell the Nephites was not without warning (2 Nephi 25:9). The Lord informs us that He sent prophet after prophet to them, but they would not listen (3 Nephi 9:10). Nibley put it this way: "They need not cry and say, 'Why did this happen to us? Why weren't we warned?' . . . You knew perfectly well what you were doing—you brought this on yourselves."⁹ Such is the case in our own lives. The Lord isn't going to punish us for sinning in ignorance. Sadly, however, the major sins we commit are seldom due to ignorance. Much like the Nephites of old, we often sin knowingly, and contrary to the repeated warnings of the Lord's anointed. President Boyd K. Packer highlighted an important truth:

> I will make a promise to you, and you can test it. I have no hesitancy in making this promise. . . . As you move forward in life, you cannot

make a major mistake, any mistake that will have lasting consequences in your life, without having been warned and told not to do it. It cannot be done in this Church. It doesn't work that way. You try to do something that is wrong, and the Spirit will say no. Now you may plug your ears—you don't plug your ears, you plug your feelings, and you [may] let your desires or some other thing get hold of you. But you cannot make a mistake that is going to have any consequence without knowing about it. . . . You will be warned of danger. . . . You cannot make a major mistake in your life without being warned.[10]

If we listen to the Spirit, we will be warned. Each time we hear the voice of living apostles and prophets, we are being warned. We may choose to ignore their warnings, but we cannot claim that God has not warned us of the dangers afoot and the consequences of sin. Even in our most tempting hours, when Satan makes it nearly impossible for the Spirit to get our attention, we still receive that warning voice—though we sometimes place ourselves in tempting situations that make it difficult to hear and obey.

As a final application, it is interesting that the Lord doesn't say that those who were preserved were "perfect" or "sinless." Rather, He simply calls them "more righteous" than those who were destroyed (3 Nephi 9:13); and He emphasizes that His "arm of mercy is extended towards" all who will "come unto" Him (3 Nephi 9:14). God does not require that we be flawless in order to be saved.[11] We should strive for personal holiness—as we assume many of the surviving Nephites had. But He can save us in spite of our weaknesses *if* we are regularly seeking out the care of the Great Physician of our souls.

Notes

1. Nyman (2003–2004), 5:102.
2. Gardner (2007), 5:313–14.
3. See Tresidder (2000), 108, 111.
4. Ryken, Wilhoit, and Longman (1998), 471.
5. Ibid., 471–72.
6. See Ibid., 918–19.
7. Gardner (2007), 5:313. See also Delbert L. Stapley, cited in Bassett (2007–2008), 3:34.
8. McConkie, Millet, and Top (1992), 40.
9. Nibley (2004), 3:335.
10. Boyd K. Packer (2008), 130–31.

11. We should be cautious to remember that "more righteous" doesn't necessarily mean "more successful at being obedient to commandments." A person who has not faith in God but who lives a very moral, honest, and good life still needs the Atonement of Christ. We are not "more righteous" because of the number of good or holy things we do. We are "more righteous" because we believe in Christ and apply His atoning blood and, thereby, Jesus became "sin for us . . . that we might be made the righteousness of God in him" (2 Corinthians 5:21).

A Voice *from* Heaven *Is* Heard *but* Initially *Not* Understood

3 Nephi 11:3–6

The Miracle

After the destruction that had taken place at the death of Christ, a "great multitude" gathered to the temple in the land of Bountiful (3 Nephi 11:1). As they surveyed "the great and marvelous change which had taken place," they "conversed" (verses 1–2) about Christ—and the sign of His death that had been given in fulfillment of the words of Samuel (Helaman 14:20–27).

As they talked they unexpectedly heard a "small voice" coming from heaven (3 Nephi 11:3). Though they could not understand the words spoken by the voice—and though the voice was neither harsh nor loud—it did cause their frames to shake and their hearts to burn. The voice pierced them to their very souls.

Three times they heard this same voice, and the first two times they couldn't understand the words spoken. However, the third time the voice spoke to them, they focused intently on the voice and the place of its origin. They "opened their ears to hear it" and fixed their eyes on the heavens, "from whence the sound came" (verse 5). And this third time they were able to understand what the voice was saying to them.

BACKGROUND

This narrative highlights an important point about how revelation is received. The Holy Ghost speaks to our personal spirits—not to our physical ears. President Boyd K. Packer has repeatedly spoken of the fact that the Spirit is something you feel more than it is something you hear: "That sweet, quiet voice of inspiration . . . comes more as a feeling than it does as a sound."[1] "These delicate, refined spiritual communications are not seen with our eyes, nor heard with our ears. And even though it is described as a voice, it is a voice that one feels, more than one hears."[2] "Revelation is the process of communication to the *spiritual* eyes and to the *spiritual* ears that were ours before our mortal birth."[3] "You don't *hear* the words of an angel, you *feel* the words of an angel, because 'angels speak by the power of the Holy Ghost.'"[4] When we receive revelation, we do so independent of our physical bodies—as though we had no bodies at all.[5]

> The voice of God, received through the spirit of revelation, does not have to be heard with ears, nor necessarily be transmitted by auditory nerves. It speaks to the soul of man. Hence it can be a "small voice" but can cause a person to "quake" or tremble. It is not volume but rather the spiritual power of this "small voice" that makes it unique. Compare Helaman 5:30; see also 1 Kings 19:11–12; D&C 8:2–3; D&C 9:8; D&C 85:6.[6]

This does not mean that there is no physical response when we feel the Spirit. On the contrary. Our spirits and our bodies are intimately tied together, for "the spirit and the body are the soul of man" (D&C 88:15). But the point of spiritual contact *is* Spirit to spirit.

Brant Gardner points out that the timing of this gathering, and the appearance of Jesus, is not clear from the text. It may have happened almost immediately after the three days of darkness had ended, in which case we would assume that Bountiful had not sustained much damage. Or it may have happened quite some time later, after they had addressed the priorities of tending to the wounded and burying those who had been killed. Nephi simply does not record for us many of the details necessary for ascertaining how soon after the destruction and darkness this miracle took place.[7]

SYMBOLIC ELEMENTS

Because the number three was often associated with divine things, the thrice-repeated message in this miracle may be more than a simple coincidence. It may be that Nephi is trying to highlight for us that what is about to happen to the Nephites would be an encounter with the divine.

Nephi's craftsmanship is obvious in these verses. The people are conversing with one another when they hear something they do not understand. Again they listen but still do not understand. The third time, after they have exerted considerable effort, they hear comprehensible words. This triple repetition is a literary technique, used earlier when Nephi said the destruction lasted three hours, even though he had no way of measuring that passage of time. He also asserted that the darkness lasted for three days, even though there was no way to tell the difference between day and night. . . .

Nephi is telling us that this occasion is another "three" that points to the Messiah. Nephi is also telling us that the people had to believe before they could have this manifestation.[8]

APPLICATION AND ALLEGORIZATION

As we are told repeatedly in scripture, the Spirit speaks as a "still small voice" (1 Kings 19:12; 1 Nephi 17:45; D&C 85:6). It requires that we listen and focus. It requires that we have a spirit of reverence about us, as "reverence invites revelation."[9] As President Henry B. Eyring has said, the Spirit will not "shout" in order to gain our attention.[10] Thus, if there is too much external or internal noise in our heads and hearts, we are liable to miss its whisperings—its revelation. President Boyd K. Packer taught: "There are so many places to go, so many things to do in this noisy world. We can be too busy to pay attention to the promptings of the Spirit."[11] President David O. McKay told the following story, illustrative of this principle:

One day in Salt Lake City a son kissed his mother good morning, took his dinner bucket, and went to City Creek Canyon where he worked. He was a switchman on the train that was carrying logs out of the canyon. Before noon his body was brought back lifeless. The mother was inconsolable. She could not be reconciled to that tragedy—her boy just in his early twenties so suddenly taken away. The funeral was held, and words of consolation were spoken, but she was not consoled. She couldn't understand it. One forenoon, so she says, after her husband had gone to his office to attend to his duties as a member of the Presiding Bishopric, she lay in a relaxed state on the bed, still yearning and praying for some consolation. She said that her son appeared and said, "Mother, you needn't worry. That was merely an accident. I gave the signal to the engineer to move on, and as the train started, I jumped for the handle of the freight car, and my foot got caught in a sagebrush, and I fell under the wheel. I went to Father soon after that, but he was so busy in the office I couldn't influence him—I couldn't make any impression upon him, and I tried again. Today I come to you to give you that comfort and tell you that I am happy."[12]

God certainly seeks to communicate with His children upon the earth. However, the thinness of the veil that separates us from God is determined by you and me—not by Him. As we simplify our lives, and as we make time for prayer, meditation, and contemplation, God will be more able to speak to our hearts and minds. However, if we allow our lives to become too busy—even with Church work—we run the risk of limiting God's power to provide the revelation we need. As with the Nephites who could not understand what God was saying until they intently focused, so also you and I must find a quiet place to go each day to focus and listen. That quiet place needs to be both a physical location as well as a state of mind. In other words, we need to learn to quiet our hearts and minds as much as our surroundings. President Eyring noted that "you must be very quiet inside" if you wish to hear the Spirit speaking.[13] Similarly, Mother Teresa said, "In the silence of the heart God speaks."[14] Even if we spend time in prayer each day, if our minds are racing and not focused, we will not recognize His words to us. Like the Nephites, we must "open [our] ears" and "look steadfastly towards heaven" (3 Nephi 11:5) when we seek to hear His voice and know His will.

As an additional application, it will be noted that the Nephites were at the temple, but they were somewhat distracted by all that had recently happened in their lives and to their community. Thus, when God spoke to them, they didn't recognize what He was saying. They heard the voice but twice missed the message. One commentator applied this experience to our own time at the temple: "Some of us attend the temple . . . more times than we are really there, because our mind is focused on outside influences. . . . Each time we attend the temple we should say, 'Today I am going to the temple, will I be in the temple completely?' "[15] Like the Nephites, you and I may find ourselves "at" the temple. But are we completely focused on what is taking place therein? Or are we, too, hearing the words but missing the message God has for us because our hearts and minds are focused on the things happening in our lives? Inattentively attending the temple still blesses the dead; but it does minimal for the patron—as the Spirit cannot speak to the distracted soul.

NOTES

1. Packer, in Williams (2008), 121.
2. Ibid., 122–23.
3. Ibid., 122; emphasis added.
4. Ibid., 123; emphasis in original.
5. See Joseph Smith, in Smith (1976), 355.
6. McConkie, Millet, and Top (1992), 52.
7. See Gardner (2007), 5:333. See also Nyman (2003–2004), 5:126–29.
8. Gardner (2007), 5:344.
9. Boyd K. Packer, "Reverence Invites Revelation," *Ensign*, November 1991.
10. Henry B. Eyring, "To Draw Closer to God," *Ensign*, May 1991, 67.
11. Boyd K. Packer, in Conference Report, April 2000, 8.
12. David O. McKay, *Gospel Ideals* (Salt Lake City: Bookcraft, 1998), 525–26.
13. Eyring (1991), 67.
14. Mother Teresa (2010), 11.
15. Marshal Burton, cited in Bassett (2007–2008), 3:37.

Nephite Children *Are* Encircled *by* Fire *and* Ministered *to by* Angels

3 NEPHI 17:21–24

THE MIRACLE

In the midst of His post-Resurrection ministry among the Nephites, Jesus instructed the parents to bring forth their little children. The Lord "one by one" blessed them and prayed to the Father on behalf of them (3 Nephi 17:21). When He had done so, He openly wept. He then turned to the adults gathered around Him and said, "Behold your little ones" (verse 23).

As the parents gazed upon the scene, suddenly the heavens were opened and angels began to descend in the midst of a pillar of fire. These divine beings encircled the children so that they too were encompassed by fire, and the angels ministered unto the little ones who had been seated at Jesus's feet.

BACKGROUND

In examining this miracle, John Welch suggested that it might be part of a larger temple text, and that which is described therein may actually be an account of the sealing of the Nephite children to their parents. Welch wrote:

I . . . imagine, although this cannot be known for sure, that Jesus did more than pray, for it seems that he did things that the people saw just as he spoke words that they heard. This produced unspeakable joy. First the parents heard what Jesus prayed for them, the parents: "No one can conceive of the joy which filled our souls at the time we heard him pray for us unto the Father" (3 Nephi 17:17). The adults were overcome. Jesus asked them all to arise, and he blessed them and pronounced his joy to be full (see 3 Nephi 17:18–20). He then touched the children "one by one, and blessed them, and prayed unto the Father for them" (3 Nephi 17:21). This was done in the presence of God (Jesus), witnesses (the parents who "[bore] record of it"; 3 Nephi 17:21), and angels (who came down and encircled the children with fire and ministered to them; 3 Nephi 17:24). In the end, Jesus turned to the parents and said, "Behold your little ones" (3 Nephi 17:23). It seems to me that Jesus is not just inviting the parents to look at their children and admire them. Although that simple reading is possible, I would suggest that he is saying, "Behold, your little ones"—they are yours. While it cannot be said exactly what transpired that afternoon, the children apparently now somehow belonged to the parents in a way they had not belonged before. [1]

Welch is right that we cannot know for sure. But the idea is intriguing and may offer some context for the otherwise unexplained miracle.

Nibley interprets the passage in a slightly different way, conjecturing, "Jesus gave each child his patriarchal blessing . . . as he met the people one by one, not in the plural." [2] Perhaps! Either way, what is clear is that Jesus did more than simply pray for these children. He did something powerful and priestly on their behalf.

Jesus is said to have blessed each of the children "one by one" (3 Nephi 17:21). The amount of time this would have taken seems staggering. Even if He only spent a few minutes per child, with several hundred children before Him, this would have taken several hours to accomplish. Couple that with the time He spent allowing each of the 2,500 plus adults to come forth and feel the nail prints in His body, blessing those who were sick or afflicted—and you get a picture of how attentive Jesus is to the "one." [3]

SYMBOLIC ELEMENTS

The text of this miracle records that the Nephite children were "encircled about with fire" (3 Nephi 17:24). One commentary on the Book of Mormon points out: "Being encircled about with fire is a tangible symbol of the outpouring of the Holy Spirit (compare Nephi and Lehi's experience in Helaman 5:23–49)."[4] Of course, fire is a common symbol in scripture for the Holy Ghost (see *JST* Genesis 6:69; Matthew 3:11; 2 Nephi 31:13–17; D&C 19:31; Moses 6:66). The description of this miracle brings to mind the happenings that took place on the Eastern Hemisphere on the day of Pentecost (Acts 2:1–4).[5] What happened here among the Nephites is a comparable Pentecostal outpouring.

Circles are curious symbols. They can represent a number of things, including that which is eternal, the rejection of the world or worldliness, and divinely sent protective forces. As it relates to the latter of these symbolic connotations, one text states: "In forming the prayer circle one excludes the outer world." The participants "form closed circles with their backs all turned on the outer world."[6] The focal point in a prayer circle is not that which is outside of the circle, but the altar at the center of the circle.[7] Altars were traditional symbols of God, Christ, and sacrifice. Curiously, in this miracle Christ prays for the children, and they are encircled by fire with Him at the center of that circle. He is their focus—and the world is excluded from their sacred circle.

Here, as in John 11:35 and Moses 7:28–29, we read of Jesus weeping. While this act is quite literal, it has symbolic implications. We know that in heaven there is no sorrow, no pain, no crying, and no tears.[8] Thus, while Jesus may have cried here in order to teach us, it would probably be best to not assume God cries each time something bad happens to one of His children upon one of His endless earths (Moses 1:33–35). Were God to do so, He would be in a state of never-ending sadness—as sad things never cease to happen. In other words, rather than assuming God—who dwells in a place where there is no "sorrow" or "crying" (Revelation 21:4)—weeps, we should understand this symbolic act as a representation of the truth that He cares deeply about us; He loves us and feels for us in our darkest and our brightest hours. Weeping is a sign and a symbol that God is not cold and hardened, but warm and loving. It represents that God is not removed from His creations, their lives, or their emotions. The representation of God weeping does not so much define what He does as it depicts for us that He deeply cares.

APPLICATION AND ALLEGORIZATION

Little children are "alive in Christ" (Moroni 8:12) and, thus, have a spirituality and faith that is beyond that of many adults. They are receptive to God's Spirit because they are worthy of it. It is commonly pointed out that adults are commanded to become as little children (see Matthew 18:4; 3 Nephi 9:22), and here the little children exemplify what Jesus is offering each of us: profound spiritual outpourings for those who are holy. Previously we noted that circles are sometimes symbols of rejecting the world. Little children care little for the world. Indeed, they are seldom conscious of it. The encircling of the children in this narrative reminds us of that truth. Perhaps you and I can learn something about our own spiritual journeys from this miraculous episode. If we wish to have greater endowments of the Spirit—as these little ones had—we must turn our backs on worldliness as little children typically do.

On a related note, Sister Michaelene P. Grassli, former Primary general president of the Church, highlighted this miracle and Jesus's choice to call the little children forth. She said,

> Jesus waited "till they had *all* been brought to him." He wasn't looking for a representative sample, and he wasn't content with just some of the children. He wanted them *all* to be there, and he ministered to them *all*.
>
> Then Jesus prayed unto the Father so powerfully that "no tongue can speak, neither can there be written by any man, neither can the hearts of men conceive so great and marvelous things." (3 Ne. 17:17.) And the children were there! They heard that prayer; they saw that event, and they were affected by it. Children can understand and should witness marvelous events—events like priesthood blessings, special ward and family fasts, the testimonies and prayers of their parents and leaders, and gospel discussions with people they love.[9]

This should cause us to take pause the next time we are tempted to dismiss the children prior to the performance of an ordinance. Having them present is what Christ would want. Having them there is how they will learn to feel the spirit of sacred things. Sister Grassli added: "Let us not underestimate the capacity and potential power of today's children to perpetuate righteousness. No group of people in the Church is as receptive to the truth."[10]

Jesus's choice to spend hours addressing the needs of individuals—one at a time—is unfathomable. Yet this miracle attests to the fact that He did just that. And, thus, it is a testament to His awareness of each of us. He loves us individually. He answers our individual prayers. He cares about us personally. Mother Teresa counseled: "I want you to spend your time being alone with Jesus. What does it mean to be alone with Jesus? . . . It means that you know that He is close to you, that He loves you, that you are precious to Him, that He is in love with you. . . . You belong to Him. If you know that, you will be all right anywhere; you will be able to face any failure, any humiliation, any suffering, if you realize Jesus' personal love for you."[11]

This miracle reminds me of a comment by President Joseph F. Smith, who spoke of our deceased ancestors and their awareness of us, even though they now dwell beyond the veil. He taught, "We are closely related to our kindred . . . who have preceded us into the spirit world. . . . Those who have been faithful, who have gone beyond, are still engaged in the work for the salvation of the souls of men. . . . They see us, they are solicitous for our welfare, they love us now more than ever."[12] One would assume, therefore, when sacred ordinances are engaged in and covenants are made, our faithful kindred dead are aware of those rites of passage and are overjoyed at such happenings. In that vein, D. Kelly Ogden shared the following experience:

> One day at the Provo Utah Temple, [I] stopped by the office of . . . temple recorder Kurt Jensen. Brother Jensen looked up and asked: "You're a grandfather. When one of your grandchildren is blessed or baptized, where do you want to be?"
>
> "There at the ordinance, of course."
>
> "Well," Brother Jensen said, "I was reading in 3 Nephi 17, where the children are surrounded by fire, and angels came down and ministered to them. Who do you think those angels were? Wouldn't they be grandparents and great-grandparents? Who in all the universe would most want to be there for such a sacred occasion?"[13]

We certainly do not know the identity of the angels who descended from the heavens to minister to these little children. Nevertheless, Brother Jensen's suggestion makes sense on both a doctrinal and emotional level. Who indeed would want to be there more than our kindred dead? If, as President Smith suggests, they are working on our behalf on the "other side," then we would assume that they would want to be present to see the fruits of their labors.

This miracle also reminds us that *sometimes* God sends His angels or His influence to protect His little ones. This may happen in the form of spiritual protection when they are in the home of a disbelieving parent. It may come in the form of physical protection when they are in the presence of one who would harm them. It may come in the form of emotional protection when they *have been* harmed by another (allowing them to either forget or be less affected by the sins of others). Either way, just as the Nephite children were encircled by fire, Jesus has the power (when it fulfills His will) to encircle and protect His little children from whatever harm threatens them. Some will query, "Why then did He not protect me?" or "Why then did my child become the victim of someone else's evil acts?" As in this episode—where not all of the world's children had this experience with Jesus and the angels—in the wisdom of God, sometimes we are called to bear a cross that we wish we had not been asked to take up. However, God can enable all of us to endure with grace if we give our burdens to Him (Mosiah 24:14–15). And were we actually able to see all of the details, I suspect each of us would attest to the fact that we have been protected in many ways unseen and unrecognized.

Finally, as a general symbolic message one can draw from this miracle, McConkie, Millet, and Top explained:

> His love for little children is not only evidence of his divine compassion but was and is also symbolic of the requirements of the gospel. The Savior reminds us that, in order to partake of his greatest blessing, even eternal life, ye must "be converted and become as little children" (Matthew 18:3). The tender mercies extended by the Savior and his blessings of the little children serve also as a symbolic teaching that through the atonement of Jesus Christ we are able to put off the natural man and become as little children (see Mosiah 3:19)—literally born again as the spiritual sons and daughters of Jesus Christ (see Mosiah 5:7; Mosiah 27:25).[14]

In so many ways, this miracle testifies of how Christ loves the little children—and how you and I may gain His acceptance and access to spiritual endowments if we seek to live lives of purity and holiness, as little children do.

NOTES

1. John W. Welch, *The Sermon at the Temple and the Sermon on the Mount* (Provo, UT: Foundation for Ancient Research and Mormon Studies, 1990), 80. See also Ogden and Skinner (2011), 2:186.

2. Nibley (2004), 3:363.

3. See Nyman (2003–2004), 5:257.

4. McConkie, Millet, and Top (1992), 118.

5. See Gardner (2007), 5:490.

6. Hugh Nibley, *Mormonism and Early Christianity* (Provo, UT: Foundation for Ancient Research and Mormon Studies, 1987), 70.

7. Cyril of Jerusalem stated that, while "the Presbyters . . . stand round God's altar . . . the Priest cries aloud, 'Lift up your hearts.'" In the early Christian liturgy of James (the brother of Jesus) the language is "Let us lift up our minds and our hearts." Cyril continues: "In effect therefore the [officiating] Priest bids all in that hour to dismiss all cares of this life, or household anxieties, and to have their heart in [or focused on] heaven with the merciful God" [Cyril of Jerusalem, "Catechetical Lectures," Lecture 23:4, in Philip Schaff and Henry Wace, *Nicene and Post-Nicene Fathers*, fourteen volumes (Peabody, MA: Hendrickson Publishers, 2004), 7:153–54. Regarding James's alternate wording, see "The Divine Liturgy of James," Section 3:28, in "Early Liturgies," in Roberts and Donaldson (1994), 7:543].

8. See Orson Pratt, *Millennial Star*, Vol. 28, 722, November 17, 1866, cited in L. G. Otten and C. M. Caldwell, *Sacred Truths of the Doctrine & Covenants*, two volumes (Springville, UT: LEMB, Inc., 1982), 2:342; Sidney Rigdon, *Messenger and Advocate* (Feb. 1835), 67; Sidney Rigdon, *Messenger and Advocate* (Aug. 1835), 165; John Taylor, *The Government of God* (Liverpool: no publisher given, 1852), chapter 5, paragraph 13; Isaiah 25:8; Revelation 7:17; 21:4. See also John Taylor, in *Journal of Discourses*, 10:118; McConkie (1980–1981), 1:95–96; James E. Talmage, *Articles of Faith* (Salt Lake City: The Church of Jesus Christ of Latter-day Saints, 1924), 377; Parley P. Pratt, *A Voice of Warning* (New York: no publisher listed, 1837), 135; Bruce R. McConkie, *The Millennial Messiah* (Salt Lake City: Deseret Book, 1982), 306; B. H. Roberts, *The Mormon Doctrine of Deity* (Salt Lake City: Deseret News, 1903), 281; Orson Pratt, *Journal of Discourses* 14:236; 18:322; 21:326.

9. Michaelene P. Grassli, cited in Bassett (2007–2008), 3:84.

10. Ibid., 3:85.

11. Mother Teresa (2010), 12–13.

12. Joseph F. Smith, *Gospel Doctrine* (Salt Lake City: Bookcraft, 1998), 430, 431.

13. Ogden and Skinner (2011), 2:186.

14. McConkie, Millet, Top (1992), 118.

Nephi Raises His Brother Timothy *from the* Dead

3 Nephi 7:19; 19:4

The Miracle

While the details are not given, Nephi's brother Timothy had died prematurely. "In the name of Jesus" (3 Nephi 7:19), Nephi raised him from the dead—presumably via the priesthood he held.

Background

In relation to this miracle, Gardner pointed out that Nephi's raising of his brother from the dead was a "pre-figuring" of the resurrection that would be brought to pass by Christ. Gardner wrote: "We have no more information about" Timothy, but we "may assume that he was also righteous" (like his brother Nephi) "because he was worthy of this pre-figuring [of the] 'resurrection.'[1] We may also assume that he was stoned by the people for his preaching, given the antagonism that met Nephi."[2] Gardner, who sees a strong Mesoamerican influence in the Book of Mormon, highlights the fact that "stoning as a means of execution was known among the Maya and the Aztecs."[3] Timothy would eventually serve in the first Quorum of the Twelve among the Nephites.

As for the name Timothy, some have puzzled why a seemingly Greek name would appear among the Hebrew names of the Book of Mormon. Nibley explained: "Here are the names of the Twelve Apostles. Notice they're a mixture of Aramaic and Hebrew and Greek, . . . which is exactly the mixture of the population at the time of Lehi in Palestine, showing that these names had circulated among the people."[4] Elsewhere Nibley wrote:

> The occurrence of the names *Timothy* and *Lachoneus* in the Book of Mormon is strictly in order, however odd it may seem at first glance. Since the fourteenth century B.C. at latest, Syria and Palestine had been in constant contact with the Aegean world, and since the middle of the seventh century Greek mercenaries and merchants, closely bound to Egyptian interests (the best Egyptian mercenaries were Greeks), swarmed throughout the Near East. Lehi's people, even apart from their mercantile activities, could not have avoided considerable contact with these people in Egypt and especially in Sidon, which Greek poets even in that day were celebrating as the great world center of trade. It is interesting to note in passing that Timothy is an Ionian name, since the Greeks in Palestine were Ionians (hence the Hebrew name for Greeks: "Sons of Javanim"), and—since "Lachoneus" means "a Laconian"—that the oldest Greek traders were Laconians, who had colonies in Cyprus (BM Akish) and of course traded with Palestine.[5]

Gardner reasoned:

> Most of the names in this verse come from Nephite New World milieu or from the brass plates. The exception is Timothy, a name of Greek origin. While it is plausible that both "Timothy" and "Lachoneus" (3 Ne. 3:2) were Greek names that crossed the ocean, it is perhaps unusual that they were preserved for six hundred years in the New World. Most probably, they were family names, possibly borne by someone who crossed the ocean.[6]

While we cannot say for certain which theory is right, the presence of these names in the Book of Mormon can be explained by a number of probabilities.

SYMBOLIC ELEMENTS

The raising of Timothy by his brother has been seen by some as a type for how Jesus (our "elder Brother") will raise us during the resurrection. And, just as Nephi likely performed this miracle via the priesthood, so do we also know that resurrection is a priesthood ordinance.[7]

APPLICATION AND ALLEGORIZATION

The most important application of this miracle is the truth that you and I can be "raised" from spiritual death through Christ Jesus. He has the power to soften the hardest heart and heal the most wounded of souls. As with any physician, the spiritual patient must seek out his or her doctor. However, if we earnestly do, He will heal us. Of course, not all cures—whether physical or spiritual—come quickly. But Christ promises healing for all those who turn to Him.

Similarly, just as Timothy's healing came through one of Christ's earthly representatives, often in our own lives Jesus will employ one of His other sons or daughters to minister to his sin-sickened or spiritually starved children. Whether it be through the teachings of living prophets and apostles, or via the ministration of some ward or stake officer (bishops, Relief Society and priesthood leaders, faithful and inspired home and visiting teachers), Jesus can and will heal the earnest in heart. And, like Nephi, you and I should seek for opportunities to "raise" our "spiritually dead" brothers and sisters, helping them find the life and love they once knew. As President Spencer W. Kimball taught: "God does notice us, and he watches over us. But it is usually through another mortal that he meets our needs. Therefore, it is vital that we serve each other in the kingdom."[8]

NOTES

1. Of course, Timothy was not resurrected at this point. Christ was "the firstfruits of them that slept" (1 Corinthians 15:20). Timothy being raised from the dead was only a "pre-figuring" or "foreshadowing" of the resurrection.
2. Gardner (2007), 5:298.
3. See Ibid., 5:298.
4. Nibley (2004), 3:368.
5. Nibley (1988), 33.
6. Gardner (2007), 5:510.
7. President Brigham Young stated: "If we ask who will stand at the head of the resurrection in this last dispensation, the answer is—Joseph Smith, Junior, the Prophet of God. He is the man who will be resurrected and receive the keys of the resurrection, and he will seal this authority upon others, and they will hunt up their friends and resurrect them when they shall have been officiated for, and bring them up . . . until the chain is made perfect back to Adam, so that there will be a perfect chain of Priesthood from Adam to the winding-up scene" [*Journal of Discourses* 15:139]. Similarly, President Spencer W. Kimball taught: "We talk about the gospel in its fulness, but do you realize how large a part of it is still not available as we prepare,

perfect and become more like God? . . . It is supposed by this people that we have all the ordinances in our possession for salvation and exaltation, and that we are administering in these ordinances. This is not the case. We are in possession of all the ordinances that can be administered in the flesh, but there are other ordinances and administrations that must be administered beyond this world. . . . There [is] one ordinance in particular that is not given to men in the flesh, nor can men receive it. It is the ordinance and the keys of resurrection. . . . The keys will be given to those who have passed off this stage of action . . . and have received their bodies again. They will be ordained by those who hold the keys of the resurrection and go forth to resurrect the saints just as we receive the ordinance of baptism and the keys of the authority to baptize others for the remission of sins" ["Conference Issues," *The Church News*, 1970–1987, 12; see also, William J. Critchlow, in Conference Report, October 4, 1963, 29; Brigham Young, *Discourses of Brigham Young*, John A. Widtsoe, compiler (Salt Lake City: Bookcraft, 1998), 372–73, 397–98].

8. Kimball (1998), 252.

NEPHITES *Were* ENCIRCLED *by* FIRE, ANGELS MINISTERED *to* THEM, *and* JESUS MINISTERED *to* THEM

3 NEPHI 19:14–15

THE MIRACLE

Jesus had been with the Nephites, ministering to them and teaching them. After He had ordained the Twelve, a cloud overshadowed the crowd—so Jesus could no longer be seen. While He was obscured from their view, He ascended into heaven.

Immediately after Jesus's Ascension, those who had been present went to their homes and informed their neighbors, family members, and friends (who had not been in attendance) of what had taken place, letting them know that Jesus would return the next day.

As the believing gathered on the morrow the Twelve taught the things Jesus had taught them, "nothing varying" (3 Nephi 19:8). Then Nephi went down into the water and was baptized. After he had been baptized, he in turn baptized the remaining members of the Twelve. Once they had been baptized, the Holy Ghost fell upon them and they were filled with the Spirit.

Suddenly fire came down from heaven, encircling the Nephite Apostles, and angels descended to minister unto them. Likewise, Jesus appeared also and ministered unto the Twelve.

BACKGROUND

President Joseph Fielding Smith pointed out that the baptism of the Nephite Twelve highlighted here was not their first baptism but was instead a rebaptism. According to President Smith, they had each been baptized earlier in their lives for the remission of sins. Here, however, they were being rebaptized for membership in the newly formed Church, which Jesus had organized among them.[1] President Smith pointed out:

> For the same reason Joseph Smith and those who had been baptized prior to April 6, 1830, were again baptized on the day of the organization of the Church. Joseph Smith and Oliver Cowdery were baptized on the 15th day of May, 1829, Samuel Smith a few days later, Hyrum Smith a little later, and a few others, before the Church was organized. That baptism was for the remission of sins.
>
> When the Church was organized, each of the brethren who organized the Church, and the others who had been baptized, were baptized again. They had to be in order to come into the Church by the door. Suppose Joseph Smith had overlooked that. It is just a little thing, but how vital it is. You will find all through the ministry of Joseph Smith that all these little things are there; not a thing is overlooked that is vital to the story.[2]

This would explain why Jesus appeared to have ordained the Twelve prior to their baptism (see 3 Nephi 18:36–37; 19:11–14). In actuality, as President Smith points out, they most likely had each been baptized for the remission of sins earlier, but here were ordained and then subsequently rebaptized for membership in the newly formed Church.

BYU's Monte Nyman suggested that the "touching" of the Twelve by Jesus was not an ordination to the Melchizedek Priesthood—as they already held the authority. Rather, Nyman conjectures that it was either their ordination to the office of Apostle or the conferring upon them some additional apostolic keys they had not yet received from Christ.[3]

The text tells us that prior to this miracle, the Twelve "ministered those same words" to the people "which Jesus had spoken—nothing varying from the words which Jesus had spoken" (3 Nephi 19:8). Of this, one commentator suggested the following interpretation: "The fact that the twelve ministered to the people in combination with repeating Jesus's exact words suggests an ordinance. Because 'they desired that the Holy Ghost should be given unto them,' the particular ministration seems to have been conferring the gift of the Holy Ghost, as Jesus had done for the twelve the previous day (3 Ne. 18:36–37)."[4]

Nephi's baptism here has been said to "reenact Alma's baptism at the waters of Mormon (Mosiah 18:14–16)."[5] If that is the case, then one might assume that Nephi immersed himself as Alma had. (The account in 3 Nephi certainly leaves the reader with the impression that Nephi could have immersed himself—as no one else is highlighted as having performed the rite, and Nephi is certainly depicted as the presiding authority at the time.)[6]

SYMBOLIC ELEMENTS

Mormon's phrase "he touched with his hand the disciples . . . one by one" (3 Nephi 18:36) means He performed the rite of the laying on of hands.[7] The laying on of hands represents the transferal of authority, power, or blessings. One commentary pointed out:

> All ordinances are physical; they all involve touch. Touch can provide a tangible transmission of power and love. When we experience a scene like this in our own lives, it is, as we say, "touching," because it affects us emotionally and spiritually. As with the ancient leaders, we hope Jesus will continue to touch our souls and symbolically place his hands upon our lives, so that we may live.[8]

The "fire" described in this narrative is a traditional symbol of the glory of God and divine beings, often referred to as the *shekinah* (literally "the dwelling" of God among us). "The symbol of the Holy Ghost is fire. The people were encircled about 'as if it were by fire'—again, not our usual fire, but the radiance, brilliance, light, or glory that accompanied angelic ministrations from heaven."[9]

Baptism is a well-known symbol for the "death" of the old man and the "birth" of a new man. As the Apostle Paul taught, "We are buried with him by baptism into death: that like as Christ was raised up from the dead by the glory of the Father, even so we also should walk in newness of life" (Romans 6:4). Here, the Nephites consciously get rebaptized as a statement of their recommitment to live holy lives—particularly as recipients of the fulness of the gospel that Jesus was bringing them.[10]

APPLICATION AND ALLEGORIZATION

We see the Nephite Twelve in this miracle "encircled about *as if it were* by fire" (3 Nephi 19:14). Oh how God wishes to bathe us in His glory and light. He desperately desires to be with us and to overshadow us. His disciples manifested a recommitment to Him through their rebaptism. In response to that sincere act of consecration, the "fire" of the Spirit was poured out upon them, and they received a visitation from Christ. *Only we* can prevent God's Spirit from being operative in powerful ways in our lives. We are promised time and again in scripture that God will give us His Spirit if we will turn our hearts and ways toward Him. How can one not want that in his or her life? What need you change that you might be "encircled about *as if it were* by fire"? If you have God's Spirit and power with you, spiritual encounters *will* be yours.

On a related note, the Lord and His angels seek to minister to us. Christ may do so personally (John 14), or through His representatives (Hebrews 13:2). It really doesn't matter, for as the Lord has declared, "Whether by mine own voice or by the voice of my servants, it is the same" (D&C 1:38). If we are spiritually in tune, we will see His face in any whom He sends to minister to us.

As we have suggested previously (3 Nephi 17:21–24), being encircled by the Spirit implies protection. From this miracle we can draw a symbolic reminder that the Lord protects His anointed servants until they have finished their work upon the earth. The prophet can expect such protection, as can the Apostles and other General Authorities and general auxiliary officers of the Church. But so can a faithful stake president, bishop, home or visiting teacher, Relief Society or elders quorum president. If we have a calling from God to minister to His children, until we have completed what He desires of us, we can assume we will have His protection *and* His guidance—so long as we are living worthy of it.

NOTES

1. See Smith (1998), 2:336.
2. Smith (1998), 2:336. See also Gardner (2007), 5:511; Nibley (2004), 3:368.

3. See Nyman (2003–2004), 5:283.

4. Gardner (2007), 5:510–11.

5. Gardner (2007), 5:512.

6. Monte Nyman thinks one of the other members of the Twelve baptized Nephi, and then Nephi baptized that brother after—much like Joseph Smith and Oliver Cowdery did after the appearance of John the Baptist (Joseph Smith—History 1:69–71). See Nyman (2003–2004), 5:286.

7. See Gardner (2007), 5:504.

8. Ogden and Skinner (2011), 2:188–89.

9. Ogden and Skinner (2011), 2:190.

10. See Gardner (2007), 5:512.

JESUS PROVIDES BREAD *and* WINE *When* NONE *Is* AVAILABLE

3 NEPHI 20:6–7

THE MIRACLE

During Jesus's second day among the Nephites, He introduced those who were not present on the first day to the ordinance of the sacrament. While the description of the ordinance seems quite familiar, the miracle is found in the following statement: "Now, there had been no bread, neither wine, brought by the disciples, neither by the multitude; but he truly gave unto them bread to eat, and also wine to drink" (3 Nephi 20:6–7).

BACKGROUND

The persons who were the focus of the command to "arise" (3 Nephi 20:2) can be interpreted in two ways, contingent upon what the antecedent of who "them" is. Jesus could have been speaking to the Twelve only or to the whole multitude. If the former, then Jesus would have commanded them to arise so that He could administer the sacrament to them, which reminds us of the practice today in the modern Church. The members of the Aaronic Priesthood traditionally stand in front of the sacrament table while the sacrament is administered to them. If, on the other hand, Jesus's command was to the entire multitude, we are reminded of how covenants have (in times past) been made in the temple. One commentator on this miracle wrote:

Of course, if it is read to imply that all in attendance stood, then this section of scripture is very temple oriented. Praying in preparation for an ordinance, standing to receive an ordinance, giving the ordinance to ordinance workers, who then in turn give it to those standing (Vv:1–4). Then starting in vs. 6 we see the symbols of the covenant cannot be produced by ourselves. We are dependent upon Christ for those. He is giving the multitude present the symbols of the covenant which they had not yet received, bringing them from heaven to give them to His faithful followers until all present had received them (V:8). Then in vs. 9, when all had received the symbols and the signs of the Atonement of their own free will and in a unified vocal commitment, Jesus brings them into His glory—that they might see and hear Him.[1]

I suppose it is impossible to say for certain whom Jesus was commanding to "arise." Either way, the parallels with our modern practice seem curious.

Regarding Jesus making bread in what appears to be an act of creation *ex nihilo* ("out of nothing"), Daniel H. Ludlow explained:

A miracle has been defined as the use of natural law in a way that is not fully understood. In this sense the term miracle could be used to describe electricity, for no scientist professes to understand all the laws upon which electricity is based. Certainly the Savior's providing bread and wine for the sacrament could be termed a miracle. The Savior did not circumvent natural law; rather, he used the law in a way we do not fully understand. Many people can make bread by taking wheat and adding other ingredients such as yeast and sugar; this process also requires the presence of the ingredients plus heat and time. However, Jesus Christ, the Creator of the heavens and the earth, was able to apply these natural laws almost instantaneously. That is, although there was no bread present, he was able to reach out his hands, gather the elements, and break bread that could be used in the sacrament.[2]

SYMBOLIC ELEMENTS

In reading this miracle, one cannot help but be reminded of Jesus's miracle (in the Eastern Hemisphere) of multiplying "loaves and fishes" (see Matthew 14:14–21; 15:29–38; Mark 6:33–44; 8:1–9; Luke 9:11–17; John 6:1–14). In both cases it appears that the miracle was provoked by the circumstances: a large group of faith-filled followers and no food available. Hence, the necessity of performing a miracle. One commentator wrote:

> In the Old World, an impossibly small amount miraculously becomes an abundance. The New World version does not stress quantity but rather the fact that the food and drink appeared where none had been before. Because the focus of the New World miracle is on providing the items themselves, gathering up the remainder is not required to support the claim that a miracle has occurred. . . .
>
> In this [New World] case, the miracle was that something appeared where there had been nothing before. In the Old World, since the episode explicitly mentioned a pre-existing something (the five loaves and two fishes), then the miracle could be shown only through their multiplication. Both forms show a miracle; and that purpose, not a doctrinal exposition on the possibility of *creation ex nihilo*, is Nephi's purpose in making his record.[3]

Eating is generally seen as a symbol of communion. The ancients ate, not only to satiate hunger but to also show communion with or acceptance of those with whom they broke bread.

> The act of eating together implies a relationship of closeness and trust (Ps 41:9). Conversely, people who do not wish to be intimately related do not eat together (Gen 43:32). The social bonding function of eating together, which is widespread if not universal in human cultures, probably originates in the shared meals of families. . . . Groups . . . eat together, thus binding themselves into a quasi-family. . . . To absent oneself from a family meal is to communicate feelings of alienation and anger.[4]

In the case of this Book of Mormon miracle, eating is a perfect representation of communion with God both here and in the hereafter. It reminds us of our efforts to be adopted into the family of God through the making of sacred covenants. The following is worth considering: "That the ordinance of the sacrament was conducted two times in as many days by the very Being to be remembered in the ordinance ought to teach us something about its true significance. Of the many ordinances we participate in for ourselves during our lifetime, most are only done once in our behalf, but the sacrament is not one of those."[5] Eating is an act of communion (and, therefore, of acceptance), and

God seeks our daily communion with Him—as this episode symbolically reminds us.

Jesus's command for the Twelve to stand seems significant. This symbolic posture is mentioned more than a thousand times in the standard works of the Church. It can be an expression of reverence, such as standing when a prophet or apostle enters a room. It can represent prayer, as when we pray standing in the house of the Lord. Standing is often associated with commitment to some godly purpose, as when one "stands" for a cause. Sometimes it implies a defensive posture, as when one stands if an enemy enters the room. Often standing is associated with authority (a king stands at the head of a nation, the prophet at the head of the Church, or the officiator at the head of the company in the temple). Standing is also an image of permanence (a building that stands as opposed to one that has collapsed). In the case of this miracle, the three most obvious implications of the Apostles' act of standing are the act of prayer, the presence of authority, and the sense of reverence. All seem potentially applicable here.[6]

As Jesus Himself explains, the bread and wine (water) in this miracle are standard symbols of His body and blood—shed for the guilty that they might inherit His purity (Matthew 26:26; Mark 14:22–24; 1 Corinthians 11:23–25; D&C 20:77, 79).

APPLICATION AND ALLEGORIZATION

While this miracle attests to many things—including the omnipotence of Jesus—one truth it highlights is that temporally speaking, the Lord can and does provide for us in quite miraculous ways. Those with grateful hearts can typically attest to the many "providing miracles" Jesus had done in their lives, miracles that seem to happen time and again when our means are insufficient.

On a related note, this miracle stands as a testament to the fact that Jesus can give us that which we need and do not have—in our work *and* our callings. In other words, none of us is sufficient for that which he or she has been called to do, particularly within the kingdom. Bishops feel inadequate, as do Relief Society presidents. Those who feel fully confident of their ability to perform the holy task to which they have been called likely do not understand the complete parameters of the assignment. For, surely if they did, they would see their need for the Lord's intervention. As President Thomas S. Monson stated, "Whom the Lord calls, the Lord qualifies."[7] But the Lord can only qualify those who reach out to Him with humble manifestations of acknowledged dependence.

Just as the disciples and the great multitude had no bread and no wine but Jesus provided all, likewise, you and I have *nothing* aside from that which God and Christ make available to us. In this miracle the Lord miraculously provided for His faithful followers. For you and me, He similarly provides each and every day—and in quite extraordinary ways. Jesus is the source of *all* that we have, though few of us truly see how good He is to us and how fully He blesses us day in and day out. I have never been fond of this line, often uttered in corporate prayers: "We're grateful for all of our blessings . . ." Oh, no, we are not! We miss the vast majority of what God does for us. We may be grateful for our blessed lives, but we are hardly grateful for all of our blessings. The sad reality is, we never notice most of them. Jesus is the source of all! And, thus, our lives are truly miraculous each and every day.

As with the many temporal blessings Jesus provides us, so also He grants us salvation in a miraculous and incomprehensible way. No matter how firmly we believe, what Christ has done for us in and through His Atonement is absolutely incomprehensible to any finite being. We cannot grasp how it was accomplished, all that it encompasses, the degree to which we are reliant upon His enabling power, or the depth of the love of a being who would give so much for those who obey Him so seldom. In the words of the hymn, "I stand all amazed!"[8]

NOTES

1. Andy Skelton, review of *Miracles of the Book of Mormon*.
2. Ludlow (1976), 277.
3. Gardner (2007), 5:522–23.
4. Alan W. Jenks, "Eating and Drinking in the Old Testament," in David Noel Freedman, *The Anchor Bible Dictionary*, six volumes (New York: Doubleday, 1992), 2:252.
5. Ogden and Skinner (2011), 2:194.
6. See Ryken, Wilhoit, and Longman (1998), 812–13.
7. Thomas S. Monson, in *Church News*, April 9, 1988, 14.
8. "I Stand All Amazed," Charles H. Gabriel, composer, in *Hymns of the Church of Jesus Christ of Latter-day Saints*, second revised edition (Salt Lake City, UT: Intellectual Reserve, Inc., 2002), hymn number 193.

THE DEAD MINISTER
to the LIVING

3 NEPHI 23:7–13

THE MIRACLE

In counseling with the Nephites during His post-Resurrection ministry in the Americas, Jesus commanded them to "diligently" search the words of Isaiah—because the prophet had taught many things pertaining to those who are of the house of Israel (3 Nephi 23:1–2).

Jesus then asked Nephi, the senior Apostle in the Church of the Americas, to bring forth the records that had been kept by the leadership.[1] As Jesus looked over that which they had kept, He expressed concern that they had not recorded a miracle prophesied of by Samuel the Lamanite, namely that upon Jesus's Resurrection numerous deceased Saints would arise from the dead, appear unto many, and minister unto them.

Jesus commanded Nephi that this be written, and so they did as He commanded them.

BACKGROUND

Though they had not recorded Samuel's prophecy, it is evident that Nephi (and likely others) knew of it and well remembered it, for Mormon records: "And . . . Nephi remembered this thing had not been written" (3 Nephi 23:12). What Nephi and the other disciples likely did not know was the scope of the fulfillment of Samuel's prophecy. In Jerusalem, Matthew recorded:

Jesus, when he had cried again with a loud voice, yielded up the ghost. And, behold, the veil of the temple was rent in twain from the top to the bottom; and the earth did quake, and the rocks rent; And the graves were opened; and many bodies of the saints which slept arose, And came out of the graves after his resurrection, and went into the holy city, and appeared unto many. Now when the centurion, and they that were with him, watching Jesus, saw the earthquake, and those things that were done, they feared greatly, saying, Truly this was the Son of God. (Matthew 27:50–54)

McConkie, Millet, and Top wrote: "The same miraculous events took place in the New World but, for some reason, the Nephites had failed to record them."[2] The Nephites knew what Samuel had predicted and saw a partial fulfillment of his words. However, it is likely that it was not until Jesus's appearance on the Western Hemisphere that they knew of its complete fulfillment and the details of the miracle, as they had unfolded on the opposite side of the world.

On a related note, one commentary on the Book of Mormon highlights the paradox this story presents:

> Even with this command to complete the records, it is interesting that Mormon elected to include the instruction to write this information, but not the information itself. Apparently Mormon felt that the injunction to keep the records of the prophets was more important than [recording] a fulfillment of a prophecy of resurrection. The fact that the resurrected Lord appeared in Bountiful was probably ample proof of that doctrine.[3]

Thus, the Nephites created a record of the prophecy—and an attestation that it was fulfilled—but the Book of Mormon does *not* chronicle for us the details of its fulfillment—only their witness that what Samuel had said would happen did indeed happen.

SYMBOLIC ELEMENTS

The most central symbol in this miracle story would be the grave and Christ's power to free its captives. Of its standard symbolism, one dictionary of biblical symbols notes:

> The grave conjures up many kinds of images, most of them negative.
> The grave is the epitome of darkness (Job 17:13; 18:18; Lam 3:6).

Spatially, its abode is the farthest recess from light, a prison detaining one from life and activity in the upper world. It is described as "the pit," and its entrance as going down "into the dust" (Job 17:14, 16). The grave is ritually unclean (Num 19:16) and is a place where such detestable nighttime activities as necromancy take place (1 Sam 28:8; Is 45:18–19; 65:4).

Loneliness and solitude (Ps 31:17–18; Is 47:5) represent the chief epithets on the gravestone. It is a place where one's only companions are worms (Job 17:12, 14), consuming the last vestiges of the flesh that represent the experience of pleasures in the life above. In this sense, experience in the grave is the very antithesis of the enjoyment of life. It is the absence of companionship, the love between man and woman, the sounds of joy and laughter, sampling the fruits of one's labor or participation in worship (Ps 88:10–12; Is 38:18). . . .

For the wicked dead the grave represents a place of punishment and eternal torment (Mt 10:28) and of separation from all sources of help or rescue (Lk 16:24).

The grave and death are also personified as having insatiable appetites (Is 5:14; Hab 2:5; Prov 27:20; 30:15–16). Here the grave as Sheol is associated with swallowing (Prov 1:12; Ps 141:7). . . . In an interesting play on this metaphor, the Lord reverses the curse of the grave by "swallowing up death for ever" (Is 25:8 RSV; cf. 1 Cor 15:54–57). Here the grave is transformed into a profoundly positive symbol in which those who "die in Christ" are not in Hades but rather are united with Christ (Lk 23:43; 2 Cor 5:8; Phil 1:23). For the righteous, then, the grave becomes a symbol of ultimate hope.[4]

The grave is a fitting symbol of spiritual death, imprisonment, and bondage—from which Christ frees us through His Atonement and our faith in His ransom act.

APPLICATION AND ALLEGORIZATION

The most obvious application of this miracle is the truth that, because of Christ, we shall all live again: "If they be good, to the resurrection of endless life and happiness; and if they be evil, to the resurrection of endless damnation, being delivered up to the devil, who hath subjected them, which is damnation" (Mosiah 16:11).

Both Matthew and Mormon record that the dead that came forth from their graves at the time of Jesus's Resurrection appeared to many and, 3 Nephi informs us, "ministered" unto those to whom they appeared (3 Nephi 23:9). Latent in this miracle is the reality that those on the other side of the veil do at times minister to those of us who remain here in mortality. Often such ministrations are in association with temple work but, at other times, they may be for the purpose of comfort or direction. As a singular example, Parley P. Pratt described a visitation he received from his deceased wife, Thankful Halsey, while he was incarcerated in a Richmond, Missouri, prison during the 1838 extermination order:

> After some days of prayer and fasting, and seeking the Lord . . . I lay in silence, seeking and expecting an answer to my prayer, when suddenly I seemed carried away in the spirit, and . . . a personage from the world of spirits stood before me with a smile of compassion in every look, and pity mingled with the tenderest love and sympathy in every expression of the countenance. A soft hand seemed placed within my own, and a glowing cheek was laid in tenderness and warmth upon mine. A well known voice saluted me, which I readily recognized as that of the wife of my youth, who had for near two years been sweetly sleeping where the wicked cease from troubling and the weary are at rest. . . . She was sent to commune with me, and answer my question.[5]

In one of the most touching stories in his autobiography, Elder Pratt tells of how he learned through the ministration of his deceased wife that he would soon be released from the living nightmare he was then encountering. Though Parley encountered the wife of his youth— one who was yet a spirit awaiting the resurrection—the Prophet Joseph interacted with many resurrected beings (Moses, Elijah, John, Moroni), and they ministered to him as part of the restoration of all things. Of the deceased Saints, President Joseph F. Smith taught:

> Sometimes the Lord expands our vision from this point of view and this side of the veil, that we feel and seem to realize that we can look beyond the thin veil which separates us from that other sphere. . . . I have a feeling in my heart that I stand in the presence not only of the Father and of the Son, but in the presence of those whom God commissioned, raised up, and inspired, to lay the foundations of the work in which we are engaged. . . . So I feel quite confident that the eye of Joseph, the prophet, and of the martyrs of this dispensation, and of Brigham, and John, and Wilford, and those faithful men who were associated with them in their ministry upon the earth, are carefully

guarding the interests of the kingdom of God in which they labored and for which they strove during their mortal lives. I believe they are as deeply interested in our welfare today, if not with greater capacity, with far more interest, behind the veil, than they were in the flesh. . . . Surely those who have passed beyond, can see more clearly through the veil back here to us than it is possible for us to see to them from our sphere of action. I believe we move and have our being in the presence of heavenly messengers and of heavenly beings. . . . We are closely related to our kindred, to our ancestors, to our friends and associates and co-laborers who have preceded us into the spirit world. . . . Those who have been faithful, who have gone beyond, are still engaged in the work for the salvation of the souls of men, in the opening of the prison doors to them that are bound and proclaiming liberty to the captives. . . . They see us, they are solicitous for our welfare, they love us now more than ever. For now they see the dangers that beset us; they can comprehend better than ever before, the weaknesses that are liable to mislead us into dark and forbidden paths. They see the temptations and the evils that beset us in life, and the proneness of mortal beings to yield to temptation and to wrong doing [sic]; hence their solicitude for us and their love for us and their desire for our well being [sic] must be greater than that which we feel for ourselves.[6]

The miracle described in 3 Nephi 23 and Matthew 27 is a testament to the fact that angels *do* minister from the other side of the veil—doing God's bidding and accomplishing that which we cannot do for ourselves. Like the dead who rose with Jesus and ministered to many, our kindred dead minister on our behalf on the other side of the veil—aware of our needs, trials, and weaknesses and solicitous for our welfare.

In this miracle we can also find a message about the importance of holding sacred not just the prophecies and miracles of the past but those of our own day too. "Scriptures are valuable according to the truth they contain, not their relative age. Even Samuel's 'new' scriptures were important and must be recorded. . . . It is easy to think of the scriptures as ancient records; here, [Jesus] tells the Nephites that some scriptures are the words of the living oracles as well."[7] Perhaps Nephi's neglect was due not to his lack of reverence for prophetic utterance but to the tendency of many to cherish the printed words of the past while forgetting the paramount place of the words of the living prophets. It is easy to forget that words not bound in the standard works of the Church may actually take precedence over those that are.

Finally, this miracle reminds us of the ancient law of witnesses—well attested to in scripture (Deuteronomy 17:6; 19:15; Matthew 18:16; 2 Corinthians 13:1; 2 Nephi 27:14; Ether 5:4; D&C 6:28; 42:81; 128:3)—wherein we are promised that God will provide multiple attestations to salvific truths and events. Of Jesus's concern about the Nephites not recording the fulfillment of Samuel's words, one commentator suggested: "Apparently Jesus desired another witness of the resurrection so that his law of witnesses would be met."[8] While it matters little whether we are aware that others have seen or experienced the sacred, what does matter is that you and I (when we are privy to manifestations of the hand of God) record such things as we experience them. The Lord will determine later if our witness needs to come forth to support the testimony of others. However, it is not for us to worry about that. All that matters is this: when we recognize God working in and around us, we should record that sacred event and, where directed, bear testimony of it. Wilford Woodruff wrote:

> I have never spent any of my time more profitably for the benefit of mankind than in my Journal writing for a great portion of the Church History has been Compiled from my Journals and some of the most glorious Gospel Sermons truths and revelations that were given from God to this people through the mouth of the Prophets Joseph, Brigham, Heber and the Twelve Could not be found upon the Earth on record only in my Journals and they are Compiled in the Church History and transmitted to the Saints of God in all future Generations. Does not this pay me for my trouble? It does.[9]

Time and again you and I are witnesses to the sacred. How can we not hold these events and experiences as holy and worthy of note? How can we not preserve that which God has allowed us to learn and receive? Surely Nephi was mortified that such sacred things had been neglected by the leaders of the Lord's Church. Will you and I be any less ashamed if, upon the Judgment Day, the Lord asks us, "Where is the record of those holy and sacred experiences I sent you?" President Spencer W. Kimball opined that, as we make a record of the sacred events of our lives (and those we witness in the lives of others), perhaps "the angels may quote from it for eternity."[10]

NOTES

1. Some have debated as to whether the Nephite Twelve were Apostles or simply disciples of a higher order (since Jesus doesn't use the term *Apostle* in reference to them in the Book of Mormon). President Joseph Fielding Smith addressed this question: "While in every instance the Nephite Twelve are spoken of as disciples, the fact remains that they had been endowed with divine authority to be special witnesses for Christ among their own people. Therefore, they were virtually apostles to the Nephite race, although their jurisdiction was, as revealed to Nephi, eventually to be subject to the authority and jurisdiction of Peter and the Twelve chosen in Palestine. According to the definition prevailing in the world, an apostle is a witness for Christ, or one who evangelizes a certain nation or people, 'a zealous advocate of a doctrine or cause.' Therefore, in this sense the Nephite Twelve became apostles, as special witnesses, just as did Joseph Smith and Oliver Cowdery in the dispensation of the fulness of times" [Smith (1998), 3:158].

2. McConkie, Millet, Top (1992), 159. See also Nyman (2003–2004), 5:351. The fact that the Nephites would testify to Christ, "Yea, Lord, Samuel did prophesy according to thy words, and they were all fulfilled" (3 Nephi 23:10), indicates that some miraculous things had taken place on the Western Hemisphere, though for some reason they had neglected to record these events.

3. Gardner (2007), 5:553.

4. Ryken, Wilhoit, and Longman (1998), 349–50. From an LDS perspective, of course, the dead are initially in the spirit world—not yet in heaven [see Alma 40:11–15].

5. *Autobiography of Parley Parker Pratt*, 5th edition, Parley P. Pratt Jr., editor (Salt Lake City: Deseret Book, 1961), 238, 239.

6. Smith, *Gospel Doctrine* (1998), 430, 431. President Smith also said: "When messengers are sent to minister to the inhabitants of this earth, they are not strangers, but from the ranks of our kindred, friends, and fellow-beings and fellow-servants. . . . Our fathers and mothers, brothers, sisters and friends who have passed away from this earth, having been faithful, and worthy to enjoy these rights and privileges, many have a mission given them to visit their relatives and friends upon the earth again, bringing from the divine Presence messages of love, of warning, of reproof and instruction to those whom they had learned to love in the flesh" [Joseph F. Smith, *Journal of Discourses*, 22:351].

7. Gardner (2007), 5:553, 552.

8. Nyman (2003–2004), 5:351.

9. Wilford Woodruff, March 17, 1857, in *Wilford Woodruff's Journal*, nine volumes, Scott G. Kenney, editor (Midvale, UT: Signature Books, 1984), 5:37; irregular capitalization in original.

10. Kimball (1998), 351.

JESUS LOOSES *the* TONGUES *of the* CHILDREN

3 NEPHI 26:14, 16

THE MIRACLE

During His post-Resurrection ministry among the Nephites, Jesus taught and expounded to the multitude many great and important doctrines pertaining to the kingdom. "In the midst of this teaching, the Lord loosed the tongues" of the children that they did speak "great and marvelous things"—truths even greater than that which He had revealed to the adults (3 Nephi 26:14).

The multitude gathered did both see and hear children—"even babes"—speaking things so sacred that the people were forbidden to write them down (verse 16).

BACKGROUND

Mormon is silent on the context of the "great" and "marvelous" things these children spoke, primarily because he was forbidden to write them (verse 11). It may also be the case that he was not fully aware of all of the details of these miraculous events. If 3 Nephi 26:16 is to be taken literally, then even the great editor of the Book of Mormon received no record of their words. McConkie, Millet, and Top note,

> We are left to conjecture about their messages. Was the veil parted to allow them to speak of life in the first estate? Did they discourse upon life among the Gods in a celestial environment? Did they reveal doctrinal mysteries which today's world could not receive? Such an event

epitomizes that of which the prophet Joel prophesied, albeit of a later time: "And it shall come to pass afterward, that I will pour out my spirit upon all flesh; and your sons and daughters shall prophesy" (Joel 2:28; see also Alma 32:23.)[1]

Whatever it was that these little children said, those who were privileged to witness the outpouring were left with no doubt about its miraculous and humanly impossible nature. Ogden and Skinner suggested: "Verse 14 describes what can happen when all of God's people are spiritually prepared, worthy, and receptive—with no wicked distracting."[2]

In a November 1832 letter to W. W. Phelps, the Prophet Joseph wrote: "Oh Lord God, deliver us in thy due time from the little, narrow prison—almost as it were total darkness—of paper, pen, and ink, and a crooked and broken scattered and imperfect language."[3] In this same spirit, one commentary on this miracle suggests that the reason the people were forbidden to write the words of the children was "that mortal language could not adequately capture the true meaning and intent" of the words.[4] Perhaps; though there seems to be more behind this than that. The rites of the temple are sacred beyond words—and yet we use words to convey them, knowing that many will not fully grasp their meaning. One can only conjecture, but I suspect that some of the content of the words spoken by the children that day were of such a sacred nature that, while hearers might grasp them, some might also treat them in profane ways. Perhaps the Lord was simply seeking to keep the "pearls" away from the "swine" (3 Nephi 14:6; D&C 41:6; Matthew 7:6).

As Mormon's account stands, it appears that the children spoke "great" and "marvelous" things on both the second and third days of Jesus's visit to the Nephites. One commentator has suggested that perhaps the miraculous speaking only took place on the third day, and that Mormon started to mention it (3 Nephi 26:14) but then realized he needed to first point out that Christ had ascended at the end of the second day (verse 15), which then potentially gives the reader the impression that the speaking happened twice instead of just once.[5] This reading is certainly possible, but not necessarily provable. It may be that the children spoke on both days—though we have no way of telling for sure.[6]

SYMBOLIC ELEMENTS

In this miracle we are told that the "tongues" of the children—even those of the Nephite babies—were loosed that they might speak "great and marvelous things" (3 Nephi 26:14). "Just as the words uttered by the tongue are symbols, so too the word *tongue* occurs frequently with symbolic import."[7] The tongue is sometimes a symbol of "eloquence and wisdom."[8] The binding of the tongue, therefore, often represents the silencing of the individual and, thus, a loss of power and truth. Consequently, the loosing of the tongue carries the exact opposite meaning—denoting freedom, empowerment, and wisdom. And as the tongue is a fitting symbol for the whole person—one's "thoughts and attitudes"—the fact that these children spoke holy things is a doctrinal statement about the nature of children and their status before God.[9]

APPLICATION AND ALLEGORIZATION

Elder Neal A. Maxwell shared the following modern application of how little children can teach us divine truths, as they had in this miracle:

> Some time ago Nate, then just over three, said: "Mommy, there is another little girl who is supposed to come to our family. She has dark hair and dark eyes and lives a long way from here."
> The wise mother asked, "How do you know this?"
> "Jesus told me, upstairs."
> The mother noted, "We don't have an upstairs," but quickly sensed the significance of what had been communicated. After much travail and many prayers, the Barker family were in a sealing room in the Salt Lake Temple in the fall of 1995—where a little girl with dark hair and dark eyes, from Kazakhstan, was sealed to them for time and eternity. Inspired children still tell parents "great and marvelous things" (3 Ne. 26:14).[10]

As with the children of the Nephites, today the Lord still inspires His little ones with utterance beyond their own. Our children are one of the many ways in which the Lord speaks to us.

The Prophet Joseph indicated that the primary purpose of the gift of tongues was to preach the gospel to those who did not speak the preacher's same language—that they might hear the word of the Lord in their own tongue.[11] In a sense, the children in this miracle are manifesting a form of the gift of tongues. Even those too young to speak were given utterance, much as young missionaries are the recipients of the power to convey gospel truths in a tongue they do not personally have access to.

On a related note, Jesus can give us profundity beyond our own. Like these children who were inspired to speak that which they did not know, God often inspires His faithful followers with spiritual endowments beyond their own. President Marion G. Romney is said to have commented: "I always know when I am speaking under the inspiration of the Holy Ghost because I always learn something from what I've said."[12] God can do that for us, wherein He gives us knowledge, wisdom, and words that are not our own. "Open your mouths and they shall be filled" (D&C 33:8, 10). Compared to God, we are each spiritually children. But, like the Nephite infants who were given utterance, God can use us to speak "great and marvelous" truths the world needs to hear.

One commentary reports: "The conference lasted for three days, but the minutes of only two are given in detail."[13] Indeed, Jesus commanded that some of what He gave the Nephites be held back. Not all that was shared or experienced was to be recorded (3 Nephi 26:16). This element in the miracle reminds us of the need to keep sacred things sacred. A number of years ago I was at Church, wrapping up some of the responsibilities of my calling. A woman whom I did not know walked past and—recognizing me—said: "Do you want to hear a spiritual experience I had?" To which I replied, "No." Sacred things should be kept sacred, and only on rare occasions does the Spirit prompt us to share them with others. President Boyd K. Packer shared the following:

> Everywhere we go . . . we are often asked the question, "Have you seen the Lord? You are an Apostle. Have you seen the Lord?"
>
> I always have the same answer. I say that when I was called to the Twelve, I answered that question in a general conference. . . . In substance [I said] this: I have not asked that question of anyone. I have never asked that question of my Brethren. I know the answer, but I have never asked it, supposing that would be so sacred and so personal that it would be among the things that the Lord had in mind when He said, "It is given unto many to know the mysteries of God; nevertheless they are laid under a strict command that they shall not impart only

according to the portion of this word which he doth grant unto the children of men, according to the heed and diligence which they give unto him." [See Alma 12:9]

I bear witness that the Lord lives, that Jesus is the Christ. This I know. I know that He lives. I know that He directs this Church. Sometimes I wish that there were the authorization to say more, [to] say it plainer, but that is the way we say it.[14]

Jesus's reserve about recording the sacred is instructive. The Brethren exemplify this cautiousness about sacred and spiritual things. We should each follow their lead on this. If we desire for the Spirit to reveal sacred things to us, we need to be trustworthy of those things; we need to be the type of men and women who can keep those experiences and impressions to ourselves. The Prophet Joseph said: "The reason we do not have the secrets of the Lord revealed unto us, is because we do not keep them but reveal them."[15] As we learn to keep the sacred secret, the Lord will open the windows of heaven and reveal to us many important and precious things.

NOTES

1. McConkie, Millet, and Top (1992), 172. Ogden and Skinner similarly wrote: "The children's tongues were 'loosed,' apparently speaking things beyond their mortal years, possibly penetrating the veil, using the language of God, and revealing 'great and marvelous things' about the premortal life and even the post-mortal life—things even greater than what Jesus had taught these righteous disciples" [Ogden and Skinner (2011), 2:220].

2. Ogden and Skinner (2011), 2:220.

3. Joseph Smith to W. W. Phelps, 27 November, 1832, in Godfrey, et al (2013), 320; spelling and punctuation standardized.

4. See McConkie, Millet, and Top (1992), 172.

5. See Gardner (2007), 5:572.

6. See M. Gawain Wells, "The Savior and the Children in 3 Nephi," in *Journal of Book of Mormon Studies*, Volume 14, Number 1 (2005), 64.

7. Ryken, Wilhoit, and Longman (1998), 875.

8. See Tresidder (2000), 17.

9. See Ryken, Wilhoit, and Longman (1998), 876.

10. Neal A. Maxwell, "Becometh As a Child," *Ensign*, May 1996, 69–70.

11. See Dahl and Cannon (1998), 670–71.

12. Marion G. Romney, quoted in Boyd K. Packer, *Teach Ye Diligently* (Salt Lake City: Deseret Book, 1979), 304.

13. Reynolds and Sjodahl (1955–1961), 7:208.

14. Packer (2008), 579.
15. Joseph Smith, in Smith (1976), 194.

JESUS HEALS *All* MANNER *of* AFFLICTIONS

3 NEPHI 26:15

THE MIRACLE

While the details of this series of miracles are not given, we are informed that Jesus healed the sick, the lame, those who were blind or deaf, and even the dead (bringing one man back to life).[1]

BACKGROUND

The text is not entirely clear as to whether these miraculous healings happened on both the first and second day, or only on the first one. 3 Nephi 17:7–9 explicitly refers to many healing miracles on day one of Jesus's visit. It appears that 3 Nephi 26:15 is referencing miracles He performed on the second day of His Nephite ministry.[2]

SYMBOLIC ELEMENTS

Healing the physically sick (whether lame, deaf, blind, or dumb), though real, is often employed as a metaphor—particularly in the New Testament—for healing those who are spiritually ill.[3] Likewise, raising one from the dead is frequently seen as a representation of how Christ and His Church can resuscitate even those who are suffering from spiritual death.[4]

APPLICATION AND ALLEGORIZATION

This miracle reminds us of the reality that, according to our faith *and His will,* Jesus can heal all manner of physical afflictions. Stories abound in the Church of such healing miracles, wherein the Lord, through His servants, has healed the sick. As a singular example, we offer this experience from the life of William D. Huntington (as reported by Joseph Curtis):

> In Nauvoo he lived in the family of and worked for Joseph Smith at the time . . . when nearly everybody was stricken down and he himself was among the afflicted, and was one of those who were healed by Joseph. He . . . had been sick some weeks and kept getting weaker, until he became so helpless that he could not move. Finally he got so low he could not speak. . . . He saw friends come to the bedside, look at him a moment and commence weeping, then turn away. . . .
>
> Observing his situation [he] found that he was in the upper part of the room near the ceiling, and could see the body he had occupied lying on the bed, with weeping friends, standing around as he had witnessed in many cases where people had died under his own observation.
>
> About this time he saw Joseph Smith and two other brethren come into the room. . . . They stepped to the bed and laid their hands upon the head of his body, which at that time looked loathsome to him, and as the three stretched out their hands to place them upon the head, he by some means became aware that he must go back into that body, and started to do so. The process of getting in he could not remember; but when Joseph said "amen," he heard and could see and feel with his body. . . .
>
> As soon as the brethren had taken their hands from his head he raised up in bed, sitting erect, and in another moment turned his legs off the bed. . . .
>
> Joseph asked him if he had not better be careful, for he was very weak. He replied, "I never felt better in my life," almost immediately adding, "I want my pants." . . .
>
> Then he signified his intention to sit in a chair at or near the fireplace. Joseph took hold of his arm to help him along safely, but William declared his ability to walk alone, notwithstanding which, the help continued.
>
> Astonishment had taken the place of weeping throughout the room. Every looker-on was ready to weep for joy; but none were able or felt inclined to talk.
>
> Presently William said he wanted something to eat. Joseph asked him what he would like, and he replied that he wanted a dish of bread and milk.
>
> Emma immediately brought what he called for, as one may easily

comprehend, every hand was anxious to supply the wants of a man who, a few moments before was dead, really and truly dead! Brother Huntington ate the bowl of bread and milk with as good a relish as any he ever ate. . . .

Joseph . . . remarked that they had just witnessed as great a miracle as Jesus did while on the earth. They had seen the dead brought to life.

At the close of his narrative to me William Huntington remarked: "Now I have told you the truth, and here I am a live man, sitting by the side of you on this log, and I testify that Joseph Smith was a Prophet of God."[5]

William Huntington was quite literally raised from the dead. This miracle is a profound testament to the powers of the priesthood. That being said, this life is not about surviving *this life*. As beautiful as stories like these are, much more important than physical healing is the healing of the spirit. While Jesus can certainly heal our bodies—even to the extent of raising the dead—He can also heal us spiritually. He can heal the sin-sick, the spiritually lame (or inactive), the doctrinally deaf and blind, even the spiritually dead. Just as Jesus healed all manner of diseases among the Nephites, He can heal whatever ails you and me—and He cares most deeply about those diseases of the soul that keep us from being worthy of His companionship.

NOTES

1. The reference to raising "a man from the dead" in this verse could be an allusion to the miracle associated with Nephi's brother Timothy.

2. See, for example, Ogden and Skinner (2011), 2:221. While it is certainly possible that 3 Nephi 26:15 is saying that Jesus performed these miracles on the second day, just before He ascended, not all commentators perceive the verse as saying that.

3. See Ryken, Wilhoit, and Longman (1998), 99, 197–98, 209–10. This is not to suggest that those whom Jesus healed in this miracle were "spiritually dead." Indeed, the fact that they survived the destructions recorded is evidence that they were spiritually well—at least to the degree that any of us fallen sinners can be considered such.

4. See Ryken, Wilhoit, and Longman (1998), 198–99.

5. Levi Curtis, "Recollections of the Prophet Joseph Smith," in Juvenile Instructor, Volume 27, Number 12 (June 15, 1892): 385–86. See also Trevan G. Hatch, *Visions, Manifestations and Miracles of the Restoration* (Orem, UT: Granite Publishing, 2008), 90–91.

THE THREE NEPHITES
Are TRANSLATED

3 NEPHI 28
4 NEPHI 1:32–34

THE MIRACLE

Jesus had been teaching the Nephites for three days. After informing them of what they should call the Church, teaching them about
His Atonement, encouraging them to preach repentance and baptism,
and urging them to be even as He is, the Lord turned His attention to
the Twelve.

Jesus asked them "one by one" what they desired of Him (3 Nephi
28:1). Nine of the Twelve asked for the blessing that, once they had
finished their lives, they could "speedily come unto" Christ in His
"kingdom" (3 Nephi 28:2). The Lord promised them that their earnest
desires would be granted and, at the age of seventy-two, they would
pass from this life and find rest in His kingdom.

Though nine of the Twelve were quite open about their wishes,
three of the Nephite Apostles did not respond to Jesus's query. They
were, perhaps, embarrassed about what it was they wished from Him.
They "sorrowed in their hearts, for they durst not speak unto him
the thing which they desired" (3 Nephi 28:5). But Jesus knew their
thoughts. He knew that, like John the Beloved, these three wanted to
be translated so that they could remain upon the earth, preaching and
teaching the people about Christ and His gospel.

Jesus promised the three Nephite Apostles that their wish would be granted and, like John, they would remain—in an altered state—until the Judgment Day.

BACKGROUND

The doctrine of translation is one of the most intriguing and uniquely LDS beliefs. Of these quasi-immortal beings, the Prophet Joseph Smith taught:

> Now the doctrine of translation is a power which belongs to this Priesthood. . . . Many have supposed that the doctrine of translation was a doctrine whereby men were taken immediately into the presence of God, and into an eternal fullness, but this is a mistaken idea. Their place of habitation is that of the terrestrial order. . . . [They are] held in reserve to be ministering angels unto many planets. . . . Translation obtains deliverance from the tortures and sufferings of the body, but their existence will prolong as to the labors and toils of the ministry.[1]

In concert with Joseph's statement, 3 Nephi 28 expounds upon the doctrine of translated beings. We learn there a number of things about their nature, powers, and the promises made to them. Among other things, we are informed

- They will never experience death or its accompanying pains (3 Nephi 28:7–8).[2]

- They will experience no pain or sorrow—except for the sins of the world (3 Nephi 28:9).

- Their calling and election is made sure, and thus, they have the promise of eternal life (3 Nephi 28:10).[3]

- They cannot be retained against their will (3 Nephi 28:19).

- They cannot be harmed by man or beast (3 Nephi 28:21–22).

- They can show themselves to whomever they choose (3 Nephi 28:30).

- Satan has no power to tempt them (3 Nephi 28:39).

- Their state of translation will last until Christ's return (3 Nephi 28:40).[4]

As a point of clarification, the promise that they will remain translated until the Judgment Day does not apply to those beings translated prior to Christ's Resurrection. Elder Bruce R. McConkie explained: "Those who were translated before the resurrection of our Lord 'were with Christ in his resurrection.' (D. & C. 133:55.) Those who have been translated since the resurrection of Christ shall continue to live as mortals until the Second Coming when they shall receive their immortal glory. It will be resurrected, not translated beings, who shall return with the city of Enoch."[5]

Many Saints have been translated throughout the history of the Church. Of course, it would be impossible to create an exhaustive list of all those who have experienced this change. But, among others, we know of the following translated beings: Moses[6] (Alma 45:19); Elijah[7] (2 Kings 2); Alma the Younger[8] (Alma 45:18–19); Nephi,[9] the son of Helaman (3 Nephi 1:2–3; 2:9); John the Beloved (D&C 7; John 21:22–23); Enoch, and his city (Moses 7:21); Melchizedek, and his city (*JST* Genesis 14:32–34); the three Nephite disciples; and many "holy men that ye know not of" (D&C 49:8).[10]

President Harold B. Lee noted that he had wondered why God, in His infinite wisdom, had made translated beings part of the plan.[11] President Lee indicated that his question was answered in a statement made by President J. Reuben Clark Jr., of the First Presidency:

> President Clark said something that startled some folks years ago. He said, "It is my faith that the gospel plan has always been here, that His priesthood has always been here, that His priesthood has been here on the earth, and that it will continue to be so until the end comes." When that conference session was over there were many who said, "My goodness, doesn't President Clark realize that there have been periods of apostasy following each dispensation of the gospel?"
>
> I walked over to the Church Office Building with President Joseph Fielding Smith and he said, "I believe there has never been a moment of time since the creation but what there has been someone holding the priesthood on the earth to hold Satan in check." And then I thought of . . . the three Nephites. Why were they translated and permitted to tarry? For what purpose? An answer was suggested when I heard President Smith, whom we have considered one of our well-informed theologians, make the above statement. . . . These individuals were translated for a purpose known to the Lord. There is no question but what they were here.[12]

In 3 Nephi 19:4 we are given the names of the original Nephite Twelve: Nephi, Timothy, Jonas (the son of Timothy), Mathoni, Mathonihah, Kumen, Kumenonhi, Jeremiah, Shemnon, Jonas, Zedekiah, and Isaiah. Three of these men became the famed Three Nephites. Mormon informs us: "Behold, I was about to write the names of those who were never to taste of death, but the Lord forbade; therefore I write them not, for they are hid from the world. But behold, I have seen them, and they have ministered unto me" (3 Nephi 28:25–26). Nearly two millennia later, Oliver B. Huntington, an early Latter-day Saint, wrote the following entry in his journal (on February 16, 1895): "I am willing to state that the names of the 3 Nephites who do not sleep in the earth are Jeremiah, Zedekiah and Kumenonhi."[13] While Huntington often attributes such tidbits—which his journal is sprinkled with—to Joseph Smith, in this case he offers no source for this curious insight.

In 3 Nephi 28:13–14 we learn that the three translated Nephite Apostles were "caught up into heaven, and saw and heard unspeakable things" of which they were "forbidden" to speak. Elder Franklin D. Richards explained,

> He took them into the heavens and endowed them with the power of translation, probably in one of Enoch's temples, and brought them back to the earth. Thus they received power to live until the coming of the Son of Man. I believe He took them to Enoch's city and gave them their endowments there. I expect that in the city of Enoch there are temples; and when Enoch and his people come back, they will come back with their city, their temples, blessings and powers. . . . It is a good thing to take a glimpse once in a while into, and contemplate the glories of the future.[14]

Elder Richards's insight is interesting, to say the least, particularly in light of the Prophet Joseph's declaration that those who are sent out to proclaim the gospel—and the Three Nephites would spend the next 2,000 years proclaiming the gospel—need an endowment first.[15] In support of Elder Richards's view, one commentator pointed out: "Mormon explains that they did not speak of that heavenly experience, lending support to the hypothesis that it was preparation for their mission, not part of the message they would impart."[16]

Stories of appearances of the Three Nephites abound in the early

Church. Volumes have been written about them and latter-day encounters with them.[17] One expert on LDS folklore wrote:

> The basic structure of these stories seems to be this: someone has a problem; a stranger appears; the stranger solves the problem; the stranger miraculously disappears. A story may have more to it than this, but it must have these features. Any account that is taken into the Nephite cycle will be adjusted (probably unconsciously) to fit the pattern. The remarkable disappearance is particularly interesting. I see no compelling reason why the Nephites must disappear. In Book of Mormon times they were thrown into prison, dens of wild beasts, and into furnaces, and in none of these instances did they solve their problems by disappearing. But in the modern stories, they vanish from the back seats of speeding cars; they vaporize before one's eyes; or they walk away and someone later tracing their footsteps in the snow finds that they abruptly end. The Nephites disappear, I believe, because the story requires it. The disappearance is the climax toward which the narrative builds, overshadowing in many instances the kindly deeds the Nephites came to perform in the first place.[18]

Acknowledging that Latter-day Saints have sometimes embellished details, one commentator noted: "It is important to remember . . . that while there is certainly folklore concerning the Three Nephites, that fact does not mean that the Three Nephites *are* folklore."[19] Monte Nyman suggested: "Each story should be tested by the purpose given in the Third Nephi account; does the incident bring souls to Christ?"[20] (3 Nephi 28:9).

Symbolic Elements

Death is frequently seen as a symbol of sin, spiritual sickness, a person's unsaved state, and a lack of receptivity to the things of the Spirit.[21] Thus, the promise that the translated Nephites will not taste of death can be seen as a representation of how they would be preserved from sin, damnation, and the spirit of the adversary.

From a more general perspective, it seems that Mormon uses the Three Nephite disciples to develop a motif that would be common in the sacred text.

> Mormon begins a series of references to incidents in the lives of the three that parallel scriptural stories of deliverance. From his perspective,

some four hundred years later, these events (3 Nephi 28:19–22) have been made into super-history, stories of the three that place them in the context of scriptural miracles. They are stories that, regardless of the events they describe, have been phrased in language that makes the correlation to scripture clear. The message is the complete righteousness and power of these three special emissaries. It appears that the tendency of the Three Nephites to enter into a community's active lore has a long history.[22]

This same source gives examples of this motif making, such as how the casting of the three translated beings into pits recalls the mistreatment of Joseph of Egypt at the hands of his resentful brothers (Genesis 37:23–24), or how the Nephite three were protected when cast into a fire, much like Shadrach, Meshach, and Abed-nego (Daniel 3:16–26). When the three are cast into a den of wild beast but are preserved, we are reminded of the story of Daniel in the lions' den (Daniel 6:16).[23]

APPLICATION AND ALLEGORIZATION

The doctrine of translation is not a symbol but a theological reality. Nevertheless, in it we see a type for what God seeks to do in each of us. Metaphorically, God can translate or change us (3 Nephi 28:37–38), as He did the Three Nephites, so that we do not sorrow or feel pain, save it be for the sins of the world. And like the three Nephite Apostles, we too can be preserved from our enemies (verses 19–22). As in this miracle, our joy can also be full as we become "even as He is." Of course, each of these changes—these transfigurations—requires the exercise of our faith (Ether 12:17). But it is God's will, His earnest desire, that all of His children believe so fully in Him (and in His plan) that pains are alleviated, protection is enabled, and joy is achieved. Of course, we are the ones who determine the realization of these blessings.

On a related note, just as the Nephite Apostles' change was not full—but a fuller change would come in the future (verses 39–40)—so also our change or divine development will not be full here in mortality. Each of us struggles to repent, improve, develop, and live a holy and faithful life. But like the Three Nephites, who awaited a full and permanent change at the coming of Christ, you and I will never achieve in mortality a full measure of our spiritual potential. However, like the three, if we hold out faithful here, in the next life we will be like Him, for His grace will be sufficient to make it so (2 Corinthians 12:9–10; Ether 12:27).

The Lord's promise that the Nephite Twelve will not "taste of death" (3 Nephi 28:7) reminds us of the beautiful promise made to all who are faithful to covenants: "And it shall come to pass that those that die in me shall not taste of death, for it shall be sweet unto them" (D&C 42:46). For some this promise is fulfilled through a painless passing from this world to the next. For others, because of their faith in the great plan of happiness (Alma 42:8), death is "sweet" because they know that it is the gate to the next stage of existence—to that better world we all seek and anticipate. And so, though they may suffer, that suffering is tempered and "sweet" because it certainly leads to exaltation in the celestial kingdom of their God.

As in the miracle where Jesus "loosed the tongues of the children" (3 Nephi 26:14, 16), here also we find emphasized the principle of keeping sacred things sacred. President Brigham Young taught:

> If a person understands God and godliness . . . and the Lord reveals anything to that individual, no matter what, unless He gives permission to disclose it, it is locked up in eternal silence. And when persons have proven to their messengers that their bosoms are like the lock-ups of eternity, then the Lord says, *I can reveal anything to them, because they never will disclose it until I tell them to.*[24]

During this miracle, the three Nephite Apostles learned sacred things and had hallowed experiences. But, in accordance with the command of Christ (3 Nephi 28:16) and the dictates of the Holy Spirit, they locked those things tightly in their bosom. The Lord needs to see in us this kind of sensitivity to the sacred, or He will not reveal to us all that He is willing and able to impart.

NOTES

1. See Ehat and Cook (1980), 41–42; see also Smith, in Smith (1976), 170–71.
2. Regarding translated beings never dying, note the following quotations: "Death [is a] separation of body and spirit (1 Cor. 15; Alma 11:37–46; 12:12–18)" [McConkie (1979), 637]. "Translated bodies cannot enter into rest until they have undergone a change equivalent to death" [Smith, in Smith (1976), 190]. "In the case of translated beings and the righteous persons who shall live during the millennial era, death and the resurrection shall take place instantaneously. They shall be changed from

mortality to immortality in the twinkling of an eye, the spirit never having occasion to separate from the body, and in their cases this change is called death. (D. & C. 63:49–52; 3 Ne. 28.) But it is not death according to the most common usage of the word (D. & C. 101:29–31; Isa. 65:20.)" [McConkie (1979), 185]. "All translated beings undergo another change in their bodies when they gain full immortality. This change is the equivalent of a resurrection" [McConkie (1982), 644]. "At the conclusion of his mortal life, Elijah was translated; that is, he experienced some type of change from mortality without experiencing mortal death" [Franklin D. Day, "Elijah," in Daniel H. Ludlow, editor, *Encyclopedia of Mormonism*, four volumes (New York: Macmillan, 1992), 2:450]. "Translated beings . . . escape the normal process of death. . . . When their ministries as translated beings have been completed, in a 'twinkling of an eye' they experience a change equivalent to death, as they go from a translated state to a resurrected state" [Clyde Williams, in Largey (2003), 758]. "These [translated beings] have to pass through a change equivalent to that of death; notwithstanding their translation from the earth, a certain change has to be wrought upon them that is equivalent to death, and probably equivalent also to the resurrection of the dead" [Orson Pratt, *Journal of Discourses*, 17:149–50]. "Will translated beings ever die? Remember John's enigmatic words relative to his own translation: 'Then went this saying abroad among the brethren, that that disciple should not die: yet Jesus said not unto him, He shall not die; but, If I will that he tarry till I come, what is that to thee?' (John 21:23.) Note the distinction between avoiding death as such and living till the Lord comes. Then note that Jesus promises the Three Nephites, not that they shall not die, but that they 'shall never taste of death' and shall not 'endure the pains of death.' Again it is an enigmatic declaration with a hidden meaning. There is a distinction between death as we know it and tasting of death or enduring the pains of death. As a matter of doctrine, death is universal; every mortal thing, whether plant or animal or man, shall surely die. Jacob said: 'Death hath passed upon all men, to fulfil the merciful plan of the great Creator.' (2 Ne. 9:6.) There are no exceptions, not even among translated beings. Paul said: 'As in Adam all die, even so in Christ shall all be made alive.' (1 Cor. 15:22.) Again the dominion of death over all is acclaimed. But the Lord says of all his saints, not that they will not die, but that 'those that die in me shall not taste of death, for it shall be sweet unto them; And they that die not in me, wo unto them, for their death is bitter.' (D&C 42:46–47.) The distinction is between dying as such and tasting of death itself. Again the Lord says: 'He that liveth when the Lord shall come, and hath kept the faith, blessed is he; nevertheless, it is appointed to him to die at the age of man. Wherefore, children shall grow up until they become old; old men shall die; but they shall not sleep in the dust, but they shall be changed in the twinkling of an eye.' (D&C 63:50–51.) Thus, this change from mortality to immortality, though almost instantaneous, is both a death and a resurrection. Thus, translated beings do not suffer death as we normally define it, meaning the separation of body and spirit; nor do they receive a resurrection as we ordinarily describe it, meaning that the body rises from the dust and the spirit enters again into its fleshly home. But they do pass through death and are changed from mortality to immortality, in the eternal sense, and they thus both die and are resurrected in the eternal sense. This, we might add, is why Paul wrote: 'Behold, I shew you a mystery; We shall not all sleep, but we shall all be changed, In a moment, in the twinkling of an eye, at the last trump: for the trumpet shall sound, and the dead shall be raised incorruptible, and we shall be changed.' (1 Cor. 15:51–52.)" [McConkie (1980–1981), 4:389–90]. "Latter-day Saint scriptures speak of a unique class of beings, persons whom the Lord has 'translated' or changed from a mortal state to one in which they are temporarily not subject to death, and in which they experience neither pain nor sorrow except for the sins of the world. Such beings appear to have much greater power than mortals. All translated beings will eventually experience physical death and resurrection (MD, p. 807–808). Translation is a necessary condition in special instances to further the work of the Lord. Translated beings are not resurrected beings, though all translated beings either have since been or yet will be resurrected or 'changed in the twinkling of an eye' to a resurrected state (3 Ne. 28:8). In effect, this last change is their death, and they therefore receive what amounts to an instantaneous death and resurrection" [Mark L. McConkie, in Ludlow (1992), 4:1485].

3. See Clyde J. Williams, "The Three Nephites and the Doctrine of Translation," in Monte S. Nyman and Charles D. Tate Jr., editors, *The Book of Mormon: 3 Nephi 9–30, This Is My Gospel* (Provo, UT: Brigham Young University Religious Studies Center, 1993), 242–43.

4. See McConkie, Millet, and Top (1992), 190, 192.

5. McConkie (1979), 807. See also McConkie, Millet, and Top (1992), 190. Elder McConkie added: "Enoch and his city were all translated and taken up into heaven without tasting death. So also were Moses and Elijah and Alma and many others of whom we have no record. Indeed the whole focus of life among the worthy saints from the day of Enoch to the day of Abraham was so to live that they would be caught up and receive an inheritance in that city whose builder and maker was God. All these were with Christ in his resurrection; that is, they received their resurrected and immortal bodies at that time. John the Revelator and the Three Nephites and others whose identity is unknown have been translated since the day of Christ. They are all carrying on their ministries of preaching and prophesying and will do so until the Second Coming, when they will receive their resurrected and immortal bodies" [McConkie (1982), 647].

6. See Josephus, *Antiquities of the Jews*, Book 4, Chapter 8, Verse 48; Clement of Alexandria, *Stromata*, Book 6, Chapter 15, in Roberts and Donaldson (1994), 2:511; Clement of Alexandria, *Fragments from Cassiodorus*, Chapter 2, in Roberts and Donaldson (1994), 2:573; Ginzburg (1967–1969), 6:166n960, 6:162n951; Philo of Alexandria, "On the Birth of Abel and the Sacrifices offered by Him and by His brother Cain," 3:8–10, in C. D. Yonge, translator, *The Works of Philo: Complete and Unabridged* (Peabody, Massachusetts: Hendrickson Publishers, 1997), 94–95.

7. McConkie (1979), 223.

8. Smith (1993), 5:38.

9. McConkie, Millet, and Top (1992), 4:4.

10. McConkie (1979), 806; McConkie (1987–1988), 1:396–97; McConkie and Ostler (2000), 376.

11. Harold B. Lee, cited in Ludlow, Pinegar, Allen, Otten, and Caldwell (2007), 463.

12. Lee (1998), 485–86.

13. See Oliver B. Huntington, *Typescript of the Diary of Oliver B. Huntington*, two volumes (Salt Lake City: Utah State Historical Society, no date given), 2:377; see also Ogden Kraut, *The Three Nephites*, third edition (Salt Lake City: Pioneer Press, 1993), 30.

14. Franklin D. Richards, in *Journal of Discourses*, 25:236–37.

15. Smith, in Smith (1976), 91.

16. Gardner (2007), 5:589.

17. See, for example, Hector Lee, *The Three Nephites The Substance and Significance of the Legend in Folklore* (New Mexico: The University of New Mexico Press, 1949); Bruce E. Dana, *The Three Nephites and other Translated Beings* (Springville, UT: Bonneville, 2003); Douglas and Jewell Beardall, *About the Three Nephites* (Provo, UT: LDS Book Publications, 1992); Kraut (1993).

18. William A. Wilson, "The Paradox of Mormon Folklore," in *BYU Studies,* Volume 17, Number 1 (Autumn 1976), 42.

19. Gardner (2007), 5:586. See also Nyman (2003–2004), 5:411.

20. Nyman (2003–2004), 5:411.

21. See Wilson (1999), 111, 112.

22. Gardner (2007), 5:590.

23. See Gardner (2007), 5:590–91. Mormon can't be drawing on the book of Daniel as his source for these parallels, since it was not written until after Lehi left Jerusalem and, therefore, would not appear on the brass plates. Thus, the parallels are either coincidental or Mormon is being inspired to tell the stories in such a way that the parallels will be evident to latter-day readers, even if those in Mormon's day would not see them.

24. Brigham Young, in Van Wagoner (2009), 3:1243–44; emphasis added.

THE NEPHITES BRING
to PASS MIRACLES *in the*
NAME *of the* LORD

4 NEPHI 1:5

THE MIRACLE

In the years immediately after the visit of Christ to the Nephites, the Church grew in strength and "the people were all converted unto the Lord" (4 Nephi 1:2). They lived a law akin to the united order, holding "all things common among them" (verse 3), and thus all were blessed and provided for, and peace reigned in the land.

The twelve disciples Jesus appointed to serve in the apostolic office performed "great and marvelous works" among the people (verse 5), healing the sick, raising the dead, enabling the lame to walk, the blind to receive their sight, and the deaf their hearing. All kinds of miracles were had among the people—and in nothing did they work miracles except "in the name of Jesus Christ" (verse 5).

BACKGROUND

In the book of 4 Nephi, Mormon offers us an abridgement of the plates of Nephi from around the end of AD 34 to the end of AD 320, a period of about two hundred and eighty-six years. His abridgement of nearly three centuries of history is a total of four pages in length. Thus, more than a quarter of the thousand-year-plus history of Lehi and his posterity is covered in a small, four-page book.[1]

Of the Nephites during these "golden years" of their existence, we learn "surely there could not be a happier people among all the people who had been created by the hand of God" (4 Nephi 1:16). One commentator pointed out, "The small, one-chapter book of 4 Nephi . . . briefly describes the most glorious, happy, progressive, and enlightened time in all the combined Jaredite, Nephite, and Lamanite civilizations."[2] Without question, this period in the history of the Nephites was their "Zion" period. Righteousness reigned and blessings were poured down upon them. No other period in Nephite history was more glorious than this—because of the faithfulness of the people.[3]

SYMBOLIC ELEMENTS

Physical healing, in any form, often serves as a symbol for God's power to cure us of our spiritual ills.[4] Miracles such as healing the sick or raising the dead frequently serve as a representation of how Christ and His Church can resuscitate even the most sin-sick soul.[5]

The fact that the Nephite Apostles imitate the acts and miracles of Christ serves as a reminder of the source of the authority by which they operate, and whose power ultimately performs the miracle. They act "in the name of Jesus Christ" (verse 5), and thus, all holiness they bring to pass is attributed to Him and is the result of His operation in and through them.

APPLICATION AND ALLEGORIZATION

When Peter healed the lame man at the Beautiful Gate (Acts 3:1–11), it was evident that the mantle of Christ had fallen upon him. That healing was the first of Peter's miracles in the post-Ascension era, and it evidenced that he was now the presiding prophet—performing the miracles Christ had once performed.[6] Similarly, in the description in 4 Nephi we see the new Nephite Apostles doing the things Jesus had done before them (see 3 Nephi 26:15). With Jesus now gone, the Apostles of the Western Hemisphere received of His mantle and engaged in His works.

Just as the Nephite disciples worked miracles in the name of Christ, we too can work miracles in the name of Christ. All we do should be "in the name of Christ," acting *in* His name but also *as* He would. Being a true Christian requires that we live a Christian life. If we "act" in His name but are not Christlike in our demeanor, then we may do more damage than good—and we will certainly be accountable for the miracles we should have done but did not do because of the way we lived and acted toward others.

> We are the servants of the Lord, who is our Master, and he has commanded us to labor in his fields—plowing, sowing, cultivating, and harvesting. That is, we are the *agents* of the Lord, who is our *eternal principal*, and he has empowered us to represent him and do the things he would do if he were personally present. When we do all things in his name in righteousness, it means that we put ourselves in his place and stead, that we think and speak and act as he would in the same situation. It means we live our lives as though we were the one whose blessed name we bear. Our acts become his acts—they are done in his name.[7]

"What manner of men ought ye to be?" Jesus asked. "Verily I say unto you, even as I am" (3 Nephi 27:27). Our lives must reflect the message we bear. One of the things that results in the most and best converts is the lives of the members of the Church. Those who live as they should get noticed by others—and this facilitates conversion. President Gordon B. Hinckley said the most "meaningful expression of our faith" should be "the lives of our people."[8]

> We cannot hope to influence others in the direction of virtue unless we live lives of virtue. The example of our living will carry a greater influence than will all the preaching in which we might indulge. We cannot expect to lift others unless we stand on higher ground ourselves. . . .
>
> The most persuasive gospel tract is the exemplary life of a faithful Latter-day Saint. . . .
>
> If we as a people will walk with integrity, will be honest and moral in our actions, will put into our lives the simple and basic and wonderful principles of the Golden Rule, others will be led to inquire and learn. . . .
>
> Beginning with you and me, there can be an entire people who, by the virtue of our lives in our homes, in our vocations, even in our amusements, can become as a city upon a hill to which men may look and learn, and an ensign to the nations from which the people of the earth may gather strength.[9]

There can be no situational ethics. We are called to be Latter-day Saints, not Latter-day Sinners. Too many of our people have their Church behaviors and ethics and then separate behaviors for work and home. There must be only one you—the Christian one, who lives, acts, and loves as Christ did. If we are to work miracles "in the name of Christ," we must always be worthy of that name.

The introduction to 4 Nephi declares: "And it came to pass in the thirty and sixth year, the people were all converted unto the Lord, upon all the face of the land" (4 Nephi 1:2). The greatest miracle is the miracle of conversion and consequent change.[10] Just as the Nephites worked to convert "all . . . unto the Lord" (verse 2), you and I have a duty to share and convert those around us. We are reminded of the oft-quoted passage from the eighteenth section of the Doctrine and Covenants: "And if it so be that you should labor all your days in crying repentance unto this people, and bring, save it be one soul unto me, how great shall be your joy with him in the kingdom of my Father!" (D&C 18:15). So often we teach that that "one soul" is likely you! We seek first to convert ourselves—changing our hearts so that we love that which God loves and we reject that which God rejects. Once we are converted, our hearts naturally turn to others and their needs; and then the miracle can spread. The Nephites who were firmly converted to Christ healed the sick; and we are each called to help heal the spiritually sick whom God places around us. Just as they raised the dead, we can help bring back to spiritual life those who have lost their testimonies or commitment to Christ and His Church. Just as they caused the lame to walk, we can help those who are paralyzed with fears or inabilities to take steps toward God, service in the Church, success in life, and so on. Just as they caused the blind to see, we can be instruments in helping those who are too blind to see the truth overcome that blindness and see things as they really are. Just as they caused the deaf to hear, we can help those who have refused to hear the message of the restored gospel change their hearts and open up their ears to hear the word.

One of the beauties of the book of 4 Nephi is the description of the spirituality of the people. In those opening verses we read of a society that had largely overcome the world through their faith in Christ and their obedience to His ways.

> The salient reason given for the lengthy period of peace and happiness among the Nephites after Jesus' ministry was the absence of contention. The phrase 'no contention' is repeated in verses 2, 13, 15, and

18. . . . Other reasons for the peaceful, friction-free life include the following: "They had all things common among them." . . . They were living the law of consecration. "Every man [was] seeking the interest of his neighbor, and doing all things with an eye single to the glory of God" (D&C 82:19).[11]

The world in which we live has so much potential for good. We have sufficient resources to bless all of mankind. We have the intellectual capacity to create nearly anything we need to solve technological gaps, poverty, disease, concerns about energy, and more. We really do live in a remarkable time with unbelievable resources at our fingertips. If we use all with which we have been blessed, a Zionic society will reign. If we act in selfishness, then suffering will continue. One may argue, "But there is simply no way to get the *entire world* on board. Most will always choose mediocrity, or self-serving behaviors over selflessness and self-sacrifice." While that is most certainly true, it also doesn't matter. Zion is "the pure in heart" (D&C 97:21). The emphasis must be on the word *in*—"pure *in* heart" (see also Moses 7:18). Zion is to be found, not in a world that obeys (for that is a distant ideal), but in a heart that obeys. If my heart is right, I will find Zion. If my heart is right, I will have peace. If my heart is right, I will experience healing. And if my heart is right, my joy will be full. Just as the Nephite spirituality brought the people Zion, as you and I heighten our personal spirituality, Zion will be realized. It may only be in our state, our city, our neighborhood, our ward, or our family—but it will be realized. Whenever Zion exists upon the earth, it is because the individual hearts of its members are pure. It is never because the nation or city is right with God. It is always because the individual is right with God.[12] Let us, like those of 4 Nephi, build Zion—one heart at a time!

NOTES

1. See Nyman (2003–2004), 6:1.
2. Ogden and Skinner (2011), 2:228.
3. See Byron R. Merrill, "There Was No Contention," in Monte S. Nyman and Charles D. Tate Jr., *The Book of Mormon: Fourth Nephi Through Moroni, From Zion to Destruction* (Provo, UT: Brigham Young University Religious Studies Center, 1995), 167–84; Andrew C. Skinner, "Zion Gained and Lost: Fourth Nephi as the Quintessential Model," in Nyman and Tate (1995), 289–302.
4. See Ryken, Wilhoit, and Longman (1998), 99, 197–98, 209–10.

5. Ibid., 198–99.

6. See Gaskill, *Miracles of the New Testament* (2014), 268–69.

7. McConkie, Millet, and Top (1992), 200; emphasis added.

8. Hinckley (1997), 182.

9. Ibid., 182, 183, 184.

10. Elder Dallin H. Oaks said, "Changing bodies or protecting temples are miracles, but an even greater miracle is a mighty change of heart by a son or daughter of God (see Mosiah 5:2). A change of heart, including new attitudes, priorities, and desires, is greater and more important than any miracle involving the body. I repeat, the body will be resurrected in any event, but a change affecting what the scripture calls the 'heart' of a spirit son or daughter of God is a change whose effect is eternal. If of the right kind, this change opens the door to the process of repentance that cleanses us to dwell in the presence of God. It introduces the perspective and priorities that lead us to make the choices that qualify us for eternal life, 'the greatest of all the gifts of God' (D&C 14:7). My dear brothers and sisters, I pray that each one of us may experience and persist in that miracle of the mighty change of heart, that we may realize the destiny God has prescribed for all of His children and the purpose of this Church to bring to pass the eternal lives of men and women. This is the Church of Jesus Christ, and He is our Savior, our Redeemer, and our Resurrector. We are His spiritual children, spiritually begotten by His sacrifice in Gethsemane and on Calvary and possessing the opportunity to qualify for eternal life. May God bless us to do so" [Dallin H. Oaks, "Miracles," *Ensign*, June 2001, 17].

11. Ogden and Skinner (2011), 2:228.

12. Elder Dale E. Miller taught that "Zion has . . . an intensely personal . . . context. . . . It is the perfecting process within us. Those willing to serve are invited to labor in the vineyard of the Lord, steadily transforming themselves to become the pure in heart" [Dale E. Miller, cited in Bassett (2007–2008), 3:131]. Brigham Young said: "When we are swallowed up in the will of Him who has called us; when we enjoy the peace and the smiles of our Father in Heaven, the things of His Spirit, and all the blessings we are capacitated to receive and improve upon, then are we in Zion, *that is Zion*" [Brigham Young, in *Journal of Discourses*, 1:3].

Nephites' Strength *in* War Goes *beyond* Their Own

Mormon 2:25–26

The Miracle

In only his sixteenth year of life, Mormon was tapped by the Nephites to lead them in battle against the Lamanites. While this young, but gifted, military leader loved his people, he also lamented their unwillingness to repent of their sinful behaviors.

In one of many clashes with the Lamanites, the Nephites were outnumbered by twenty thousand soldiers: the Lamanites having fifty thousand, and Mormon's army having only thirty thousand men. But in a miraculous twist, the Nephites successfully contended against them, causing them to flee. Mormon's troops pursued them and beat them—though the strength of the Lord was not with them because of their sinful state.

Background

It may be that we are more indebted to Mormon than to any other Book of Mormon prophet. Named after his father, and also after the land of Mormon (where Alma established the Church), he was the author-editor of this sacred companion to the Bible—along with being a "sure witness" of Jesus Christ (see Mormon 1:15). He served as a Nephite general, a historian, a prophet, and a preacher to a people who could not hear his witness or his warning. Of him, one text states: "It was nothing short of miraculous that a child born and reared in a society glutted with iniquity could remain spiritual, loving, and tenderhearted."[1] Such was the character of Mormon, who greatly lamented the wickedness of his people (see Mormon 6:17). "It would be impossible to overstate Mormon's achievements spiritually, physically, and intellectually."[2]

The Nephites may have missed the miraculous nature of their victory because of seeming temporal and natural causes. For example, it may be that the Lamanites (and their Gadianton counterparts) "suffered unusually heavy casualties" as they attacked "the fortified city of Shem," thus "prompting a retreat." Or perhaps "their supply lines had been over-extended" causing a weakening of the Lamanite forces.[3] Either way, it may have seemed to the Nephites that this was not the hand of God, but simply evidence of their luck or superior skills in battle. Truth be told, the miraculous often happens in very mundane ways. Seeing the hand of God in what seems natural is a sign of one's attention to the Spirit and His workings. Not seeing His intervention is evidence of spiritual decay and imperception.

SYMBOLIC ELEMENTS

Regarding the number of soldiers fighting in the battle represented in this miracle, one commentator on the Book of Mormon states: "The difference between the two contending armies is an even 20,000. . . . Naturally, obtaining an accurate count of one's enemy poses great practical difficulties. . . . I read this figure as symbolic, representing superior troop strength."[4] If indeed this number is intended as a symbol, it may be representative of the truth that the Nephites did not have the Lord with them, and thus, though they may have won *this* skirmish, they would in a short time be destroyed by the Lamanites, whose power exceeded their own.

We are told that the power of the Lamanites was such that the Nephites were frightened by them and thus fled "towards the north countries" (Mormon 2:3). North is the traditional direction that means "apostate," "left-handed," "darkness," and so on.[5] The Nephites, whom Mormon describes as a spiritually bankrupt people, headed the very direction symbolic of their spiritual state.

APPLICATION AND ALLEGORIZATION

This miracle *should be* a reminder that God can magnify us beyond our own natural skills and abilities. The Nephites were up against an army that had 40 percent more soldiers than they, and yet Mormon's army won. When we live a life of personal righteousness, the Lord can do great things to and through us. However, in this particular episode, the details inform us of a darker side to this story. Mormon lamented: "The strength of the Lord was not with us; yea, we were left to ourselves, that the Spirit of the Lord did not abide in us; therefore we had become weak like unto our brethren. And my heart did sorrow because of this the great calamity of my people, because of their wickedness and their abominations" (Mormon 2:26–27). He added:

> And now, because of this great thing which my people, the Nephites, had done, they began to boast in their own strength. . . .
>
> And I did cry unto this people, but it was in vain; and they did not realize that it was the Lord that had spared them, and granted unto them a chance for repentance. And behold they did harden their hearts against the Lord their God. . . .
>
> And they have repented not of their sins. (Mormon 3:9, 3, 13)

In this miracle the Nephites remind us of all those who forget the origin of their successes and the source of their strength. Just as the Nephites attributed their "great thing" accomplished to their own strength, some of us erroneously assume that our successes are our own rather than acknowledging them for what they are—the blessings of the Lord poured out upon us. While individuals, relying upon their own gifts and skills, might have some measure of success—even significant success—it will never be what it could have been had the Lord been included in their works. As the Apostle Paul reminded us, "I can do all things through Christ which strengtheneth me" (Philippians 4:13). Jesus is the source of our strength. Jesus is the source of our success. Jesus is the means by which we will accomplish the most we possibly can in our lives.[6] If we, like the Nephites, attribute to ourselves that which God has done, like them, we should expect to be "cut off from the face of the earth" (Mormon 3:15). The Lord Himself has warned us: "And in nothing doth man offend God, or against none is his wrath kindled, save those who confess not his hand in all things" (D&C 59:21).

On a related note, Confucius taught: "Those who are virtuous always take caution to speak appropriately, but those whose speech is appropriate may not always be virtuous. Men of principle tend to be bold, but just because someone is bold does not mean that he is necessarily a man of principle."[7] This principle seems applicable to the miracle under discussion. If we live moral and righteous lives, we will be blessed; but just because someone is successful we should not assume he or she is moral or righteous. Mormon saw great success in his own people—even if it was only for a time. However, he boldly testified that their lives were filled with sin and self-aggrandizement. Appearances of success should not be taken as testaments of personal righteousness, nor should setbacks and struggles be taken as evidence of one's unworthiness. Many holy people suffer. Some whose lives are spiritually exemplary have children who stray, suffer financial setbacks, have struggles with their health, or have other trials. And some whose personal lives are the epitome of sinfulness seem to live lives relatively free of pain or challenges. The Lord's plan offers us the experiences we need to grow and become like Him. But the outward appearances of our personal mortal journeys do not tell the story of our inward experiences—and our lives simply cannot be accurately read by outside observers. We must each be cautious not to make judgment calls based on what we see in the lives of others while being cautious about necessarily assuming that our own trials are evidence of God's displeasure.

NOTES

1. See Marilyn Arnold, "Mormon," in Largey (2003), 547.
2. Arnold, in Largey (2003), 548.
3. Gardner (2007), 6:69.
4. Ibid., 6:68.
5. See Nibley (2004), 4:213; Gaskill (2003), 162–66.
6. Ogden and Skinner pointed out, "Without the Lord's Spirit as a constant source of rejuvenation, all things wind down, all things are overtaken by entropy—from people, to planets, to universes. The Nephites were left to themselves in a state of complete weakness and vulnerability" [Ogden and Skinner (2011), 2:237–38].
7. The Confucian Analects, Book 15.

THE LORD TOUCHES *the* SIXTEEN STONES MOLTEN *by the* BROTHER *of* JARED

ETHER 2:19, 22–25; 3:1, 3–6; 6:2–3

THE MIRACLE

The Lord had confounded the language of the people, because of their wickedness; and He scattered them upon the face of the earth. However, the brother of Jared prayed to God that He would have compassion upon his family and not confound their language, and the Lord heeded his request.

God gave Jared's brother counsel that he and his people gather together all of their flocks and possessions, for He was going to "go before" them and lead them to "a land which is choice above all the lands of the earth" (Ether 1:42). And so the Jaredites heeded God's command and built eight barges to carry them across the waters to this promised land.

In the process of making his preparations, the brother of Jared became aware of a problem posed by the nature of their ships. Owing to the fact that their eight barges had no windows, the Jaredite prophet worried that his people would spend the entirety of their journey dwelling in utter darkness.[1] And so he approached the Lord, requesting a solution to their darkness dilemma.

Though God was willing to provide a resolution to the problem of how to get air in the barges, He expected Jared's brother to come up with the solution as to how to have light onboard their ships. The

Lord's response to the question "Wilt thou suffer that we shall cross this great water in darkness?" (2:22) was simply, "What will ye that I should do?" (verse 23).

The prophet climbed to the top of Mount Shelem and heated sixteen small stones until they became transparent, like glass. He then approached the Lord, acknowledged his personal unworthiness—but also God's omnipotence—and then asked that He touch them with His finger so they would shine in the darkness, providing the Jaredites with the light they needed to cross the ocean. The Lord did as the brother of Jared had asked Him, and the stones glowed.

The sixteen stones were then placed in the eight barges—one in each end of the ships—and "they did give light unto the vessels" (6:2).

BACKGROUND

The Prophet Joseph learned Jared's brother's name while pronouncing a priesthood blessing upon an infant in Ohio.

> While residing in Kirtland, Elder Reynolds Cahoon had a son born to him. One day, while the Prophet Joseph Smith was passing by his door, he called the Prophet in and asked him to bless and name the baby. Joseph did so and gave the baby the name of Mahonri Moriancumer. When he had finished the blessing he laid the child upon the bed, and turning to the father, Elder Cahoon, he said, "The name I have given your son, is the name of the Brother of Jared; the Lord has just shown [or revealed] it to me." Elder William F. Cahoon, who was standing nearby, heard the Prophet make this statement to his father; and this was the first time the name of the Brother of Jared was known in the Church in this dispensation.[2]

While the name of Mahonri Moriancumer is never given in the text of the Book of Mormon, the surname of the family does appear (Ether 2:13). The Jaredites named the place on the coast where they dwelt for some four years "Moriancumer," much like how many of Utah's communities are named after the individual who homesteaded them.[3]

One wonders where Mahonri got the idea to request that the Lord touch stones to make them glow so as to illuminate their way. He certainly didn't get the inkling from his conversation with God. Indeed, in that discussion he is largely told to figure it out himself (Ether 2:23,

25). Nibley, McConkie, Millet, Top, and Gardner conjectured that Mahonri may have been drawing on an experience from the life of one of his prophetic predecessors who experienced a similar miracle less than a century and a half prior to this one.

> But who gave the brother of Jared the idea about stones in the first place? It was not the Lord, who left him entirely on his own; and yet the man went right to work as if he knew exactly what he was doing. Who put him on to it? The answer is indicated in the fact that he was following the pattern of Noah's ark, for in the oldest records of the human race the ark seems to have been illuminated by just such shining stones.[4]

Curiously, the Hebrew word translated "window" in Genesis 6:16 is *tsahar*, which means literally "light" or "noon day."[5] The suggestion that Noah may have had a glowing stone in the ark finds support in the LDS edition of the Holy Bible.[6] A parallel tradition also exists among rabbis. As one Jewish text notes: "The ark was illuminated by a precious stone."[7] Of the commonality of such stones, Nibley wrote:

> Now the oldest traditions of India have a good deal to say about a wonderful stone that shines in the dark. This gem can be produced only by subjecting certain types of stone (or the heart of a poisoned person) to terrific heat—it must in fact be kept in an exceedingly hot fire for no less than nine years! By this process was supposed to be produced a perfectly clear, transparent crystal, which "would illuminate even the deepest darkness and sometimes shine as brightly as the sun." Now this strange belief did not originate in India, though it is very ancient there; Meyer and Printz have both traced it to distant China and the West. It receives prominent mention by certain leading thinkers of the Middle Ages, including the great Albertus Magnus. . . .
>
> The common name by which this wonderful shining stone was designated was *pyrophilus* or "friend of fire," usually described as a perfectly transparent crystal and called in the Indian sources (which are the fullest) "Moonfriend" and *Jalakanta*. The last term is significant, for it means "that which causes the waters to part," the peculiar power and virtue of the stone, the most celebrated of all its many miraculous powers being a strange capacity for enabling its possessor to pass unharmed through the depths of the waters.
>
> So we have a very ancient, widespread tradition of a clear, transparent stone, formed by a smelting process requiring terrific heat, that

shines in the dark and guides and preserves its owner beneath the waves. . . .

In Western Asia . . . was the famous shrine of . . . the Dea Syra, where . . . most remarkable object in this temple was . . . "a stone which is called *lynchnis*, and the name is very appropriate; for by night it gives off a good deal of light, which illuminates the whole shrine just like a lamp, though by day the glow is weak." This recalls, of course, the peculiar Zohar described by some of the rabbis.[8]

Nibley added: "In short, we could show how the shining stones of the ancients were thought not to contain the light-giving power within themselves, but to have received the illumination from a higher source."[9] All of this being said, it is quite possible that Mahonri was aware of the story of Noah's glowing stone and simply used this scriptural story as the motivation and justification for his request that God make his sixteen small stones glow too.[10]

One commentary suggested the following regarding the name of the mount on which Mahonri crafted his sixteen small stones: "Moriancumer ascended a mount to which the pilgrims had given the name, Shelem. *Zebach Shelem* is the Hebrew for thank offering, wherefore we safely conclude that this mount had been set apart for sacred purposes (See Leviticus 7:12, 15; 22:27). Hence the name."[11]

SYMBOLIC ELEMENTS

Though perhaps not necessarily germane to this particular miracle, nevertheless, one commentator suggested that Mahonri Moriancumer is a type for Christ, as all prophets are.[12]

THE BROTHER OF JARED	JESUS THE CHRIST
He was a large and mighty man, highly favored of the Lord (Ether 1:34).	"Jesus increased in wisdom and stature, and in favour with God and man" (Luke 2:52).
He was an intermediary for his people (Ether 1:34–39).	There is one mediator between God and men, namely Christ Jesus (1 Timothy 2:5).
He was commanded to gather his people, flocks, and seeds (Ether 1:40–43).	The Lord rhetorically asked, "How often would I have gathered thy children together" (Luke 13:34).

THE BROTHER OF JARED	JESUS THE CHRIST
He was commanded to lead his people in their trek (Ether 2:1–13).	All are commanded to follow Christ (Matthew 4:19; 10:38).
He was visited by the Lord in a cloud (Ether 2:4–5, 14).	Jesus was visited by the Father in a cloud (Matthew 17:5; Mark 9:7; Luke 9:34).
He procured small, transparent stones for the Lord to touch for light in the barges (Ether 3:1–4).	He is the light that leads us through the darkness (John 8:12; 9:5; 12:46). He is also the "stone" or "rock" of Israel (Acts 4:11; 1 Corinthians 10:4; Helaman 5:12).
He had a great vision of the Lord on top of an exceedingly high mountain (Ether 3).	He received divine messengers and was transfigured on a high mountain (Matthew 17:1–3).
He was forbidden to write many of the things he had seen (Ether 4:1).	He charged His disciples after descending the mountain to "tell the vision to no man" (Matthew 17:9).

In antiquity, the number eight was often associated with the concepts of resurrection,[13] new beginnings,[14] rebirth,[15] and baptism.[16] The Jaredites prepared eight barges so that they could cross the waters and obtain the promised land (Ether 3:1). This crossing has been compared by one LDS author to the ordinance of baptism, and as a step on the voyage to the celestial promised land.[17]

On a related note, Jared was the name of the brother of the prophet Mahonri Moriancumer. This name means "he that descends" or "he that goes down."[18] Jared, along with his brother, built barges in which they and their families would cross the great deep—literally descending into the deep "as a whale in the midst of the sea" (Ether 2:24), or as one who had been "swallowed up in the depths of the sea" (Ether 2:25). Of Jared, and the significance of his name, one source notes, "Jared, whose name in Hebrew means 'to go down,' was one of those sent forth when the tower fell. Like Adam and many before and many after, Jared embarked on a new beginning."[19]

As we have pointed out elsewhere, mountains were used anciently as temples—and often symbolized temples. One commentary on the Book of Mormon notes:

When the brother of Jared has a solution to take to Yahweh, he climbs a very high mountain they called Shelem. This mountain echoes Moses's ascent of Mount Sinai to speak to Yahweh (Ex. 19:18–20). In the days before constructed temples, the ancients used mountains as natural temples. Jared and his brother had left a people who built towers as artificial mountains because mountains were a symbolic connecting point between humankind and deity. Mountains moved the ascender closer to God's realm. If one were to meet God, it would be there—in the place of nature's temple. The brother of Jared was therefore going up to his natural temple.[20]

In this miracle we see the intentional incorporation of the temple into the equation that results in the receipt of revelation.

The reference to the "finger of God" is symbolically parallel to the common biblical phrase "the hand of God." Both represent manifestations of God's power. Thus, one commentator noted, "Both 'finger of God' and the more common 'hand of God' use anthropomorphic language metaphorically. That is, they describe a human aspect, but the intent is to describe Yahweh's interaction with the world rather than his physicality. . . . It is not Yahweh's physical finger but his power that effects the miracle."[21]

It has been suggested that the experiences of the Jaredites have a symbolic parallel to our own mortal journey and our participation in God's great plan of salvation.[22]

THE JAREDITES	YOU AND I
Mahonri mediated for his people (Ether 1:33–35).	Jesus mediates for His people—you and me.
The Jaredites brought "Deseret" along with them as they headed to the promised land (Ether 2:3). *Deseret* has been said to be the Egyptian word for "Holy Land."[23] Thus, the Jaredites took with them the very symbol of where they were headed—the promised land.	You and I have embarked on this mortal journey with the intent of arriving (in the end) in the promised land—the celestial kingdom.
If they were faithful to God's directives, they will receive an inheritance in the promised land.	If you and I are faithful to God's directive, we will receive an inheritance in the promised land—the celestial kingdom.

THE JAREDITES	YOU AND I
The Jaredites named the valley they descend into during their journey the "valley of Nimrod." This valley was in the north (Ether 2:1, 4).	Nimrod was a symbol for Satan—and that valley in the wilderness reminds us of this fallen, telestial world, where Satan is ever present. Just as the Jaredites descend into it, so also you and I descend into mortality—having left God's heavenly abode. North is the direction that represents darkness, gloominess, and apostasy, attributes indicative of our fallen world.[24]
The Jaredites crossed the waters in barges or boats—being buried in the water (Ether 6:6).	The Apostle Paul spoke of crossing the waters of the Red Sea as a symbol for engaging in saving ordinances, such as baptism (see 1 Corinthians 10:1–4). Thus, the Jaredite crossing stands as a strong type for our need, during this mortal probation, to engage in the revealed ordinances of the priesthood.
The Jaredites barges were built to exact specifications given by the Lord (Ether 2:16–17).	The temples are built to exact specifications, as revealed by the Lord.
The barges protected the Jaredites from the dangerous elements they would have to pass through (Ether 2:24–25; 6:5–6).	The temple and its covenants protect us from the dangerous elements of mortality that we have to pass through.

Many elements of this story remind us of the plan of salvation and our place within it.

APPLICATION AND ALLEGORIZATION

Among the many potential applications to be drawn from this miracle, we note this one: as we seek the Lord's guidance and use our own ingenuity, the Lord can take our small acts of faith and obedience and turn them into significant offerings—as He did for the brother of Jared. As one commentary on the Book of Mormon suggests,

A practical application to our own spiritual lives of this account of Moriancumer praying for light, is the lesson that when a servant of the Lord has done all he can to overcome the difficulties he is sure to encounter, he may confidently ask the Lord to do for him what he cannot do for himself. That is the privilege of a child in his father's house. And

> When God has touched our efforts
> With the finger of His might,
> Then every worthless pebble
> Is a bright and shining light.[25]

Nibley was wont to say, "Work we must, but the lunch is free."[26] In other words, the miracles performed are always God's. We can take no responsibility for them. However, like Mahonri Moriancumer, we must work. We must do our part. Mahonri initially tried to give the work—the burden of solving the problem—to the Lord; but the Lord dropped it back on the plate of his beseeching servant. In this we find a pattern for our own prayers.

What is doctrinally significant about these verses is not so much the content of the Lord's instructions concerning the shape of the barges, the means whereby oxygen was made available, or the lighting of the interior, but rather the process whereby the brother of Jared came to acquire this important information. "What will ye that I should do . . . ?" was the Lord's response to the brother of Jared's prayerful petitions that outlined the group's predicament and their special needs. Implicit in the Lord's question is the Lord's expectation—he expects Moriancumer, and expects each of us as well, to use his intellect and his common sense as he seeks solutions to his problems. Oliver Cowdery learned this lesson the hard way, when the Lord told him that he could not translate because he had erroneously assumed that He would grant him his desires merely for the asking. "Behold, you have not understood; you have supposed that I would give it unto you, when you took no thought, save it was to ask me. But, behold, I say unto you, that you must study it out in your mind; then you must ask me if it be right." (D&C 9:7–8.) It may be that we approach our prayers the way Oliver did. It may be that all too often when we are praying about our problems and our own unique needs the Father may be saying to us: "What will ye that I should do?" We may be forfeiting greater personal revelation and inspired instructions from the Lord because, expecting the Lord to do all the work, we give no serious study or thought to the solutions but merely ask. Receiving revelation is often a strenuous endeavor that requires intellectual effort coupled with faith and spiritual yearning.[27]

The LDS Bible Dictionary famously states: "Blessings require some work or effort on our part before we can obtain them. Prayer is a form of work, and is an appointed means for obtaining the highest of all blessings."[28] Like Mahonri Moriancumer and Oliver Cowdery, we must do our work if we wish to gain God's aid and intervention. God expects that of us. Prayer becomes powerful only when we do our part. "Of course, he wants us to come to him for advice, but not in such a way that we abdicate our agency and God-given intelligence."[29] If we simply seek to shift the work to the Lord, we must also assume He will be the one deserving of the blessings. In this miracle we have a marvelous pattern for how successful prayers are accomplished: we seek to intellectually solve our own problems, we do the work necessary to create a solution, and then we ask the Lord for a confirmation and for His intervention—particularly on those parts we cannot do ourselves. "The prayer of Moriancumer might profitably be made a special study of every reader of the Book of Mormon. It should be used as a pattern for [our] own private devotions."[30]

As a separate application, we are reminded that the Lord gave light to the Jaredites so that they didn't have to traverse the ocean in the dark. He similarly offers us light as we go through our mortal experience—so that we don't have to negotiate this telestial world "in the dark" *per se*. There is tremendous power available to you and me through faithfully living the teachings of the gospel and through nurturing light in our lives—much like Mahonri nurtured the stones he would have the Lord touch. Significantly, it was allowing the Lord's finger to touch the stones that caused the light to develop in them and radiate from them. So also, in our own lives it is through allowing the Lord to touch us—to stir our hearts and souls—that His light wells up within us and is enabled to radiate from us. The degree to which we allow His hands to touch the various aspects of our lives is the degree to which we will come to know Him and be used by Him. Like Mahonri, we too should stress about the darkness and be fixated on having light in our lives. Too often, unfortunately, we seem quite content with the natural dimness this fallen world affords us. All too frequently we are content living "far beneath our privileges."[31]

In this miracle we are informed that Mahonri Moriancumer went to the mountain (a symbol of the temple) to commune with the Lord about pressing matters in his own life, and in the lives of his people.

This is instructive. We too should avail ourselves of the temple as a place of prayer and as a house of revelation. Too many of us do not attend as frequently as we should—and do not, therefore, reap the blessings associated with (and available through) the house of the Lord. To not seek out an opportunity to enter into the sacred covenants of the temple is a terrible mistake in the life of any Latter-day Saint. To have received those covenants but then not frequently return to the temple is a travesty! How can we be faithful to the covenants we initially made there when we were endowed or sealed if we do not attend regularly? No Latter-day Saint who lives in reasonable proximity to the house of the Lord can keep the covenants he or she made there if he or she does not return on a regular basis after those covenants have been made. Admittedly, not everyone lives close to a temple. But with more than 83 percent of members of the Church living within two hundred miles of one, more should be attending regularly than they are.[32] Like the brother of Jared, you and I can receive instruction from the Lord as we go to the "mountain of the Lord's house" with a prayerful and attentive spirit (Isaiah 2:2; 2 Nephi 12:2).

D. Kelly Ogden and Andrew C. Skinner offered the following application of this miracle to the lives of Latter-day Saints:

> After the stones had been prepared, "the Lord caused [the] stones to shine in darkness, to give light unto men, women, and children." This passage refers to the real, physical stones he prepared for providing light in the barges for the Jaredite colony, but we also note the symbolic message here. The Savior is the Stone of Israel, the Rock of our salvation, and he gives light to the world. Stone and rock represent in the scriptures something firm, solid, immovable. All who follow the Savior also become, in a sense, "stones" for Israel and all the earth and "rocks" of salvation to [the] earth's inhabitants.[33]

Are we letting our light so shine that such might be the case (see Matthew 5:16; 3 Nephi 12:16)?

As a final application, it seems that this miracle emphasizes the truth that Christ can do miraculous things through "small and simple" means (Alma 37:6). Elder Jeffrey R. Holland pointed out, "Here, standing next to the Lord's magnificent handiwork, the impeccably designed and marvelously unique seagoing barges, the brother of Jared offered for his contribution rocks. . . . It was a moment of genuine humility."[34] Wow! Rocks! And yet God did great things through them. And so He can through you and me, and through our own seemingly minuscule offerings. The Lord is less concerned about our capabilities than He is about our willingness to roll up our sleeves and give our best. If we're willing to contribute to the kingdom—putting whatever gifts we *do have* to work—God will magnify our unsophisticated offerings into something worthwhile. And as Mahonri's rocks became the stuff of miracles, our meager offerings can too.

NOTES

1. The Jaredites were some 344 days on the ocean, encapsulated in their barges (Ether 6:11).
2. George Reynolds, "The Jaredites—Part II," in *The Juvenile Instructor*, volume 27, number 9 (May 1, 1892): 282, note *; bracketed words in original.
3. Payson, Utah, is named after James Pace, one of sixteen pioneers who settled it. Park City, Utah, was initially named Parley's Park City (after Parley P. Pratt, who settled it). Draper, Utah, was named after William Draper III, one of the first to dwell in that location; St. George, Utah, was named after George A. Smith, who did not settle it, but who personally selected many of the pioneers who were sent there to organize a community.
4. Nibley (1988), 352. See also McConkie, Millet, and Top (1992), 273; Gardner (2007), 6:197–98.
5. See Brown, Driver, and Briggs (1999), 843, #6672.
6. See footnote 16a in Genesis 6:16, which states that "some rabbis believed" Noah had "a precious stone that shone in the ark." See also Ogden and Skinner (2011), 2:270; Bassett (2007–2008), 3:162.
7. Ginzberg (1967–1969), 1:162. See also 5:183n41, where we are informed that "the glistening precious stone was fetched by Noah from the river Pishon, at God's behest."
8. Nibley (1988), 353, 356.
9. Nibley (1988), 357.
10. One of my peer reviewers noted, "We should never inquire of the Lord for a special revelation—only in the case of there being no previous revelation on the subject. [See *History of the Church*, 1:339; Smith, in Smith (1976), 22.] There was a previous revelation to Noah, and the brother of Jared had access to it (Ether 1:3–4). The Lord expects us to check for previous revelations before we seek new ones" [Todd Parker, in review of *Miracles of the Book of Mormon*].
11. Reynolds and Sjodahl (1955–1961), 6:75; emphasis added. Nibley interpreted this word differently. He wrote: "*Shelem* means *high, safe, secure*. The word *shalom* is derived from that. Remember, *shalom* means you're safe. *Shalom* is a 'ladder, a high place.' If you're going to a high place, it is a safe place, a secure place, a *shelem*" [Nibley (2004), 4:289].

12. See Thomas R. Valletta, "Jared and His Brother," in Charles D. Tate Jr., *The Book of Mormon: Fourth Nephi through Moroni, From Zion to Destruction* (Provo, UT: Religious Studies Center, Brigham Young University, 1995), 307–08.

13. Cooper (1995), 118; Robert D. Johnston, *Numbers in the Bible: God's Design in Biblical Numerology* (Grand Rapids, MI: Kregel Publications, 1990), 75; Julien (1996), 135; E. W. Bullinger, *Number in Scripture: Its Supernatural Design and Spiritual Significance* (Grand Rapids, MI: Kregel Publications, 1967), 200; Davis (2000), 122.

14. Johnston (1990), 75; Cirlot (1971), 233; Julien (1996), 135; Bullinger (1967), 196, 200.

15. Julien (1996), 135.

16. Cirlot (1971), 233; McConkie and Parry (1990), 46. "According to Clement of Alexandria, Christ placed those whom he gave a second life under the sign of eight" [Julien (1996), 135].

17. Valletta, in Nyman and Tate (1995), 304, 318.

18. Judson Cornwall and Stelman Smith, *The Exhaustive Dictionary of Bible Names* (North Brunswick, NJ: Bridge-Logos Publishers, 1998), 125.

19. Valletta, in Nyman and Tate (1995), 307.

20. Gardner (2007), 6:196.

21. Gardener (2007), 6:199. This is not to say that the brother of Jared didn't literally see God's finger, only that the physical finger symbolizes a greater truth—that through this event (and others) God's power was manifest in the world, bringing to pass mighty miracles.

22. See Valetta, in Nyman and Tate (1995), 303–22.

23. Hugh Nibley, *Ancient Documents and the Pearl of Great Price* (Provo, UT: Foundation for Ancient Research and Mormon Studies, 1989), Lecture 8, 12; Nibley (2004), 3:272.

24. See Gaskill (2003), 162–66.

25. Reynolds and Sjodahl (1955–1961), 6:75.

26. Hugh Nibley, "Work We Must, but the Lunch is Free," in Nibley, *Approaching Zion* (Provo, UT: Foundation for Ancient Research and Mormon Studies, 1989), 202–51.

27. McConkie, Millet, and Top (1992), 271–72. See also Nyman (2004), 6:188.

28. LDS Bible Dictionary (Salt Lake City: The Church of Jesus Christ of Latter-day Saints, 1979), 753, s.v. "Prayer."

29. Gardner (2007), 6:190. Nibley put it this way: "The Lord always answers him this way, 'What ideas do you have on the subject?' He must contribute—that's the whole idea" [Nibley (2004), 4:289]. See also Nyman (2004), 6:190.

30. Reynolds and Sjodahl (1955–1961), 6:75.

31. Dieter F. Uchtdorf, "Your Potential, Your Privilege," *Ensign*, May 2011, 58–61; see Brigham Young, in Widtsoe (1998), 32.

32. Thomas S. Monson, "Welcome to Conference," *Ensign*, November 2009, 4.

33. Ogden and Skinner (2011), 2:270.

34. Jeffrey R. Holland, *Christ and the New Covenant* (Salt Lake City: Deseret Book, 1997), 16–17.

THE LORD PROVIDES *the* BROTHER *of* JARED *with a* URIM *and* THUMMIM *and* A PANORAMIC VISION

ETHER 3:22–28

THE MIRACLE

Through his deep and abiding faith, the brother of Jared parted the veil and saw the finger of the Lord—not only His finger, but His whole person. In addition, many things theretofore unknown were revealed to Mahonri Moriancumer, as the Lord ministered unto him.

Having revealed all that He did, the Lord then commanded the Jaredite prophet to not allow the things he had seen and heard to "go forth unto the world" but to instead "treasure [them] up" until the time came that Jesus glorified His name in the flesh (Ether 3:21).

The Lord further commanded Mahonri to write down (in a confounded language) what he had seen and learned, but then to seal the account up so that no one could interpret it. The Lord then conveyed to the brother of Jared two stones—a Urim and Thummim—which the prophet was to "seal up" alongside of his record (verse 23). When the time arrived for his experiences to be known, God would direct someone to those records and the Urim and Thummim accompanying them, which would allow them to be translated and the context to be known.

BACKGROUND

The Lord told the brother of Jared "the language [in] which ye shall write I have confounded" (Ether 3:24). Of this, one source states: "The original Semitic language spoken by Noah and Shem was lost when the Tower was destroyed, except as far it was preserved by Jared and his brother, their families and a few of their friends (Ether 1:35–37). The twenty-four plates must have been written in that vernacular (v. 24)."[1] Elsewhere we read, "Presumably Moriancumer was writing in Adamic, or the language of God."[2]

The Urim and Thummim prepared for and delivered by the Lord to Mahonri Moriancumer were the same ones delivered by the angel Moroni to the Prophet Joseph Smith (D&C 17:1).[3] Indeed, this same Urim and Thummim went from the Lord to Mahonri, and from Mahonri to Ether. Then they were passed to Mosiah (who used them to translate Ether's record), and then they were given to Moroni. Finally, it was given to Joseph Smith when he received the plates under the direction of Moroni.[4]

Regarding the content of that which the brother of Jared saw and learned—that which he was commanded by God to "seal up"— McConkie, Millet, and Top explained:

> The brother of Jared was granted a panoramic vision, that vision which the scriptures tell us has been given to prophet-leaders of dispensations, a vision of things from the beginning to the end. This he was instructed to seal up; it constitutes or is included in what we know as the sealed portion of the Book of Mormon. This "sealed book" is described in Nephi's record as containing "a revelation from God, from the beginning of the world to the ending thereof." When it comes forth it will "reveal all things from the foundation of the world unto the end thereof." (2 Nephi 27:7, 10.)[5]

When God instructed Moriancumer to seal up his writings and experience so others could not read it, that command is sometimes interpreted to mean that Mahonri "placed it under lock and key," so to speak. However, one commentary on the Book of Mormon explained:

> The commandment to "write [these things] and . . . seal them up" to prevent their being interpreted was not a physical sealing, since Mosiah interpreted them. Rather, they were a mental "sealing," since the

brother of Jared wrote "in a language that . . . cannot be read." Moroni had made the same statement about his own writings (Morm. 9:34). They were sealed because they could not be read by typical human means.[6]

SYMBOLIC ELEMENTS

The Hebrew words *Urim and Thummim* mean literally "lights and perfections." While "the possession and use of these stones were what constituted 'seers' in ancient or former times" (Joseph Smith—History 1:35), they also symbolically anticipate the powers and gifts of all exalted beings who will themselves, in their state of exaltation, be "seers"—knowing all things, "past, present, and future" (D&C 130:7). In the Doctrine and Covenants we are told that "the earth, in its sanctified, immortal, and eternal state" will become a great Urim and Thummim to all those who dwell thereon (D&C 77:1). The Lord revealed, "The place where God resides is a great Urim and Thummim. This earth, in its sanctified and immortal state, will be made like unto crystal and will be a Urim and Thummim to the inhabitants who dwell thereon, whereby all things pertaining to an inferior kingdom, or all kingdoms of a lower order, will be manifest to those who dwell on it" (D&C 130:8–9). Expounding on this, the Prophet Joseph said, when the earth is finally celestialized and becomes like a sea of glass, it will function as "one great Urim and Thummim," and the Saints dwelling thereon will be able to look "in it and see as they are seen."[7] Thus, while the Urim and Thummim is "associated with . . . the giving of guidance"[8] generally, it is also a symbol for the revelation that flows to and from the exalted—representative of omniscience. Thus, one text suggests that it represents "the perfect Jesus, who, as the 'light of the world,' reveals his truths to the prophets."[9] And as you and I become as He is, we too will be the source of light and truth to those for whom we have stewardship.

The image of "sealing" something is common in scripture. To seal something can imply its authenticity (it has not been tampered with—it is pure and uncorrupted) and also its ownership (the seal indicates its source and to whom it belongs). Sealing also symbolizes the secrecy of that which is sealed (a rite is kept sacred, or the content of a text is kept hidden).[10] To "seal up" words, truth, and rites is to withhold them from they who are unworthy or unauthorized.

APPLICATION AND ALLEGORIZATION

The receipt of the Urim and Thummim in this account may seem less miraculous than the device itself. However, a gift from God— regardless of its nature—is, itself, a miracle. In the case of the seer stones received my Mahonri, two rocks hardly seem miraculous. Indeed, as one who had himself already "moltened out of rock sixteen small stones" (Ether 3:1), perhaps such a gift may have initially seemed quite unremarkable. Nevertheless, our point is that God gives us many gifts—and often those seem small in significance or initially unim- pressive in nature. However, like the Urim and Thummim given to Mahonri—which would ultimately bless the lives of millions because of what it would reveal—we should recognize that the smallest gift from God to us can be the source of great miracles in our lives, and in the lives of others. For, "by small and simple things are great things brought to pass" (Alma 37:6). If nothing else, this miracle reminds us to take no gift from God for granted.

As we noted previously, the Parry brothers explained that the Urim represents "the perfect Jesus, who, as the 'light of the world,' reveals his truths to the prophets." That being the case, when we have the Lord's Spirit with us, we are guaranteed revelations. The Prophet Joseph taught: "Salvation cannot come without revelation; it is in vain for anyone to minister without it. No man is a minister of Jesus Christ without being a prophet. No man can be a minister of Jesus Christ except he has the testimony of Jesus; and this is the spirit of prophecy."[11] Thus, when we live in such a way as to have the Lord's Spirit with us, we are equipped metaphorically with our own Urim and Thummim, as we are promised revelations from the Lord.

Of course, Mahonri Moriancumer had been called to be the Lord's prophet to his people. An obvious application of this miracle is the truth that Christ provides the means by which prophets and apostles can know His will and speak His mind. God endowed the brother of Jared with such gifts, as He does those fifteen presiding prophets that serve in our dispensation. By virtue of their call, their ordina- tion, and their great faith, they—like Moriancumer—become seers to the people. This is an endowment to them from God. And like the

Jaredite people, it is our privilege to sustain them in their sacred calling—something we cannot do if we do not heed their counsel and obey their commands.

The fact that the brother of Jared received "two stones" as a means of getting revelation reminds us of the two "foundations" of personal revelation mentioned in the eighth section of the Doctrine and Covenants: "Yea, behold, I will tell you in your mind and in your heart, by the Holy Ghost" (D&C 8:2). Notice that the Lord promises revelation to our mind *and* our heart, not simply to one or the other. Certainly a singular seer stone could have been sufficient for the brother of Jared to know the Lord's will, but He gave him two. And so it is with us: the Lord promises us answers to our prayers in our minds and in our hearts. He promises that He will reveal both the logic of His commands while giving us the confirming feeling of the rightness of His ways. "In the mouth of two or three witnesses every word may be established" (Matthew 18:16; 2 Corinthians 13:1; D&C 6:28). This dual confirming process enables us to insure that, if we seek to be Spirit directed—and if we are attentive to both our thoughts and feelings—we need not worry that we will ever be led astray.

NOTES

1. Reynolds and Sjodahl (1955–1961), 6:86.
2. McConkie, Millet, and Top (1992), 279. See also Nyman (2003–2004), 6:202.
3. See McConkie, Millet, and Top (1992), 279–80; Reynolds and Sjodahl (1955–1961), 6:87.
4. See Gardner (2007), 6:210.
5. McConkie, Millet, and Top (1992), 280.
6. Gardner (2007), 6:209. Perhaps God's command to some to "seal" something up is also simply a command to lock it unto themselves. In other words, the command may sometimes be less of a dictate to lock something away and more of a command to keep something private.
7. Smith (1978), 5:279.
8. Ryken, Wilhoit, and Longman (1998), 609.
9. Donald W. Parry and Jay A. Parry, *Symbols and Shadows: Unlocking a Deeper Understanding of the Atonement* (Salt Lake City: Deseret Book, 2009), 133–34.
10. See Ryken, Wilhoit, and Longman (1998), 766.
11. Smith, in Smith (1976), 160.

THE JAREDITES *Are*
DRIVEN *upon the* SEA

ETHER 6:4–12

THE MIRACLE

The Jaredites placed their sixteen glowing stones in their barges, gathered the food and supplies they would need for the next year, and then got aboard their ships—commending their lives to the Lord.

The next 344 days were spent being tossed about by "furious wind" and "waves" (Ether 6:5). At times they were completely buried by the waters, and the wind never ceased to blow as they sailed toward the promised land.

Because their barges were "tight" in their construction (verse 7), though they were tossed about rather violently, the elements were unable to harm them—and their ships consistently surfaced to the top of the water.

Throughout the ordeal, the Jaredites sang praises to God and, upon landing in the promised land, bowed themselves to the earth, thanking God for "the multitude of his tender mercies over them" (verse 12).

BACKGROUND

The barges were of such a nature that they had no sails. Thus, the ocean's currents were the means by which the Jaredites were driven toward the promised land. "Without any means of propulsion but natural forces, tempered and shaped by God, the vessels required faith to safely reach the promised land."[1]

A number of parallels might be drawn between the experience of

Noah (some 150 years earlier) and that of the Jaredites—including the fact that the Old Testament prophet was in his ark some 370 days, and the Jaredites were in their barges nearly as long (at 344 days).[2] One commentator suggested, "The parallel to Noah's ark is intentional. The people gather animals and provisions as commanded, enter their vessels, and set forth upon the waters, trusting in Yahweh just as Noah did."[3] While it is assumed that these parallels are historic, the editor may be hoping that the reader will see the connections.

One commentary on the Book of Mormon suggests that "the Jaredites simply could not have carried enough food and fresh water for themselves and their livestock. A journey of nearly a year required landing to reprovision."[4] Thus, this same source states, "I hypothesize that they did, indeed, stop to reprovision, although the record does not say so."[5] Perhaps; though it seems the Lord could also cause their supplies to last as long as necessary—as He did for the widow of Zarephath (1 Kings 17:14). Beyond the need for additional supplies, this same commentator argues that the length of time it would have taken to make an Atlantic or Pacific crossing doesn't seem to match the 344 days described—particularly in light of the fact that "the wind did never cease to blow towards the promised land *while they were upon the waters*" (Ether 6:8; emphasis added). In other words, since they constantly had a tailwind (when they were on the waters), there must have been times that they camped during the trek—certainly for supplies but, perhaps, also to rest from the rigors of the journey.[6] Again, this is possible, but it seems the jury is still out on this element of the Jaredite journey.

SYMBOLIC ELEMENTS

"The sea," *The New Jerome Biblical Commentary* informs us, is "a common symbol for chaos and death."[7] One scholar notes that the sea "is used often in the LXX [as] the symbol of chaos and disorder."[8] Lockyer sees it as a symbol of "the restless and sinful world."[9]

Wind is often a symbol for "adverse forces" of various kinds.[10] Life's trials and tests are appropriately symbolized by wind and waves that toss us about violently. "Any kind of adversity tempting us to disobedience and disbelief" can also be depicted by wind or waves.[11] Even spiritual doubts are represented as being like "the sea driven with the wind and tossed" (James 1:6).

Boats and ships are often symbols for divinely provided "shelter from life-threatening danger."[12] The early Christians sometimes saw them as symbols for the Church that carry us safely to heaven.[13] They can symbolize "human vulnerability" in a "fearful and threatening world."[14] Setting sail has been seen as a symbol for "crossing from this world to the next"—for "setting out on the sea of life."[15] Thus, sailing corresponds to "the voyage of life,"[16] and distress upon the seas symbolically suggests "disaster on one's life journey."[17] Thus, in this episode—and in various utilizations of boats—the vessel can simply represent the life of the person, or their journey through mortality and toward the eternal resting place we each seek.[18]

The promised land well symbolizes the heavenly abode, or the state of exaltation the faithful seek to obtain.[19]

APPLICATION AND ALLEGORIZATION

This narrative seems an obvious type for our mortal experience. Detail after detail in the Jaredite account mirrors that which God calls us to encounter and endure in our journey toward the "promised land."

THE JAREDITES	YOU AND I
In anticipation of the journey, the Jaredites prepared themselves to have what was necessary to successfully make the trek to the promised land (Ether 6:4).	Prior to our entrance into mortality, you and I prepared ourselves for this journey toward the promised land—even the celestial kingdom. Once here, and as we embark on some of the most challenging parts of life, we again must anticipate and prepare ourselves for the rough waters and the strong winds that will push up against us and threaten to prevent us from reaching our destination.
The Jaredites got into their vessels and commended themselves to the trusting care of the Lord (Ether 6:4).	As you and I prepared to leave the premortal world and enter the mortal vessels (bodies) that would carry us through this life, no doubt we too commended ourselves to the trusting care of the Lord—well aware that the only way we would safely traverse this temptation-strewn existence was with His aid and protection.

THE JAREDITES	YOU AND I
Once they began, "furious wind" blew, and the Jaredites were "tossed upon the waves of the sea" (Ether 6:5).	As you and I move forward in our lives, "furious winds" of adversity buffet us, and we are "tossed" about by the chaos that is common during the mortal experience.
Moroni informs us that "the Lord caused that there should be a furious wind . . . and . . . waves of the sea" (Ether 6:5).	God, by design, made tests and trials part of the mortal experience. Only through such encounters do we develop the character necessary to qualify us to dwell with Him.
The furious winds and the choppy waves of the sea "did never cease" (Ether 6:8).	The trials of life are unending. At no point is there a lull of any significant duration. As Vivian Greene famously noted, "Life isn't about waiting for the storm to pass. . . . It's about learning to dance in the rain."
The Jaredites were "many times buried in the depths of the sea" and "great and terrible tempests" came upon them (Ether 6:6).	Time and again in mortality, you and I will feel completely consumed—buried in our trials.
The winds and waves drove the Jaredites toward the promised land (Ether 6:5, 8).	The trials God allows us to endure are all for the purpose of "driving us toward the promised land"—the celestial kingdom of our God.[20] The Father is not trying to break us; and He is certainly not trying to learn if we will obey. He is teaching us about us—and developing us into the beings we need to be in order to do what He does. His "pushing" and "driving" is an act of love that, ultimately, will make us like Him, not only in our attributes but in the joys we will have for eternity.

THE JAREDITES	YOU AND I
Because their vessels were "tight like unto a dish" the ferocious elements that beat upon them could have no effect. They were entirely protected from the winds and waves. Indeed, though they were often completely buried in the waters, the Lord "did bring them forth again upon the top" (Ether 6:7).	If you and I consistently keep our lives "tight"—not allowing the things of the world to get a foothold—we will be protected from the storms that come. Oh, they will toss us and bump up against us, but they will have no effect on us. We will be entirely protected—and the Lord will eventually "bring us forth again."
In the midst of the jolting, the submerging in water, the blowing, and the tossing by the wind and the waves, the Jaredites "did sing praises unto the Lord; yea . . . they did not cease to praise the Lord" (Ether 6:9).	Perhaps one of the most important things you and I can do is to praise God and to acknowledge the blessings that are ours—even amidst the trials.
While they were "driven forth" upon the storm-tossed sea, "they did have light continually, whether it was above the water or under the water" (Ether 6:10).	If our faith is strong and our trust is placed in Him, then whether we are buried in our trials or riding high (during a lull in the mortal storm), we too can have light continually. God is with us through the thick and the thin, through the dark times and the bright days. If we don't see the light during our dark hours, it isn't because it's not there; it is because we've turned our back toward it or shut our eyes in the midst of it.
When the Jaredites arrived at the promised land, they fell to the ground, humbled themselves before the Lord, and "did shed tears of joy . . . because of the multitude of his tender mercies over them" (Ether 6:12).	At the Judgment Day we too will fall at Christ's feet, be overwhelmed with feelings of dependence, and shed tears of joy because of the multitude of tender mercies that will have been ours throughout our mortal experience. Let us not wait until that day to so act. Let us each and every day exhibit this type of gratitude and humility toward God for His goodness and grace toward us.

NOTES

1. See Gardner (2007), 6:229; see also 6:228.

2. Ogden and Skinner (2011), 2:271. See also Nyman (2003–2004), 6:230.

3. Gardner (2007), 6:227. See also Ogden and Skinner (2011), 2:271.

4. See Gardner (2007), 6:229.

5. Gardner (2007), 6:230.

6. See Ibid., 6:229–30.

7. Kselman and Barré, in Brown, Fitzmyer, and Murphy (1990), 541.

8. Joseph Fitzmyer, *The Anchor Bible: The Gospel According to Luke I–IX* (New York: Doubleday, 1970), 739n31. "LXX" is the standard abbreviation for the Septuagint, the Greek version of the Old Testament commonly used in Jesus's day.

9. Lockyer (1965), 184. See also Richard C. Trench, *Notes on the Miracles of the Lord* (Grand Rapids, MI: Eerdmans, 1962), 92.

10. Ryken, Wilhoit, and Longman (1998), 951.

11. Ibid.

12. Ibid., 101, 102. See also Tresidder (2000), 132; Fontana (1994), 112; Wilson (1999), 364; Cirlot (1971), 295.

13. See James Hall, *Dictionary of Subjects & Symbols*, revised edition (New York: Harper & Row, 1974), 281.

14. Ryken, Wilhoit, and Longman (1998), 786.

15. Cooper (1995), 152.

16. Hugh T. Henry, *Catholic Customs and Symbols* (New York: Benziger Brothers, 1925), 17. See also Todeschi (1995), 233.

17. Todeschi (1995), 233.

18. See Cirlot (1971), 30, 95; Julien (1996), 42.

19. See Valletta, in Nyman and Tate (1995), 319; D. Kelly Ogden and Andrew C. Skinner, *Verse by Verse: Acts Through Revelation* (Salt Lake City: Deseret Book, 1998), 260; Leon Morris, "Hebrews," in Gaebelein (1976–1992), 12:121.

20. If we seek to do things the Lord's way, we will be driven in the direction He wants us to go. If, however, we seek to do things our own way, we will get tossed about more and driven back from our desired destination—as Nephi and his family were (1 Nephi 18:12–15).

A Drought *and* Poisonous Serpents Take Over *the* Land *of the* Jaredites

Ether 9:28–35; 10:19

The Miracle

During the reign of the wicked Jaredite king Heth, the Lord sent prophets to the people, calling them to repentance for their wicked ways—which included their embracing of secret combinations. The prophets warned that, if the Jaredites did not repent, a curse would come upon the land and a great famine would destroy many of them. However, the Jaredites would not repent but, instead, rejected the prophets, casting some out from among them and murdering others.

As a result of their unrepentant attitudes, a great dearth struck their land. There was no rain and, thus, no water to drink and with which to grow crops. The people began to die at a rapid rate, and there was nothing any man could do to change their situation, other than to repent and follow the words of the Lord.

Along with the drought came an infestation of poisonous snakes, biting and thereby killing many of the Jaredites. The flocks of the people—their last remnant of food—began to flee southward in order to escape the snakes. The poisonous serpents hedged up the way between the north and the south, trapping the people in the north and their game in the south, thereby making their conditions even worse.

When the people finally began to realize that they would perish for want of food and drink, they began to soften their hearts, cry unto the Lord for deliverance, and repent of their iniquities. In response to their humiliation, the Lord sent rain upon the face of the earth, which relieved them of their suffering—providing water to drink, causing crops to grow, and provoking the withdrawal of the serpents (thereby enabling the people to head southward to again hunt game).

BACKGROUND

Heth was a descendant of Jared and led the Jaredite people some eight generations after that nation's founder.

> Heth [is] a noun that means "terror." It was the name of the progenitor of the Hittites, the children of Heth, in Genesis, who were the inhabitants of Palestine during the time of Abraham. . . .
>
> Heth, the son of Com, was what his name signified, a terror. He joined some criminal, secret organization, murdered his father and usurped his office. (v. 27)
>
> The wickedness of the king had its corrupting influence on the people. His subjects imitated him. Lawlessness in high places is particularly contagious. As a rule, the moral status of a nation is at the level of the leading and ruling classes. The Jaredites under Heth became as wicked as he was.[1]

This king was an evil man who embraced both secret combinations and murder. During his reign as monarch he persecuted the prophets, encouraging his people to cast them out. In some cases, the people under his reign even murdered the prophets, casting them into pits to starve to death. The wickedness of Heth and his people brought a great dearth upon the land, along with an infestation of poisonous serpents. That same dearth, in part brought on by this unrighteous king, actually took his life.[2]

Lib was the antithesis of King Heth. Whereas Heth was wicked and rejected the prophets, Lib was righteous and found favor with the Lord. As one commentator put it, "With the rain came food and, symbolically, a new king."[3] The people were exceedingly blessed during the reign of Lib, who presided over the people about halfway between Jared (the nation's founder) and Ether (the last of the Jaredites).[4]

SYMBOLIC ELEMENTS

The dichotomy between drought and rain in this miracle seems potentially significant. Drought is a common symbol for the loss of God's blessings (or for being cursed), whereas rain is often associated with outpourings of the Holy Ghost, revelation, blessings, heavenly influences, sanctification, or grace.[5]

· The contrast between north and south here also strikes us as potentially significant. As we have noted elsewhere in this text, north is the traditional direction that means "apostate," "left-handed," in "darkness."[6] South, on the other hand, is often symbolically associated with "covenant status," "facing eastward" (or facing God), the pouring out of "moisture," or the "downpour of rain."[7] The former symbol is traditionally negative, whereas the latter is usually a positive one.

Although serpents as symbols can carry both positive and negative connotations,[8] poisonous serpents typically conjure up images of the latter. Symbolically speaking, they remind us of Satan and his teachings, buffetings, temptations, and pitfalls.[9]

In this miracle the food (which becomes scarce)—including the game or animals—potentially symbolize those things that keep us alive: physical food, which preserves us temporally, but also spiritual food (truth, covenants, and the like), which preserves us spiritually (Isaiah 55:1; John 4:34; 6:27, 35; Deuteronomy 8:3).[10]

Of Heth and the symbolic implications of his wickedness, one commentary on the Book of Mormon explains: "On this second mission of the prophets, Heth, unlike Shule (Ether 7:23), does not protect them. Indeed, he orders their persecution. Heth therefore becomes the symbol of apostasy, triggering the curse that accompanies faithlessness. In this case, the curse manifests itself as drought followed by famine (v. 30)."[11]

APPLICATION AND ALLEGORIZATION

This rather curious and miraculous story can be read in highly symbolic ways. As a general summary, the narrative speaks of a group of people who reject and kill prophets. As a consequence, a great drought (a loss of blessings) comes upon them. They are overwhelmed by an infestation of poisonous serpents (satanic influences and temptations). In order to escape the influence of the snakes (Satan) a small percentage of the people[12] make their way southward (toward the things of the covenant), as does their game (those things they need to survive spiritually). The majority stays in the land northward (in darkness and apostasy), living without rain (revelation or the companionship of the Spirit). The snakes (Satan) keeps the two groups apart, preventing those in the north (darkness) from having what those in the south (the covenant) have—rain and food (blessings, ordinances, revelation). Upon repentance, the rain (Spirit and blessings) are restored, though it takes some time for the fruits of the field to grow and the beasts of the field to return (fuller blessings, covenants, rites).

A number of applications can be drawn from this miracle. A basic principle is this: when we reject the words of the prophets, we bring trials upon ourselves and those around us, and the blessings of the Lord are often withdrawn. As demonstrated in this narrative, repentance—if sincere—can bring a return of the Lord's aid and blessings (D&C 130:20–21).

An important additional application, however, is to be found in the fact that the return of the rain did not bring immediately fruits of the field, a return of the flocks, or a banishment of the poisonous snakes. Even though the rain fell, it took time for these other blessings—once had but lost through sin—to completely return to the Jaredites. Such is the case in our own lives. When we sin, the process of repentance takes a while, and it may be some time before we regain *all* that we forfeited through our sins. Indeed, some of what we forfeited may never come back to us. As with the Jaredites, through sincere repentance, some blessings return immediately. But some can take many years to regain. We must be patient with the Lord as we traverse the process that is sincere repentance.

As a final application, we look at the missionary side of this narrative. Just as the snakes kept the two groups (those in the north and those in the south) apart, so also Lucifer seeks to keep those in bondage and sin (or those just outside the covenant) from those who have the fulness of the gospel. He may do that through causing distrust and fear (as he did in this miracle) or through causing us to feel a measure of condescension toward each other. Either way, we must be aware of Satan's ability to use such things to keep those with the gospel away from those who do not have it.

Additionally, like the Jaredites—who feared the poison of the snakes—we too must be cautious that, in the process of sharing the gospel, we do not place ourselves in danger. The "poison" of the adversary is real; and Satan will gladly "bite" us if we place ourselves in a situation wherein we make that possible. I have watched a number of good-intending youth make the choice to affiliate closely in social settings with those whose standards were far beneath their own. Many fall, despite inspired warnings. Young people should not avoid those who are not members of the Church simply because they are not members of the Church. However, when someone's standards include things such as immorality or substance abuse, the active Latter-day Saint needs to choose upon which ground he or she stands; and this miracle reminds us that, when sharing the gospel, we must always stay in the "southern" territory. Never visit the "north"!

NOTES

1. Reynolds and Sjodahl (1955–1961), 6:146–47.
2. See Ed J. Pinegar and Richard J. Allen, *Book of Mormon Who's Who: A Comprehensive Guide to the People in the Book of Mormon* (American Fork, UT: Covenant Communications, 2007), 66–67; Kip Sperry, "Jared, Posterity of," in Largey (2003), 432.
3. Gardner (2007), 6:267.
4. See Sperry in Largey (2003), 432; Pinegar and Allen (2007), 112.
5. See, for example, McConkie (1985), 268; Cooper (1995), 188–89, 136; Ryken, Wilhoit, and Longman (1998), 221, 694; Wilson (1999), 125, 332–33; Julien (1996), 343–45; Todeschi (1995), 104, 214, 281–82; Fontana (1994), 113.
6. Nibley (2004), 4:213; Gaskill (2003), 162–66.
7. Gaskill (2003), 157–61.
8. See Skinner, in Ricks and Parry (2000), 359–84.
9. See Ryken, Wilhoit, and Longman (1998), 773–74; Cooper (1995), 150; Julien (1996), 383; Hall (1979), 285; Todeschi (1995), 239.
10. See Ryken, Wilhoit, and Longman (1998), 298–99.
11. Gardner (2007), 6:264.
12. See Gardner (2007), 6:266.

THE BROTHER *of* JARED
REMOVES MOUNT ZERIN

ETHER 12:30

THE MIRACLE

In a discourse on faith, Moroni informs his readers that God works in the lives of the children of men "according to their faith" (Ether 12:29). To illustrate this, he tells us of how Mahonri Moriancumer commanded the mountain named Zerin to "remove" (verse 30), and it moved! The last Nephite prophet then informs us (in his narrative) that this should be an example to us: in our works we must have faith as the brother of Jared did, that the Lord can use that faith to perform miracles.

BACKGROUND

As we have previously noted, in the *Lectures on Faith* we are informed that faith "is the principle of power in the Deity as well as in man. Hebrews 11:3: 'Through faith we understand that the worlds were framed by the word of God, so that things which are seen were not made of things which do appear.' (Lecture 1:14–16.)"[1] This first of seven lectures goes on to say,

> Secondly, [faith] is the principle of power in man also. . . . The mountain Zerin, by the faith of the brother of Jared, is removed.
>
> How do you convey to the understanding more clearly [than through such an example] that faith is the first great governing principle which has power, dominion, and authority over all things? By it

they exist, by it they are upheld, by it they are changed; . . . and without it there is no power.[2]

When Jesus, therefore, taught, "If ye have faith as a grain of mustard seed, ye shall say unto this mountain, Remove hence to yonder place; and it shall remove; and nothing shall be impossible unto you" (Matthew 17:20), He was speaking of the power resident in faith; and, apparently, He was *not* speaking in hyperbole. One commentator suggested that when Jesus taught this discourse on faith, He "may actually have been referring to this literal event."[3]

One might ask, Under what circumstance would you or I need to move a mountain? Moroni gives us no details surrounding this miraculous movement. However, one commentator suggested that

> it is, by no means improbable, that the Jaredites during their migrations from the coast to the interior of the Continent of Asia, encountered some mountainous obstacle which the Lord removed in answer to the prayers of faith of the great Jaredite Moses. It may have been done by some physical adjustment of the earth such as an earthquake, or by some supernatural agency unknown to us. Whatever it was, be it either case, it was a miracle, a divine reward of Faith.[4]

While the act of physically moving a mountain is likely something you and I would never need to accomplish, the aforementioned possibility reminds us that the brother of Jared would never have performed such a miracle as a shameful display of personal power but, instead, *only* in a circumstance where no other option was available to him and his people. Thus, whatever the reason for the miracle, it was his only option; and because of his great faith, God granted his request.

SYMBOLIC ELEMENTS

Mountains are often symbols for the temple. However, in this miracle it seems evident that Mount Zerin is a symbol for the obstacles of life. As one text notes, mountains are often symbols of a "great challenge or obstacle that is to be overcome."[5] Elsewhere we read that their "visible immensity makes them the benchmark for enormity"—such as the enormity of a challenge.[6]

APPLICATION AND ALLEGORIZATION

The most obvious application of this miracle is the need for each of us to have faith that God can work in our lives and through our lives. One commentator on this miracle wrote, "Moroni teaches us that God works in the lives of people *after* they have faith in him (Ether 12:30–31)."[7] Or, as Ogden and Skinner put it, "Our spiritual attainments in this life are directly proportional to our faith or our lack thereof. Moroni attested, 'I know that thou workest unto the children of men according to their faith; . . . wherefore thou workest *after* men have faith.' "[8] Faith is the foundation of every miracle, and of all *meaningful* religious experiences.

Knowing that you and I will likely never need to move a physical, rocky mountain, a more symbolic application seems appropriate. As all who have faith have learned, God can and does remove "mountains" or obstacles in our lives when we turn to Him for aid and comfort. True it is that He often requires that you and I—through our faith—do some of the heavy "lifting" (as He did with the brother of Jared). Nevertheless, we should be under no illusions: God is the one who really does the moving. One commentator wrote: "Troubles, hindrances, problems and difficulties are represented in the [scriptures] as mountains. Those who know the Lord intimately and believe Him fully may address themselves to these problems and see the Lord solve them and remove them. Spirit-filled men [and women] see miracles happen in their lives."[9] God offers each of us this kind of encounter with His power, if we can but live faith-filled lives. "Doubt not, but be believing" (Mormon 9:27)!

NOTES

1. *Lectures on Faith* (1985), 7.
2. Ibid., 7, 8–9.
3. McConkie, Millet & Top (1992), 303. See also Ludlow (1988), 325.
4. Reynolds and Sjodahl (1955-1961), 6:170-171. Another commentator suggested that perhaps a volcanic eruption was the means by which the mountain was removed. See Gardner (2007), 6:296.
5. Todeschi (1995), 176. See also Wilson (1999), 283.
6. Ryken, Wilhoit and Longman (1998), 573.
7. H. Dean Garrett, "Light in Our Vessels: Faith, Hope, and Charity," in Nyman and Tate (1995), 83.
8. Ogden and Skinner (2011), 2:281.
9. Wilson (1999), 283.

THE NEW JERUSALEM
DESCENDS *out of* HEAVEN

ETHER 13:3

THE MIRACLE

Near the end of his abridgement of the book of Ether, Moroni informs his reader that (after the flood of Noah) the Americas became a "choice land above all other lands, and chosen land of the Lord" (Ether 13:2). The last of the Nephite prophets tells us that whoever dwells on that sacred continent should serve God.

Then Moroni adds a brief description, *not* of a miracle that has taken place but of one that *will happen* many years after the passing of his people. He promises the reader that the dwelling place of the Nephites and Jaredites—the Western Hemisphere—would be the "place of the New Jerusalem," which, Moroni says, would "come down out of heaven" (verse 3).[1]

BACKGROUND

Technically this miracle may not belong in a compilation such as this because it is more of a prophecy than an actual miracle; at least it is such until its fulfillment. However, because it seems to highlight God's miraculous work in the world—and in our personal lives—it seemed appropriate to address it here.

SYMBOLIC ELEMENTS

The New Jerusalem is a symbol for the presence of a covenant-making, covenant-keeping community of God. Is the New Jerusalem a singular location? It is! But that location is ultimately not Independence, Missouri, or Salt Lake City, Utah. Rather, it is the temple of our God! Wherever a temple is built, Zion is present. Wherever a temple is raised, a place of gathering is established. Thus, while we often equate Zion or the "New Jerusalem" with a physical city, it is better seen as a symbol of the pure in heart who enter the house of the Lord, make sacred covenants, and then live those covenants throughout their lives in a consecrated and holy way. [2]

APPLICATION AND ALLEGORIZATION

The most important application of this miracle is not about a physical city descending out of the heavens. Rather, our focus should be on the truth that the city is of God; its laws, rites, ordinances, and ways have been sent from heaven by God to man upon the earth. One commentary points out,

> The establishment of Zion and the New Jerusalem will come "down out of heaven" in both a literal and a symbolic way. In the symbolic way, the New Jerusalem will be built upon heavenly principles and under the influence of revelation to the Lord's chosen officers. In this way, it will come down from heaven, and then mortals who are cleansed and purified through the atonement of Jesus Christ will build up a new City of Holiness, even a New Jerusalem.[3]

Under the instrumentality of the latter-day prophets and apostles, Zion has returned. The New Jerusalem is here—not solely in Jackson County, Missouri, but wherever the "pure in heart" are found (D&C 97:21; 101:18). Indeed, all that we have that is Zionic in nature "comes down out of heaven"—as God is the source of all that is good (see Ether 4:12). Those who were reared outside the Church—who converted as adults—can often testify of the good the restored gospel has brought to them. It is truly the purveyor of heavenly gifts. As we seek to live the teachings of Christ, engage in the covenants restored by Joseph, and practice the principles provided by the prophets, Zion will grow in our hearts and in our homes. Our natures will be changed, and a bit of heaven will be apparent in our countenances and in our communications. That is the "New Jerusalem" we must seek! That is the Zion we must foster! Indeed, *in our personal lives,* that is the only one that truly matters.

NOTES

1. The tenth article of faith states, "We believe . . . that Zion (the New Jerusalem) will be built upon the American continent."

2. See Alonzo L. Gaskill, "Location Veneration: Independence, Missouri, in Latter-day Saint Zionist Tradition and Thought," in *Mormon Historical Studies*, Volume 14, Number 1 (Spring 2013), 163–83. Zion, the New Jerusalem, also becomes a type for the celestial kingdom.

3. McConkie, Millet, and Top (1992), 307. Andy Skelton pointed out: "I think Zion is a miracle. For members of our selfish and violent species to dwell in one heart and one mind is evidence of the miracle of Atonement. I think that is one of the most missed definitions—to again be at one with each other as presumably we were in premortality. This Zion *should* occur in every marriage and home and ward." [Andy Skelton, in review of *Miracles of the Book of Mormon*].

EPILOGUE

It seems that miracles have ever been a part of revealed religion, and they are certainly part of the Restoration of the gospel in the latter days. The prophets of the Old Testament were miracle workers. Jesus was unquestionably a miracle worker. Every prophet of the Book of Mormon had the gift of working miracles.[1] Indeed, the Book of Mormon is saturated in the miraculous, from its detailed narratives to its coming forth and inspired translation. Yet, in almost a spirit of resignation, one modern commentator on scriptural miracles penned this: "It is safe to say that the miracles that occurred in the days of Jesus and the apostles no longer happen today. No human being has the power to . . . give sight to someone . . . blind, make the deaf to hear, . . . or command both storm and wind to cease."[2] I can only say I disagree. God is a God of miracles. He lives, and because He lives, miracles still happen! One of the signs of the Restoration was the reopening of the heavens, outpourings of revelation, and a return of miracles, including those performed through restored priesthood power. All of this is true! And it is a precious component of the Restoration—particularly in the lives of those who have experienced firsthand such miracles (as many of us have).

In what feels like a response to our aforementioned naysayer, Moroni penned these words about the eternal connection between the existence of God and the presence of miracles in the world:

And now, O all ye that have imagined up unto yourselves a god who can do no miracles, I would ask of you, have all these things passed, of which I have spoken? Has the end come yet? Behold I say unto you, Nay; and God has not ceased to be a God of miracles.

Behold, are not the things that God hath wrought marvelous in our eyes? Yea, and who can comprehend the marvelous works of God?

Who shall say that it was not a miracle that by his word the heaven and the earth should be; and by the power of his word man was created of the dust of the earth; and by the power of his word have miracles been wrought?

And who shall say that Jesus Christ did not do many mighty miracles? And there were many mighty miracles wrought by the hands of the apostles.

And if there were miracles wrought then, why has God ceased to be a God of miracles and yet be an unchangeable Being? And behold, I say unto you he changeth not; if so he would cease to be God; and he ceaseth not to be God, and is a God of miracles.

And the reason why he ceaseth to do miracles among the children of men is because that they dwindle in unbelief, and depart from the right way, and know not the God in whom they should trust. (Mormon 9:15–20)

The brother of Jared "said unto the mountain Zerin, Remove—and it was removed" (Ether 12:30). Jesus promised those who place their trust in Him that they would possess this same power (see Matthew 17:20). Of course, one cannot help but ask, "Under what circumstance would I need to literally, physically move a mountain?" For nearly all of us, this promise is metaphorical; it is symbolic. It reminds us that mortality is filled with obstacles, mountains we must climb or remove. These may be weaknesses, or they may consist of some trial of faith, finance, or family. But they are, nevertheless, seemingly insurmountable when we are confronted with them. They seem impossible to bear and crushing in their weight. And yet Jesus promised us, if we will exercise faith in Him, He will give us the strength to make it over the mountain, or to remove the mountain altogether. He is a God of miracles, and we—through our faith—can expect miracles in our lives. The Book of Mormon testifies of this truth over and over again.

That being said, as wonderful as the miracle of Jesus providing the sacrament to the Nephites without any bread was, and as amazing as the night without a day (at Jesus's birth) seemed, the miracles you and I need in our lives today are different than that. What we need today is more personal and more practical. We may or may not need to be healed from physical blindness (3 Nephi 26:15), but each of us needs to be healed from our spiritual blindness—from our inability to see "things as they really are" (Jacob 4:13). Elder Neal A. Maxwell was once asked, "Where is the joy in this rigorous living" that is required of Latter-day Saints? To which Elder Maxwell responded,

> Seeing a prodigal return . . . is a marvelous thing [Alma 36:6–24]. To see someone, in the words of Scripture, who comes to himself and resolves that "I will go to my Father" is a marvelous journey for someone to make. The joy comes in seeing someone who has been crusty and difficult to deal with become more meek, or to see a family really come to love and appreciate each other. Those are the real miracles. The multitude were fed five thousand loaves and fishes, yet they were hungry again the next day. But Jesus is the Bread of Life, and if we partake thereof then we will never be hungry again. The most lasting miracles are the miracles of transformation in people's lives. These give one much joy, and while we can't cause these to happen, the Lord lets us, at times, be instruments in that process. This brings great joy.[3]

Our review of the miracles of the Book of Mormon has been filled with such "transformations." We have examined many miracles, historical events that testify not only of Christ's power *over* life, death, and the elements of nature, but that (through application) have also reminded us of the more important power He has *in* our lives. While He literally blessed the little children of the Nephites—encircling them with fire and endowing them with supernatural gifts—what seems to matter more to me today is that I can turn to Him (when I feel spiritually or emotionally fragile like a child), knowing that He will bless me, encircle me with His light and power, and endow me with the gifts I need—gifts beyond what I would naturally have. *That* is the great miracle of the gospel of Jesus Christ; *that* is the great promise of the Lord.

In the dozens of miracles we have examined, we have offered applications and allegories that various authors have drawn—all with the intent of making the events of the past applicable to the needs and trials of the present. We have sought to follow Jacob's council and read the scriptures for application, looking for ways that "they may be likened unto" our lives today (2 Nephi 6:5; see also 1 Nephi 19:23). While fully believing in the value of the intended message of the original author of the text, we've sought to emphasize the additional value of looking for personal applications beyond the original meaning of the story, to look for ways to find personal meaning in the events of scripture that originally had nothing to do with you or me or the day in which we live. It is my hope that via this little study, you have felt the power of the Book of Mormon and have sensed the Spirit speaking to you regarding the miracles Christ has performed in your personal life. But it is also my hope that you have sensed the timelessness of scripture and its ability to speak to you and me today about the trials we face, and Christ's ability to lift our burdens, heal our spiritual sicknesses, and save our sin-stained souls.

NOTES

1. If every prophet of the Book of Mormon worked miracles, one might query as to why I have not included any herein from the book of Moroni. There are certainly miracles in that sacred record. For example, we read of the miracle of gaining a testimony (Moroni 10:3–5). We also find in the book of Moroni the miracle of being perfected in Christ (Moroni 10:33–34). That same section of the Book of Mormon speaks of the miraculous gifts of the Spirit (Moroni 10:8–19). These, and others, appear in the book of Moroni. However, since the focus of our text has been on the narrative portions of the Book of Mormon and their described miracles, it seemed best to not examine here the type of miracles the book of Moroni discusses. Moroni worked mighty miracles, and he invites us to experience a number of those ourselves. However, the miracles he leaves us in his record are not narrative miracles but potential miracles you and I must seek out. They are not less significant, but unique in their own right—and less suited to being allegorized.

2. Simon J. Kistemaker, *The Miracles: Exploring the Mystery of Jesus's Divine Works* (Grand Rapids, MI: Baker Books, 2006), 254.

3. Neal A. Maxwell, "A Conversation with Elder Neal Maxwell," in Hugh Hewitt, *Searching for God in America* (Dallas, TX: Word Publishing, 1996), 143. Andy Skelton wrote: "To link this idea with Alma the Younger in Alma 36 is a very relevant miracle. I have also begged for forgiveness and have been granted it as soon as I have asked. This may be the most powerful and relevant miracle of the Book of Mormon. Everyone that asks for forgiveness gets it. Starting with Laman, Lemuel, and Nephi" [Skelton, review of *Miracles of the Book of Mormon*].

BRIEF BIOGRAPHICAL SKETCHES

OF ANCIENT AND MODERN
NON-LDS SOURCES CITED

ANCIENT SOURCES

- Ambrose of Milan—Circa AD 333–397—Bishop of Milan and teacher of Augustine.
- Augustine of Hippo—AD 354–430—Bishop of Hippo and one of the most influential voices in Christianity.
- Athanasius of Alexandria—Circa AD 295–373—Bishop of Alexandria and influential figure at the Council of Nicaea.
- Bede the Venerable—Circa AD 673–735—British Father who was responsible for the practice of dating events from the birth of Christ by using the designation AD, or *anno Domini* (in the year of the Lord).
- Caesarius of Arles—Circa AD 470–543—A popular sixth-century preacher and Bishop of Arles.
- Chromatius—Flourished AD 400—Bishop of Aquileia and friend of St. Jerome.
- Cyril of Alexandria—AD 375–444—The Patriarch of Alexandria and the driving force behind the declaration of the Council of Ephesus (AD 431) that the Virgin Mary is the Theotoks or "Mother of God."
- Ephrem the Syrian—Circa AD 306–373—A Syrian Christian commentator and composer of hymns.
- Gregory the Great—Circa AD 540–604—Influential pope, unifying source in Western Christianity, and source for the style of chant known as "Gregorian."
- Gregory of Nyssa—Circa AD 335–394—Bishop of Nyssa and influential in early clarifications regarding post-Nicene Trinitarian doctrines.
- Jerome—Circa AD 347–420—Translator of the Latin Vulgate Bible and staunch defender of the dogma of the perpetual virginity of Mary.
- John Chrysostom—Circa AD 344–407—Bishop of Alexandria. Famous for his orthodoxy and his attacks on Christian laxity.
- John of Damascus—Circa AD 650–750—Arab monastic and theologian whose writings greatly influenced both Eastern and Western Christian traditions.
- Justin Martyr—Circa AD 100–165—Palestinian philosopher and convert to Christianity. Wrote against pagan and Jewish beliefs. Combined Greek philosophy and Christian theology in his writings. Died as a martyr for the faith.
- "Life of Adam and Eve"—Circa first century AD—Jewish pseudepigraphical text recounting the lives of Adam and Eve after their expulsion from Eden.
- Maximus of Turin—Died circa AD 423—Bishop of Turin, Italy.
- Origen—Circa AD 185–254—An influential expositor and theologian in

Alexandria. Believed in the preexistence of the soul—a belief for which he was eventually condemned.

- Paulus Orosius—Born circa AD 380—Student of St. Augustine and outspoken critic of Pelagius. Considered by some to be the first author of a history of Christianity.
- Peter Chrysologus—Circa AD 380–450—Latin archbishop of Ravenna who emphasized the relationship between grace and Christian living.
- Philo of Alexandria—Circa 20 BCE–AD 50—Jewish-born exegete. Greatly influential over Christian patristic interpretations of the Hebrew Bible.
- "Revelation of Moses"—Circa first century AD—Sometimes known as the "Life of Adam and Eve," this document is a Jewish pseudepigraphical text recounting the lives of Adam and Eve after their expulsion from Eden.
- Tertullian—Circa AD 160–225—Born in Carthage, he was the Church's first Latin Father. Wrote of his discomfort with the laxity of some Christians.
- "The Divine Liturgy of James"—Circa fourth century AD—Oldest surviving Christian liturgy developed for general use in the Church.
- "The First Gospel of the Infancy of Jesus Christ"—Circa fifth–sixth century AD—One of several texts in the New Testament Apocrypha that chronicle the infancy of Jesus.
- "The Gospel of Pseudo-Matthew"—Circa sixth century AD—One of the texts part of the New Testament Apocrypha. Offers details regarding the childhood of Jesus, expanding on that which appears in the New Testament Gospels of Matthew and Luke.
- "The Protevangelium of James"—Circa AD 145—An infancy Gospel which expands on Matthew's and Luke's accounts of Jesus's childhood.
- Theodore of Heraclea—Died circa AD 355—Pre-Nicene Bishop of Thrace who sought reconciliation between Eastern and Western Christianity.
- Theodore of Mopsuestia—Circa AD 350–428—Bishop of Mopsuestia and founder of the Antiochene school of exegesis (which emphasized a literal interpretation of the scriptures).

MODERN SOURCES

- Allen, Ronald B.—Lutheran Biblical Scholar and professor of Bible exposition at the Evangelical Dallas Theological Seminary.
- Barclay, William—Church of Scotland biblical scholar.
- Barré, Michael L.—Catholic clergyman and biblical scholar.
- Blackbourne, Lorne H.—Medical doctor specializing in critical care surgery.
- Bowden, John—Anglian theologian.
- Briggs, Charles A.—Presbyterian minister and Hebrew scholar.
- Brown, David—Free Church of Scotland minister and professor of theology.
- Brown, Francis—American Hebrew Bible scholar and linguist.
- Brown, Raymond E.—Catholic biblical scholar and theologian.
- Bullinger, Ethelbert William—Anglican biblical scholar.
- Cirlot, Juan E.—Catholic hermeneutist and symbologist.
- Clarke, Adam—Methodist biblical scholar and theologian.
- Cole, R. Alan—Evangelical biblical scholar and exegete.

- Conner, Kevin J.—Leader and author in the charismatic movement of the Pentecostal faith.
- Cooper, Jean C.—Scholar of comparative religion and symbolism.
- Cornwall, Judson—Charismatic Christian pastor and author.
- Cross, Frank Leslie—Anglican patristic scholar.
- Davis, John J.—Evangelical biblical scholar.
- Donaldson, James—Scottish Episcopal patristic scholar and theologian.
- Drinkard, Joel F., Jr.—Baptist biblical scholar and theologian.
- Driver, Samuel R.—English Hebrew Bible scholar and linguist.
- Fairbairn, Patrick—Scottish theologian and minister in the Free Church of Scotland.
- Fausset, Andrew—English clergyman and biblical scholar.
- Ferguson, Everett—Church of Christ patristic scholar.
- Fitzmyer, Joseph A.—Catholic biblical scholar and theologian.
- Fontana, David—Psychologist and author.
- Ford, J. Massyngberde—Catholic biblical scholar and theologian.
- France, Richard Thomas—Anglican biblical scholar.
- Freedman, David Noel—Biblical scholar and Hebraist.
- Freyne, Sean—Irish theologian and New Testament Scholar.
- Gabriel, Charles H.—American composer of gospel music.
- Gabriel, Richard A.—Professor of history and military studies.
- Gaebelein, Frank E.—Evangelical biblical scholar and theologian.
- Ginzberg, Louis—Conservative Jewish scholar and Talmudist.
- Habershon, Ada R.—Baptist symbologist and hymnist.
- Hall, James—Art historian.
- Hastings, Thomas—American composer of sacred music.
- Hamilton, Victor P.—Professor of Bible and Theology.
- Henry, Hugh T.—Roman Catholic symbologist, hymnologist, and ecclesiastical leader.
- Ifrah, Georges—French author and historian of mathematics.
- Jamieson, Robert—Scottish exegete and minister.
- Jenks, Alan W.—Hebrew Bible scholar.
- Johnson, Alan F.—Protestant scholar of New Testament and Christian Ethics.
- Johnson, Luke Timothy—Catholic biblical exegete and historian of Christianity.
- Johnston, Robert D.—An Assemblies of Brethren teacher and author.
- Julien, Nadia—Author of several texts on myths and symbols.
- Kaiser, Walter C.—Evangelical Hebrew Bible scholar.
- Keoke, Emory Dean—Author of books on Native American history and also health and wellness.
- Kistemaker, Simon J.—Evangelical New Testament scholar.
- Kragh, John F., Jr.—Orthopedic surgeon.
- Kselman, John S.—Catholic clergyman and biblical scholar.
- La Sor, William S.—Dead Sea Scrolls and Josephus scholar.
- Lienhard, Joseph T.—Roman Catholic priest and theologian.
- Lockyer, Herbert—Evangelical biblical scholar and clergyman.
- Mabry, Richard L.—Medical doctor.

- Mann, C. S.—Catholic biblical scholar and theologian.
- McKay, Patricia L.—Orthopedic surgeon.
- McQuade, Pamela—Christian author of popular religious texts.
- Metz, Karen S.—Historian of military medicine.
- Morgan, Robert J.—Free Will Baptist pastor and author.
- Morris, Leon—Evangelical biblical scholar and theologian.
- Mother Teresa—Roman Catholic nun and Nobel Prize winner.
- Murphy, Roland E.—Catholic biblical scholar and theologian.
- Myers, Allen C.—Senior editor, Eerdmans Publishing.
- Norris, Fredrick W.—Protestant biblical scholar and church historian.
- Porterfield, Kay Marie—Author of books on medicine and health.
- Rasmussen, Todd E.—Professor of vascular surgery.
- Rich, Norman M.—Professor of vascular surgery.
- Richey, Stephen L.—Doctor of oncology.
- Roberts, Alexander—Presbyterian churchman and patristic scholar.
- Rockwood, Bruce L.—Lawyer and author.
- Ryken, Leland—Evangelical theologian and symbologist.
- Sakenfeld, Katharine Doob—Professor of Hebrew Bible and Exegesis.
- Sigourney, Lydia Howard—Nineteenth-century American poet.
- Schaff, Philip—Protestant theologian and church historian.
- Smith, D. C.—Doctor of veterinary medicine.
- Salhotra, Rashmi—Medical doctor.
- Shafi, Shahid—Clinical research scholar and trauma surgeon.
- Shama, Jai Prakash—Professor of political science.
- Smith, Stelman—Evangelical pastor and author.
- Sobrino, Justin—Medical doctor.
- Sprague, Achsa W.—Nineteenth-century American poet and spiritualist.
- Swan, K. G.—Orthopedic surgeon.
- Thompson, Daniel P.—Nineteenth-century American author and lawyer.
- Todeschi, Kevin J.—Lecturer and author on symbolism.
- Toplady, Augustus M.—Eighteenth-century English Anglican cleric and composer.
- Trench, Richard C.—Anglican churchman and theologian.
- Trent, Kenneth E.—Baptist pastor and author.
- Tresidder, Jack—Journalist and symbologist.
- Trigg, Joseph W.—Episcopal churchman and scholar.
- Trunkey, David L.—Trauma surgeon.
- Vawter, Bruce—Roman Catholic priest and biblical scholar.
- Wace, Henry—Anglican priest and professor of ecclesiastical history.
- Webster, Noah—American lexicographer and textbook pioneer.
- Welling, David L.—Surgeon.
- Wenham, Gordon J.—English Hebrew Bible scholar.
- Williamson, Lamar, Jr.—Presbyterian biblical scholar and theologian.
- Wilson, Walter L.—Non-denominational Christian physician who founded a theological seminary and authored a number of conservative theological texts.
- Zornberg, Avivah Gottlieb—Scottish Torah scholar.

BIBLIOGRAPHY

Allen, Joseph L. "Nephi, land of and city of." In *Book of Mormon Reference Companion*. Dennis L. Largey, editor. Salt Lake City, UT: Deseret Book, 2003, 593–94.

Allen, Ronald B. "Numbers." In *The Expositor's Bible Commentary*. Twelve Volumes. Gaebelein, Frank E., editor. Grand Rapids, MI: Zondervan, 1976–1992, 2:655–1008.

Ambrose of Millan. "Letter." In *Ancient Christian Commentary on Scripture: Exodus, Leviticus, Numbers, Deuteronomy*. Joseph T. Lienhard, editor. Downers Grove, IL: InterVarsity Press, 2001.

Andersen, Neil L. "The Spiritual Gifts." *Ensign*, December 2009, 48–53.

Anderson, Lavina Fielding. *Lucy's Book: A Critical Edition of Lucy Mack Smith's Family Memoir*. Salt Lake City: Signature Books, 2001.

Arnold, Marilyn. "Mormon." In *Book of Mormon Reference Companion*. Dennis L. Largey, editor. Salt Lake City: Deseret Book, 2003, 547–51.

Augustine. "Explanation of the Psalms." In *Ancient Christian Commentary on Scripture: Exodus, Leviticus, Numbers, Deuteronomy*. Joseph T. Lienhard, editor. Downers Grove, IL: InterVarsity Press, 2001.

———. "On Eighty-Three Varied Questions." In Joel C. Elowsky, editor. *Ancient Christian Commentary on Scripture: John 11–21*. Downers Grove, IL: InterVarsity Press, 2007.

———. "On The Gospel of St. John." In *Nicene and Post-Nicene Fathers—First Series*. Fourteen volumes. Phillip Schaff, editor. Peabody, Massachusetts: Hendrickson Publishers, 2004.

Barclay, William. *The Gospel of Matthew*. Revised edition. Two volumes. Louisville, KY: Westminster John Knox, 1975.

Bassett, Douglas K. *Doctrinal Insights to the Book of Mormon*. Three volumes. Springville, UT: Cedar Fort, 2007–2008.

Beardall, Douglas and Jewell. *About the Three Nephites*. Provo, UT: LDS Book Publications, 1992.

Bede the Venerable. "Homilies on the Gospels." In *Ancient Christian Commentary on Scripture: Exodus, Leviticus, Numbers, Deuteronomy*. Joseph T. Lienhard, editor. Downers Grove, IL: InterVarsity Press, 2001.

Bednar, David A. "In the Strength of the Lord." Brigham Young University Devotional, October 23, 2001. *Brigham Young University 2001–2002 Speeches*, 1–8.

Benson, Ezra Taft. *A Witness and a Warning: A Modern-Day Prophet Testifies of the Book of Mormon*. Salt Lake City: Deseret Book, 1988.

———. *Teachings of Ezra Taft Benson*. Salt Lake City: Bookcraft, 1998.

Book of Mormon (Religion 121–122) Student Manual. Second edition, revised. Salt Lake City: The Church of Jesus Christ of Latter-day Saints, 1981.

Bowden, John, editor. *Encyclopedia of Christianity*. New York: Oxford University Press, 2005.

BIBLIOGRAPHY

Brown, Francis, S. R. Driver, and Charles A. Briggs. *The Brown-Driver-Briggs Hebrew and English Lexicon*. Peabody, MA: Hendrickson Publishers, 1999.

Brown, Raymond E., Joseph A. Fitzmyer, and Roland E. Murphy, editors. *The New Jerome Biblical Commentary*. Englewood Cliffs, New Jersey: Prentice Hall, Inc., 1990.

———. *The Birth of the Messiah*. New York: Doubleday, 1993.

———. *The Death of the Messiah*. Two volumes. New York: Doubleday, 1994.

Bullinger, E. W. *Number in Scripture: Its Supernatural Design and Spiritual Significance*. Grand Rapids, MI: Kregel Publications, 1967.

Bunker, Robert L. "The Design of the Liahona and the Purpose of the Second Spindle." In *Journal of Book of Mormon Studies*. Volume 3, Number 2 (Fall 1994), 1–11.

Caesarius of Arles. "Sermon." In *Ancient Christian Commentary on Scripture: Exodus, Leviticus, Numbers, Deuteronomy*. Joseph T. Lienhard, editor. Downers Grove, IL: InterVarsity Press, 2001.

Cannon, George Q. *The Life of Joseph Smith, the Prophet*. Salt Lake City: Deseret Book, 1986.

Casper, Kevin D. "The Lord Truly Protected Us." *Liahona*, March 2010, 16–17.

Cassiodorus. "Exposition on the Psalms." In *Ancient Christian Commentary on Scripture: Exodus, Leviticus, Numbers, Deuteronomy*. Joseph T. Lienhard, editor. Downers Grove, IL: InterVarsity Press, 2001.

Cheesman, Paul R. *The Keystone of Mormonism: Early Visions of the Prophet Joseph Smith*. Provo, UT: Eagle Systems International, 1988.

Christianson, Jack R. "Lamoni." In *Book of Mormon Reference Companion*. Dennis L. Largey, editor. Salt Lake City: Deseret Book, 2003, 498–99.

Church History in the Fulness of Times. Second edition. Salt Lake City: The Church of Jesus Christ of Latter-day Saints, 2000.

Chrysostom, John. "Homilies on First Corinthians." In *Ancient Christian Commentary on Scripture: Exodus, Leviticus, Numbers, Deuteronomy*. Joseph T. Lienhard, editor. Downers Grove, IL: InterVarsity Press, 2001.

———. "Homilies on Second Corinthians." In *Ancient Christian Commentary on Scripture: Exodus, Leviticus, Numbers, Deuteronomy*. Joseph T. Lienhard, editor. Downers Grove, IL: InterVarsity Press, 2001.

Cirlot, J. E. *A Dictionary of Symbols*. Second edition. New York: Philosophical Library, 1971.

Clarke, Adam. *The Holy Bible Containing the Old and New Testaments . . . with a Commentary and Critical Notes*. Six volumes. New York: Methodist Book Concern, 1846.

Clement of Alexandria. "Cassiodorus—Fragments." In *Ante-Nicene Fathers*. Ten volumes. Alexander Roberts and James Donaldson, editors. Peabody, MA: Hendrickson Publishers, 1994, 2:571–77.

———. "Stromata." In *Ante-Nicene Fathers*. Ten volumes. Alexander Roberts and James Donaldson, editors. Peabody, MA: Hendrickson Publishers, 1994, 2:480–568.

Clement of Rome. "Letter to the Corinthians." In *Ancient Christian Commentary on Scripture: Exodus, Leviticus, Numbers, Deuteronomy.* Joseph T. Lienhard, editor. Downers Grove, IL: InterVarsity Press, 2001.

Cole, R. Alan. *Tyndale New Testament Commentaries: Mark.* Revised edition. Grand Rapids, MI: Eerdmans, 1997.

Confucius. *The Analects.* New York: Penguin Books, 1979.

Conner, Kevin J. *Interpreting the Symbols and Types.* Revised and expanded edition. Portland, OR: City Bible Publishing, 1992.

Cooper, J. C. *An Illustrated Encyclopaedia of Traditional Symbols.* London: Thames and Hudson, 1982.

Cornwall, Judson, and Stelman Smith. *The Exhaustive Dictionary of Bible Names.* North Brunswick, NJ: Bridge-Logos Publishers, 1998.

Cowley, Matthew. In Conference Report, October 1948, 155–62.

Critchlow, William J. In Conference Report, October 4, 1963, 26–30.

Cross, Frank Lloyd, and Elizabeth A. Livingstone, editors. *The Oxford Dictionary of the Christian Church.* Second edition. New York: Oxford University Press, 1990.

Curtis, Levi. "Recollections of the Prophet Joseph Smith." In *Juvenile Instructor,* Volume 27, Number 12. June 15, 1892, 385–86.

Cyril of Jerusalem. "Catechetical Lectures." In *Nicene and Post-Nicene Fathers— Second Series.* Fourteen volumes. Phillip Schaff and Henry Wace, editors. Peabody, Massachusetts: Hendrickson Publishers, 2004, 7:1–157.

Dahl, Larry E. and Donald Q. Cannon. *The Teachings of Joseph Smith.* Salt Lake City: Bookcraft, 1998.

Dana, Bruce E. *The Three Nephites and other Translated Beings.* Springville, UT: Bonneville, 2003.

Davis, John J. *Biblical Numerology.* Grand Rapids, MI: Baker Book House, 2000.

Day, Franklin D. "Elijah." In *Encyclopedia of Mormonism.* Four volumes. Daniel H. Ludlow, editor. New York: Macmillan, 1992, 2:450–51.

Drinkard, Joel F. "Direction and Orientation." In *The Anchor Bible Dictionary.* Six volumes. David Noel Freedman, editor. New York: Doubleday, 1992, 2:204.

———. "East." In *The Anchor Bible Dictionary.* Six volumes. David Noel Freedman, editor. New York: Doubleday, 1992, 2:248–49.

Ehat, Andrew F. and Lyndon W. Cook. *The Words of Joseph Smith.* Provo, UT: Brigham Young University Religious Studies Center, 1980.

Eyring, Henry B. "To Draw Closer To God." *Ensign,* May 1991, 65–67.

Fairbairn, Patrick. *Typology of Scripture.* Two volumes in one. Grand Rapids, MI: Kregel Publications, 1989.

Farbridge, Maurice. *Studies in Biblical and Semitic Symbolism.* London: Kegan Paul, Trench, Trubner, & Co., 1923.

Faust, James E. "The Light in Their Eyes." *Ensign,* November 2005, 20–23.

Ferguson, Everett, editor. *Encyclopedia of Early Christianity.* New York: Garland Publishing, 1990.

Firmage, Edwin. "Zoology." In *The Anchor Bible Dictionary.* David Noel Freedman, editor. New York: Doubleday, 1992, 6:1109–67.

Fitzmyer, Joseph A. *The Anchor Bible: The Gospel According to Luke I–IX*. New York: Doubleday, 1970.

Fontana, David. *The Secret Language of Symbols*. San Francisco, CA: Chronicle Books, 1994.

Ford, J. Massyngberde. *The Anchor Bible: Revelation*. New York: Doubleday, 1975.

France, R. T. *Tyndale New Testament Commentaries: Matthew*. Grand Rapids, MI: Eerdmans, 1997.

Freedman, David Noel, editor. *The Anchor Bible Dictionary*. Six volumes. New York: Doubleday, 1992.

Freyne, Sean. "The Sea of Galilee." In *The Anchor Bible Dictionary*. Six volumes. David Noel Freedman, editor. New York: Doubleday, 1992, 2:899–901.

Gabriel, Richard A. and Karen S. Metz. *A History of Military Medicine*. Two volumes. Westport, CT: Greenwood Press, 1992.

Gabriel, Charles H., composer. "I Stand All Amazed." In *Hymns of the Church of Jesus Christ of Latter-day Saints*. Second revised edition. Salt Lake City: Intellectual Reserve, Inc., 2002. Hymn number 193.

Gaebelein, Frank E., editor. *The Expositor's Bible Commentary*. Twelve Volumes. Grand Rapids, MI: Zondervan, 1976–1992.

Gardner, Brant A. *Second Witness: Analytical and Contextual Commentary on the Book of Mormon*. Six volumes. Salt Lake City: Greg Kofford Books, 2007.

Garrett, H. Dean. "Light in Our Vessels: Faith, Hope, and Charity." In *The Book of Mormon: 4 Nephi Through Moroni—From Zion to Destruction*. Monte S. Nyman and Charles D. Tate Jr., editors. Provo, UT: Brigham Young University Religious Studies Center, 1995, 81–93.

Gaskill, Alonzo L. *The Lost Language of Symbolism: An Essential Guide for Recognizing and Interpreting Symbols of the Gospel*. Salt Lake City: Deseret Book, 2003.

———. "Location Veneration: Independence, Missouri, in Latter-day Saint Zionist Tradition and Thought." In *Mormon Historical Studies*. Volume 14, Number 1 (Spring 2013), 163–83.

———. "Ammon and the Arms of the Lamanites: Have We Been Misreading the Book of Mormon?" In *Restoration Studies*. Volume 15 (2014), 82-94.

———. *Miracles of the New Testament: A Guide to the Symbolic Messages*. Springville, UT: Cedar Fort, 2014.

Ginzberg, Louis. *The Legends of the Jews*. Seven volumes. Philadelphia, PA: The Jewish Publication Society of America, 1967–1969.

Godfrey, Matthew C., Mark Ashurst-McGee, Grant Underwood, Robert J. Woodford, and William G. Hartley, editors. *The Joseph Smith Papers Documents—Volume 2: July 1831–January 1833*. Salt Lake City: The Church Historians Press, 2013.

Gregory of Nyssa. "On the Baptism of Christ." In *Ancient Christian Commentary on Scripture: Exodus, Leviticus, Numbers, Deuteronomy*. Joseph T. Lienhard, editor. Downers Grove, IL: InterVarsity Press, 2001.

Habershon, Ada R. *Study of the Types*. Grand Rapids, MI: Kregel Publications, 1974.

————. *Hidden Pictures in the Old Testament.* Grand Rapids, MI: Kregel Publications, 1982.

Hall, James. *Dictionary of Subjects & Symbols.* Revised edition. New York: Harper and Row, 1974.

Hall, Randall L. "Amulek." In *Book of Mormon Reference Companion.* Dennis L. Largey, editor. Salt Lake City: Deseret Book, 2003, 52–54.

Hamblin, William, and A. Brent Merrill. "Swords in the Book of Mormon." In *Warfare in the Book of Mormon.* Stephen D. Ricks and William J. Hamblin, editors. Salt Lake City: Deseret Book, 1990, 329–51.

————. "Weapons." In *Book of Mormon Reference Companion.* Dennis L. Largey, editor. Salt Lake City: Deseret Book, 2003, 783–84.

Hamilton, Victor P. *Handbook on the Pentateuch.* Grand Rapids, MI: Baker Book House, 1982.

Hatch, Trevan G. *Visions, Manifestations and Miracles of the Restoration.* Orem, UT: Granite Publishing, 2008.

Hedges, Andrew H., Alex D. Smith, and Richard Lloyd Anderson, editors. *The Joseph Smith Papers—Journals, Volume 2: December 1841–April 1843.* Salt Lake City: The Church Historian's Press, 2011.

Henry, Hugh T. *Catholic Customs and Symbols.* New York: Benziger Brothers, 1925.

Hewitt, Hugh. *Hugh Hewitt. Searching for God in America.* Dallas, TX: Word Publishing, 1996.

Hilton, Lynn M. and Hope Hilton. *In Search of Lehi's Trail.* Salt Lake City: Deseret Book, 1976.

Hinckley, Gordon B. "Let Not Your Heart Be Troubled." Lecture delivered at Brigham Young University, October 29, 1974.

————. *Teachings of Gordon B. Hinckley.* Salt Lake City: Deseret Book, 1997.

History of The Church of Jesus Christ of Latter-day Saints. Seven volumes. Brigham H. Roberts, editor. Salt Lake City: Deseret Book, 1978.

Holland, Jeffrey R. "The Inconvenient Messiah." *Ensign*, February 1984, 68–73.

————. *Christ and the New Covenant.* Salt Lake City: Deseret Book, 1997.

————. "The Tongue of Angels." *Ensign*, May 2007, 16–18.

Holzapfel, Richard Neitzel, and Kent P. Jackson, editors. *My Redeemer Lives!* Provo, UT: Brigham Young University Religious Studies Center and Deseret Book, 2011.

Hunter, Howard W. "Reading the Scriptures." *Ensign*, November 1979, 64–66.

Huntington, Oliver B. *Typescript of the Diary of Oliver B. Huntington.* Two volumes. Sat Lake City: Utah State Historical Society, no date given.

Ifrah, Georges. *The Universal History of Numbers.* New York: John Wiley and Sons, 2000.

Jackson, Kent P. and Robert L. Millet, editors. *Studies in Scripture Volume Five: The Gospels.* Salt Lake City: Deseret Book, 1986.

Jamieson, Robert, Andrew Fausset, and David Brown, editors. *Jamieson, Fausset and Brown One Volume Commentary.* Grand Rapids, MI: Associated Publishers and Authors Inc., no date given.

Jenks, Alan W. "Eating and Drinking in the Old Testament." In *The Anchor*

Bible Dictionary. Six volumes. David Noel Freedman, editor. New York: Doubleday, 1992, 2:250–54.

Jessee, Dean C., Mark Ashurst-McGee, and Richard L. Jensen, editors. *The Joseph Smith Papers—Journals Volume 1: 1832–1839.* Salt Lake City: The Church Historian's Press, 2008.

John of Damascus. "Exposition of the Orthodox Faith." In *Nicene and Post-Nicene Fathers—Second Series.* Fourteen volumes. Phillip Schaff and Henry Wace, editors. Peabody, Massachusetts: Hendrickson Publishers, 2004.

Johnson, Alan F. "Revelation." In *The Expositor's Bible Commentary.* Twelve volumes. Gaebelein, Frank E., editor. Grand Rapids, MI: Zondervan, 1976–1992, 12:397–603.

Johnson, Jennifer, Claire Koltko, Brittany McEwen, and Natalie Ross, compilers. *The Eyewitness History of the Church, Volume Three, Journey to Zion's Hill, 1845–1869.* Springville, UT: Cedar Fort, 2006.

Johnson, Luke Timothy. *Sacra Pagina: The Acts of the Apostles.* Collegeville, Minnesota: The Liturgical Press, 1992.

Johnson, Robert D. *Numbers in the Bible: God's Design in Biblical Numerology.* Grand Rapids, MI: Kregel Publications, 1990.

Julien, Nadia. *The Mammoth Dictionary of Symbols.* New York: Carroll and Graf Publishers, 1996.

Kaiser, Walter C., Jr. "Exodus." In *The Expositor's Bible Commentary.* Twelve volumes. Frank E. Gaebelein, editor. Grand Rapids, MI: Zondervan, 1976–1992, 2:285–497.

Keoke, Emory Dean, and Kay Marie Porterfield. *Encyclopedia of American Indian Contributions to the World.* New York: Facts On File, 2002.

Kimball, Spencer W. "Conference Issues." *The Church News,* 1970–1987, 12.

———. *The Miracle of Forgiveness.* Salt Lake City: Bookcraft, 1989.

———. *The Teachings of Spencer W. Kimball.* Edward L. Kimball, editor. Salt Lake City: Bookcraft, 1998.

———. *Faith Precedes the Miracle.* Salt Lake City: Bookcraft, 2001.

Kistemaker, Simon J. *The Miracles: Exploring the Mystery of Jesus's Divine Works.* Grand Rapids, MI: Baker Books, 2006.

Kragh, J. F. Jr, K. G. Swan, D. C. Smith, R. L. Mabry, and L. H. Blackbourne. "Historical Review of Emergency Tourniquet Use to Stop Bleeding." In *The American Journal of Surgery* (2012), 242–52.

Kraut, Ogden. *The Three Nephites.* Third edition. Salt Lake City: Pioneer Press, 1993.

Kselman, John S. and Michael L. Barré. "Psalms." In *The New Jerome Biblical Commentary.* Raymond E. Brown, Joseph A. Fitzmyer, and Roland Murphy, editors. New Jersey: Prentice Hall, 1990, 523–52.

La Sor, Willaim S., translator. *The Complete Works of Josephus.* Grand Rapids, MI: Kregel Publications, 1981.

Lambert, Neil E. "Liahona." In *Book of Mormon Reference Companion.* Dennis L. Largey, editor. Salt Lake City: Deseret Book, 2003, 519–20.

Largey, Dennis L. *Book of Mormon Reference Companion.* Salt Lake City: Deseret Book, 2003.

———. "Korihor." In *Book of Mormon Reference Companion*. Dennis L. Largey, editor. Salt Lake City: Deseret Book, 2003, 483–85.

———. "Samuel the Lamanite." In *Book of Mormon Reference Companion*. Dennis L. Largey, editor. Salt Lake City: Deseret Book, 2003, 697–700.

LDS Bible Dictionary. Salt Lake City: The Church of Jesus Christ of Latter-day Saints, 1979.

Lectures on Faith. Salt Lake City: Deseret Book, 1985.

Lee, Harold B. *The Teachings of Harold B. Lee*. Clyde J. Williams, complier. Salt Lake City: Bookcraft, 1998.

Lee, Hector. *The Three Nephites—The Substance and Significance of the Legend in Folklore*. New Mexico: The University of New Mexico Press, 1949.

Liefeld, Walter L. "Luke." In *The Expositor's Bible Commentary*. Twelve volumes. Frank E. Gaebelein, editor. Grand Rapids, MI: Zondervan, 1976–1992, 8:795–1059.

Lienhard, Joseph T., editor. *Ancient Christian Commentary on Scripture: Exodus, Leviticus, Numbers, Deuteronomy*. Downers Grove, IL: InterVarsity Press, 2001.

"Life of Adam and Eve." In *The Old Testament Pseudepigrapha*. Two volumes. James H. Charlesworth, editor. New York: Doubleday, 1983, 1985, 2:249–495.

Lockyer, Herbert. *All the Miracles of the Bible: The Supernatural in Scripture—Its Scope and Significance*. Grand Rapids, MI: Zondervan, 1965.

Ludlow, Daniel H. *A Companion to Your Study of the Book of Mormon*. Salt Lake City: Deseret Book, 1976.

———. *A Companion to Your Study of the Doctrine and Covenants*. Two volumes. Salt Lake City: Deseret Book, 1978.

———. *Encyclopedia of Mormonism*. Four volumes. New York: Macmillan, 1992.

———, Ed J. Pinegar, Richard J. Allen, Leaun G. Otten, and C. Max Caldwell. *Unlocking the Book of Mormon*. American Fork, UT: Covenant Communications, 2007.

Martyr, Justin. "Dialogue with Trypho." In *Ancient Christian Commentary on Scripture: Exodus, Leviticus, Numbers, Deuteronomy*. Joseph T. Lienhard, editor. Downers Grove, IL: InterVarsity Press, 2001.

MacKay, Michael H., Gerrit J. Dirkmaat, Grant Underwood, Robert J. Woodford, and William G. Hartley, editors. *The Joseph Smith Papers— Documents Volume 1: July 1828–June 1831*. Salt Lake City: The Church Historians Press, 2013.

Madsen, Truman G. *Joseph Smith the Prophet*. Salt Lake City: Bookcraft, 1989.

Mann, C. S. *The Anchor Bible: Mark*. New York: Doubleday, 1986.

Marsh, W. Jeffrey. "Lamoni, Father Of." In *Book of Mormon Reference Companion*. Dennis L. Largey, editor. Salt Lake City: Deseret Book, 2003, 499–500.

Matthews, Robert J. "Abinadi." In *Book of Mormon Reference Companion*. Dennis L. Largey, editor. Salt Lake City: Deseret Book, 2003, 22–24.

Maxwell, Neal A. *That My Family Should Partake*. Salt Lake City: Deseret Book, 1974.

———. *All These Things Shall Give Thee Experience.* Salt Lake City: Deseret Book, 1979.

———. "Willing to Submit." *Ensign,* May 1985, 70–73.

———. *But for a Small Moment.* Salt Lake City: Bookcraft, 1986.

———. "Becometh As A Child." *Ensign,* May 1996, 68–70.

———. *The Neal A. Maxwell Quote Book.* Cory H. Maxwell, complier. Salt Lake City: Bookcraft, 1992.

———. "A Conversation with Elder Neal A. Maxwell." In *Hugh Hewitt. Searching for God in America.* Dallas, TX: Word Publishing, 1996, 121–44.

———. *CES Evening with A General Authority.* February 2, 2001.

———. "Plow in Hope." *Ensign,* May 2001, 59–61.

———. *The Promise of Discipleship.* Salt Lake City: Deseret Book, 2001.

McConkie, Bruce R. *Mormon Doctrine.* Second edition. Salt Lake City: Bookcraft, 1979.

———. *The Mortal Messiah.* Four volumes. Salt Lake City: Deseret Book, 1980–1981.

———. *The Millennial Messiah.* Salt Lake City: Deseret Book, 1982.

———. "The Caravan Moves On." *Ensign,* November 1984, 82–85.

———. *Doctrinal New Testament Commentary.* Three volumes. Salt Lake City: Bookcraft, 1987–1988.

McConkie, Joseph Fielding. *Gospel Symbolism.* Salt Lake City: Bookcraft, 1985.

McConkie, Joseph Fielding, and Robert L. Millet. *Doctrinal Commentary on the Book of Mormon.* Three volumes. Salt Lake City: Deseret Book, 1987–1991.

McConkie, Joseph Fielding, and Donald W. Parry. *A Guide to Scriptural Symbols.* Salt Lake City: Bookcraft, 1990.

McConkie, Joseph Fielding, Robert L. Millet, and Brent L. Top. *Doctrinal Commentary on the Book of Mormon.* Volume four. Salt Lake City: Deseret Book, 1992.

McConkie, Joseph Fielding. *Witnesses of the Birth of Christ.* Salt Lake City: Bookcraft, 1998.

McConkie, Joseph Fielding, and Craig J. Ostler. *Revelations of the Restoration.* Salt Lake City: Deseret Book, 2000.

McConkie, Mark L. "Translated Beings." In *Encyclopedia of Mormonism.* Four volumes. Daniel H. Ludlow, editor. New York: Macmillan, 1992, 4:1485–86.

McKay, David O. Conference Report. October 1968, 84–87.

———. *Gospel Ideals.* Salt Lake City: Bookcraft, 1998.

McQuade, Pamela. *The Top 100 Miracles of the Bible.* Uhrichsville, OH: Barbour Publishing, 2008.

Merrill, Byron R. "There Was No Contention." In *The Book of Mormon: 4 Nephi Through Moroni—From Zion to Destruction.* Monte S. Nyman and Charles D. Tate Jr., editors. Provo, UT: Brigham Young University Religious Studies Center, 1995, 167–84.

Millet, Robert L. "The Birth and Childhood of the Messiah." In *Studies in Scripture Volume Five: The Gospels.* Kent P. Jackson and Robert L. Millet, editors. Salt Lake City: Deseret Book, 1986, 140–59.

Monson, Thomas S. In *Church News*, April 9, 1988, 14.

———. "Welcome to Conference." *Ensign*, October 2009, 4–6.

———. *Teachings of Thomas S. Monson*. Lynne F. Cannegieter, compiler. Salt Lake City: Deseret Book, 2011.

Morgan, Robert J. *On This Day in Christian History*. Nashville, TN: Thomas Nelson, 1997.

Morris, Leon. "Hebrews." In *The Expositor's Bible Commentary*. Twelve volumes. Frank E. Gaebelein, editor. Grand Rapids, MI: Zondervan, 1976–1992, 12:1–158.

———. *Tyndale New Testament Commentaries: Luke*. Revised edition. Grand Rapids, MI: Eerdmans, 1999.

———. *Tyndale New Testament Commentaries: Revelation*. Revised edition. Grand Rapids, MI: Eerdmans, 1999.

Mother Teresa. *Where There is Love, There is God*. Brian Kolodiejchuk, compiler. New York: Image Books, 2010.

Myers, Allen C. *The Eerdmans Bible Dictionary*. Grand Rapids, MI: Eerdmans, 1997.

Nibley, Hugh. *Mormonism and Early Christianity*. Provo, UT: Foundation for Ancient Research and Mormon Studies, 1987.

———. *An Approach to the Book of Mormon*. Third edition. Provo, UT: Foundation for Ancient Research and Mormon Studies, 1988.

———. *Lehi in the Desert/The World of the Jaredites/There Were Jaredites*. Provo, UT: Foundation for Ancient Research and Mormon Studies, 1988.

———. *Since Cumorah*. Provo, UT: Foundation for Ancient Research and Mormon Studies, 1988.

———. *Ancient Documents and the Pearl of Great Price*. Provo, UT: Foundation for Ancient Research and Mormon Studies, 1989.

———. *Approaching Zion*. Provo, UT: Foundation for Ancient Research and Mormon Studies, 1989.

———. "Work We Must, but the Lunch is Free." In *Approaching Zion*. Provo, UT: Foundation for Ancient Research and Mormon Studies, 1989, 202–51.

———. *Teachings of the Book of Mormon: Transcripts of Lectures Presented to an Honors Book of Mormon Class at Brigham Young University, 1989–1990*. Four volumes. Provo, UT: Foundation for Ancient Research and Mormon Studies, 2004.

Norris, Fredrick W. "Antioch." In Everett Ferguson, editor. *Encyclopedia of Early Christianity*. New York: Garland Publishing, 1990, 52–54.

Nyman, Monte S. and Charles D. Tate Jr., editors. *The Book of Mormon: Second Nephi, The Doctrinal Structure*. Provo, UT: Brigham Young University Religious Studies Center, 1989.

———, editors. *The Book of Mormon: Mosiah: Salvation Only Through Christ*. Provo, UT: Brigham Young University Religious Studies Center, 1991.

———, editors. *The Book of Mormon: Helaman Through 3 Nephi 8, According To Thy Word*. Provo, UT: Brigham Young University Religious Studies Center, 1992.

————, editors. *The Book of Mormon: 3 Nephi 9–30, This Is My Gospel.* Provo, UT: Brigham Young University Religious Studies Center, 1993.

————, editors. *The Book of Mormon: 4 Nephi Through Moroni—From Zion to Destruction.* Provo, UT: Brigham Young University Religious Studies Center, 1995.

————. *Book of Mormon Commentary.* Six volumes. Orem, UT: Granite Publishing, 2003–2004.

Oaks, Dallin H. "Bible Stories and Personal Protection." *Ensign*, November 1992, 37–40.

————. "Scripture Reading and Revelation." *Ensign*, January 1995, 6–9.

————. "Miracles." *Ensign*, June 2001, 6–17.

Ogden, D. Kelly, and Andrew C. Skinner. *Verse by Verse: Acts Through Revelation.* Salt Lake City: Deseret Book, 1998.

————. *Verse by Verse: The Book of Mormon.* Two volumes. Salt Lake City: Deseret Book, 2011.

Orosius, Paulus. "Seven Books of History Against the Pagans." In *Ancient Christian Commentary on Scripture: Exodus, Leviticus, Numbers, Deuteronomy.* Joseph T. Lienhard, editor. Downers Grove, IL: InterVarsity Press, 2001.

Otten, L. G. and C. M. Caldwell. *Sacred Truths of the Doctrine and Covenants.* Two volumes. Springville, UT: LEMB, 1982.

Packer, Boyd K. *Follow the Brethren. Brigham Young University Speeches.* Provo, UT, 23 March 1965.

————. *Teaching Ye Diligently.* Salt Lake City: Deseret Book, 1979.

————. "The Cloven Tongues of Fire." In Conference Report. April 2000, 6–9.

————. "The Edge of the Light." In *BYU Magazine.* March 1991, 22–25.

————. *Mine Errand From the Lord: Selections from the Sermons and Writings of Boyd K. Packer.* Clyde J. Williams, complier. Salt Lake City: Deseret Book, 2008.

————. "The 20-Mark Note." *Liahona*, June 2009, 20–24.

Parry, Donald W. and Jay A. Parry. *Symbols and Shadows: Unlocking a Deeper Understanding of the Atonement.* Salt Lake City: Deseret Book, 2009.

Penrose, Charles W. "School Thy Feelings." In *Hymns of the Church of Jesus Christ of Latter-day Saints,* revised edition. Salt Lake City: Intellectual Reserve, 1998. Hymn number 336.

Philo of Alexandria. "On the Birth of Abel and the Sacrifices Offered by Him and by His Brother Cain." In *The Works of Philo: Complete and Unabridged.* C. D. Yonge, translator. Peabody, MA: Hendrickson Publishers, 1997, 94–111.

Pinegar, Ed J. and Richard J. Allen. *Teachings and Commentaries on the Book of Mormon.* American Fork, UT: Covenant Communications, 2003.

————. *Book of Mormon Who's Who: A Comprehensive Guide to the People in the Book of Mormon.* American Fork, UT: Covenant Communications, 2007.

————. *Commentaries and Insights on The Book of Mormon: 1 Nephi–Alma 29.* American Fork, UT: Covenant Communications, 2007.

Pratt, Orson. Discourse given February 18, 1855. In *Journal of Discourses,* 2:334–47.

———. "Past and Future Existence." In *Millennial Star*. Volume 48 (November 17, 1866), 721–23.

———. Discourse given December 27, 1868. In *Journal of Discourses*, 12:338–46.

———. Discourse given August 20, 1871. In *Journal of Discourses*, 14:233–45.

———. Discourse given July 19, 1874. In *Journal of Discourses*, 17:145–54.

———. Discourse given December 3, 1876. In *Journal of Discourses*, 18:314–23.

———. Discourse given August 1, 1880. In *Journal of Discourses*, 21:319–31.

Pratt, Parley P. *A Voice of Warning*. New York: no publisher listed, 1837.

———. *Autobiography of Parley Parker Pratt*. Fifth edition. Parley P. Pratt Jr., editor. Salt Lake City: Deseret Book, 1961.

"Prayer." In *LDS Bible Dictionary*. Salt Lake City: The Church of Jesus Christ of Latter-day Saints, 1979, 752–53.

Rasmussen, Ellis T. *A Latter-day Saint Commentary on the Old Testament*. Salt Lake City: Deseret Book, 1993.

Read, Lenet Hadley. *Unveiling Biblical Prophecy*. San Francisco, CA: Latter-day Light Publications, 1990.

Rector, Hartman, Jr. "The Gospel." *Ensign*, November 1985, 74–77.

"Revelation of Moses." In *Ante-Nicene Fathers*. Ten volumes. Alexander Roberts and James Donaldson, editors. Peabody, MA: Hendrickson Publishers, 1994, 8:565–70.

Reynolds, George, and Janne M. Sjodahl. *Commentary on the Book of Mormon*. Seven volumes. Salt Lake City: Deseret Book, 1955–1961.

———. "The Jaredites—Part II." In *The Juvenile Instructor*. Volume 27, Number 9 (May 1, 1892), 282–85.

Richards, Franklin D. Discourse given May 17, 1884. In *Journal of Discourses*, 25:230–37.

Richey, Stephen L. "Tourniquets for the Control of Traumatic Hemorrhage: A Review of the Literature." In *World Journal of Emergency Surgery*. Volume 2 (2007): epublished at http://www.ncbi.nlm.nih.gov/pmc/articles/PMC2151059/.

Ricks, Richard L. *Partly Cloudy: 76 Miracles from the Book of Mormon*. No publication information available: 2006.

Ricks, Stephen D. and William J. Hamblin, editors. *Warfare in the Book of Mormon*. Salt Lake City: Deseret Book, 1990.

Rigdon, Sidney. "Millennium." In *Messenger and Advocate*. February 1835, 67–68.

———. In *Messenger and Advocate*. August 1835, 165.

Robert, Alexander, and James Donaldson, editors. *Ante-Nicene Fathers*. Ten volumes. Peabody, MA: Hendrickson Publishers, 1994.

Roberts, Brigham H. *The Mormon Doctrine of Deity*. Salt Lake City: Deseret News, 1903.

Rockwood, Bruce L. "The Good, the Bad, and the Ironic: Two Views on Law and Literature." In *Yale Journal of Law and the Humanities*. Volume 8, Number 2 (1996), 533–58.

Ryken, Leland, James C. Wilhoit, and Tremper Longman III, editors. *Dictionary of Biblical Imagery*. Downers Grove, IL: InterVarsity Press, 1998.

Sakenfeld, Katharine Doob. *International Theological Commentary: Numbers—Journeying with God*. Grand Rapids, MI: Eerdmans, 1995.

"Mormon Missions: Did You Know . . . ?" In *Salt Lake Tribune*. September 30, 2011.

Schaff, Philip. *Nicene and Post-Nicene Fathers—First Series*. Fourteen volumes. Peabody, Massachusetts: Hendrickson Publishers, 2004.

———, and Henry Wace, editors. *Nicene and Post-Nicene Fathers—Second Series*. Fourteen volumes. Peabody, Massachusetts: Hendrickson Publishers, 2004.

Shama, Jai Prakash, and Rashmi Salhotra. "Tourniquets in Orthopedic Surgery." In *Indian Journal of Orthopedics*. Volume 46, Number 4 (July–August 2012), 377–82.

Sigourney, Lydia Howard. *Sketches*. Philadelphia: Key and Biddle, 1834.

Skinner, Andrew C. "Nephi's Ultimate Encounter with Deity: Some Thoughts on Helaman 10." In *The Book of Mormon: Helaman Through 3 Nephi 8, According To Thy Word*. Monte S. Nyman and Charles D. Tate Jr., editors. Provo, UT: Religious Studies Center, Brigham Young University, 1992, 115–27.

———. "Zion Gained and Lost: Fourth Nephi as the Quintessential Model." In *The Book of Mormon: 4 Nephi Through Moroni—From Zion to Destruction*. Monte S. Nyman and Charles D. Tate Jr., editors. Provo, UT: Brigham Young University Religious Studies Center, 1995, 289–302.

———. "Savior, Satan, and Serpent: The Duality of a Symbol in the Scriptures." In *The Disciple as Scholar: Essays on Scripture and the Ancient World in Honor of Richard Lloyd Anderson*. Stephen E. Ricks, Donald W. Parry, and Andrew H. Hedges, editors. Provo, UT: Foundation for Ancient Research and Mormon Studies, 2000, 359–84.

———, and Gaye Strathearn, editors. *Third Nephi: An Incomparable Scripture*. Provo, UT: Maxwell Institute for Religious Scholarship, 2012.

Smith, Hyrum G. Conference Report, October 1928, 81–82.

Smith, Joseph Fielding. *Doctrines of Salvation*. Three volumes. Salt Lake City: Bookcraft, 1998.

Snow, Erastus. Discourse given May 6, 1882. In *Journal of Discourses*, 23:181–89.

Sperry, Kip. "Jared, Posterity of." In *Book of Mormon Reference Companion*. Dennis L. Largey, editor. Salt Lake City: Deseret Book, 2003, 430–33.

Royal Skousen. *Analysis of Textual Variants of the Book of Mormon: Part Three, Mosiah 17–Alma 20*. Provo, UT: Foundation for Ancient Research and Mormon Studies, 2006.

———. *The Book of Mormon: The Earliest Text*. New Haven, CT: Yale University Press, 2009.

Rust, Richard Dilworth. "Recurrence in Book of Mormon Narratives." In *Journal of Book of Mormon Studies*. Volume 3, Number 1 (1994), 39–52.

Smith, George Albert. *The Teachings of George Albert Smith*. Robert and Susan McIntosh, compilers. Salt Lake City: Bookcraft, 1998.

Smith, Hyrum M. and Janne M. Sjodahl. *Doctrine and Covenants Commentary.* Revised edition. Salt Lake City: Deseret Book, 1978.

Smith, Hyrum W. *Pain is Inevitable, Misery is Optional.* Salt Lake City: Deseret Book, 2004.

Smith, Joseph. *Teachings of the Prophet Joseph Smith.* Joseph Fielding Smith, editor. Salt Lake City: Deseret Book, 1976.

Smith, Joseph F. Discourse given January 29, 1882. In *Journal of Discourses,* 22:350–53.

———. *Gospel Doctrine.* Salt Lake City: Bookcraft, 1998.

Smith, Joseph Fielding. *Answers to Gospel Questions.* Five volumes. Salt Lake City: Deseret Book, 1993.

———. *Doctrines of Salvation.* Three volumes. Bruce R. McConkie, compiler. Salt Lake City: Bookcraft, 1998.

Sobrino, Justin, and Shahid Shafi. "Timing and causes of death after injuries." In *Baylor University Medical Center Proceedings.* Volume 26, number 2 (2013), 120–23.

Sorenson, John. "When Lehi's Party Arrived in the Land, Did They Find Others There?" In *Journal of Book of Mormon Studies.* Volume 1, Number 1 (Fall 1992), 31–34.

Sprague, Achsa W. *The Poet and Other Poems.* Boston: William White and Co., 1865.

Swift, Charles L. *"I Have Dreamed a Dream": Typological Images of Teaching and Learning in the Vision of the Tree of Life.* Doctoral Dissertation. Provo, UT: Brigham Young University.

———. "Three Stories." In *My Redeemer Lives!* Richard Neitzel Holzapfel and Kent P. Jackson, editors. Provo, UT: Brigham Young University Religious Studies Center and Deseret Book, 2011, 123–46.

———. "'So Great and Marvelous Things': The Literary Portrait of Jesus as Divine Lord in 3 Nephi." In Andrew C. Skinner and Gaye Stratharn, editors. *Third Nephi: An Incomparable Scripture.* Provo, UT: Maxwell Institute for Religious Scholarship, 2012, 235–60.

Talmage, James E. *The Articles of Faith.* Salt Lake City: The Church of Jesus Christ of Latter-day Saints, 1924.

Taylor, John. *The Government of God.* Liverpool, England: no publisher listed, 1852.

———. Discourse given February 22, 1863. In *Journal of Discourses,* 10:113–20.

"The Divine Liturgy of James." In *Ante-Nicene Fathers.* Ten volumes. Alexander Roberts and James Donaldson, editors. Peabody, MA: Hendrickson Publishers, 1994, 7:537–50.

"The First Gospel of the Infancy of Jesus Christ." In *The Lost Books of the Bible.* New York: Bell Publishing, 1979, 38–59.

"The Gospel of Pseudo-Matthew." In *Ante-Nicene Fathers.* Ten volumes. Alexander Roberts and James Donaldson, editors. Peabody, MA: Hendrickson Publishers, 1994, 8:368–83.

The Lost Books of the Bible. New York: Bell Publishing, 1979.

"The Protevangelium of James." In *Ante-Nicene Fathers.* Ten volumes. Alexander

Roberts and James Donaldson, editors. Peabody, MA: Hendrickson Publishers, 1994, 8:361–67.

Thompson, Daniel P. *The Adventures of Timothy Peacock, Esquire, or, Freemasonry Practically Illustrated*. Vermont: Knapp and Jewett, 1835.

Todeschi, Kevin J. *The Encyclopedia of Symbolism*. New York: The Berkley Publishing Group, 1995.

Toplady, Augustus M. and Thomas Hastings. "Rock of Ages." In *Hymns of the Church of Jesus Christ of Latter-day Saints*, revised edition. Salt Lake City: Intellectual Reserve, 1998. Hymn number 111.

Trench, Richard C. *Notes on the Miracles of the Lord*. Grand Rapids, MI: Eerdmans, 1962.

———. *Miracles and Parables of the Old Testament*. Grand Rapids, MI: Baker Book House, 1974.

Trent, Kenneth E. *Types of Christ in the Old Testament*. New York: Exposition Press, 1960.

Tresidder, Jack. *Symbols and Their Meanings*. London: Duncan Baird Publishers, 2000.

Trigg, Joseph W. "Allegory." In *Encyclopedia of Early Christianity*. Everett Ferguson, editor. New York: Garland Publishing, 1990, 23–26.

Trunkey, Donald. "Trimodal Distribution of Death." In *Scientific America*. Volume 249, number 2 (1983), 20–27.

Turner, Rodney. "The Lamanite Mark." In *The Book of Mormon: Second Nephi, The Doctrinal Structure*. Monte S. Nyman and Charles D. Tate Jr., editors. Provo, UT: Brigham Young University Religious Studies Center, 1989, 133–57.

Tuttle, A. Theodore. "Developing Faith." *Ensign*, November 1986, 72–73.

Valletta, Thomas R. "Jared and His Brother." In *The Book of Mormon: 4 Nephi Through Moroni—From Zion to Destruction*. Monte S. Nyman and Charles D. Tate Jr., editors. Provo, UT: Brigham Young University Religious Studies Center, 1995, 303–22.

Vawter, Bruce. *On Genesis: A New Reading*. New York: Doubleday, 1977.

Webster, Noah. *Noah Webster's First Edition of an American Dictionary of the English Language—Facsimile [1828] Edition*. San Francisco, CA: Foundation for American Christian Education, 1967.

Wenham, Gordon J. *Tyndale Old Testament Commentaries: Numbers*. Downers Grove, IL: InterVarsity Press, 1981.

Welch, John W. *The Sermon at the Temple and the Sermon on the Mount*. Provo, UT: Foundation for Ancient Research and Mormon Studies, 1990.

———. "Why Study Warfare in the Book of Mormon?" In *Warfare in the Book of Mormon*. Stephen D. Ricks and William J. Hamblin, editors. Salt Lake City: Deseret Book, 1990, 3–24.

———. "Zeezrom." In *Book of Mormon Reference Companion*. Dennis L. Largey, editor. Salt Lake City: Deseret Book, 2003, 800–01.

Welling, David L., Patricia L. McKay, Todd E. Rasmussen, and Norman M. Rich. "Historical Vignettes in Vascular Surgery." In *Journal of Vascular Surgery*. Volume 55, Issue 1 (January 2012), 286–90.

Wells, M. Gawain. "The Savior and the Children in 3 Nephi." In *Journal of Book of Mormon Studies*. Volume 14, Number 1 (2005), 62–73.

Whitmer, David. *An Address to All Believers in Christ.* Richmond, Missouri: David Whitmer, 1887.

Williams, Clyde J. "Deliverance From Bondage." In *The Book of Mormon: Mosiah: Salvation Only Through Christ.* Monte S. Nyman and Charles D. Tate Jr., editors. Provo, UT: Brigham Young University Religious Studies Center, 1991, 261–74.

———. "The Three Nephites and the Doctrine of Translation." In *The Book of Mormon: 3 Nephi 9–30, This Is My Gospel.* Monte S. Nyman and Charles D. Tate Jr., editors. Provo, UT: Brigham Young University Religious Studies Center, 1993, 237–51.

———. "Translation." In *Book of Mormon Reference Companion.* Dennis L. Largey, editor. Salt Lake City: Deseret Book, 2003, 758–59.

Williamson, Lamar, Jr. *Interpretation—A Bible Commentary for Teaching and Preaching: Mark.* Atlanta, GA: John Knox Press, 1983.

Wilson, Walter L. *A Dictionary of Bible Types.* Peabody, Massachusetts: Hendrickson Publishers, 1999.

Wilson, William A. "The Paradox of Mormon Folklore." In *BYU Studies.* Volume 17, Number 1 (Autumn 1976), 40–58.

Woodruff, Wilford. Discourse given February 23, 1873. In *Journal of Discourses* 15:341–47.

———. *Wilford Woodruff's Journal.* Nine volumes. Scott G. Kenney, editor. Midvale, UT: Signature Books, 1984.

———. In *Things in Heaven and Earth: The Life and Times of Wilford Woodruff.* Thomas G. Alexander. Salt Lake City: Signature Books, 1993.

———. In *The Discourses of Wilford Woodruff.* G. Homer Durham, editor. Salt Lake City: Bookcraft, 1998.

Young, Brigham. Discourse given January 16, 1853. In *Journal of Discourses,* 1:1–6.

———. Discourse given June 28, 1857. In *Journal of Discourses,* 4:367–74.

———. Discourse given April 6, 1868. In *Journal of Discourses,* 12:192–96.

———. Discourse given August 24, 1872. In *Journal of Discourses,* 15:135–39.

———. *Discourses of Brigham Young.* John A. Widtsoe, compiler. Salt Lake City: Bookcraft, 1998.

———. *The Complete Discourses of Brigham Young.* Five volumes. Richard S. Van Wagoner, compiler. Salt Lake City: The Smith-Pettit Foundation, 2009.

Zornberg, Avivah Gottlieb. *The Particulars of Rapture: Reflections on Exodus.* New York: Doubleday, 2001.

INDEX

INDEX

INDEX

ABOUT *the* AUTHOR

Alonzo L. Gaskill is a professor of Church history and doctrine at Brigham Young University. He holds a bachelor's degree in philosophy, a master's in theology, and a PhD in biblical studies. Brother Gaskill has taught at BYU since 2003. Prior to coming to BYU, he served in a variety of assignments within the Church Educational System—most recently as the director of the LDS Institute of Religion at Stanford University (1995–2003).

SCAN TO VISIT

WWW.ALONZOGASKILL.WORDPRESS.COM